Gender and Heritage

Gender and Heritage brings together a group of international scholars to examine the performance, place and politics of gender within heritage. Through a series of case studies, models and assessments, the significance of understanding and working with concepts of gender is demonstrated as a dynamic and reforming agenda. Demonstrating that gender has become an increasingly important area for heritage scholarship, the collection argues that it should also be recognised as a central structuring device within society and the location where a critical heritage studies can emerge.

Drawing on contributions from around the world, this edited collection provides a range of innovative approaches to using gender as a mode of enquiry. From the politics of museum displays, the exploration of pedagogy, the role of local initiatives and the legal frameworks that structure representation, this volume's diversity and objectives represent a challenge for students, academics and professionals to rethink gender. Rather than featuring gender as an addition to wider discussions of heritage, this volume makes gender the focus of concern as a means of building a new agenda within the field.

This volume, which addresses how we engage with gender and heritage in both practice and theory, is essential reading for scholars at all levels and should also serve as a guide for practitioners.

Wera Grahn is Associate Professor in Gender Studies, Senior Lecturer and Head of Unit at Linköping University, Sweden. She is also Director of Postgraduate Research Training and Director of the Master's Programme, Gender Studies – Intersectionality and Change. Previously, she has worked as a Senior Research Fellow at the Norwegian Institute for Cultural Heritage Research (NIKU) in Oslo, Norway (2007–2011) and was affiliated to Upplandsmuseet for research (2006–2007). Before that, she was a PhD student at Tema Genus in Linköping (1999–2006).

Ross J. Wilson is Professor of Modern History and Public Heritage at the University of Chichester, UK. His research interests include the experience, representation and memory of the First World War and he also focuses on issues of museum, media and heritage representations in the modern era.

Key Issues in Cultural Heritage
Series Editors:
William Logan and Laurajane Smith

Also in the series:

Heritage and Globalisation, Sophia Labadi and Colin Long

Intangible Heritage, Laurajane Smith and Natsuko Akagawa

Places of Pain and Shame, William Logan and Keir Reeves

Cultural Diversity, Heritage and Human Rights, Michele Langfield, William Logan and Máiréad Nic Craith

Heritage, Labour and the Working Classes, Laurajane Smith, Paul Shackel and Gary Campbell

The Heritage of War, Martin Gegner and Bart Ziino

Managing Cultural Landscapes, Ken Taylor and Jane L. Lennon

Children, Childhood and Cultural Heritage, Kate Darian-Smith and Carla Pacoe

Heritage and Tourism, Russell Staiff, Robyn Bushell and Steve Watson

The Future of Heritage as Climates Change, David Harvey and Jim Perry

Urban Heritage, Development and Sustainability, Sophia Labadi and William Logan

Managing Heritage in Africa, Webber Ndoro, Shadreck Chirikure and Janette Deacon

Intellectual Property, Cultural Property and Intangible Cultural Heritage, Christoph Antons and William Logan

Emotion, Affective Practices, and the Past in the Present, Laurajane Smith, Margaret Wetherell and Gary Campbell

For more information on the series, please visit https://www.routledge.com/Key-Issues-in-Cultural-Heritage/book-series/KICH

Gender and Heritage

Performance, Place and Politics

Edited by Wera Grahn and
Ross J. Wilson

LONDON AND NEW YORK

First published 2018
by Routledge
2 Park Square, Milton Park, Abingdon, Oxon OX14 4RN

and by Routledge
711 Third Avenue, New York, NY 10017

Routledge is an imprint of the Taylor & Francis Group, an informa business

© 2018 selection and editorial matter, Wera Grahn and Ross J. Wilson; individual chapters, the contributors

The right of Wera Grahn and Ross J. Wilson to be identified as the authors of the editorial material, and of the authors for their individual chapters, has been asserted in accordance with sections 77 and 78 of the Copyright, Designs and Patents Act 1988.

All rights reserved. No part of this book may be reprinted or reproduced or utilised in any form or by any electronic, mechanical, or other means, now known or hereafter invented, including photocopying and recording, or in any information storage or retrieval system, without permission in writing from the publishers.

Trademark notice: Product or corporate names may be trademarks or registered trademarks, and are used only for identification and explanation without intent to infringe.

British Library Cataloguing-in-Publication Data
A catalogue record for this book is available from the British Library

Library of Congress Cataloging-in-Publication Data
A catalog record for this book has been requested

ISBN: 978-1-138-20816-2 (hbk)
ISBN: 978-1-138-20814-8 (pbk)
ISBN: 978-1-315-46009-3 (ebk)

Typeset in Times New Roman
by Swales & Willis Ltd, Exeter, Devon, UK

Contents

Figures	viii
Acknowledgements	x
List of contributors	xi
Series general co-editors' foreword	xvii

PART I
Introduction   1

1 The tyranny of the normal and the importance of being liminal   3
   ROSS J. WILSON

PART II
Performance   15

2 Johanna, Moa and I'm every lesbian: gender, sexuality and class in Norrköping's industrial landscape   17
   BODIL AXELSSON AND DAVID LUDVIGSSON

3 Gender, heritage and changing traditions: Russian Old Believers in Romania   30
   CRISTINA CLOPOT AND MÁIRÉAD NIC CRAITH

4 Handicrafting gender: craft, performativity and cultural heritage   44
   ANNELI PALMSKÖLD AND JOHANNA ROSENQVIST

5 Naturing gender and gendering nature in museums   61
   SMILLA EBELING

PART III
Place   79

6 It's a man's world. Or is it? The 'Pilgrim Fathers', religion,
   patriarchy, nationalism and tourism   81
   ANNA SCOTT

7 The fleshyness of absence: the matter of absence in
   a feminist museology   99
   ARNDÍS BERGSDÓTTIR AND SIGURJÓN BALDUR HAFSTEINSSON

8 Taller than the rest: the Three Dikgosi Monument,
   masculinity reloaded   113
   KELETSO G. SETLHABI

9 Exploring identities through feminist pedagogy   129
   VIV GOLDING

10 Impasse or productive intersection? Learning to 'mess with
   genies' in collaborative heritage research relationships   148
   JONI LARIAT

PART IV
Politics   167

11 Transversal dances across time and space: feminist strategies
   for a critical heritage studies   169
   ASTRID VON ROSEN, MONICA SAND AND MARSHA MESKIMMON

12 Gendering 'the other Germany': resistant and residual
   narratives on Stauffenbergstraße, Berlin   185
   JOANNE SAYNER AND RHIANNON MASON

13 Gender and intangible heritage: illustrating the
   inter-disciplinary character of international law   207
   JANET BLAKE

14 Women of Steel at the Sparrows Point Steel Mill,
   Baltimore, USA   221
   MICHELLE L. STEFANO

15 'Does it matter?' Relocating fragments of queer heritage in
post-earthquake Christchurch   **239**
ANDREW GORMAN-MURRAY AND SCOTT MCKINNON

PART V
Conclusion   **253**

16 The politics of heritage: how to achieve change   **255**
WERA GRAHN

Index   269

Figures

2.1	Statue of Moa, Norrköping, Sweden	24
3.1	Women attending the Easter service in an Old Believers' church, April 2015	36
3.2	Children learning how to apply shadows during the iconography workshop, August 2015	39
4.1	Lace braiding	50
4.2	Lace braiding	52
4.3	Tunisian crochet	55
5.1	Logo of the Werratalmuseum Gerstungen	65
5.2	Poster in the Nationalpark-Haus Museum Fedderwardersiel, "Migrating birds at the coast of the North Sea"	66
5.3	Plate in the Nationalpark-Haus Museum Fedderwardersiel, "The seal—circle of the year"	68
5.4	Poster in the Landschaftsmuseum Angeln (Unewatt milkmaid leaning against a cow on a historical advertisement)	69
5.5	Poster in the Lötschentaler Museum. Original picture of a group of Tschäggätta participants	72
6.1	Pilgrim Father Bassetlaw Museum	85
6.2	Scrooby Manor trail board	88
8.1	The Three Dikgosi Monument, Gaborone, Botswana	117
8.2	Boitshoko Pillar at the Three Dikgosi Monument	121
8.3	A group of friends at the Three Dikgosi Monument	123
12.1	Commemorative Courtyard of the German Resistance Memorial Centre	190
12.2	Statue by Richard Scheibe	191
12.3	German Resistance Memorial Centre: plan of the permanent exhibition	192
12.4	Room 10: 'co-conspirators'	196

12.5	View from room 8 to room 9, picturing Claus Schenk Graf von Stauffenberg and Albrecht Ritter Mertz von Quirnheim	198
12.6	Permanent exhibition, topic 04 'Resistance from the workers' movement'	199
16.1	Gender blind model	263

Acknowledgements

The editors would like to thank all the staff at Routledge for their support. Special thanks are due to Professor William Logan and Professor Laurajane Smith for their scholarship and guidance, which has inspired and structured this volume.

Contributors

Bodil Axelsson is Associated Professor at Linköping University, Sweden. Her interdisciplinary research and teaching examine heritagisation, that is processes in which cultural institutions, associations and individuals produce meaningful pasts. She uses dynamic combinations of interviews, participant observation and text interpretations so as to understand contemporary and historical processes where relevant pasts are actualised, restored and reinserted into present and future actions. She is currently co-authoring a book on guides and city walks, including guided tours of the industrial heritage of Norrköping, Kiruna and Malmberget. Moreover she does fieldwork on the digital practices of cultural institutions. Previous research projects have focused on historical theatre plays, popular history magazines, cultural history museum's contemporary collecting and artistic work.

Arndís Bergsdóttir has a PhD in Museology from the University of Iceland and is a GEXcel open position scholar participating within the intersectional critical heritage research strand. Her PhD research focused on the reflection of gender politics in museum materialities with particular emphasis on absence as part of that materiality.

Janet Blake is an Associate Professor of Law at the University of Shahid Beheshti (Tehran) where she teaches International, Environmental and Human Rights Law and is a member of the UNESCO Chair for Human Rights, Peace and Democracy and the Centre for Excellence in Education for Sustainable Development, both based at the university. She is also a member of the Cultural Heritage Law Committee of the International Law Association and has acted as an International Consultant to UNESCO since 1999, mostly in the field of intangible cultural heritage and implementing the 2003 Convention. Her research monograph, *International Cultural Heritage Law*, was published by Oxford University Press in 2015.

Cristina Clopot is a Research Assistant at the Intercultural Research Centre, Heriot Watt University (Edinburgh, UK) working on CoHERE, a Horizon

2020 research project focused on European heritage. Her work explores the intersection of heritage studies, folklore and anthropology and her doctoral research focused on the heritage of Russian Old Believers in Romania. Cristina is a member of the board of the ICH network in the Association of Critical Heritage Studies and a founding member of its new Early Career Researchers' network. Her publications include, 'Liminal Identities of Migrant Groups: The Old Russian Believers of Romania' (Chapter 7 in the edited collection *Landscapes of Liminality*, Rowman & Littlefield, 2016) and 'Weaving the Past in a Fabric' (*Folklore* 66 (2016): 115–132).

Smilla Ebeling is a Senior Research Scientist at the University of Oldenburg, Germany. As a research scientist, she has been devoting herself to the question of how gender knowledge is constituted for more than 15 years. For example, she looks at the interplays between biological knowledge about sex and gender and societal gender relations. In the project 'Neue Heimatmuseen at Institutions of Knowledge Production', she was especially interested in the interaction of museum actors, exhibition objects, presentation forms and visitors. Her current project 'Gender Knowledge in and Between Disciplines: Critique, Transformation, and "Dissident Participation" in Academia', investigates the conditions for the development of critical gender knowledge in women's and gender studies.

Viv Golding joined the University of Leicester's School of Museum Studies in 2002 following a varied career in London as Head of Formal Education at the Horniman Museum (1992–2002) and Ceramic Arts at Community Education Lewisham (1980–1992). At Leicester she is Associate Professor and Joint Director of Postgraduate Research. Her academic research on museums and diversity is closely linked to the profession and she was elected President of ICME in 2013 and 2016 having served on the Board as Newsletter Editor (2004–2007) and Secretary (2010–2013). Viv is widely funded to speak on her research themes internationally (AHRC 2010–2011; AHRC 2011–2013; JSPS 2012–2013; 2014–2015; DAIWA 2011–2012; MA Australia 2011). She publishes widely, including most recently *Learning at the Museum Frontiers: Identity, Race and Power* (Routledge, 2016); *Museums and Truth* (Cambridge Scholars Publishing, 2014, with A. Fromm and P. Rekdal); and *Museums and Communities: Curators, Collections, Collaboration* (Berg, 2013, with W. Modest). For further details see www2.le.ac.uk/departments/museumstudies/people/dr-viv-golding.

Andrew Gorman-Murray is an Associate Professor in Social Sciences (Geography and Urban Studies), Leader of the Urban Research Program and Research Theme Champion for Urban Living and Society at Western Sydney University. He is a social, cultural and political geographer. His research encompasses: gender, sexuality and space; home and belonging; mobilities and place-making; emotional geographies and well-being; urban and rural studies; visual and material cultures; and social and cultural dimensions of disasters, climate change and sustainability. He co-edited *Material Geographies of Household Sustainability* (Ashgate, 2011, with Ruth Lane), *Sexuality, Rurality, and Geography* (Lexington, 2013, with Barbara Pini and Lia Bryant) and *Masculinities and Place* (Ashgate, 2014, with Peter Hopkins). He is co-editor of the journal *Emotion, Space and Society*.

Wera Grahn is Associate Professor in Gender Studies, Senior Lecturer and Head of Unit at Linköping University, Sweden. Furthermore, she is also Director of Postgraduate Research Training and Director of the Master's Programme, Gender Studies – Intersectionality and Change, as well as researching, teaching and supervising commitments. Previously, she has worked as a Senior Research fellow at the Norwegian Institute for Cultural Heritage Research (NIKU) in Oslo, Norway (2007–2011) and been affiliated to Upplandsmuseet for research (2006–2007). Before that, she was a PhD student at Tema Genus in Linköping (1999–2006). Her academic background is based in gender studies, ethnology, and theory and history of science, and she also has a BA in Journalism. She has a broad empirical interest in the field of cultural heritage, ranging from museums to monuments, historical sites, places and landscapes. Her main research questions have focused on how we use history today, how it is created, what it does to people and societies, what interests are working as driving forces in these processes, whose history is promoted and regarded and whose is not, and how can we find new more inclusive and diverse ways to use various parts of cultural heritage to tell alternative histories.

Sigurjón Baldur Hafsteinsson is Professor at the University of Iceland. His latest books in English are *Indigenous Screen Cultures in Canada* (University of Manitoba Press, 2010), *Unmasking Deep Democracy* (Intervention Press, 2013) and *Phallological Museum* (LIT Verlag, 2014). Hafsteinsson's fields of research have included indigenous media and democracy, visual culture and identities, death, representation, subjectivities, ethics and power and museums and cultural politics.

Joni Lariat is a PhD Candidate in the Department of Social Sciences and International Studies at Curtin University in Perth, Western Australia.

David Ludvigsson is Associate Professor of History at Linköping University, Sweden, where he works with History Teacher Training Programmes. He is the president of the Swedish Association of History Teachers and serves as Associate Editor of *Arts and Humanities in Higher Education: An International Journal of Theory, Research and Practice* (Sage). His research interests are mainly in the fields of uses of the past, history of historiography, teaching and learning of history and history of education. His books include

The Historian-Filmmaker's Dilemma: Historical Documentaries in Sweden in the Era of Häger and Villius (Uppsala Universitet, 2003) and *Enhancing Student Learning in History: Perspectives on University History Teaching* (Swedish Science Press, 2012). His current research, financed by the Swedish National Heritage Board, deals with modern uses of historical sites.

Scott McKinnon is a Vice-Chancellor's Postdoctoral Research Fellow in the School of Geography and Sustainable Communities, University of Wollongong. His research investigates the collective memory of disasters in Australia. He was previously Postdoctoral Research Fellow at the University of Western Sydney where he worked on the project 'Queering Disasters in the Antipodes: Investigating the Experiences of LGBTI People in Natural Disasters'. Scott has also worked as a Research Officer in the Department of Modern History and International Relations at Macquarie University and the School of Social Sciences and Psychology, University of Western Sydney. His primary research interests include geographies of memory, the social and cultural dimensions of disaster and historical geographies of sexuality and gender,

Rhiannon Mason is Professor of Museum, Heritage and Cultural Studies at Newcastle University. She joined Newcastle University in January 2001. Prior to this, she studied for a PhD at the Centre for Critical and Cultural Theory, Cardiff University, and taught at the universities of Cardiff and Glamorgan. She has previously been the Director of the International Centre for Cultural and Heritage Studies, Director of Research for the School of Arts and Cultures, Director of Postgraduate Studies for the School of Arts and Cultures, UoA 36 coordinator, and the Head of Media, Culture, Heritage. She is the current Head of the School of Arts and Cultures.

Marsha Meskimmon is Professor of Modern and Contemporary Art History and Theory and was Director of the School of the Arts from 2005–2011. Meskimmon's research has been recognised through the award of several international fellowships, including the Paul Mellon Visiting Senior Fellowship at the Centre for Advanced Study in the Visual Arts (CASVA), at the National Gallery of Art in Washington, DC, a Senior Research Fellowship at the Humanities Research Centre at The Australian National University and a period of AHRC-funded research leave. Most recently, she was Visiting Professor of Art History and Visual Studies at the University of Gothenburg in Sweden

Máiréad Nic Craith is Professor of Culture and Heritage and Director of Research at the School of Social Sciences at Heriot-Watt University (Edinburgh, Dubai, Malaysia). Her research has focused on different aspects of living heritage: including literary heritage, intercultural heritage, World Heritage sites, heritage and conflict, and heritage and law. An elected member of the Royal Irish

Academy, Máiréad's recent publications have advocated a holistic approach to heritage and include numerous journal essays on topics such as the role of heritage in a UK City of Culture and the implications of Wim Wenders' documentary (*Cathedrals of Culture*) for the concept of heritage more broadly. Along with William Logan and Ullrich Kockel, Máiréad is co–editor of *A Companion to Heritage Studies* (Blackwell, 2015). Her TEDx talk on intangible cultural heritage can be viewed at: www.youtube.com/watch?v=d9ZHj4ihTog

Anneli Palmsköld holds a PhD in Ethnology, her focus is on crafts in the Department of Conservation at the University of Gothenburg. She has done research on topics such as material culture and making, textiles and needlework from historical as well as contemporary points of view, craft and home craft as idea and phenomenon, and sloyd and craft as cultural heritage. She has also conducted a study on the reuse of textiles.

Johanna Rosenqvist is Senior Lecturer in History and Theory of Craft at Konstfack (Stockholm, Sweden), besides her tenure as Senior Lecturer in Art History and Visual Studies at Linnaeus University (Växjö/Kalmar, Sweden). She wrote her thesis, 'An Aesthetics of Sexual Difference? On Art and Artistry in Swedish Handicraft of the 1920s and 1990s' (2007) at Lund University, and has since continued to investigate the field of handicraft in relation to a wider field of cultural production with craft and performativity as a special point of interest. Together with Christina Zetterlund and Charlotte Hyltén-Cavallius she co-edited and contributed to the most recent overview of craft in Sweden, *Konsthantverk i Sverige del 1* (Mångkulturellt centrum, 2015).

Monica Sand is an artist and researcher with a PhD in Architecture from the Royal Institute of Technology, KTH, Stockholm, Sweden. Her present position at the Swedish Centre for Architecture and Design involves both artistic research and research coordination. In artistic practice, workshops and courses she collaborates with artists, dancers, architects and researchers to collectively explore public space through walking, performances and experimentations on resonance.

Joanne Sayner is Senior Lecturer in Cultural and Heritage Studies at Newcastle University. She completed her PhD at Cardiff University in 2002 and held her first lecturing post at the University of Bath. She then taught memory, media and German Studies at the University of Birmingham for 12 years before joining Media, Culture, Heritage at Newcastle University in January 2017.

Anna Scott is an Associate Lecturer in the School of History and Heritage at the University of Lincoln, with a PhD from the University of Lincoln.

Keletso G. Setlhabi is a Senior Lecturer in Archaeology at the University of Botswana. Her research interest is the study of material culture, its documentation and its role in defining and shaping past and present societies. She is further interested in intangible cultural heritage, its documentation and preservation.

Michelle L. Stefano is a Folklife Specialist (Research and Programs) at the American Folklife Center, Library of Congress (Washington, DC). She earned her BA in Art History (Brown University, 2000), MA in International Museum Studies (Gothenburg University, Sweden, 2004) and PhD in Heritage Studies at the International Centre for Cultural and Heritage Studies at Newcastle University (UK) in 2010. From 2011–2016, Stefano worked for Maryland Traditions, the folklife program of the state of Maryland, of which she was its Co-Director from 2015–2016. From 2012–2016, she led the partnership between Maryland Traditions and the University of Maryland, Baltimore County, where she was Visiting Assistant Professor in American Studies. She co-edited the *Routledge Companion to Intangible Cultural Heritage* (Routledge, 2017), *Engaging Heritage, Engaging Communities* (Boydell & Brewer, 2017) and *Safeguarding Intangible Cultural Heritage* (Boydell & Brewer, 2012).

Astrid von Rosen is a Senior Lecturer in Art History and Visual Studies, at the University of Gothenburg, Sweden, and a Research Coordinator for the Embracing the Archives cluster at the Centre for Critical Heritage Studies. Her research interests include historiographical and participatory approaches to independent dance community archives and archiving, the power of images in relation to social change and transformation, and border-crossing methodological development. Recent publications include (editor and contributor) *Dream-Playing Across Borders: Accessing the Non-Texts of Strindberg's A Dream Play in Düsseldorf 1915–18 and Beyond* (Makadam, 2016) and '"Dream no Small Dreams!" Impossible Archival Imaginaries in Dance Community Archiving in a Digital Age', in *Rethinking Dance History* (Routledge, 2017).

Ross J. Wilson is Professor of Modern History and Public Heritage at the University of Chichester, UK. His research interests include the experience, representation and memory of the First World War in Britain and the United States. His wider research focuses on issues of museum, media and heritage representations in the modern era. He is the author of *Representing Enslavement and Abolition in Museums* (Routledge, 2011), *Landscapes of the Western Front* (Routledge, 2012), *Cultural Heritage of the Great War in Britain* (Routledge, 2013), *New York and the First World War* (Routledge, 2014), *The Language of the Past* (Bloomsbury Academic, 2016) and *Natural History: Heritage, Place and Politics* (Routledge, 2017).

Series general co-editors' foreword

The interdisciplinary field of Heritage Studies is now well established in many parts of the world. It differs from earlier scholarly and professional activities that focused narrowly on the architectural or archaeological preservation of monuments and sites. Such activities remain important, especially as modernisation and globalisation lead to new developments that threaten natural environments, archaeological sites, traditional buildings and arts and crafts. But they are subsumed within the new field that sees 'heritage' as a social and political construct encompassing all those places, artefacts and cultural expressions inherited from the past which, because they are seen to reflect and validate our identity as nations, communities, families and even individuals, are worthy of some form of respect and protection.

Heritage results from a selection process, often government-initiated and supported by official regulation; it is not the same as history, although this, too, has its own elements of selectivity. Heritage can be used in positive ways to give a sense of community to disparate groups and individuals or to create jobs on the basis of cultural tourism. It can be actively used by governments and communities to foster respect for cultural and social diversity, and to challenge prejudice and misrecognition. But it can also be used by governments in less benign ways, to reshape public attitudes in line with undemocratic political agendas or even to rally people against their neighbours in civil and international wars, ethnic cleansing and genocide. In this way there is a real connection between heritage and human rights.

This is time for a new and unique series of books canvassing the key issues dealt with in the new Heritage Studies. The series seeks to address the deficiency facing the field identified by the Smithsonian in 2005 – that it is 'vastly under-theorized'. It is time to look again at the contestation that inevitably surrounds the identification and evaluation of heritage and to find new ways to elucidate the many layers of meaning that heritage places and intangible cultural expressions have acquired. Heritage conservation and safeguarding in such circumstances can only be understood as a form of cultural politics and that this needs to be reflected in heritage practice, be that in educational institutions or in the field.

It is time, too, to recognise more fully that heritage protection does not depend alone on top-down interventions by governments or the expert actions of heritage industry professionals, but must involve local communities and communities of interest. It is critical that the values and practices of communities, together with traditional management systems where such exist, are understood, respected and incorporated in heritage management plans and policy documents so that communities feel a sense of 'ownership' of their heritage and take a leading role in sustaining it into the future.

This series of books aims then to identify interdisciplinary debates within Heritage Studies and to explore how they impact on the practices not only of heritage management and conservation, but also the processes of production, consumption and engagement with heritage in its many and varied forms.

William S. Logan
Laurajane Smith

Part I

Introduction

Chapter 1

The tyranny of the normal and the importance of being liminal

Ross J. Wilson

There is a strange status that exists within the study of gender and heritage, which ensures that the subject is perennially cast aside upon the outer extremities from the central focus of the subject area. Gender appears fated to be regarded as a niche topic as assessments of power, discourse, identity, consumerism and authority have become the established fields of enquiry within heritage studies. Indeed, despite the articles and books on gender that have been published since the 1980s and that appear ready to launch this concern into the mainstream and secure a degree of prominence and respect, the breakthrough has not been achieved in an Anglo-American context (Porter 1987). Within Scandinavia, gender has become a central part of heritage studies, serving as a critical perspective on the representation of the past (see Grahn 2012). However, elsewhere, gender is frequently reduced to a secondary status; it functions as an interest, an extra layer of analysis, an addition to a complex study, but not a subject in its own right. Seemingly obscured by the 'major' topics, gender can almost be viewed and dismissed as a fashion or passing trend within the wider fluctuations of theory and method in heritage studies. This would seem to mirror the study of gender across the humanities and social sciences, even within wider Western society, where discussions of gender are frequently neglected or reduced to temporary debating points before attention is swiftly fixed elsewhere. Therefore, this collection of articles on gender and heritage might have the rescuing of 'gender' from this neglect as its primary aim. However, primarily, this volume seeks not to provide the long-awaited declaration of acceptance for gender within heritage studies and the discarding of its niche status in some sectors. Rather, within the work of the authors that has been gathered here to reflect current agendas within the field, this is a reiteration and celebration of gender as a 'liminal' area of concern. Developing from the model of Scandinavian studies, it is through this character that the position of gender as a mode of critique par excellence can serve scholars, heritage practitioners and wider society. This collection of chapters challenges the tyranny of the normal from the powerful perspective of the margins.

Defining gender for a critical heritage studies

The use of gender within heritage studies has been complicated by the manner in which scholars have consistently offered new definitions of this field before any assessment. Because the analysis of gender varies in different contexts it could be construed to be lacking in any firm grounding in data; this is a subject that appears almost ephemeral and ethereal. Clarifications of this area can ascribe gender as a product of power relations, the subject of consumerism, the expression of the psyche, the effect of discourse, the gaze of institutions, the consequence of the material environment or the result of social performances. This is the consequence of the trajectory of gender studies within philosophy and the social sciences over the course of the twentieth century. From de Beauvoir's (1949) existential analysis of women's subordinate role within society; Freud's (1919) and Lacan's (1936) psychoanalytical assessment of gender identities; Cixous's (1975) development of 'écriture feminine'; Irigaray's (1977) dissection of the semiology of gendered economics; and Foucault's (1976) examination of the 'genealogy' of sexualities, a rich basis of enquiry has developed. The development of gender studies has also been enhanced and indeed entwined with the growth of second-wave feminist theory from the 1960s onwards that assessed the limits placed upon women's identities within Western society (Friedan 1963; Greer 1970). This lineage has provided an array of theoretical approaches for the discussion of gendered identities and processes within society for gender studies, queer theory, sexuality studies and masculinity studies (see Grosz 1994). As a result of this work, a distinct concern for gender studies programmes emerged in the 1970s and the notion of masculinity and femininity as biologically determined binary opposites was dismissed, with scholars examining the controls, nuances and fluidity of gendered identities (see Connell 1987; Kessler and McKenna 1978).

Within philosophy, literature studies, politics and sociology, gender became a point of reflection for scholars after the 1970s. One of the most prominent of these works to emerge within gender studies was Butler's (1990) discussion of 'gender performativity', which assessed gender as a social role that is acted out by individuals to assume a place within society (see Turner 1988). Within this study, gender becomes a matter of negotiation between individual agency and societal expectations; the corollary of this analysis being that such performances are the site of control but also resistance. This analysis of gender as a conceptual category with socio-political effect had been earlier undertaken by Haraway (1989). This analysis revealed how specific disciplines and modes of enquiry have been tacitly gendered in both their conception and their research as a 'mode of production'. Bordo's (1987, 1993) examination of 'body politics' extends this study of symbolism onto the human form where the corporeal is transformed into an ideology composed of a series of signs formed through the effects of late capitalism, which are then established as 'real'. Barad (2007) has also examined how it is the interaction of agents, both human and non-human, which enables concepts such as 'gender' to emerge. This assessment of gendered identities as the site of multiple processes was explored within the development of 'intersectionality' as African American feminist scholars highlighted how gender is entangled with issues of race, ethnicity and class (Crenshaw 1989, 1991; Hill Collins 1990; hooks 1982). Through this work, the 'function' of gender, intertwined with other social categories such as ethnicity and class, was examined and recognised as a central structuring device within society.

It was during the 1970s and 1980s that this increasing awareness for both feminist studies and gender identity emerged within the field of cultural heritage, anthropology and archaeology in Anglo-American and European scholarship (see Ortner and Whitehead 1981). Drawing upon the work of theorists within the social sciences, the role of gendered identities within the representation of the past became a distinct area of concern for curators and heritage practitioners (see Anderson and Winkworth 1991; Gifford-Gonzalez 1993; Nenadic 1994; Porter 1987, 1991). These examinations focused upon the gendered assumptions within museums, galleries and heritage sites that reinforced normative values within contemporary society (after Glaser and Zenetou 1994). In this manner, institutions served as a means by which gendered identities were formed and reiterated (Devonshire and Wood 1996). This has led to a range of studies within museology that focus upon asserting gender and sexual equality within collections and displays (see Horn 2010; Liddiard 2004; Machin 2008). This focus on gender as a means to assert ideas and identities that have been repressed or obscured has also become part of wider practices within cultural resource management (Buckley 1993; Smith and du Cros 1994; Smith et al. 2003; Sørensen 1999; Whittlesey 1994). Indeed, over the last two decades a strong area of concern for the analysis of gender and heritage has developed, which has enabled emerging and established scholars, museum professionals and heritage practitioners to include gendered perspectives as a considered part of their work (see Levin 2010).

This position is reflected in the appearance of sections on 'gender' within handbooks, dictionaries, discussions and overviews of heritage and cultural resource management (see Ashworth et al. 2007; Graham and Howard 2008; Tunbridge and Ashworth 1996). However, critical concepts of gender within heritage studies have emerged through the work of scholars engaging in the use and value of heritage within society:

> Heritage is gendered. It is gendered in the way that heritage is defined, understood and talked about and, in turn, in the way it reproduces and legitimizes gender identities and the social values that underpin them. A range of assumptions about the experiences of men and women are embedded in the definitions and discourses of heritage.
>
> (Smith 2008: 161)

The role of gender in heritage policy and practice has also been recognised at an international level through the UNESCO (2014) report on gender equality and culture. This document outlined the significance of establishing a role for gender equality and representation within the heritage industry. In fact, one of the main findings of the report was stated as: 'Support interdisciplinary research on gender equality in heritage and the creative industries that involve groups and communities concerned, and consider the complexity and diversity of gender relations and the underlying power structures' (UNESCO 2014).

However, despite this acknowledgement of gender as an important subject to both study and to address, scholars still note that regardless of such prominence, gender within heritage studies still appears to be at the margins of the major concerns of the subject area (Reading 2015; Smith 2008). Though there is now over three decades of established scholarship on the subject, there still appears to be an obstacle or barrier preventing gender assuming a central role within research and practice especially within the Anglo-American tradition. This condition has been exposed through the emergence of a 'critical heritage studies' that places a greater role on for scholarship and practice to take an active and analytical role within society (Harrison and Linkman 2010; Winter 2013). In these circumstances, it appears that gender is something that heritage studies engages with as an associated concern but only rarely is it regarded as a central focus of assessment. Placed at the periphery, a gender perspective on the construction and consumption of heritage is seemingly obscured as the established themes of the subject area dominate scholarship.

The importance of being liminal

Where the place of gender studies at the edges of research has often been the cause of lament and criticism from scholars working in this field, it is the locus where a 'critical gender heritage studies' can emerge. Rather than seeking to place gender in the mainstream of academic research, it is from the periphery where an engaged and analytical study of gender and heritage can most benefit scholarship and wider society. The importance of being liminal or residing upon the periphery has been explored by political scientists, economists and philosophers as a means of understanding wider processes within society (after Wallerstein 1983). While the periphery can be disregarded, oppressed and exploited it is from the edges where a critique of the operation of power emerges. However, this critique should not be regarded as a fait accompli, this exchange between core and periphery is a constant process that defines the identity of both (see Derrida 1976: 98). In this understanding, the edge is always the area where the costs of the excesses of society are most keenly experienced but where the agenda to reform and reshape will develop (see Said 1978). This follows from the work of the Argentinian-Mexican philosopher Enrique Dussel, who argued in his work for a rereading of classic Marxist texts. Dussel (1978) asserted that Marx had too often been interpreted by Western scholars as operating from a site of privilege in the 'centre'. Through this assessment, Dussel forwarded the notion of 'exteriority', defined as the periphery and the liminal, as the site of liberation: 'In order to create something new, one must have a new world that bursts in from the exteriority. This exteriority is the people itself which, despite being oppressed by the system, is totally foreign to it' (Dussel 2012: 33).

It is the location of the periphery where the emergence of alternative, dissident and transforming ideas are created and can then effect the operation of power and authority at the core (see Fanon 1961). This value of the liminal and its relationship to a dominant perspective has been discussed by Stalybrass and White (1986) as both exploitative but also revelatory. While that which is placed upon the edges of society and politics and regarded as separate from the mainstream is obscured by practice, it serves as a site of symbolic resistance to those same hegemonic structures (after Gramsci 1971).

This is the location of a critical gender heritage studies rather than attempting to ensure its place within the conventional. From this position, scholarship can act to inform practice and policy by challenging established norms. Indeed, it is the importance of being liminal that must be vaunted to oppose the tyranny of 'normal'; this is undertaken not just for those who are cast aside from what is defined by tradition, creed or custom as 'regular' but also to liberate those who are weighed down under those same definitions. This tyranny of normative values and ideals that shape our identities can be exposed for the constructed, contingent and pervasive influence that they are upon society. In an assessment of moral norms, Korsgaard (1996) details the function of the common, the everyday or the 'regular': 'They do not merely describe a way in which we, in fact, regulate our conduct. They make claims on us; they command, oblige, recommend or guide. Or at least, when we invoke them, we make claims on one another' (Korsgaard 1996: 8).

As such, to be regarded as normal is to exist within a site of control and domination as much as those who are cast beyond the boundaries of that defined status of 'normal' (Foucault 1976). The rationale for reform from the periphery must be partly to secure liberation for those at the core. Such a transformation is pertinent in the study of gender where the 'tyranny of the normal' is particularly acute and laden with issues of power and identity. It is within this area of debate that 'queer theory' developed as a distinct concern to undermine and redefine notions of gender and sexuality (de Lauretis 1991; Halperin 1990; Kosofsky Sedgwick 1990). In this assessment, the binary notions of masculine and feminine, heterosexual and homosexual, normal and other, emerged as a consequence of historical processes. From medieval religious doctrine, modes of civil government or the psychoanalytical assessment of deviance and subversion in the early twentieth century, a series of controls and regulations have defined the status of 'normal' in contrast to what is seen as 'deviant' (see Freud 1901). As a process of challenging this division, queer theorists have emphasised the need to undermine the assumed subjective, authoritative power of the normal. As Halperin (1990: 52) states, 'queer is by definition whatever is at odds with the normal, the legitimate, the dominant'. While this position deconstructs the established values of society, in the process it ensures the liberty of individuals from the rigid categories of being that outline notions of agency and identity. From these assessments, the value of gender studies emerges not as a rigid set of principles or methods, but as a critical perspective from the periphery that sets itself against the operation of power that defines and limits humanity.

A critical gender heritage studies

This is the position forwarded by this volume; a critical gender heritage studies that is marked by a variety of approaches, methods and encounters with data, but is framed by its position at the periphery. An area of study that orientates itself on the edge as a deliberate challenge to the structures of power and authority that persist within academic scholarship as well as wider society. As it is from this place on the margins that a counter-narrative can emerge that works towards the liberation of both the core and the periphery. This enables a redefining of gender within heritage studies as a critical tool for examining the form, function and use of the most intimate and fundamental aspect of human identity (after Ridgeway 2011). Over the last three decades as gender has been recognised within heritage studies there has been a tendency to attempt a definition of 'gender' and 'gendered identities' as a means of establishing the field as a legitimate concern. While this has been highly important in bringing greater recognition to a topic that has been obscured, the consequence of such work has entailed that gender has become focused on identifying masculine, feminine, 'queer' and transgender performances and roles within museums and heritage sites (after Levin 2010). This identification does highlight the issues, but it also constrains the way in which gender can be used as more than a definition but as a critique against the operation of power (Sandell 2007). Rather than define how gender within heritage studies is a construct, an identity formed from acquiescence or resistance against the social, cultural and political norms that structure society, a critical gender heritage studies can be a tool through which the central condition of the experience of humanity is assessed. In this manner, to take a 'gender' perspective is to look upon the world as an unceasing process of criticism to secure liberation (Marx 1977: 131).

If this new approach to study is incorporated, then the role of gender as the fundamental mode of critique regarding society can be considered; rather than seeking to define and characterise gender identities this forms a means of examining everyday life as it is through gender that we perceive and structure the world. While heritage studies have included gender as an area of concern, where this use of gender perspectives as an analytical tool has been explored is within the cognate field of tourism studies (Kinnaird and Hall 1994; Swain 1995; Thea Sinclair 1997; Veijola and Jokinen 1994). It is within this area that gender assessments, encompassing a range of approaches and theories, are nevertheless used as a conceptual device, to examine identity and place but also economics, resources, development, commercialism, politics and human rights (see Ferguson 2010a, 2010b). In this approach, gender is not about identity, it is about understanding how the world is experienced and used by individuals, groups and communities (Hall *et al.* 2003). Tourism can be regarded in this work as a sector that is entirely framed by gender issues and it is through that frame that issues of social justice and equality can be pursued (Aitchison 1996a, 1996b, 2000). Edensor and Kothari's (1994) study of the masculine form and content of the heritage sites within the Scottish city of Stirling is an example of this agenda within tourism studies. Whether through visual culture, materials, landscapes, discourse, corporeal performances or body politics, the critical study of gender serves as the basis of assessment of the function, representation and experience within tourism (see Pritchard 2007; Swain 2004; Swain and Momsen 2002).

It is this perspective that can be developed for a critical gender heritage, a broad area of study encompassing a variety of approaches and theories. This perspective is informed by the notion of intersectionality, which stresses how gender is underscored with issues of ethnicity, power and class. Rather than undermining the approach of specifically 'gender' heritage, this mode of assessment supports the role of gender as the primary point of critique for modern society. If gendered identities and perspectives are formed through this nexus, then it is gender as an analytical instrument through which an understanding of the world must be considered. Therefore, this reveals the significance of a critical gender heritage, while located on the periphery it possesses the scope and significance to engage with issues at the very core of politics, society and economics. Gender constitutes a key means of disrupting and amending the 'Authorized Heritage Discourse' (Smith 2006). This edited collection is, therefore, not a statement of gender as a mainstream subject within the field of heritage studies. It is a demonstration of what can be achieved from the edges and a recognition that gender can address more than the process of identity formation. It is the fundamental mode of critique for the modern era.

Outline of the book

The following chapters represent the diversity of scholarship within current gender and heritage studies as well as emphasising a common concern for addressing issues of equality and social justice. To reflect this strength, these chapters have been arranged across three major themes of performance, place and politics as a means of demonstrating the way in which gender studies offers a critique of central concerns while operating at the margins. The division of these chapters highlights what can be possible within a critical gender studies as scholars use a variety of data, from museum displays and historic walks, legal principles and educational agendas, to assert gender as a critical mode of enquiry. While chapters within these three sections may well reflect performance, place and politics in one, the division of this edited volume into this tripartite scheme has been undertaken not to limit or define the work of scholars but to emphasise the diversity of practice with gender and heritage studies.

Part II focuses upon issues of performance within gender and heritage. Performance refers to the personal and intimate as well as the public and collective displays of gender that take place through concepts of heritage. A range of different cultural and political contexts are explored within this section as authors engage with how gender is constructed through sites, habits and values by individuals, communities and government bodies. The chapters form distinct case studies that examine these concerns from a global context. In this manner, the juxtaposition of examples of the formation of identities and progressive values within a Swedish post-industrial landscape can be contrasted with similar processes at religious sites in Romania. Rather than forming a demonstration of cross-cultural comparisons, these studies reveal the way gender is performed as more than a means of identity but as a means of establishing networks of power, capital, authority and as a process of resistance. This is clearly demonstrated in the opening chapter of the section by Axelsson and Ludvigsson, whose assessment of gendered perspectives of historic walking tours in the eastern Swedish city of Norrköping provides a challenge to normative ideas and a means of liberating both the dominant and liminal elements of society.

Part III provides a direct line of continuation with Part II by focusing on issues of place within the study of gender and heritage. The chapters within this section address how specific sites, museums, heritage parks, monuments or teaching facilities serve as delineated locales where gender values are learnt, acculturated or challenged. In this section, importance is attached to how spaces serve as both transformational arenas where dissonant voices can be rehearsed and recognised but also where normative roles are asserted. In these chapters, a concern for tourism, museums, monuments and education will reveal the gendered constructions of heritage representations and the modes of resistance and reform present within each of these fields. Place is examined within this volume as a site or locale that is divided and interpreted on the basis of gender, an arena where normalising values and ideals constrain its inhabitants and exclude others. It is from the study of these spaces that a critical gender studies can be observed as the scholars within this collection engage with how gendered perspectives constitutes a counter-discourse. This is most succinctly defined by Lariat's use of anthropology, queer theory and feminist studies to create collaborative heritage partnerships in Sabang, Indonesia.

Part IV will advance the debate presented within the initial sections of the volume by examining the issues of gender, heritage and politics. The chapters within this section address issues of gender politics within heritage sites in the United States and Germany alongside the formation of a feminist critique of heritage practice, the role of gender with international law regarding heritage and the political agenda in forming gender as a central concern within the heritage sector. All of the chapters engage with the politics of gender at varying levels to reveal how structures of power delineate expectations and definitions regarding gender and gender roles. However, each of these chapters utilises the role of authority, whether of the museum, legal principles or governments, as a means by which a hegemonic discourse can be altered. As such, this section provides a fitting conclusion to the edited volume as it explores the politics of gender and heritage and its potential in serving individuals and communities. This work exemplifies the function of a critical gender heritage, a study that assesses the policy, practice, economics and ethics of cultural heritage to ensure a movement towards social justice.

This is demonstrated by the chapters provided by Grahn and by Blake, who both challenge the institutional models of power and authority through subversive narratives and agendas from the periphery. For Grahn, this is demonstrated in the hegemonic power of the museum, while for Blake this is reflected in the international structures for managing and preserving heritage.

Conclusions

This volume emphasises the significance of gender perspectives within heritage studies and calls for a formation of a critical gender heritage to emphasise the rationale and relevance for this area within the field of study. However, this is not undertaken to establish gender as a mainstream concern for heritage studies. The place of gender has been debated by heritage scholars over the past two decades as increasing numbers of studies have drawn attention to the role of gender identity in the construction and consumption of heritage within society. This has seen the inclusion of gender within handbooks and guides to heritage studies but there has been a resistance to acknowledge gender as a defining issue within the field. As heritage studies discuss hegemony, power, consumerism, capitalism or identity, a concern for gender has been obscured or eclipsed. The flaw in this process has been highlighted by theories of intersectionality, which demonstrate how these concerns are underscored by the experience of class, ethnicity and gender. However, the central concerns of heritage studies have rendered gender liminal. In effect, gender has been cast to the periphery by the tyranny of the normal. As such, this volume asserts not the necessity of gender as a core area of debate but as a critical tool of enquiry that exists upon the edges. It is from this position that a critical gender heritage studies can thrive, serving as a means of addressing inequality and absence for communities as well as undermining the forces that constrain the majority. Whereas gender within heritage has struggled in being recognised and used by scholars as a fundamental part of how the past is experienced and represented, in this collection we seek to make plain the 'vital importance' of being liminal.

Bibliography

Aitchison, C.C. 1996a. Monumentally male? A guided tour of the heritage tourism industry. *Trouble and Strife: A Radical Feminist Journal* 14(2): 53–61.

Aitchison, C.C. 1996b. The masculinisation and militarisation of Scotland's heritage. *Leisure Studies Association Newsletter* November: 16–23.

Aitchison, C.C. 2000. Locating gender: space, place and heritage tourism. In K. Atkinson, S. Oerton and G. Plain (eds) *Feminisms on Edge: Politics, Discourses and National Identities*. Cardiff: Cardiff Academic Press, 93–102.

Anderson, M. and Winkworth, K. 1991. Museums and gender – an Australian critique. *Museum* 171: 147–151.

Ashworth, G.J., Graham, B.J. and Tunbridge, J.E. 2007. *Pluralising Pasts: Heritage, Identity and Place in Multicultural Societies*. London: Pluto Books.

Barad, K. 2007. *Meeting the Universe Halfway: Quantum Physics and the Entanglement of Matter and Meaning.* Durham, NC: Duke University Press.

Bordo, S. 1987. *The Flight to Objectivity: Essays on Cartesianism and Culture.* Albany, NY: SUNY Press.

Bordo, S. 1993. *Unbearable Weight: Feminism, Western Culture and the Body.* Berkeley, CA: University of California Press.

Buckley, K. 1993. Cultural resource management and gender issues. In H. du Cros and L. Smith (eds) *Women in Archaeology: A Feminist Critique.* Canberra: Australian National University, Department of Prehistory, Research School of Pacific Studies, Occasional Papers in Prehistory, No. 23, 173–174.

Butler, J. 1990. *Gender Trouble: Feminism and the Subversion of Identity.* New York: Routledge.

Cixous, H. 1975. The Laugh of the Medusa. Trans. by K. Cohen and P. Cohen. *Signs* 1: 875–893.

Connell, R. 1987. *Gender and Power: Society, the Person, and Sexual Politics.* Stanford, CA: Stanford University Press.

Crenshaw, K. 1989. Demarginalizing the intersection of race and sex: a Black feminist critique of antidiscrimination doctrine, feminist theory and antiracist politics. *University of Chicago Legal Forum* 1: 136–167.

Crenshaw, K. 1991. Mapping the margin: intersectionality identity politics and violence against women of color. *Standard Law Review* 43(6): 1241–1299.

De Beauvoir, S. 1949. *Le deuxième sexe.* Vols. I and II. Paris: Gallimard.

de Lauretis, T. 1991. Queer theory: lesbian and gay sexualities: an introduction. *differences: A Journal of Feminist Cultural Studies* 3(2): iii–xviii.

Derrida, J. 1976. *Of Grammatology.* Baltimore, MD: Johns Hopkins University Press.

Devonshire, A. and Wood, B. (eds) 1996. *Women in Industry and Technology from Prehistory to Present Day: Current Research and the Museum Experience.* London: Museum of London.

Dussel, E. 1978. *Ethics and the Theology of Liberation.* Maryknoll, NY: Orbis.

Dussel, E. 2012. Transmodernity and interculturality: an interpretation from the perspective of philosophy of liberation. *Transmodernity: Journal of Peripheral Cultural Production of the Luso-Hispanic World* 1(3): 28–59.

Edensor, T. and Kothari, U. 1994. The masculinisation of Stirling's heritage. In V. Kinnaird and D. Hall (eds) *Tourism: A Gender Analysis.* Chichester: Wiley, 164–187.

Fanon, F. 1961. *Les Damnés de la Terre.* Paris: Seuil.

Ferguson, L. 2010a. Interrogating 'gender' in development policy and practice: the World Bank, tourism and microenterprise in Honduras. *International Feminist Journal of Politics* 12(1): 3–24.

Ferguson, L. 2010b. Tourism development and the structuring of social reproduction in Central America. *Review of International Political Economy* 17(5): 860–888.

Foucault, M. 1976. *La Volonté de savoir.* 2nd edition, vol. 1. Paris: Gallimard.

Freud, S. 1901. *The Psychopathology of Everyday Life.* London: T. Fisher Unwin.

Freud, S. 1919. Lines of advance in psycho-analytic therapy. In J. Strachey (ed.) *The Standard Edition of the Complete Psychological Works of Sigmund Freud.* vol. 17, 159–168. London: Hogarth Press.

Friedan, B. 1963. *The Feminine Mystique.* New York: Dell.

Gifford-Gonzalez, D. 1993. You can hide, but you can't run: representation of women's work in illustrations of palaeolithic life. *Visual Anthropology Review* 9: 3–21.

Glaser, J. and Zenetou, A. (eds) 1994. *Gender Perspectives: Essays of Women in Museums*. Washington, DC: Smithsonian Institution Press.

Graham, B. and Howard, P. (eds) 2008. *Companion to Heritage and Identity*. Aldershot: Ashgate.

Grahn, W. 2012. Theorizing gender in heritage studies. *Session presented at the inaugural conference of the Association of Critical Heritage Studies*, 5–8 June 2012. Gothenburg, Sweden: University of Gothenburg. Available at: www.gu.se/digitalAssets/1358/1358499_s015wera-grahn.pdf (accessed 15 July 2015).

Gramsci, A. 1971. *Selections from the Prison Notebooks*. Trans. Q. Hoare and G.N. Smith (ed.). New York: International Publishers.

Greer, G. 1970. *The Female Eunuch*. London: MacGibbon & Kee.

Grosz, E.A. 1994. *Volatile Bodies: Toward a Corporeal Feminism*. Bloomington, IN and Indianapolis, IN: Indiana University Press.

Hall, D., Byrne Swain, M. and Kinnaird, V. 2003. Tourism and gender: an evolving agenda. *Tourism Recreation Research* 28(2): 7–11.

Halperin, M. 1990. *One Hundred Years of Homosexuality: And Other Essays on Greek Love*. New York: Routledge.

Haraway, D. 1989. *Primate Visions: Gender, Race and Nature in the World of Modern Science*. New York and London: Routledge.

Harrison, R. and Linkman, A. 2010. Critical approaches to heritage. In R. Harrison (ed.) *Understanding the Politics of Heritage*. Manchester: Manchester University Press, 43–80.

Hill Collins, P. 1990. *Black Feminist Thought: Knowledge, Consciousness and the Politics of Empowerment*. Boston, MA: Unwin Hyman.

hooks, b. 1982. *Ain't I a Woman? Black Women and Feminism*. London: Pluto Press.

Horn, A. 2010. *Queering the Museum Catalogue*. Birmingham: Birmingham Museum.

Irigaray, L. 1977. *Ce Sexe qui n'en est pas un*. Paris: Editions de Minui.

Kessler, W. and McKenna, S.J. 1978. *Gender: An Ethnomethodological Approach*. New York: Wiley.

Kinnaird, V. and Hall, D.R. (eds) 1994. *Tourism: A Gender Analysis*. Chichester: Wiley.

Korsgaard, A. 1996. *The Sources of Normativity*. Cambridge: Cambridge University Press.

Kosofsky Sedgwick, E. 1990. *Epistemology of the Closet*. Berkeley, CA: University of California.

Lacan, J. 1936. The mirror stage as formative of the I as revealed in psychoanalytic experience. In J. Lacan, *Ecrits: The First Complete Edition in English*, trans. by Bruce Fink. New York: W.W. Norton, 2006.

Levin, A.K. 2010. *Gender, Sexuality and Museums: A Routledge Reader*. New York: Routledge

Liddiard, M. 2004. Changing histories: museums, sexuality and the future of the past. *Museum and Society* 2(1): 15–29.

Machin, R. 2008. Gender representation in the natural history galleries at the Manchester Museum. *Museum and Society* 6(1): 54–67.

Marx, K. 1977. *A Contribution to the Critique of Hegel's Philosophy of Right*. Trans. by A. Jolin and Joseph O'Malley. Cambridge: Cambridge University Press.

Nenadic, S. 1994. Museums, gender and cultural identity in Scotland. *Gender & History* (6)3: 426–434.

Ortner, S.B. and Whitehead, H. 1981. *Sexual Meanings: The Cultural Construction of Gender and Sexuality*. Cambridge: Cambridge University Press.

Porter, G. 1987. Gender bias: representations of work in history museums. Bias in museums. *Museum Professional Group Transactions* 22: 11–15.

Porter, G. 1991. How are women represented in British history museums? *Museum* 171: 159–162.

Pritchard, A. (ed.) 2007. *Tourism and Gender: Embodiment, Sensuality and Experience*. Wallingford: CABI.

Reading, A. 2015. Making feminist heritage work: gender and heritage. In E. Waterton and S. Watson (eds) *The Palgrave Handbook of Contemporary Heritage Research*. Basingstoke: Palgrave Macmillan, 397–410.

Ridgeway, C.L. 2011. *Framed by Gender: How Gender Inequality Persists in the Modern World*. New York: Oxford University Press.

Said, E. 1978. *Orientalism*. New York: Pantheon.

Sandell, R. 2007. *Museums, Prejudice and the Reframing of Difference*. London and New York: Routledge.

Smith, L. 2006. *Uses of Heritage*. London and New York: Routledge.

Smith, L. 2008. Heritage, gender and identity. In B. Graham and P. Howard (eds) *The Ashgate Research Companion to Heritage and Identity*. Aldershot: Ashgate, 159–178.

Smith, L. and du Cros, H. 1994. Equity and gender in Australian archaeology: a survey of the Women in Archaeology Conference, 1991. In M.C. Nelson, S.M. Nelson and A. Wylie (eds) *Equity Issues for Women in Archaeology: Archaeological Papers of the American Anthropological Association*. Washington, DC: Archaeological Papers of the American Anthropological Association, No. 5, 115–120.

Smith, L., Morgan, A. and van der Meer, A. 2003b. The Waanyi women's history project: a community partnership, Queensland, Australia. In L. Derry and M. Malloy (eds) *Archaeologists and Local Communities: Partners in Exploring the Past*. Washington, DC: Society for American Archaeology, 147–165.

Sørensen, M.L.S. 1999. Archaeology, gender and the museum. In N. Merriman (ed.) *Making Early Histories in Museums*. Leicester: Leicester University Press, 136–150.

Stallybrass, P. and White, A. 1986. *The Politics and Poetics of Transgression*. Ithaca, NY: Cornell University Press.

Swain, M. 1995. Gender in tourism. *Annals of Tourism Research* 22(2): 247–266.

Swain, M. 2004. (Dis)embodied experience and power dynamics in tourism research. In J. Phillimore and L. Goodson (eds) *Qualitative Research in Tourism*. London: Routledge, 102–118.

Swain, M. and Momsen, J.H. (eds) 2002. *Gender/Tourism/Fun?* New York: Cognizant Communication.

Thea Sinclair, M. (ed.) 1997. *Gender, Work and Tourism*. London: Routledge.

Tunbridge, J.E. and Ashworth, G.J. 1996. *Dissonant Heritage: The Management of the Past as a Resource in Conflict*. Chichester: Wiley.

Turner, V. 1988. *The Anthropology of Performance*. New York: PAJ Publications.

UNESCO 2014. *Gender Equality, Heritage and Creativity*. Paris: UNESCO.

Vanegas, A. 2002. Representing lesbians and gay men in British social history museums. In R. Sandell (ed.) *Museums, Society, Inequality*. London: Routledge, 98–109.

Veijola, S. and Jokinen, E. 1994. The body in tourism. *Theory, Culture & Society* 11(3): 125–151.

Wallerstein, I. 1983. *Historical Capitalism*. London: Verso.

Whittlesey, S.M. 1994. The sociology of gender in Arizona archeology. *Archeological Papers of the American Anthropological Association* 5(1): 173–181.

Winter, T. 2013. Clarifying the critical in critical heritage studies. *International Journal of Heritage Studies* 19: 532–545.

Part II
Performance

Chapter 2

Johanna, Moa and I'm every lesbian
Gender, sexuality and class in Norrköping's industrial landscape

Bodil Axelsson and David Ludvigsson

> Work. I have almost not met any homophobia at all. On the contrary, everyone close to me has been super supportive about me being a lesbian. I work in an academic environment where it is not socially acceptable to be neither [sic] homophobic, nor [sic] racist or sexist. Maybe that's one of the reasons why I got so shocked when two summers ago a man at work all of a sudden made this very homophobic statement in the break room. Of course I argued against him but it didn't help at all. He just got more and more angry and started to attack me on a very personal level. I remember that he said that because I was a lesbian I had destroyed all of my students for life and that if his children had me as a teacher he would take them out of school.[1]

The homophobic harassment (which led to six months of sick leave for the female and a warning from the employer to the harassing male) is included in the city walk 'I'm every lesbian', and the scene is in one of the university buildings in central Norrköping, Sweden. It represents one of 24 stops included in a guided tour of the city donated to the museum by the artist and lesbian activist Sofia Hultin. In this chapter, we will use the competing narratives and performances of Hultin's tour and three other guided walks as the basis for a discussion of heritage in the intersection of gender, sexuality and class in the urban landscape of Norrköping. While three walks focus on the life of straight, white, working-class women, Hultin's 'I'm every lesbian' walk disrupts these other walks. Based on interviews that have been transformed to first-person stories with use of the artist's poetic license, the walk places lesbian experiences in the local landscape. As stated by its creator, the purpose of the 'I'm every lesbian' walk is to make a marginalized group visible by connecting individual experiences to social and political contexts. Thus, Hultin uses the city walk as a political tool (Hultin 2015).

Hultin's city walk is now part of an audio-guide published on the website of the Norrköping City Museum. Hultin has created similar walks in Belgrade and Tirana as well as in other towns in Sweden. In all these towns there are also other established guided walks that offer interpretations of the place and its former or present inhabitants. Investigating the competing narratives of such guided walks can provide us with important information about how heritage is produced (Bryon 2012; Io and Hallo 2011; Reisinger and Steiner 2006;

Sarmento 2010). We understand heritage as a process in which the pasts that are understood to be meaningful are confronted with modern-day relationships between people, their words, their actions and their material environments. In other words, cultural heritage is an active process also associated with future-oriented values (Harrison 2013).

By contrasting Hultin's activism with how femininity and class intersect in the three additional city walks, the chapter will raise questions concerning competing social and political agendas. The issue is pertinent as public institutions such as museums increasingly apply social agency and intervene politically by, for example, confronting prejudice and representing social diversity (Oram 2011; Sandell 2007). Feminist scholars such as Nina Lykke have pointed to the difficulties in including divergent political and theoretical concerns regarding intersecting power-imbued social categories in research as well as in social mobilization. In different ways and from different positions, conflicting feminist branches have critically pointed to how the category 'woman' masks differences between women and have challenged the concept of a global and all-encompassing feminist white heterosexual middle-class 'we' (Lykke 2010). The subsequent analysis will point to how this is also a dilemma in heritage-making (see also Grahn 2011).

Routes and paths

The site of the guided tours, known as the Industrial Landscape of Norrköping, is quite a spectacular area of red brick and yellow plaster factory buildings erected in the nineteenth century and located along the river Strömmen. A run-down area in the 1970s, most buildings have since been renovated and transformed into museums, a university campus, a concert hall, conference facilities and local innovation incubators. The historical architecture has become a source of local pride and it is now widely perceived as a unique heritage site (Alzén 1996). Thus, like many other places in the Global North, Norrköping is, in the words of Anna Storm, 'experiencing a post-industrial situation' (Storm 2014: 9). No longer the seat of industrial production, old industrial landscapes have been abandoned and sometimes turned into resources for memorialization as well as for attracting tourists and affluent inhabitants (Dicks 2004). Many industrial heritage sites are entwined with struggles for social justice and the equitable distribution of resources; therefore, to working-class people, they can be sources of pride, just as they can be perceived as a symbolic terrain dominated by images of defeat and subjection (Dicks 2008).

Whereas female achievements have often been neglected in historical culture (e.g. Deufel 2011; McDowell 2008), women's history is highlighted in Norrköping. Female workers formed a large share of the workforce at these mills and they were a crucial part of the industrial revolution in Norrköping, just as in Manchester (Clark 1995; Horgby 1989). This is emphasized in the local memorial landscape and manifested, for instance, in public art and at the museums. Two of the walks analysed in this chapter are even named after women, Johanna and Moa respectively. Thus, the Industrial Landscape is made to echo with 'herstories'. The common denominator of the three established walks is that they all focus on the lives of straight white women. In line with Sara Ahmed's work on queer phenomenology, one could argue that heterosexuality is such a well-trodden path, a line so normative, that it is performative. For most women, heterosexuality and the associated nuclear family comprise the dominant femininity, depending on 'the repetitions of norms and conventions, of routes and paths taken, also created as an effect of this repetition' (Ahmed 2006: 16). In Ahmed's phenomenological take on sexual orientation, routes and paths are more than metaphors; rather they point to how actions take place in space, how bodies, histories and spaces co-direct one another. Repetitive inhabitancy of space makes some paths more preferable than others, also making some bodies and orientations more comfortable and at home than others.

Even if Ahmed's approach is not explicitly intersectional, her queer phenomenology opens up for critical consideration of how power relationships intersect. With reference to black feminist theory, she concludes that both bodies and institutions are 'meeting points' for many lines, arguing that how a body moves along a line is affected by the other lines one follows (Ahmed 2006: 136). Where the 'I'm every lesbian' walk draws on contemporary memories to create a purposefully disruptive future heritage, the other walks dealt with in this chapter are intended to inform, entertain and even promote the city. They move in the borderlands of social history and local lore and have been offered for some years. The trails cross, sometimes literally, as the walks stop at the same spots, while at other instances they intersect thematically, as they adopt similar interpretations of the past. The analysis takes as its starting point diverging interpretations, but will note resonances. With the exception of the 'I'm every lesbian' walk, where we draw from an online version, the chapter is based on participant observation. One of the authors accompanied the walks together with guides and participants, making an audio recording of the walks and photographing the stops. This author lives in the locality and the analysis of the city walks is a continuation of earlier fieldwork (Axelsson 2010, 2013). We have also recorded interviews with the guides leading these walks, but the interviews are used only to a minor degree.

Reiterating the line: the West End walk

The contrasting of city walks in the same area accentuates how heritage-making is always a matter of selecting a perspective. There are a number of routes available in any area and even if the city walks stop at the same locations, the stories told may differ. This becomes clear when contrasting the initial quote with the words of the guide at the same stop in what is here referred to as the West End walk. The walk in the western part of the Industrial Landscape is led by a member of the Norrköping guide club in her sixties, who does several different walks in the city. In the West End walk, the building in which the homophobic incident is placed becomes part of the official story about the city, which has been presented, for example, at local museums in exhibitions produced in 2012 and in a leaflet presenting the Industrial Landscape. In this overarching story, Norrköping becomes a phoenix, rising from the ashes of the textile mills into a new post-industrial life. After explaining that the building is named for an earlier building whose first owner christened it after his hometown in Lithuania, the guide points out that this was the last of the textile mills to close down. She charges the place emotionally by describing what a difficult moment it was for the city when the mill closed and 900 workers were laid off in 1970. In line with the official story, she points to how this very same building today is the centre of a university campus with 6,000 students.

Sexual orientation as a complex and contested issue is not included in the West End walk. This becomes particularly apparent when comparing the ways in which the two walks approach the Arbis Theatre, which is located close to the university building. While the West End walk tells its participants of the importance of the theatre for the cultural and social empowerment of workers in the nineteenth and twentieth centuries, the 'I'm every lesbian' walk highlights its current use as a meeting spot for RFSL, the Swedish Federation for Lesbian, Gay, Bisexual and Transgender Rights, not mentioning its original purpose of educating and entertaining workers. The West End city walk starts from an implicitly heterosexual position and orients its participants to a gender divided historical space, directing the participants towards a discrete and binary division between women and men. The moral emphasis is on women's double oppression, how they were economically oppressed by being used as cheap labour in the textile mills and how they had to do all the housework. The division between the sexes is projected onto the former textile mills as the guide points out that some mills housed wool production, whereas others were used for the manufacturing of cotton. She explains that men were assigned to work with wool and women with cotton, and that this division of labour was based on the view that women were better suited for the lighter work with cotton and men more suitable for handling wool. For the sake of simplicity, the guide's interpretation smooths over the complex gender system in the factories indicated by historical research. In fact, men and women had different tasks in the same mills. According to the historian Björn Horgby (1989), these differences were crucial for the level of social organization. They were derived not only from gender but also from type of employment, background and lifestyle.

No structural explanations are given by the guide to account for the differences between the sexes, and the ways in which the issue of class is dealt with without highlighting conflict is striking. At the stop at Skvallertorget Square, a mansion that has been relocated to one end of the square and a statue opposite honouring female textile workers and the female Socialist agitator Kata Dalström (1858–1923) are pointed out. When stopping here, the guide tells about an early owner of the mansion, a widow who made a fortune from textile manufacturing in the eighteenth century. Then the guide changes the subject to talk about how difficult it was for women who worked in the factories to follow Kata Dalström's call in the beginning of the twentieth century to become involved in the union due to the heavy workload they had. Not only did they work in the mills, says the guide, they also had their hands full with taking care of husbands, children and doing domestic labour. Instead of taking up the thread of class inequality by highlighting how the widow's fortune was derived from other women's work, this city walk evokes solidarity among women across time. When the guide directs the attention to a former prison first used as a spinning mill she recounts a morally imbued story of how factory owners, in collaboration with the authorities, used the loitering statutes of the time to imprison women to work. In the midst of the story, she says: 'We haven't had easy lives'.

The guide's use of the first-person, plural pronoun 'we' invites the women participating in the walk to transcend their own time as if they were part of the same society and historical specific circumstances as the women in eighteenth-century Norrköping. According to Joan W. Scott, the identity and transcendental category of woman is an outcome of an effort to mobilize collectivity rather than a natural fact. As in the case of this city walk, it often masks conflicts and contradictions in relations between women in the same way that contrasting women with men does. In such processes of identification, women are mobilized by the repetition of scenes. It is the very repetitions that stabilize identity and allow for women in past time to become 'us'. Scott introduces the notion of a fantasy that echoes as a reminder of the inexactness of such temporal condensations (Scott 2001). As will follow from the subsequent interpretations of the Johanna and Moa walks, the Industrial Landscape is a space imbued with working-class heterosexuality. However, the existing walks cause the fantasy of the working-class heterosexual woman to be reflected back in different ways, allowing for some slight variations in how to walk the line.

Circling the line: the Johanna walk

Women's hardships in past times recur in the so-called Johanna walk, which is organized by the local tourist office, Destination Norrköping. This walk has been available for some years, and it was designed to offer drama and entertainment within the traditional format for city walks.[2] Even if this walk takes place in the eastern part of the Industrial Landscape, and thus has a different set of stops than the West End walk does, the two walks deal with similar themes. The Johanna walk has two guides, one of them piloting the group between the stops and the other showing up at the various stops, impersonating the invented historic character Johanna who is said to have worked in one of the textile mills. Johanna represents a woman from 1910; she is dressed in period clothes with a long skirt, apron, shawl and kerchief. She speaks in a broad local dialect and addresses the participants of the walk as if they were her contemporaries, thus inviting the visitors to transcend time.

The heterosexual orientation, which is presupposed in the West End walk, makes up a strong theme in the Johanna walk. It is as if the actress impersonating Johanna performs or echoes heterosexuality by returning to this path in circular movements, both literally and metaphorically. In doing this, the walk charges the space with heterosexual actions and orientations, and thus projects heterosexuality into the Industrial Landscape. Extending Ahmed's argument on the ways in which objects work and are modified by people's actions, the buildings and the area are modified by the guides so as to produce this fit (cf. Ahmed 2006: 50–51). Every time Johanna turns up, she has some new details to add. In her first performance, she praises herself for moving to the city from the countryside where she was born and for finding such a good-looking, sober husband. In her second performance, she tells about his proposal and embellishes it with some prerequisites of the everyday life in her nuclear family. She gives the impression of being in a constant hurry homebound to feed her family of four children in the one-room apartment that is part of her husband's salary. Furthermore, she tells the audience how she takes care of a week elderly colleague. Her words thus demonstrate the classical female virtues of caretaking.

Similar to the West End walk, the Johanna walk directs attention to Kata Dalström's struggle for equality and the difficulties married women like Johanna faced when trying to find time to join her. According to Johanna, her own husband opposes women's suffrage, a statement the female participants in the walk responded to by booing. Johanna then questions her husband's point of view and invites the audience, who she calls 'girls', to agree with her. Addressing the audience in such a spirit of comradeship is again an example of how a female guide invites contemporary women to identify with historical women, asking for female solidarity and implicitly for them to unite against oppressive men.

The format with an actress performing historical working-class femininity and interacting with the audience evokes retrospective identification with women of the past. Here, the scenes suggested in the West End walk are instead re-enacted. Sometimes the guide supports Johanna's scenes and the fantasies they echo. For example, as a parallel to Johanna's mentioning of her husband's proposal, the guide gives a vivid description of a romantic proposal she once came across on one of her walks in the Industrial Landscape. According to our interview with the guide, this anecdote is not normally included in the Johanna walk. It was included on the spot as the guide thought it might suit the all-female group taking part in this particular city walk.[3] The Johanna walk also reiterates the overarching story of the re-birth of Norrköping. It ends at the same spot as the West End walk, outside some brand new university buildings, with the guide suggesting there will be a bright future. Thus, even if these two walks start at different locations, they both invite their participants to embody heterosexuality and walk the forward moving path of Norrköping toward individual affluence and social mobility through education and cultural consumption.

Stretching the line: the Moa walk

The West End walk and the Johanna walk recast two common fantasies (in Scott's sense of the word) in feminist politics: the female orator and the feminist maternal figure (cf. Scott 2001), Kata Dalström being the orator intervening in the masculine public sphere of politics and Johanna pointing to the ways in which an ordinary Norrköping woman could orient herself to men, reproduction and caretaking. The fantasy of maternity has echoes in Sofia Hultin's walk as well as in the last walk introduced in this chapter. One of the stories of the 'I'm every lesbian' walk takes place at the Museum of Work, also one of the stops in the Johanna walk. Hultin's first-person story here provides information about how this museum has hosted debates on the right for lesbians to have the same insemination rates as straight couples have.

In the Moa walk, the fantasy of feminist maternity once again interacts with one of the female orators. This walk is named after Moa Martinson, an author born and raised in Norrköping in the early part of the twentieth century and whose work is strongly associated with working-class women of that period. A trilogy of autobiographical novels connects her childhood and adolescence to the textile mills, although she herself never worked in the factories. The walk is organized by the City Museum and is written and performed by a curator at the museum. Originally the walk stems from the 1990s when it was created in conjunction with a national series of fairs focusing on women's work and entrepreneurship.

The story of Moa Martinson's life is told as the story of a woman who challenges the line, as Ahmed would say, by not following the trajectory set out for working-class women. She made a life for herself as a writer of popular novels and a public intellectual, forever becoming the 'Moa' of Swedish cultural life and a hero to many working-class women here. Tellingly, this city walk takes a detour outside the Industrial Landscape. Even so, the Moa walk thematically overlaps with both the West End and the Johanna walks by casting the female experience as one of hardship and vulnerability. Apart from the natural discussion of Moa's impact as a writer, the guide tells how both Moa and her mother gave birth to children out of wedlock and were unhappily married. In the story of Moa's life, as told by the guide, Moa comes across as an unusually strong woman, and this is also how she is portrayed in a statue gracing one of the open places in the Industrial Landscape (Figure 2.1). In the words of the guide of the West End walk: 'Here's a determined lady putting her foot down.'

The Moa walk has an underlying tone of ambiguity with regard to both gender and class norms. This is especially poignant in the retelling of a scene from the novels depicting the wedding of Moa Martinson's aunt. According to the guide, Moa describes her aunt as a bit eccentric, with a masculine appearance and a muscular body thanks to labouring in the woods and on farms. She is close to 40 years old when she marries and defies convention by being wed in church, which at that time was a privilege for the bourgeoisie, as the workers usually married in the parish office. On the morning of the wedding, a wide-eyed little Moa looks at her aunt preparing herself by washing her big muscular body, letting out her ankle long hair to wash it before braiding it and choosing underwear. The guide stresses that Martinson makes a point of the fact that this big woman had a weakness for beautiful underwear. The bride-to-be then puts on her wedding dress, a long black dress, traditionally worn by working-class women. The guide concludes that in

Figure 2.1 Statue of Moa, Norrköping, Sweden
Source: photograph by authors.

this case, the aunt stuck to the conventions, because only the daughters of the bourgeois would wear white wedding dresses.

The scene visualizes a woman with a fleshy form that is reminiscent of a man's body. It is this 'in-between' body that reaches out for feminine attributes in the preparations for the wedding ritual. This is one of many acts grounded in social fantasies and gender norms that produce 'real women' (Butler 1990). With her masculine tone, the aunt appears as slightly queer, not fully in line with the feminine woman. In accordance with this, the scene could be read as a straightening up of the queer aunt as she puts on the wedding dress in order to enter into a heterosexual relationship blessed by a powerful societal institution. At the same time, and a bit like Moa herself, she strays from the path laid out for the working-class woman, as she is out of place class-wise when choosing to walk down the aisle.

Transgressing the line: I'm every lesbian

The 'I'm every lesbian' walk disrupts the heterosexual orientation, which is taken for granted. As already pointed out, a couple of stops on the lesbian walk intersect with stops in two of the established walks. All in all, this walk has 24 stops scattered all over Norrköping's inner city. The stories connected to these places could be divided into three categories. One category, and the most encompassing, concerns the manifestations of same-sex relationships and LGBTQ issues in public space. This category includes the different locations where the local branch of RFSL has organized various activities over the years. The stories here underline the importance of having meeting places and free zones where lesbians can feel at home and be themselves. It is about community, warmth and acceptance. Other stories falling under this category highlight the importance of the Pride festivals and collaboration with cultural institutions such as museums and libraries to promote visibility and public acceptance of LGBTQ people.

The second category relates to public institutions. One story in this category is about a wedding ceremony, personally customized to provide a wonderful experience in a circle of close family and friends in a local church. An additional example is the not so pleasant encounter with the County Court in connection with an adoption. This is a reminder of the fact that both partners in a registered partnership do not automatically share parental rights to a child carried by one of the women, when the child has been conceived by artificial insemination outside Sweden. In these cases, the couples have to call on their right to adopt.

From a radical perspective, these latter stories balance on the verge of what Lisa Duggan has labeled the new homonormativity. This concept describes a move towards a greater societal visibility of those LGBTQ practices and desires that fit the heterosexual majority's lifestyle. According to this position, politics and practices supporting family-oriented constellations such as marriage and adoption sustain heteronormativity. They uphold societal institutions and connect sexual politics to private consumption that is associated with neoliberal agendas at the risk of personalizing political agendas and excluding more norm-challenging sexual orientations related to bisexual, transgender, pansexual and intersexual communities (Duggan 2002).

In some stories, the wedding ceremony is as significant as in the Moa walk. In the third category of stops, infatuation and romantic love are as important as in the Johanna walk. This third category includes personal matters, either dilemmas lesbians have experienced when telling relatives and friends about their sexual orientation, or the joys of starting a same-sex relationship. In the terminology of Ahmed, these stories are about turning points when a woman's life takes another direction, when she detours from the heterosexual path and sometimes magically arrives somewhere else (Ahmed 2006: 16–17). As if to counter the homonormative perspective and acknowledge inequalities within the LGBTQ community, Sofia Hultin's walk ends with a reflection on the privileged position of a fully functional white person with a gender that agrees with the sex she was assigned at birth. Hultin's walk is thus a way of opening up the Industrial Landscape to orientations transgressing the heterosexual straight line, also acknowledging that there might be additional paths in need of being pointed out.

Sexuality, gender and class in post-industrial heritage productions

The herstories in the three established city walks that have been analysed in this chapter are part of the many elements that are repeated and that make the Industrial Landscape into a space where heterosexuality echoes between the walls and straight bodies feel at home. The walks are all part of the numerous performances extending heterosexuality into space (cf. Ahmed 2006). They project pictures that give suggestions as to how the historic female factory workers inhabited the Industrial Landscape and extended into it – and how space affected them. They propose particular actions for women in particular places, moving back and forth between factory work and demanding housework. In doing this they present heterosexuality, including romantic love, as part of the spatial background and the heritage of the participants in the walks, also inviting them to consider it as a relevant future.

The three established city walks analysed in this chapter are performative in several respects. In addition to the stories told, they are gendered through the gendered performances of the guides (cf. Reading 2015). Female guides are acting in public space on behalf of the local guide club and public institutions. Clearly, guides in Norrköping, including the visiting artist Sofia Hultin, have made great effort to construct the heritage of women, to establish an atlas of a female historical landscape (cf. Heffernan and Medlicot 2002). This is not just a result of the guides' initiatives, but also of other activities such as the work of historians and the local museums. Even so, the guides appear to be individual heritage agents – orators in the public sphere – charging their stories morally and fusing them with personal experience of what it means to be a woman, past and present. It was also primarily women who participated in the city walks so as to reiterate (the West End walk), circulate (the Johanna walk) and expand (the Moa walk) the normative path.

The 'I'm every lesbian' walk suggests an alternative story for collective identification by inserting lesbian experiences in the Industrial Landscape. By bringing forth anonymous first-person stories, this walk also represents an alternative take on the genre of lesbian history walks. Established in the 1980s, they usually locate specific individuals, networks and communities in space by pointing out houses where lesbians or gay persons once lived or had their meeting places (Oram 2011). The anonymous first-person stories of the 'I'm every lesbian' walk invoke a lesbian 'we', mobilizing identification across class lines, generations and ethnic boundaries. This inclusiveness rings in the very name of the walk that alludes to the 1980s disco hit 'I am every woman' and perhaps even to the medieval play *Everyman.* The walk thus introduces a lesbian 'we' so as to challenge the concept of a global and encompassing white heterosexual female 'we'. So as to complicate matters, the very last stop on the walk displays consciousness of the difficulties of including the LGBTQ community in its entirety by reflecting on how passing through heterosexual space depends on following white middle-class norms.

The 'I'm every lesbian' walk aims at balancing the personal and the political, whereas the Johanna walk and the Moa walk personalize female experiences in particular. Bella Dicks (2008) explains this tendency to personalization with references to changing directions in heritage communication as well as to more general trends in popular culture that highlight the individual rather than the collective. As a consequence, the politics of class has turned into an 'absent presence' in the contemporary industrial heritage (Dicks 2008). Here contemporary heritage productions stand in sharp contrast to how Norrköping's industrial past was perceived in the 1970s, in the wake of the international leftist movement, when historians turned towards history from below and cultural politics were revised (Alzén 2011). One of the manifestations of this radicalization of the past was the 1979 lay theatre performance named after a line in the Swedish translation of the International (*Stiga vi mot ljuset: Folkets Park Norrköping 25 maj–16 juni* 1979).

In the three established city walks, class is made into a safe topic; the collective of workers, both women and men, never really comes across as oppressed. Surely, there are vestiges of a class perspective both in the West End walk and in the Moa and Johanna walks, which all implicitly deal with working-class experiences in terms of class relations that are bound up in the structure of the everyday lives of workers. However, those most clearly oppressed are the women who are portrayed as strong figures but are still repressed by men, be it their husbands or other males in society. These men appear as impressionistic figures, for example, in the Johanna walk in the form of a demanding but loving husband. The consequence of this impressionistic treatment, however, is that ultimately unequal relations between male and female bodies are left unexplained because the larger context of societal power relations is lacking. This reflects partly the form of the guided presentations, which is narrative rather than analytic.

All walks dealt with in this chapter are part of recent more encompassing projects to render female experiences visible so as to connect to current agendas and include them in the heritage for the future. They also testify to the difficulties of incorporating social complexity and intersectionality in heritage productions such as city walks. A case in point is Baltimore where Hon-festivals, playful performances of working-class femininity, mask past and present racial conflicts and inequalities (Rizzo 2010). The narrative format does not make it any easier than the analytical and the political paths taken by feminist politics and research. There is always the possibility that the chosen social and political agendas overshadow others. With its explicit focus on Lesbian experiences Hultin's audiowalk backgrounds other possible trajectories. With regard to past realities in Norrköping, the three established city walks gloss over not only class differences but also the differences within Norrköping's working class.

Acknowledgements

We wish to thank Alison Twells, Karin Hassan Jansson, Anette Kindahl and Karl-Emil Åkerö for their helpful comments on an earlier version of this chapter. This research is funded by the Swedish National Heritage Board.

Notes

1 SofiaHultin,2013.Iameverylesbian,Norrköping,4.www.sofiahultin.com/IELnorrkoping.html (accessed 15 May 2016).
2 Interview with Kerstin Volminger, 1 September 2014.
3 Interview with Kerstin Volminger, 1 September 2014.

Bibliography

Ahmed, S. 2006. *Queer Phenomenology: Orientations, Objects, Others*. Durham, NC: Duke University Press.

Alzén, A. 1996. *Fabriken som kulturarv: Frågan om industrilandskapets bevarande i Norrköping 1950–1985*. Stockholm: Symposion.

Alzén, A. 2011. *Kulturarv i rörelse. En studie av 'Gräv där du står'-rörelsen*. Mölndal: Brutus Östlings bokförlag Symposion.

Axelsson, B. 2010. Sound machine through city space: the sprawled studio and the signature at the center. In B. Axelsson and K. Becker (eds) *Art Through City Space/Konst genom staden. Tema Q Skriftserie* 1. Linköping: Linköping University Electronic Press. Available at: www.ep.liu.se/ea/temaq/2010/001/bodil/bodil.pdf (accessed 14 October 2016).

Axelsson, B. 2013. Klosterruinen och industrilandskapet: transformationer, iscensättningar, makt och handlingsutrymmen. In G. Swensen (ed.) *Å lage Kulturminner: om hvordan kulturarv formes, forstås og forvaltas*, Oslo: Novus förlag, pp. 227–248.

Bryon, J. 2012. Tour guides as storytellers: from selling to sharing. *Scandinavian Journal of Hospitality and Tourism* 12(1): 27–43.

Butler, J. 1990. *Gender Trouble*. London: Routledge.

Clark, A. 1995. *The Struggle for the Breeches: Gender and the Making of the British Working Class*. Berkeley, CA: University of California Press.

Deufel, N. 2011. Telling her story of war: challenging gender bias at Culloden Battlefield Visitor Centre. *Historical Reflections* 37(2): 72–89.

Dicks, B. 2004. *Culture on Display: The Production of Contemporary Visitability*. Milton Keynes: Open University Press.

Dicks, B. 2008. Performing the hidden injuries of class in coal-mining heritage. *Sociology* 42(3): 436–452.

Dubrow, G.L. 1992. Claiming public space for women's history in Boston: a proposal for preservation, public art, and public historical interpretation. *Frontiers: A Journal of Women Studies* 13(1): 111–148.

Duggan L. 2002. The new homonormativity: the sexual politics of neoliberalism. In R. Castronovo and D.D. Nelson (eds) *Materialising Democracy: Towards a Revitalized Cultural Politics*. Durham, NC: Duke University Press, pp. 175–194.

Grahn, W. 2011. Intersectionality and the construction of cultural heritage management. *Archaeologies: Journal of the World Archaeological Congress* 7(1): 222–250.

Harrison, R. 2013. *Heritage: Critical Approaches*. London: Routledge.

Heffernan, M. and Medlicot, C. 2002. A feminine atlas? Sacagewea, the suffragettes and the commemorative landscape in the American West, 1904–1910. *Gender, Place and Culture* 9(2): 109–131.

Horgby, B. 1989. *Surbullestan*. Stockholm: Carlsson.

Hultin, S. 2015. *I'm every lesbian.* Available at: www.sofiahultin.com/IEL.html (accessed 7 June 2015).

Io, M.U. and Hallo, L. 2011. Tour guides interpretation of the historic center of Macao as a World Cultural Heritage site. *Journal of Tourism and Cultural Change* 9(2): 140–152.

Lykke, N. 2010. *Feminist Studies: A Guide to Intersectional Theory, Methodology and Writing.* London: Routledge.

McDowell, S. 2008. Commemorating dead 'men': gendering the past and present in post-conflict Northern Ireland. *Gender, Place, and Culture* 15: 335–354.

Oram, A. 2011. Going on an outing: the historic house and queer public history. *Rethinking History: The Journal of Theory and Practice* 15(2): 189–207.

Reading, A. 2015. Making feminist heritage work: gender and heritage. In S. Watson and E. Waterton (eds) *The Palgrave Handbook of Contemporary Heritage Research.* Basingstoke: Palgrave Macmillan, pp. 397–413.

Reisinger, Y. and Steiner, C. 2006. Reconceptualising interpretation: the role of tour guides in authentic tourism. *Current Issues in Tourism* 9(6): 481–498.

Rizzo, M. 2010. Honouring the past: play-publics and gender at Baltimore's HonFest. *International Journal of Heritage Studies* 16(4/5): 337–351.

Sandell, R. 2007. *Museums, Prejudice and the Reframing of Difference.* London: Routledge.

Sarmento, J. 2010. Fort Jesus: guiding the past and contesting the present in Kenya. *Tourism Geographies: An International Journal of Tourism Space, Place and Environment* 12(2): 246–263.

Scott, J.W. 2001. Fantasy echo: history and the construction of identity. *Critical Inquiry* 27(2): 284–304.

Stiga vi mot ljuset: Folkets Park Norrköping 25 maj–16 juni (1979) Norrköping: Stadsteatern Norrköping-Linköping.

Storm, A. 2014. *Post-Industrial Landscape Scars.* New York: Palgrave Macmillan.

Chapter 3

Gender, heritage and changing traditions
Russian Old Believers in Romania

Cristina Clopot and Máiréad Nic Craith

> One cannot step twice into the same river.
> (Heraclitus)

Introduction

With the wisdom of a past age, Heraclitus once reflected on the transience of things. As Heraclitus remarked, everything is in transition in this world; the river is in continuous flux, ever-changing as water passes from stream to estuary. Using the metaphor of the river, the philosopher highlighted that nothing is as permanent as it might seem. Change creeps in the stillest of places. Smaller communities and larger international bodies alike are forced to come to terms with flow and negotiate change. This chapter analyses the fluidity of gender roles in the community of Russian Old Believers in Romania with regard to their religious heritage. Our data derives from ethnographic research conducted in a 'yo-yo' manner (Wulff 2002) among Old Believers in Romania during 2014–2015. We will analyse recent transformations in this traditional community whose ancestors had left Russia on the grounds of religious persecution. Despite this history of persecution, the community maintains its traditional faith and heritage in the new Romanian context. We have concerned ourselves with the implications of the traditional Russian Orthodox religion for Old Believer women in Romania today who have maintained their traditions over centuries.

Our quote from Heraclitus at the beginning of the chapter echoes the connectivity of time, as the past is reflected in the present and imbues future potential. Rarely is this connectivity of time frames as visible as in the field of heritage, which links past, present and future in a very particular way. Decades ago, researchers conceptualized heritage as tangible and inert emphasizing the past (Nic Craith 2008). Since the 2003 Convention on Intangible Heritage, the definition of heritage has been broadened to include intangible dimensions such as ritual, performance and traditional crafts (UNESCO 2003). As William Logan notes, this revision brings forward a 'heritage that is embodied in people rather than in inanimate objects' (Logan 2007: 39). In line with the above consideration, the concept of heritage discussed here is not an expression of a static past, *lieux de memoire* (Nora 1989). Instead, we understand heritage to be continuously produced by the very fact of 'being and/or becoming in the world' (Fairclough 2009: 29). It is thus subjected to revisions, as vulnerable to changes as the persons that embody it, both at the closer personal level as well as larger community changes. The gendered ways in which we experience living heritage are also evolving, as our case of Old Believers will show. Before considering the case study, however, we will reflect on the heritage–gender interaction more generally.

Gender and heritage

Like heritage, the concept of gender has evolved over time. Following West and Zimmerman (1987), we conceive gender not only as a social construct but as a continuous performance, not a given, gender is 'done' in the act of living. Such processes involve, as West and Zimmerman (1987: 142) argue 'self-regulating processes' whereby people place behaviours under scrutiny, judging them against a prescriptive sets of norms that have become naturalized. Different ways of 'doing gender' are linked, among others, with their specific locations (McDowell 1999); being a female Old Believer in Romania differs from being a woman in the UK in many ways. Gender is a contentious topic within the heritage sector. As Laurajane Smith (2008) has indicated, current academic debates within heritage studies have strong masculine undertones. As a reaction to these discussions projects, such as the Metropolitanka (the Metropolitan woman) in Poland, aiming to uncover the hidden imprint of women in Gdansk's shipyard's heritage, have successfully moved the agenda forward (Metropolitanka ND). In a similar vein, in this chapter we go against that grain by putting forward an analysis from a feminist standpoint. This is not to say that 'men have no gender' (Smith 2008: 159), but by looking at women in particular, we aim to rebalance some of the current 'bias in representation' (Levy 2013: 87).

International bodies such as UNESCO have strongly emphasized their commitment to gender equality (UNESCO 2014b). In a recent report, UNESCO mentions that 'cultural diversity is fully compatible with human rights' (UNESCO 2014a: 16). Feminist researchers have, however, critiqued UNESCO's approach, arguing that the use of neutral language in convention texts leaves room for inequalities (Moghadam and Bagheritari 2007). Farida Shaheed, Special Rapporteur in the field of cultural rights, outlined the particular conundrums that women face in UNESCO's publication *Gender Equality – Heritage and Creativity* and states 'that no social group has suffered greater violation of human rights in the name of culture than women' (Shaheed 2014: 5). The fight for equality in relation to cultural practices, however, is not as recent as it might seem. A key document is the 1979 Convention on the Elimination of all Forms of Discrimination against Women, which urged states to modify practices 'which are based on the idea of the inferiority or the superiority of either of the sexes or on stereotyped roles for men and women' (CEDAW 1979: introduction).

Nevertheless, Heraclitus' quote of the moving river implies continuous change. From this perspective, gendered heritage practices can be transformed following the natural course of change. Problems such as female genital mutilation (Ruggles and Silverman 2009; Talle 2010) or forced marriages (Logan *et al.* 2010) have attracted attention from researchers, activists and media alike, and changes have been registered. However, finer instances of structural inequalities are underrepresented in literature. This article focuses on those small acts that are sometimes glossed over, as 'small facts speak to large issues' (Geertz 1973: 23). The nexus between gender, heritage and religion is discussed with reference to our case study of Russian Old Believers in Romania and set in the wider debates that highlight the difficult relationship between cultural diversity and human rights (Logan 2009; Logan *et al.* 2010; Ruggles and Silverman 2009). We aim to highlight change and potentialities opened by this processual approach to understanding heritage as expressed through place or embodied in people and its effects within this community.

Gender and the Old Believers

Located in Romania, navigating the swampy terrain of post-socialist change is particularly challenging for our case study of Old Believers and their traditional way of life. As Vlad Naumescu observed: 'nowadays, caught between their increasing marginalization at the periphery of the Romanian state and the massive migration of younger generations, these communities cannot but imagine their future in apocalyptic terms' (Naumescu 2011: 60).[1]

Their tenacity in clinging to their religious heritage is rooted in the particular history of this group. Old Believers left Russia and settled in different communities across the world in the seventeenth–eighteenth centuries (Morris 1999).[2] Their departure was a reaction to persecution due to their refusal to accept a set of religious reforms that would have aligned Russian with Byzantine Orthodoxy. Old Believers viewed these changes imposed by Patriarch Nikon as heretical and fiercely defended the old faith.[3] Settling in another environment has led to an 'excessive ritualization of everyday life' (Naumescu 2011: 61) and triggered processes of resistance to changes. Old Believers' traditional way of life, defended by ancestors with their lives, has been preserved in contemporary Romania.

The outlook of the community has improved following the change of regime in December 1989. Soon after the fall of communism, some minorities in Romania, including Old Believers, formed non-governmental organizations (NGOs) to protect their heritage and defend their interests politically. The Old Believers' NGO, The Community of Lipovan Russians[4] in Romania, has branches across the whole country, in villages and cities with a large population of Old Believers. Local leaders of this structure are habitually men. In our fieldwork, meeting a female leader was a rare occurrence. Outside the NGO we have also observed that certain roles within the community are clearly gendered. Community choirs (almost every locality has one or two groups) seem to be mostly women and children based, accompanied by one or two men playing the accordion. While community leaders are mostly men, there is one exception. The official two printed publications of the Old Believers, *Zorile* (monthly magazine with news and events) and *Kitej Grad* (monthly cultural magazine), with internal circulation, are both currently led by women.

Normalized gender roles can be observed in reference to access to and participation in religious heritage also. Crafts such as icon painting, essential for the practice of Orthodoxy, are preponderantly masculine to this day. Moreover, learning Slavonic, the official language of the church, needed for Old Belief transmission (Naumescu 2010), although not forbidden for women, tends to be normalized for men only. Informal systems of learning practices within communities perpetuate this patriarchal model for younger generations as well. For instance, during one of our observations, an elderly Old Believer woman argued her niece simply did not need to know as much Slavonic as her nephew did. These practices are not surprising, as the wider majority community in Romania is also identified as lagging behind in terms of gender equality. For instance, the Gender Equality Index has recently been published by the European Institute for Gender Equality, analysing the 28 member states' performances in terms of gender equality between 2005 and 2012 promptly put Romania last in the EU with a score of 33.7 as opposed to the EU median of 52.9 (EIGE 2015).

However, it would be inaccurate to paint Russian Old Believers in Romania as a homogenous, gendered, unchanging society and the picture is becoming ever more nuanced in line with the quotation from Heraclitus. While there are clear differences in the role of women in villages and cities, with villages tending to hold onto gendered practices, the situation is clearly changing for the community overall. Census statistics show that women participate in many sectors of the economy. According to the latest national census (NSI 2011), from the total of 23,487 people registered as Old Believers, 12,369 were women. 9,192 people formed the economically active population, 4,094 of which were women. A large part of these women work in agriculture, forestry and fishing (1,770), and a further 705 work in services. Popular areas of activity for women include commerce (510 women), manufacturing (261), health (241), housekeeping (286), teaching (194) or national insurance, defense and public administration (184) (NSI 2011). Alongside these active women, the census registered 2,014 stay-at-home wives and 3,783 pensioners. It is thus a complex situation reflected in a community undergoing structural changes that represents the background for the case study outlined in the next sections.

Gender and the body

To analyse heritage as embodied in persons, we need to look at how bodies, living carriers of gendered heritage processes, can be conceptualized. Interpreting the body as place is not something new (Longhurst 2005; McDowell 1999). As Robyn Longhurst (2005: 337) argues bodies 'are deeply embedded in psychoanalytic, symbolic, and social processes yet at the same time they are undoubtedly biological, material and "real"'. It is thus important to look both at the symbolic and material expressions of the body. Materiality, as the embodied expression of the 'past of a place' (Massey 1995a: 184), includes elements of tangible (clothing) and intangible heritage (cultural norms that guide these).

The body's trajectories in social space are defined among others by social and cultural values that constitute part of our geographical imagination. Imagination plays a key role in navigating social life, as Gill Valentine (1999: 48) observed: it is 'fundamental to our understanding of space itself and how we construct our sense of self and other'. Linda McDowell argues that 'assumptions about the correct place for embodied women are drawn on to justify and to challenge systems of patriarchal domination in which women are excluded from particular spatial arenas and restricted to others' (McDowell 1999: 56). For her, it is essential to closely examine the manner in which bodies are set in place, normalized and how difference is constructed in particular contexts.

Gendered practices for Old Believers start early on in life. The earliest *rite of passage* (Turner 1969) is the christening of the child. For Old Believers, unless there are exceptional circumstances, a christening usually takes place eight days from birth. This simple ceremony is performed in the early hours of the morning in the presence of the child's father, godfather and godmother (they need not be related to each other). Other people from the family or community are permitted. The one person forbidden to take part in this ceremony is the mother, as she is considered still unclean following the birth of her child.

Gendered practices of christening are applied not just to the mother, but also to the child. There are differences in the ways names are chosen for boys and girls and these are linked to the Old Belief calendar. A boy's name is chosen from the eight different names of saints celebrated in the calendar from his birth to his christening. For girls, a period of about two weeks is considered, eight days before her birth and eight days after. An Old Believer woman reflected that this distinction is needed as otherwise there would not be enough female names to choose from, as the calendar has more male saint names. While new rite orthodoxy allows alteration of names from female to male or vice versa (i.e. St. Paul is celebrated by women named Paula also), the Old Believers only consider a saint's name in its original form.

Other traditional religious ceremonies reinforce a conservative view of gender roles. This was the case for the wedding ritual that we observed in the summer of 2015 in the Northern part of the country (Moldavia). Towards the end of the ceremony, the bride first took three bows in front of her husband before they kissed. The submissive position of the woman's body was symbolically performed in front of all the guests. Subsequently, the priest led the couple and guests to the parents of the groom and a celebratory meal took place. On the way, the followers, wedding guests and people from the village, walked in a particular order. A child carrying an icon went first, then the priest, followed by the couple holding hands with the godparents. Other followers were segregated by gender, with men first and then the women and children.

In general terms, the gendered body of a woman is marked through clothing. Married women should wear the '*kitchka*' (a small cape) and a kerchief at all times (although this does not happen so often). Priests' wives we met during our fieldwork usually keep their heads covered at all times. Before entering a church the woman must cover her head with a kerchief, while a man has to wear his head uncovered at all times while in the church. The roots of this custom are located in teachings of the New Testament. Moreover, a woman's clothing needs to include a skirt longer than knee-length and a shirt that covers the elbows. Another ritual object necessary for church is the '*poyas*', a long handmade braid worn as a belt. While fashions change and traditional clothing is replaced by current fashion trends from outside the community, the basic principles are kept. Devoted believers (of both genders) are expected to keep their body as pure as possible. For instance, one informant told us her priest asked her in confession whether she had cut her hair that year, as a woman is not supposed to make alterations such as haircuts. This purity rule also applies to any adornments, such as dying one's hair or applying any tattoos. Yet, in cities, such rules are rarely considered, and it is common for women to dye their hair. Moreover, in such cosmopolitan locations, the traditional costume is seen as out of place (Clopot 2016a).

Gender and place

The role of gender in this closed community extends beyond the personal body to issues of access to religious places and sacred places can highlight the problematic relationship of Orthodox religious sites between their universal nature and their particularism (Ferrari 2014). One of the cases, relevant to Old Belief, which is an Orthodox religion also, that has attracted particular attention is that of Mount Athos (Rössler 2014). Established in the XIX century, this sacred site is autonomous and has clear restrictions for both women and female animals, any breach is punishable with time in prison (Papastathis 2014). It is argued that women's presence would entail a distraction from the spiritual pursuits of the monks on Holy Mountain (Papastathis 2000). This rule is quite strict and the legislative measures stipulate that no ship can approach the island closer than 500 meters if there are any women on board (Papastathis 2014).

Inscribed as a World Heritage site in 1988, this restriction has made Mount Athos the subject of heated debates. Defenders of the Athonite regime base their arguments in the millennium-old regulations, emphasizing that this rule cannot be linked with patriarchal systems or discrimination (Papastathis 2000). At a meeting of the EU Council of the Ministers of Foreign Affairs in 1997, it was suggested that opposition to gender restrictions was grounded in cultural differences resulting from different religious traditions.

On a smaller scale, segregation based on gender is also evident in our case study in Romania. Upon entering the church, women are segregated from men. The church as place imposes clear norms of where each gender should stand and there is even a special 'women's entrance' in the back (see Figure 3.1).

Figure 3.1 Women attending the Easter service in an Old Believers' church, April 2015
Source: photograph by Cristina Clopot.

This contrasts with the men's entrance, which is situated towards the middle of the church. Moreover, prohibition to access places of worship extends to any woman during her menstrual period. For the duration of the menstrual cycle and eight days after, the rules say, the woman's entrance to the church is prohibited. Practices around menstruation seem less burdensome than the corresponding Jewish rituals (Steinberg 1997), yet they have been signalled several times as problematic by the women we have interviewed. During these days, if a woman wishes to come to church she must stay in the hallway of the church, '*papritea*',[5] and cannot enter its main body.

Religious rituals reinforce the gender divide. Within orthodoxy, access for women to the altar is commonly forbidden. At the end of the baptism ritual, for example, the child is walked in front of the icons. While baby boys are taken inside the altar, girls are only presented to the icons situated outside the altar. The rationale is that a female presence in the altar at any time would render the church unusable. If the altar were tainted with a female presence, it would need to be sanctified again through a special ceremony. It is only in special circumstances and with a blessing from a priest that a woman may enter the altar.

Gender segregation is also observed today in the community in ritual meals following church services. Thus, after every funeral service a 3–4 course ritual meal, '*praznic*', takes place, usually in a church annex especially built for this purpose.

Here, tables are arranged on two sides and women and men sit separately. The family of the deceased usually organizes these meals, with the help of other women who cook from the community. At one of these meals that we observed, men served alcohol, while women brought the food to the tables and cleared the plates. While there is no prohibition on women regarding alcohol consumption, men were in charge of pouring the drink. The separation of gendered bodies was also noticed at the ritual meal observed to celebrate a traditional wedding and upon asking Old Believer women about the segregation they said it has always been this way.

This comment is not just about the physicality of women and place but also about 'the cultural significance of place' (Nic Craith and Kockel 2015: 438). Laurajane Smith (2006: 75, original emphasis) has noted that 'heritage is about a sense of *place*'. Place, as gender, is equally caught in transience. Essentialist views of place as stable and unchanging are not tenable within our case study. Unlike earlier ideas about place as a bounded entity, recent scholarship conceptualizes place as 'contested, fluid and uncertain' (McDowell 1999: 4), situated at the junction of local and global relationships (Massey 2004). Place is both a concrete structure, a street, a church, but also a more ethereal idea 'constructed out of articulations of social relations' (Massey 1995a: 183). It is continuously created in everyday life both 'in imagination' and 'in material practice' (Massey 1995b: 48).

Mainstreaming gender

In the quote above, Massey is pointing to an inward-looking sense of place, resistant to changes. Yet, recent changes in the community, driven by larger processes within the Romanian society seem to be reflected in Old Believers' religious practices. Such examples include redefining access to religious sites and participation in heritage transmission. One such practice is learning Slavonic. As the official language of the Russian Old Belief Orthodox church, knowledge of this language is essential for religious practice and transmission (Naumescu 2011). Every ritual and every prayer inside or outside the church is uttered in Slavonic, using prayer books, at times hundreds of years old, some even handwritten. As a 'dead' language, Slavonic is not taught in formal education. Instead, Old Believers' communities organize reading classes, led either by the local priest or an elder. Sometimes, as it was the case during our fieldwork, classes are organized at the monastery and children from nearby villages and cities come to be taught how to read. Although the children are taught the mechanics of reading Slavonic, they have no understanding of the Slavonic text, pointing to passive reading or what Naumescu (2011: 61) has deemed as 'textualism', which turned 'reading practices into a form of religious devotion and texts into objects of piety'.

Classes organized informally by priests or monks are now mixed, with both boys and girls accepted, yet our fieldwork has shown there are differences between regions. In the Northern part of Romania, girls, even those literate in Slavonic are not allowed to stand by men who read and sing in the church. In other areas, however, women stand next to men in front of the altar reading together. In a village from the southern part of the country discussions over women's participation in the church choir revealed that only younger girls who are not married or widowers are permitted to sit in the local choir, pointing yet again to purity rules. In a further discussion with Old Believer girls, the one coming from the Southern part of the country proudly said at one point she always reads in church. Her interlocutor, a girl from the Northern part explained that in her village girls are not allowed to read in church. During our observations, one informant described this as patriarchal, pointing to the separation of women from men and her experience where women attempting to go to the front of the church are met with hostile looks.

A further activity that, according to our informants, used to be exclusively masculine is carol singing at Christmas, but the fabric of relations is changing and girls are now involved in the carol singing. In the Old Believer tradition, following the Christmas morning service, the priest listens to the carol then gives the boys and girls his blessing to go and spread the news about the birth of Jesus. After coming inside the house, the carol singers make the sign of the cross and start singing in front of the icon. As a reward, they used to receive bagels and fruits but now they are given money.

Another notable case study applies to the practice of iconography (Ipatiov 2001; Moldovan 2004), a craft essential for religious practice and until very recently, exclusively practised by men. The craft has mostly been passed on informally from painters to younger male apprentices in a studio. It was only recently that newer generations of iconographers with formal art studies appeared.

Icons are very special and they represent an essential part of orthodoxy since they are the visual counterparts of the written word. For this reason, following the Byzantine tradition, it was considered that the iconographer held a very privileged position. While the priest expresses the divine through words, the iconographer is responsible for the image. The iconographer thus needs a strong faith and stories about the link between the iconographer's gift and miracle-working icons abound. According to unwritten rules, to be allowed to paint icons the iconographer needs to receive a blessing from the Metropolitan bishop. Furthermore, as one iconographer informant noted, iconography is essentially a man's job, as the woman is not allowed to be a priest she cannot be an iconographer either (Iconographer interview n.d.).

However, even this tradition is changing among Old Believers in Romania and in our fieldwork we encountered probably the first female iconographer in the community. At 27 years of age, the iconographer is an art studies graduate. During our conversations, she told us that her first icon painting order came from an Old Believer monastery. News about her work has spread orally and more orders have meant that she now runs a small studio specializing in painting icons. Despite any barrier to women becoming priests, this lady feels deeply about her iconography as a spiritual art. In our discussions with this iconographer, she expressed an opinion that there should not be a separation between women and men in iconography

Figure 3.2 Children learning how to apply shadows during the iconography workshop, August 2015
Source: photograph by Cristina Clopot.

as both genders were priests in the old days. When asked about the tensions of being a female iconographer, our informant observed that people expressed doubt at first but gradually accepted her. She acknowledges that her work is a little different from the norm since her art studies helped her create her own style along the lines of Byzantine iconography.

In the summer of 2015, this woman iconographer conducted a summer workshop for children in one of the villages (see Figure 3.2). This workshop was initiated five years previously and was organized by the NGO that represents them, at the suggestion of a church leader. The intention was to form a new generation of iconographers who would carry on the tradition since there are now less than 10 iconographers in the Russian Orthodox community. Initially, there was some confusion regarding the participation of girls as only boys had participated previously. Some girls we met, thinking they could not participate, engaged in other activities. Once it became clear that girls were permitted, first two and later on three others from the village joined the workshop. From a total of 19 children attending the camp, 7 were girls. The acceptance of girls proved successful and produced good results.

Conclusion

Applying a patriarchal label to the Old Believer community can be easily done. With conservative approaches to gender roles, rooted in an inward-looking sense of place, Old Believers seem to be a perfect example of an unchanging tradition. Yet, the life of the community and their religious heritage is changing. The community's life is embedded in Romania's social, economic, cultural and political life, and thus subjected to wider influences. Modern communication technologies open up further communication channels. It is thus that we can discuss of a progressive sense of place (Massey 1993), where opportunities for women's imagination expand and new roles are opened up. Territories and activities that were once labelled as exclusively masculine can now be taken by women also. In moving towards a progressive sense of place, the tension between global and local leads to a double bind (Nic Craith 2010). On the one hand, it gives an opportunity to women to renegotiate their heritage roles. On the other hand, such influences result in a loss of traditions, when people, attracted by modern developments, reject rather than modify their inheritance.

Case studies such as ours raise interesting questions on the nexus between heritage, gender and religion. To what extent are gendered traditions passed on at the beginning of the twenty-first century (Clopot 2016b)? Would such traditions survive if they were rendered gender neutral? Would they lose meaning if the gender dimension were absent? To what extent do male perspectives dominate or contribute to the resolution of these questions? The tenacity that has kept Old Believers' heritage alive, along with its patriarchal structures, offers interesting insights on the tensions between heritage, gender and a traditional sense of place in a postmodern world.

Acknowledgements

Fieldwork for this project was conducted with the support of an Estella Cranziani Post-Graduate Bursary for Research from the Folklore Society.

Notes

1 Here Naumescu draws a parallel with one of the main characteristics of Old Belief, that it is considered an apocalyptic religion, as various authors have emphasiszd that Old Believers live their lives in preparation for the imminent end of times.
2 The history of Old Believers has attracted historians from different parts of the world, researchers such as Robert Crummey (1970, 2011), David Scheffel (1991), or Roy Robson (1996) have conducted extensive analyses of the Russian Schism. The anthropology of religion has represented another avenue and Vlad Naumescu (2010, 2011, 2013) presents a secluded Old Believers community in the Danube Delta, or Rogers' study in Sepych (Russia) centred on ethics (Rogers 2009).
3 These innovations promoted by Patriarch Nikon include changes to texts but also to religious practices. While the full range of changes is extensive, researchers often point to changes in the manner of crossing. These changes approved through the 1654 council

stipulated that the thumb, index and middle fingers should be joined, while Old Believers join the thumb, little and ring finger while the index and middle finger are kept straight. This annulled the profound symbolic nature of the sign, with the two straight fingers representing the dual nature of Christ and the three united fingers the Holy Trinity.
4 Lipovan is the local name used for Old Believers in Romania and Moldova.
5 This is a local pronunciation of the Russian word 'papert' (паперть).

Bibliography

CEDAW, 1979. *Convention on the Elimination of All Forms of Discrimination Against Women.* Available at: www.un.org/womenwatch/daw/cedaw/text/econvention.htm (accessed 29 May 2015).

Clopot, C. 2016a. Weaving the Past in a Fabric: Old Believers' Traditional Costume. *Folklore: Electronic Journal of Folklore* 66: 115–132.

Clopot, C. 2016b. Liminal Identities of Migrant Groups: The Old Russian Believers of Romania. In D. Downey, I. Kinane and E. Parker (eds) *Landscapes of Liminality: Between Space and Place.* London and New York: Rowman & Littlefield, pp. 153–176.

Crummey, R. O. 1970. *The Old Believers and the World of Antichrist: The Vyg Community and the Russian State, 1694–1855.* Madison, WI: University of Wisconsin Press.

Crummey, R.O. 2011. *Old Believers in a Changing World.* DeKalb, IL: Northern Illinois University Press.

European Institute for Gender Equality (EIGE), 2015. *Gender Equality Index 2015: Measuring Gender Equality in the European Union 2005–2012.* Available at: http://eige.europa.eu/sites/default/files/documents/mh0415169enn.pdf (accessed 21 August 2015).

Fairclough, G. 2009. New Heritage Frontiers. In Council of Europe (ed.) *Heritage and Beyond.* Strasbourg: Council of Europe, pp. 29–41.

Ferrari, S. 2014. Introduction: The Legal Protection of the Sacred Places of the Mediterranean. In S. Ferrari and A. Benzo (eds) *Between Cultural Diversity and Common Heritage: Legal and Religious Perspectives on the Sacred Places of the Mediterranean.* Farnham: Ashgate, pp. 1–14.

Geertz, C. 1973. *The Interpretation of Cultures.* New York: Basic Books.

Iconographer Interview. ND. *Resurse culturale.* Available at: www.resurseculturale.ro/site/?q=node/122 (accessed 20 June 2014).

Ipatiov, F. 2001. *Rușii-lipoveni din România.* Bucharest: Editura Presa Universitară Clujeană.

Levy, J.E. 2013. Gender, Feminism and Heritage. In P.F. Biehl and C. Prescott (eds) *Heritage in the Context of Globalization: Europe and the Americas.* London and New York: Springer, pp. 85–91.

Logan, W. 2007. Closing Pandora's Box: Human Rights Conundrums In Cultural Heritage Protection. In H. Silverman and D.F. Ruggles (eds) *Cultural Heritage and Human Rights.* New York: Springer, pp. 33–52.

Logan, W. 2009. Playing the Devil's Advocate: Protecting Intangible Cultural Heritage and the Infringement of Human Rights. *Historic Environment* 22(3): 14–18.

Logan, W., Langfield, M. and Nic Craith, M. 2010. Intersecting Concepts and Practices. In M. Langfield, W. Logan and M. Nic Craith (eds) *Cultural Diversity, Heritage and Human Rights: Intersections in Theory and Practice.* London and New York: Routledge, pp. 3–20.

Longhurst, R. 2005. Situating Bodies. In L. Nelson and J. Seager (eds) *A Companion to Feminist Geography*. Oxford: Blackwell, pp. 337–349.

McDowell, L. 1999. *Gender, Identity and Place: Understanding Feminist Geographies*. Minneapolis, MN: University of Minnesota Press.

Massey, D. 1993. Power-Geometry and a Progressive Sense of Place. In J. Bird, B. Curtis, T. Putnam, G. Robertson and L. Tickner (eds) *Mapping the Futures: Local Cultures, Global Change*. London and New York: Routledge, pp. 60–70.

Massey, D. 1995a. Places and their Pasts. *History Workshop Journal* 39(1): 182–192.

Massey, D. 1995b. The Conceptualization of Place. In D. Massey and P. Jess (eds) *A Place in the World: Places, Cultures and Globalization*. Oxford: Open University Press, pp. 45–77.

Massey, D. 2004. Geographies of Responsibility. *Geografiska Annaler: Series B, Human Geography* 86(1): 5–18.

Metropolitanka. ND. Gdańsk Shipyard from Women's Perspective. Available at: http://metropolitanka.ikm.gda.pl/dzialania/zwiedzanie/zwiedzanie-stoczni/gdansk-shipyard-from-womens-perspective/ (accessed 10 January 2017).

Moghadam, V. and Bagheritari, M. 2007. Cultures, Conventions, and the Human Rights of Women: Examining the Convention for Safeguarding Intangible Cultural Heritage, and the Declaration on Cultural Diversity. *Museum International* 59(4): 9–18.

Moldovan, S. 2004. *Comunitatea Rușilor Lipoveni*. Bucharest: Editura Ararat.

Morris, R.A. 1999. The Dispersion of Old Believers in Russia and Beyond. In J. Pentikäinen (ed.) *'Silent as Waters We Live': Old Believers in Russia and Abroad: Cultural Encounter with the Finno-Ugrians*. Helsinki: Suomalaisen kirjallisuuden seura, pp. 103–125.

National Institute of Statistics (NSI), 2011. *Romanian Population and Homes Census 2011*. Bucharest: National Institute of Statistics.

Naumescu, V. 2010. Le vieil homme et le livre: la crise de la transmission chez les Vieux-Croyants. *Terrain* 55: 72–89.

Naumescu, V. 2011. The Case for Religious Transmission: Time and Transmission in the Anthropology of Christianity. *Religion and Society: Advances in Research* 2: 54–71.

Nic Craith, M. 2008. 'Intangible Cultural Heritages: The Challenge for Europe', *Anthropological Journal of European Cultures* 17(1), 54–73.

Nic Craith, M. 2010. Local Cultures in a Global World. In U. Kockel and M. Nic Craith (eds) *Communicating Cultures*. Berlin: LIT, pp. 279–300.

Nic Craith, M. and Kockel, U. 2015. (Re-)Building Heritage: Integrating Tangible and Intangible. In W. Logan, M. Nic Craith and U. Kockel (eds) *Blackwell Companion to Heritage Studies*. Oxford: Blackwell, pp. 426–442.

Nora, P. 1989. Between Memory and History: Les lieux de mémoire. *Representations* 26: 7–24.

Papastathis, C.K. 2000. The Enclosure of Mount Athos in the Framework of Gender Discrimination. *Kanon* XVI: 265–281.

Papastathis, C.K. 2014. The Regime of Mount Athos. In S. Ferrari and A. Benzo (eds) *Between Cultural Diversity and Common Heritage: Legal and Religious Perspectives on the Sacred Places of the Mediterranean*. Farnham: Ashgate, pp. 273–292.

Robson, R.R. 1996. *Old Believers in Modern Russia*. Dekalb, IL: Northern Illinois University Press.

Rogers, D. 2009. *The Old Faith and the Russian Land: A Historical Ethnography of Ethics in the Urals*. Ithaca: Cornell University Press.

Rössler, M. 2014. Gendered World Heritage? A Review of the Implementation of the UNESCO World Heritage. In UNESCO (ed.) *Gender Equality Heritage and Creativity*. Paris: UNESCO, pp. 60–72.

Ruggles, F.D. and Silverman, H. 2009. From Tangible to Intangible Heritage. In F.D. Ruggles and H. Silverman (eds) *Intangible Heritage Embodied*. London and New York: Springer, pp. 1–14.

Scheffel, D. 1991. *In the Shadow of Antichrist: the Old Believers of Alberta*. Peterborough, ON: Broadview Press.

Shaheed, F. 2014. Foreword. In: UNESCO (ed.) *Gender Equality Heritage and Creativity*. Paris: UNESCO, pp. 5–6.

Smith, L. 2006. *Uses of Heritage*. London and New York: Routledge.

Smith, L. 2008. Heritage, Gender and Identity. In B. Graham and P. Howard (eds) *The Ashgate Research Companion to Heritage and Identity*. Aldershot: Ashgate, pp. 159–180.

Steinberg, J. 1997. From a 'Pot of Filth' to a 'Hedge of Roses' and Back: Changing Theorizations of Menstruation in Judaism. *Journal of Feminist Studies in Religion* 13(2): 5–26.

Talle, A. 2010. Getting the Ethnography 'Right': On Female Circumcision in Exile. In M. Melhuus, H. Wulff and J.P. Mitchell (eds) *Ethnographic Practice in the Present*. New York and Oxford: Berghahn Books, pp. 107–120.

Turner, V.W. 1969. *The Ritual Process: Structure and Anti-Structure*. London: Routledge and Keegan Paul.

UNESCO, 2003. *Convention for the Safeguarding of the Intangible Cultural Heritage*. Available at: www.unesco.org/culture/ich/en/convention (accessed 10 June 2015).

UNESCO, 2014a. *Gender Equality Heritage and Creativity*. Available at: www.uis.unesco.org/Library/Documents/gender-equality-heritage-creativity-culture-2014-en.pdf (accessed 6 January 2015).

UNESCO, 2014b. *UNESCO's Promise: Gender Equality – A Global Priority*. Available at: http://unesdoc.unesco.org/images/0022/002269/226923m.pdf (accessed 29 May 2015).

Valentine, G. 1999. Imagined Geographies: Geographical Knowledges of Self and Other in Everyday Life. In D. Massey, J. Allen and P. Sarre (eds) *Human Geography Today*. Cambridge: Polity Press, pp. 47–61.

West, C. and Zimmerman, D.H. 1987. Doing Gender. *Gender and Society* 1(2): 125–151.

Wulff, H. 2002. Yo-Yo Fieldwork: Mobility and Time in a Multi-Local Study of Dance in Ireland. *Anthropological Journal on European Cultures* 11: 117–136.

Chapter 4

Handicrafting gender
Craft, performativity and cultural heritage

Anneli Palmsköld and Johanna Rosenqvist

Introduction

To write the history of craft and heritage engages with constructing a canon of known practices parallel to deconstructing the differences incorporated in institutions dealing with craft. Craft objects have long since been considered as heritage, but craft is also recognized as 'intangible heritage'. This can be seen in UNESCO's (2009) designation of 'traditional craftsmanship' as a part of global intangible heritage. However, craft's gendered character is not equally recognized. In this chapter, we will discuss craft, heritage and gender from a performativity perspective on making. The main question is how gender patterns are reflected in the understanding of craft, and in heritage-making. The aim is to make visible the gender demarcations in the making of craft. We argue that the making of craft and its heritage status has been highly charged with gender differences. Recognizing this is of importance to be able to understand and to challenge heritage-making processes and canons when it comes to craft. After a short theoretical background focusing on performativity and the canon of gender differences, three empirical examples are outlined. The first is about organizational aspects of handicraft, the second concerning the technique of crocheting and the third considering visual representations of crafting, using empirical archival and published materials from the Home Craft Movement in Sweden.

Institutions and the canon of heritage-making

Heritage-making processes are most often connected to official authorities such as museums and other organizations working with cultural heritage management (Grahn 2011). Through their work and inscribed in collections and sites, they represent an 'official version of history' (Grahn 2011: 224) or what has been called an 'authorised heritage discourse' (Smith 2006). As Grahn and Smith have pointed out, these versions and discourses need to be deconstructed and critically analysed in order to identify under what premises they were formed (Grahn 2011; Smith 2006). Furthermore, the objects and places that have been chosen to be safeguarded in heritagization processes are representations of various ideas on society, culture and people that have developed and changed over time (see Kirshenblatt-Gimblett 1998). The authorities and institutions are in that sense examples of multi-layered and complex patchworks, containing long since abandoned ideas. Old ideologies and scientific-based theories are locked into archives and museum collections, and even though they are not valid any longer they are in many ways active (Palmsköld *et al.* 2016). One example of this is how the official version of craft and craft history has been created, from a gender perspective. The ways that craft is conserved in museums and institutions is part of a canonical, self-referring history-making.

By using old craft and sloyd techniques and adapting historical patterns to modern design, the Home Craft Movement in Sweden became a central actor in the early 1900s in the heritagization processes connected to craft and sloyd, and in creating an authorized heritage discourse; a Swedish national heritage when it comes to craft (we will return to the notion and describe the movement below). It had the position and the power to choose which techniques were to be accepted as 'traditional', 'Swedish' or 'typical local' according to the overall discourse (Hyltén-Cavallius 2007; Palmsköld 2007, 2012a, 2012b; Zickerman 1918). The Home Craft Movement was initiated and maintained by women but in the patriarchal society often spearheaded by men (Lundström 2005). The movement had soon created space in a metaphorical sense for accepted (typically 'Swedish') techniques that excluded other craft and sloyd techniques. The national discourse made it possible to exclude, for example, craft that were made in Swedish Jew, Sami and Romani communities (Hyltén-Cavallius 2004, 2007, 2015; Klein 1999; Palmsköld 2012a). In the same way, new and modern techniques that were considered of no historical or national value were excluded, and one of those was crocheting.

In *Differencing the Canon: Feminist Desire and the Writing of Art's Histories* (1999) Griselda Pollock defines three steps in feminist art historical writing that could be applied here. The first step is to fill the gaps in the male-dominated canon, i.e. adding on women pioneers within the field (see also Smith 2008). The second step has been to investigate how different power aspects based on, for example, the categories sex, class, ethnicity and sexuality has worked (Mainardi 1982; Parker 1984/1996; Parker and Pollock 1981; Pollock 1999: 23–24). To investigate, for example, the fluctuating status of textile craft made by women may be an example of this second step (Rosenqvist 2007). The third step, Pollock states:

> implies a shift from the narrowly bounded spaces of art history as a disciplinary formation into an emergent and oppositional signifying space we call the women's movement which is not a place apart but a movement across the fields of discourse and its institutional bases, across the texts of culture and its psychic foundations.
>
> (Pollock 1999: 26)

The third step is to transgress the position of otherness. To sum up, you might say the first step adds on or helps with constructing the canon – while the other two deconstructs the basis of it. By addressing crocheting as an overlooked technique and stating the Home Craft Movement as an important institution, we simultaneously add to the history of heritage-making and deconstruct the canon of craft as hitherto written. Empirical studies over time of local branches of the Home Craft Movement in Sweden show that aesthetics is discursive and understood as notions about expressions of art and limits for artistic creation (Rosenqvist 2007). Furthermore, this is not as separated from ideas about gender differences but rather as dependent on them. What happens if you treat the limitations regarding the techniques used in heritage-making as an effect of a canon formation?

Performative aspects of craft and gender

One possible theoretical point when exploring craft is to study performative aspects of making processes connected to the bodies that are in motion. The discussion herein on gender and performativity is informed by the theorists Iris Marion Young and Judith Butler (Butler 1997, 1999; Young 1980/2005). The field of craft in relation to a wider field of cultural production is confined by interrelated outlines of what is called, for example, home craft, handicraft and art (Rosenqvist and Palmsköld 2015). While the notion of words *as* actions was of initial interest in performativity studies, the relationship between saying and doing has become the centre of attention (Sedgwick 1993). Although not focusing on the actual making of craft, Butler's theories on gender concerned with 'doing' rather than 'being' are useful in looking at craft from a critical perspective on what is being done. In introducing her concept of gender performativity, Butler proposes that gender is to be understood neither as an entity nor as a set of free-floating attributes, but instead, as continuously being *done*. In her seminal text *Gender Trouble* from 1990, she writes 'gender is itself a kind of becoming or activity to be conceived [. . .] as an incessant and repeated action of some sort' (Butler 1999: 112). The attributes ascribed to gender are performative, Butler says. So if repeated action makes up the patterns, that are thought of as feminine or masculine, and in turn are making gender, this is where a pioneering work by Iris Marion Young can be considered. Her study of what it means to be 'throwing like a girl' involves examining the movements physically as well as their spatial setting (Young 1980/2005).

The expected feminine expressions of the female body are creating physical limitations. In the contemporary Western culture that she was studying, a girl is expected to smile, tilt her head and not take up too much space. The latter is what she focuses on mainly, and she describes the feminine movements to a larger extent confined to *immanence*. They are inward looking, focusing on appearance rather than functioning in contrast to the outward reaching, or *transcended*, functionality of the movements thought of as masculine. This is something taught and repeated, and if brought to attention it can be challenged and therefore changed.

Neither Young nor Butler takes craft as an example of performing gender in their studies. Butler rather draws on speech act theory when she states that it is not enough to successfully carry out the intentions of a movement for it to be recognized as such. A performance may be seen as an activity that is framed, highlighted, displayed, and that, as an act, the performance presupposes an audience (Gradén 2011). In feminist theory and practice the notion, as offered by Butler, of mimetic, socially constructed, stylized acts that appear as authentic expressions of biological sex through a process of constant repetition, is thought to be one of the more useful models (Harris 1999; Moriel 2005; Rosenberg 2012). This transposes the question of *essence* into a key that is all the more interesting than to simply state that there is a 'tendency to portray males in active and even aggressive stances, females in passive ones' in the visual representations of museums in general as well as in the society that surrounds it (Smith 2008: 164). This, in turn, legitimizes social norms and gendered power structures that effect and are in turn affected by roles and identities of men and women. A statement is successful when a subject's statement/movement echoes prior statements and accumulates their force of authority (Butler 1997). To rephrase in terms of craft heritage-making: the craft canon is made up of works and artists constantly being echoed, thus given authority to make up history forming an authorized heritage discourse.

The Home Craft Movement and heritagization of crafts

The Home Craft Movement started by the end of the nineteenth century (Lundahl 1999, 2001; Meister 2012; Palmsköld 2012a, 2012b; Rosenqvist 2007; Stavenow-Hidemark 1999a). We use the term 'Home Craft Movement' to cover the totality of related initiatives. On an organizational level, it started when Lilli Zickerman (1858–1949) founded The Association of Swedish Handicraft (Föreningen för svensk hemslöjd) in 1899.[1] Following this development, during the first decades of the 1900s, local handicraft organizations were founded in each region in Sweden, together forming the National Association of Swedish Handicraft Societies (SHR). The main issue for the movement was how to preserve historical craft and sloyd techniques that were no longer practised and how to make this craft knowledge useful within contemporary Swedish society (Hemslöjdskommittén 1918; Zickerman 1938/1999). Compared to more institutionalized and professionalized practices like museums, the early Home Craft Movement attracted members (mostly women) that were engaged in the work mainly on a voluntary basis.

The part 'home' in the notion of 'home craft', connoted a small-scale production of handmade goods that took place in households instead of in factories. It was also, on a metaphorical level, a household name for commodities necessary for homes and home decoration such as interior textiles, furniture, baskets, bowls and weavings (cf. Föreningen för svensk hemslöjd 1907: 3). From a gender perspective, it is important to recognize that home craft was foremost connected to women and femininity, defined and constructed by the modern bourgeois in late nineteenth- and early twentieth-century Sweden (Lundström 2005). The role of women in society and family was, in this discourse, to be responsible for homes and home decoration (Lundström 2005; Svensson and Waldén 2005). The founders were fully aware of the multiple associations that could be made by using the concept of 'homecraft' (Lundahl 2001; Lundström 2005: 145–147; Palmsköld 2012a: 15–16; Zickerman 1938/1999: 39), and it became a code word saying that the organization turned to women and that the commodities provided were goods for homes (Lundström 2005; Palmsköld 2012a; Rosenqvist 2007). Since then the concept home craft, and its synonym handicraft, has turned to be a more neutral expression, that stands for what people are making at home, with local materials and more or less traditional techniques. This has come to include do-it-yourself (DIY) tips and tricks on how to solve practical problems in everyday life (Åhlvik and von Busch 2009).

According to Lilli Zickerman, the craft safeguarding practices were about designing new products, based on historical techniques and patterns, and attractive in a modern context. She ordered handcrafted commodities made by a network of crafters living in the Swedish countryside, and sold the products in a shop located in the centre of Stockholm (Stavenow-Hidemark 1999b). According to Zickerman the only way old craft techniques could survive in the modern industrial society was to make them useful by offering desirable handmade commodities for the intended costumer's belonging to an urban bourgeoisie. Special efforts with aesthetic considerations were an important priority, and the aim was to create products of good design made by high-quality raw materials, and on a skilled craft level (Hyltén-Cavallius 2007; Palmsköld 2012a; Rosenqvist 2007). The Home Craft Movement adapted the same concept as Zickerman. They often started their work by identifying local crafters, and collecting samples of craft techniques and of patterns. When decisions had been made on what to produce and sell, the crafters were asked to deliver handmade products from models and descriptions designed with inspiration by historical patterns. The products were sold in shops under the trademark Swedish Sloyd (Svensk slöjd), and each organization had its own label to put on the commodities. Craft in this discourse was considered as something 'traditional', with a long history connected to regions and places, and 'authentic' as the products were handmade, using old techniques and tools, and locally produced with carefully chosen raw materials.

Zickerman's work called *Swedish Folk Textiles* is a huge inventory project that was conducted in the period 1914–1931. She travelled around Sweden documenting textiles by describing them and photographing them, leaving an archive of 24,000 photographs and catalogue cards. Since the photographs were in black and white, threads from dyed yarns were sampled and used when hand colouring parts of the photographs. The aim of the project was to create an archive to inspire future textile artists and to give them opportunities to learn more from their forerunners. The ambition was to publish a multivolume work, but only one part of the manuscript was published (Zickerman 1937). The material is structured according to Zickerman's ideas on craft as something typically local, and the archive capsules are organized first in a geographical order and second according to different textile techniques. Her ideas on craft became an important point of departure for the governmental inquiry about craft that she participated in (Hemslöjdskommittén 1918; Zickerman 1918). Swedish Folk Textiles is a document archive, and it does not contain textile material objects. If studied closer, however, it is clear that the textiles that were in focus for the inventory were often part of collections owned by museums or handicraft craft organizations. The inventory has had a major impact on how craft have been understood in Sweden. Even though it was not published as intended, researchers, textile artists, authors in the field and museum curators have used the material for different purposes. It has also become a model for how to conduct inventories and collect for archives in the Home Craft Movement. The Swedish ethnologist and antiquarian at Nordiska museet in Stockholm, Anna-Maja Nylén, wrote a standard work on Swedish handicraft in pre-industrial society called *Swedish Handcraft* (Nylén 1976, 1977). When it comes to textiles, Nylén's work is mainly based on information from Zickerman's inventory, together with her own research on folk costumes.

Apart from the shops and the product development that was going on within the Home Craft Movement, it also created an infrastructure for knowledge production concerning craft. In order to be able to practise historical craft techniques, people had to learn how to make (including efficient bodily movements) as well as about materials used, patterns and design possibilities. Courses were provided for, and during the 1900s a network of regional working handicraft consultants were implemented.[2] Learning to craft was mainly a matter of handing over a tacit knowledge about making, but the educational situations were also moments when narratives about craft history were told. Knowledge about craft was also spread through publications such as handbooks and magazines. The shops worked as inspiration for people interested in crafting, and in the 1950s and 1960s they started selling patterns, kits, tools and materials for crafters beside the craft products. The infrastructure concerning raw materials and tools was an important part of the heritagization process. Through the Home Craft Movement, sheep breeding was started in order to come up with wool qualities for different kinds of weaving, and knitting or embroidering (Rådström 1986). Another example is the cotton thread that was used to embroider historical techniques from different parts of Sweden. It was of importance to find the right material quality and to be able to order exactly the correct nuance of the dyed yarns. Cooperation with good suppliers that could fulfil the requirements was prioritized, and this is still an important aspect of how knowledge is produced and heritage is made, and in this case: remade.

The Swedish Home Craft Movement had a major impact on creating a national history of craft and sloyd. Through the network of handicraft shops, the courses and the trademark label 'Swedish Sloyd', the Home Craft Movement had the power to select which products, craft techniques and design were to be commodified or not. The shops and the workshops were display windows of the movement. They signalled that they offered handicraft both as a ready-made commodity and as things to make themselves (Rosenqvist 2007: 187). Leaders of the Home Craft

Figure 4.1 Lace braiding
Source: photograph by Emil Palmsköld.

Movement and other intellectuals expressed their view in articles and books on what was good craft and what was not. How can this craft canon and its constitution be understood from a heritage perspective? Using crocheting as an example makes it possible to deconstruct the canon.

Crocheting: a non-heritage

Crochet came into fashion within industrialized Western countries at the beginning of the 1800s, as cotton material was spread alongside colonialism and slavery (Lemire 2011; Paludan 1986; Yafa 2006). The oldest pattern description of crocheting found was published in 1824 in a Dutch ladies magazine called *Pénélope* (Paludan 1986: 22, 44). The technique became very popular and in 1844 the first crochet pattern book was published in Sweden (Hennings 1844). Weekly papers and magazines were soon publishing crochet patterns and an increasing number of craft books were also sold in Sweden (Björk 1944: 3). Crocheting activities were to be a common part of many women's everyday life and the results that were produced for home decoration or for personal use were visible in homes of different social classes.

According to Zickerman, crocheting was a 'lazy work' that could be performed while reclining, compared with techniques such as bobbin lace, weaving and embroidery that was done with a straight back and good posture and that also supposedly requires intellectual activity (Hyltén-Cavallius 2007: 111). Crochet was too simple in comparison, Zickerman said, which was reflected in what she perceived as an ugly result. It was also considered as a useless and luxury work (see Paludan 1986: 85). Zickerman brought a struggle against crochet, which, for example, literally meant she did not sell products that were made from crochet in the shop she managed. The same was true of most local handicraft shops in Sweden. Others expressed that, for example, white cotton bedspreads made by crochet was a sign of bad taste (Danielson 1991: 200). Crocheting, it was said, only gave the impression of real work, and the result brought discomfort in the interior design (Danielson 1991: 201f.). Another theme discussed was the differences between the 'national' and the 'cosmopolitan' or 'international' sloyd (Holmström 1898: 24ff). As modern and new, crocheting was considered part of an international fashion, when patterns change with the fashions of the day (Holmström 1898: 24). The national sloyd, on the other hand, was said to be based on what was unique to a place or culture, similar to Zickerman's ideas (Holmström 1898: 26). Crocheting did not belong to the Swedish textile techniques of age and tradition to be advocated and defended. It was simply not thought of as Swedish and patriotic enough, and in addition, it was argued within the Home Craft Movement, that crocheting had displaced more traditional and Swedish techniques such as lace braiding and lace embroidery.

Crocheting was also contested from a technical and aesthetic point of view. Considered as tasteless, ugly and unsightly and not 'Swedish' enough, crocheting as a textile technique was thought to be practised by slack and unenlightened people. It was not thought of as nearly as intellectually demanding as, for example, weaving and bobbin lace making. In the late 1800s crocheting was exerted by the women from the lower and service classes, those who read 'maid novels', weekly serials and who collected pattern sheets and pattern attachments from women's and family magazines, and who changed the pattern with each other and crocheted sample collections. Crocheting could according to these arguments not be included in designated rooms of the Home Craft Movement, designed as they were according to the ideas of preserving craft of age and history.

Crocheting became a very common textile technique, maybe too connected to women's everyday activities, to be appreciated. No advanced tools or material are required, nor a certain space as when, for example, weaving in a loom. Crocheting is somehow invisible, as it has mainly been practised in people's private sphere, and as such it does not have any particular economical value. The performative

Figure 4.2 Lace braiding
Source: photograph by Emil Palmsköld.

aspects of crocheting were thus hidden from the official societal recognition. The technique, as well as the women who practised it, are rather part of the non-official version of history (Grahn 2011) than the authorized heritage discourse as a canon of craft created by the Home Craft Movement.

Not only was the technique and its lack of history debated, even the crocheting female bodies were deselected in the heritagization process. Home Craft of historical value, was, according to the discourse, to be practised by rural classes, alongside their farming activity, and not by lower- and service-class women living in urban areas. The educational role of the Home Craft Movement included teaching people to distinguish what was considered tasteless, from what was thought to be of high aesthetic value. The elite connected to the movement were convinced of the importance of educating people from a top-down perspective, and according to the belief in their superiority towards others.

Practising crochet was simultaneously a very modern and desirable craft skill for women in the 1800s that was highlighted in magazines and publications on needlework. The technique became part of the contemporary needlework culture, which was directed towards women and an important part of women's everyday life. Performing crochet was – much like needlework – about performing femininity: sitting down on a chair or in a sofa, looking down at the ongoing work, holding a needle the same way as holding a pencil and making small movements when crocheting one stitch after another. In the early 1800s, the crocheting female body most certainly belonged to a woman within the growing bourgeois culture, structured according to the idea of gender separations and complementarity. In a social setting within this culture, it was suitable for young women to demonstrate their abilities to craft, and to be modest and polite by concentrating on work and only talk when asked to. Crocheting with fine yarn and a fine hook, led to small movements and by the repeated actions, for example, leading to lace for bed linen, female gender was being performed. In another setting, at the end of the 1800s, crocheting was performed by women of lower and serving classes. In this context, craft was more about socializing with other women in the same situation, and to perform and demonstrate practical capability and working morale. In both examples, textile making was a considerable responsibility for women in households and families.

Visual representations of crocheting

Visual representations of how the craft is being performed are part of how the history of a craft is canonized. When studying craft from a heritage perspective photographs in magazines have a double function: they are of documentary value but they are also part of the outreach. The consequences of them being disseminated and that certain materials and techniques are portrayed alongside the movements and poses of the craftsperson, is that a visual norm is being constructed. The magazine *Hemslöjden* (now called *Hemslöjd – Home-Craft* in English) has functioned as the official source of information for and from the Home Craft Movement in Sweden. The magazine was founded in 1933 by art historian Gerda Boëthius. Its aim has been to maintain and renew traditional folk art and craft with a focus on small-scale production, close to home and with natural, locally produced or recycled raw materials. Before 1933 you could read about handicraft or home craft in the magazine published for and by The Swedish Society of Arts and Design (Svenska Slöjdföreningen, founded in 1845). Their magazine *FORM* is now (since 2011) a specialized magazine for architecture and design. But earlier it covered a wide range of design issues, from handicraft to working environments. It started out as a newsletter for members of The Swedish Society of Arts and Design but has been distributed to a wider audience from 1905, under its current name since 1932. The pictures in magazines elicit a heritage history in the making. In *FORM*, the professional crafts are presented and since crocheting has neither been a professional craft, nor traditional enough a craft to be part of the Home Craft Movement it is largely missing visual representation.

To study the bodily styles and functional gestures of craft the magazines have been subjected to a close reading (Rosenqvist 2013). Here is where we want to point to some specifics in *Hemslöjden*. Throughout the 1900s there has been an increase in the number of images documenting making in the issues of the magazine *Hemslöjden*. From around a thousand black and white photographs in a decade to over four times as many images in the more recent issues. There are also now a wide variety of visual manifestations ranging from graphic novels for a generation of young craft people, to lavish displays of objects in colour photographs and how-to-do-it documentaries showing the process of making craft. Apart from an overall increase in use of pictures we read this as a sign of awareness that these actual processes of making craft need visual display. The analysis also shows that the number of action pictures, of craft in the making, has steadily been around 10 per cent of the total amount of pictures. A broader study of the visual representations of the process of making in art, craft and design magazines show that there are more differences in the representations of craft between the magazines than there are differences between decades, the most obvious exception of a significantly lower percentage of action – pictures in the design magazine of the later date. Compared to the design and art magazines there is more of sharing of tips and tricks of the traditional crafts in the handicraft magazine *Hemslöjden*.[3] When studying all the issues of specialized craft magazines like *Hemslöjden* what is most remarkable is the sheer quantity of pictures of hands that are being displayed. For the most part, these hands are busy doing something. Some of the images serve as pedagogical tools to transmit knowledge of certain moves in the process of making, while others show the process of making, or the production aspects (Rosenqvist 2009). The pedagogical category of pictures functions as a strengthening of the DIY character of the magazine.

A page in *Hemslöjden* (2009/4: 37; see Figure 4.3) may serve as an example of how the performative aspects are at play. The page is divided in to three parts. In the upper part there is the finished piece that looks like a simple striped potholder. Under it follows the written description of how to make it. In the lower part of the page there is a picture of a hand showing one step in the process of making. The picture has a pedagogical aim to clearly show how to hold the crochet hook and the work. The potholder looks like the simple kind of crocheting every child in school was taught in sloyd classes but it is coined 'Tunisian crochet'. The vocabulary is interesting since it places the origin of the technique outside of Sweden and the difference is actually highlighted in the picture. The picture shows on one row of stitches that are hooked on the needle, and on the second row they are casted off. Both rows are worked from the same side, unlike conventional crocheting. In examples like the one described, gender differences are not on display. The hands in these pictures don't have any insignias or other markers, and the close-up picture doesn't contextualize the making either. The text is not written to or from a person with any specific gender that is articulated or visible and it does not give away any preferred recipient. We read this omission of gender insignias as part of the Home Craft Movements ongoing strategy to engage makers outside the prevalent dichotomic gender differences.

The pictures overall contextualize the craftsperson in the process of making. They generally show more of the room or environment and more of the body. In a majority of these production pictures the depicted person has his or her

▲ Krokningstekniken ger olika effekt på rät- och avigsida.

Att kroka en hel filt i ett stycke skulle bli alldeles för tungt, eftersom alla maskor vid vartannat varv sitter samtidigt på nålen (se teknikbeskrivningen nedan). För att kunna göra större arbeten använder vissa numera en rundkroknål, som liknar en rundsticka fast med kroknålar i ändarna, och vänder tillbaka vid varje varv.

Gudrun Gjellan krokar dessutom mössor, vantar, handledsvärmare, väskor, sjalar och stora tröjor. Och grytlappar, där ränderna är horisontella på den ena sidan och vertikala på den andra. En rolig effekt av tekniken! Strukturen på slätkrokade föremål är jämfört med stickat och virkat fastare och något tjockare. Gudrun tycker att krokade ullvantar är extra värmande.

ORDET KROKNING ger 15 400 träffar på Google. Visserligen handlar bara de 300 första om handarbetstekniken krokning, sedan gäller det mest fiske. Men 300 är inte dåligt, det visar en livlig aktivitet bland krokande nätanvändare.

– Internet har haft stor betydelse, först för att stickningen så snabbt blivit populär igen, och nu för att sprida kunskap om krokning. För mig var det en hemsida som fick igång intresset. Nätet är inte bara diskussionsforum, det är också handelsplats för garn, nålar och litteratur, säger Gudrun Gjellan. Hon har köpt flera böcker om krokning på olika språk, även på japanska som hon inte alls behärskar. Bilderna i boken är så tydliga och instruktiva att hon har nytta av den ändå.

Gudrun bloggar flera gånger i veckan. Hon deltar i olika stickgrupper och håller kurser på olika håll i landet. Bland annat har hon tagit upp krokning på slöjdkvällar för hemslöjdsföreningens medlemmar i Östergötland. Sommaren 2008 gick hon en kurs för Solvor Hofsli under Nordiskt Sticksymposium i Norge.

Gudrun Gjellan vill att fler ska få chans att upptäcka tjusningen med krokning.

– Det är en rolig och snabb teknik och man får ett resultat som är stadigare än stickat och smidigare än virkat. ◆

LÄSTIPS
Lis Paludan, *Hækling, historie och teknik*. Borgens förlag 1986.
Solvor Hofsli, *Hakling, nytt liv för gammelt håndarbeid*. Endast på bibliotek och antikvariat. Fotostatkopior med 30 olika mönstertekniker från boken finns i häftet *Hakling* av Solvor Hofsli. Svensk återförsäljare Slöjdmagasinet, www.slojdmagasinet.nu.
Kirsten Trolle-Hansen: *Hakning. En bok om tunesisk hækling*. Notabene 1987. Finns bland annat på www.needleworkbooks.com.
På nätet kan du söka på *krokning, tunisisk virkning* eller *tunisian crochet*. Bland många bloggar finns Gudrun Gjellans egen, www.krokning.blogspot.com.

KROKNING FRAM OCH TILLBAKA

Krokning kallas också tunisisk virkning eller afghansk virkning. Även beteckningen rysk virkning finns nämnd på internet. I Sverige var krokningen populär under 1800- och början av 1900-talen.

Redskapet är en lång virknål med krok i ena änden och ett stopp i den andra, eller ibland med krok i båda ändar. Ett krokvarv består av *framvarv*, då nya maskor plockas upp på nålen, och *tillbakavarv*, där man drar tråden genom varje maska. Man håller hela tiden arbetet åt samma håll.

ENKEL KROKNING – SÅ HÄR GÖR DU

Lägg på vanligt sätt upp så många luftmaskor som du vill ha.
Framvarv: stick nålen genom den näst sista luftmaskan. Dra upp en ögla och låt öglan/maskan vara kvar på nålen, fortsätt att dra upp öglor/maskor ur varje luftmaska.
Tillbakavarv: Börja med en luftmaska. Gör ett omslag, dra garnet genom en maska, omslag och dra garnet genom två maskor. Fortsätt att göra omslag och dra det genom två maskor tills du bara har en maska kvar på nålen.
Det här är ett *förstavarv* som används i början av de flesta arbeten.

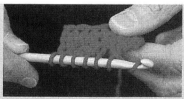

▲ Krokning liknar virkning, men alla maskorna behålls på nålen på ett framåtvarv och maskas av på ett tillbakavarv.

Fortsätt sedan så:
Tag garnet på baksidan av arbetet.
Framvarvet: stick nålen under den lodräta maskbågen, gör ett omslag och dra genom maskbågen. Fortsätt på det sättet varvet ut.
Gör *tillbakavarvet* enligt ovan.

Efter den här beskrivningen kan du prova tekniken i dess enklaste form. Gå vidare genom att läsa utförligare beskrivningar eller lär dig av någon som redan kan!

eyes directed toward the hands and what is being made. Judith Butler draws on speech act theory when she states that it is not enough to successfully carry out the intentions of a movement for it to be recognized as such. Rather a statement is successful when a subject's statement/movement echoes prior statements and accumulates their force of authority. The most repeated act in crafting is the immanent movement of and looking at hands that are making. To be portrayed in the act of making is to engage bodily with your tools and material, to have a hands-on experience, and your eyes on your hands. In all examples of visual representation of crocheting in Hemslöjden in the 2000s, regardless of the sex and age of the person crocheting (as, for example, the boys' concentration on making their own caps in *Hemslöjden* (2000/3: 18) or the fashion designer with her sculptural knitwear in *Hemslöjden* (2006/6: 31)), their focus is on the point where the material meets their hands. Iris Marion Young may say that the feminine movement is immanent. But in these examples, male craftspeople are no more or no less transgressive in their movement than their female counterpart.

If an omission can be thought of as a repeated act then the non-existent crochet work show that this technique is not part of heritage-making, as we know it. It was not until the 1990s the Home Craft Movement really became interested in the technique, and started to publish patterns and books about crocheting (for example, Gullberg and Dackenberg 1998). It is interesting to note that while crocheting was not present in the magazines before the turn of the millennium, it since has been presented a number of times. In part, these presentations are in line with some of the old ideologies of the Home Craft Movement. But in fact crocheting is also offered as a norm critical activity in a presentation of a queer craft café (*Hemslöjden* 2009/4: 24) and in an article about yarn-graffiti (*Hemslöjden* 2009/4: 18–19). Craftivism is a topic discussed with references to both pioneering craftivists and earlier issues of the magazine (*Hemslöjden* 2007/4). In Swedish handicraft organizations during the 1990s the number of men active increased, as did the use of materials traditionally thought of as masculine, and focus was now on the making of 'sloyd' instead of earlier emphasized connections to household production and the home (Rosenqvist 2007). That women and men are portrayed in equal numbers in the illustration the magazine *Hemslöjden* may not be representative of the movement as a whole – which is dominated by women – but rather a counterbalance. Difference is shown in genre rather than gender.

Crafting a new cultural heritage

Socially and culturally constructed notions of gender are central to what matters as cultural heritage. These notions are interrelated to notions of, for example, ethnicity and class and whose body counts. We have learned this by studying a handicraft context using crocheting as an example. Ideologically there were a few crucial things working against crocheting as a national heritage, such as its lack of history and the fact that it was not considered as traditional or authentic. Furthermore, it was a modern technique in a European context, and connected to an international context of fashion. The woman who was practising crocheting in the early 1800s used the technique so as to perform a modern ideal of femininity connected to the bourgeois culture. Later on, when women from lower and serving classes performed crocheting, their craft was not welcomed or included in the Home Craft Movement. They were too modern, too urban and not capable of distinguishing craft of high aesthetic value from those of low value, and they were not aware of the ongoing heritage-making conducted by the Home Craft Movement. Those who were interested in crocheting during most of the 1900s had to turn to ordinary needlework shops and magazines to get yarn, tools and patterns. When crocheting made it into the Home Craft movement it was as a re-conceptualizing craft in an activist context.

When emphasizing the word 'home', the associations went to women's responsibilities and to the home as a small world, in contrast to the public sphere reserved for men. The pioneers used it as a strategic choice to create a room of one's own. Today's activists use the same dichotomy bringing the small, previously un-noted craft out into the public, thus negotiating the terms of heritage-making, of what counts as well as of artistic practice (or indeed professional sphere as a whole). As this study shows, there were many reasons for deselecting crocheting, and not letting it into the canon of approved crafts. The effects of this non-heritage process are that cultural heritage institutions did not actively collect the objects of the practice such as tools, patterns or documents.

We argue for the importance of reiterating and recollecting not only the same old (his)story, but instead to recognize those contexts where women actually have been active. The male norm of early history of heritage collecting and writing has been mapped out, and the phase of 'adding on' from feminist scholars has been prolific for quite a few years. In what may be considered the third phase of critically transgressing the canon, the most important part might be what is outlined as an involvement phase in the actual performing of the cultural heritage in museums and at other sites, archives and institutions. The revisiting of these becomes the key point of departure for studying the reception of these efforts. This implies a social practice in which boundaries between institutional practices and individuals are created in relation to each other over time. Using a gender perspective to investigate this is not to state or define difference but rather to examine the critical imperative that lies in questioning what difference gender makes in crafting.

Notes

1 The English translation of 'Hemslöjdsrörelsen' to 'the Home Craft Movement' is inspired by the Swedish folklorist Barbro Klein (Klein 2010). Handicraft and Home Craft are synonyms that translates to the Swedish 'hemslöjd'.
2 Nämnden för hemslöjdsfrågor [The National Swedish Handicraft Council] homepage www.nfh.se (accessed 20 June 2016).
3 In Rosenqvist's research project 'Performative Handicraft. The Making of Gender in Artistic Practices' at the department of Cultural Sciences, Lund University 2011–2013, the performative aspects of practical skills or hand-made aspects of the process of making were being studied. The main empirical material was the visual representations of bodies that make design, art or craft in magazines of different genres (Rosenqvist 2013).

Bibliography

Åhlvik, C. and von Busch, O. (eds) 2009. *Handarbeta för en bättre värld*, Jönköping: Jönköpings läns museum.
Björk, G. 1944. *Svensk virkning under 100 år: ett bildhäfte med text*. Stockholm: Nordisk rotogravyr.
Butler, J. 1997. *Excitable Speech: A Politics of the Performative*. New York: Routledge.
Butler, J. 1999. *Gender Trouble: Feminism and the Subversion of Identity*. New York: Routledge.
Danielson, S. 1991. *Den goda smaken och samhällsnyttan: om Handarbetets vänner och den svenska hemslöjdsrörelsen*. PhD Thesis, Lund University. Stockholm: Nordiska museet.
Föreningen för svensk hemslöjd: dess tillkomst och verksamhet. 1907. Stockholm: Föreningen för svensk hemslöjd.
Gradén, L. 2011. *Current issues in European cultural studies*, 15–17 June. Norrköping, Sweden. *Linköping Electronic Conference Proceedings*. Available at: www.ep.liu.se/ecp_article/index.en.aspx?issue=062;article=030 (accessed 24 January 2013).
Grahn, W. 2011. Intersectionality and the construction of cultural heritage management. *Archaeologies* 7(1): 222–250.
Gullberg, M. and Dackenberg, C.B. (eds) 1998. *Tid att virka: muddar, vantar, mössor*, Umeå: Hemslöjden.
Harris, G. 1999. *Staging Femininities: Performance and Performativity*. Manchester: Manchester University Press.
Hemslöjden. 1933–2010. Stockholm: Svenska hemslöjdsföreningarnas riksförbund.
Hemslöjdskommittén. 1918. *Hemslöjdskommitténs betänkande*. Stockholm: Nordiska bokh.
Hennings, E. 1844. *Nya mönster till spets-stickning m.m. samt spets-virkning: Med plancher. Af Charlotte L-r*. Stockholm: J.J. Flodin.
Holmström, H. 1898. *Om kvinnlig hemslöjd: Några tankar om dess värde och befrämjande*. Lund: Gleerupska bokh.
Hyltén-Cavallius, C. 2004. Folk i rörelse: hemslöjdsrörelsen och det nationellas betydelse. In H. Abrahamsson and A. Sörbom (eds) *Den tömda demokratin – och vägarna tillbaka till makten*. Stockholm: Agora, pp. 146–160.
Hyltén-Cavallius, C. 2007. *Traditionens estetik: spelet mellan inhemsk och internationell hemslöjd*. PhD Thesis. Stockholm University. Stockholm: Carlsson.
Hyltén-Cavallius, C. 2015. Att göra en nation. In Hyltén-Cavallius, C. Zetterlund and J. Rosenqvist (eds) *Konsthantverk i Sverige del 1*. Botkyrka: Mångkulturellt centrum, pp. 23–31.
Intangible Heritage site at UNESCO homepage. www.unesco.org/culture/ich (accessed 10 August 2014).
Kirshenblatt-Gimblett, B. 1998. *Destination Culture: Tourism, Museums, and Heritage*. Berkeley, CA: University of California Press.
Klein, B. 1999. Den svenska hemslöjdsrörelsen och de främmande. In G. Lundahl (ed.) *Den vackra nyttan: om hemslöjd i Sverige*. Hedemora: Gidlund, pp. 130–141.
Klein, B. 2010. Cultural loss and cultural rescue: Lilli Zickerman, Ottilia Adelborg, and the promises of the Swedish homecraft movement. In H. Joas and B. Klein Sklute (eds) *The Benefit of Broad Horizons: Intellectual and Institutional Preconditions for a Global Social Science: festschrift for Björn Wittrock on the Cccasion of His 65th Birthday*. Brill: Leiden, pp. 261–280.

Lemire, B. 2011. *Cotton*. Oxford: Berg.
Lundahl, G. (ed.) 1999. *Den vackra nyttan: om hemslöjd i Sverige*. Hedemora: Gidlund.
Lundahl, G. 2001. *Karaktär och känsla: ett sekel med Svensk hemslöjd*. Stockholm: Raster.
Lundström, C. 2005. *Fruars makt och omakt: kön, klass och kulturarv 1900–1940*. PhD Thesis, Umeå University. Umeå: Umeå universitet.
Mainardi, P. 1982. Quilts: the great American art. In N. Broude and M. Garrard (eds) *Feminism and Art History: Questioning the Litany*. New York: Westview Press, pp. 330–346.
Meister, A. (ed.) 2012. *Lilli & Prinsen: 100 år av hemslöjd och textil konst*. Stockholm: Carlsson.
Moriel, L. 2005. Passing and the performance of gender, race, and class acts: a theoretical framework. *Women & Performance: A Journal of Feminist Theory* 15(1): 167–210.
Nämnden för hemslöjdsfrågor [The National Swedish Handicraft Council]. 2016. Homepage. Available at: www.nfh.se (accessed 20 June 2016).
Nylén, A.M. 1976. *Swedish Handcraft*. Lund: H. Ohlsson.
Nylén, A.M. 1977. *Swedish Handcraft*. New York: Van Nostrand Reinhold.
Palmsköld, A. 2007. *Textila tolkningar: om hängkläden, drättar, lister och takdukar*. PhD Thesis, Lund University. Stockholm: Nordiska museet.
Palmsköld, A. 2011. Hantverk som immateriellt kulturarv. In E. Löfgren (ed.) *Hantverkslaboratorium*. Mariestad: Hantverkslaboratoriet, pp. 96–105.
Palmsköld, A. 2012a. *Begreppet hemslöjd*. Stockholm: Hemslös förlag.
Palmsköld, A. 2012b. Begreppet hemslöjd idag. In A. Meister (ed.) *Lilli & Prinsen: 100 år av hemslöjd och textil konst*. Stockholm: Carlsson, pp. 130–141.
Palmsköld, A. 2016. Craft, crochet and heritage. In A. Palmsköld, J. Rosenqvist and G. Almevik (eds) *Crafting Cultural Heritage*. Gothenburg: University of Gothenburg, pp. 12–29.
Palmsköld, A., Rosenqvist, J. and Almevik G. 2016. *Crafting Cultural Heritage*. Gothenburg: University of Gothenburg.
Paludan, C. 1986. *Hækling: historie og teknik*. København: Borgen.
Parker, R. 1984/1996. *The Subversive Stitch. Embroidery and the Making of the Feminine*. Reprinted and revised edition. London: Women's Press.
Parker, R. and Pollock, G. 1981. Crafty women and the hierarchy of the arts. In R. Parker and G. Pollock (eds) *Old Mistresses: Women, Art and Ideology*. London: Routledge & Kegan Paul, pp. 50–81.
Pollock, G. 1999. *Differencing the Canon: Feminist Desire and the Writing of Art's Histories*. London: Routledge.
Rådström, A.M. 1986. *Wålstedts: mästare i ull: om en kulturgärning och ett sätt att leva*. Stockholm: LT.
Rosenberg, T. 2012. *Ilska, hopp och solidaritet: Med feministisk scenkonst in i framtiden*. Stockholm: Atlas.
Rosenqvist, J. 2007. *Könsskillnadens estetik? Om konst och konstskapande i svensk hemslöjd på 1920- och 1990-talen*. Thesis, Lund University. Stockholm: Nordiska museet.
Rosenqvist, J. 2009. Att ta saken i egna händer. In C. Åhlvik and O. von Busch (eds) *Handarbeta för en bättre värld*. Jönköping: Jönköpings läns museum, pp. 79–89.
Rosenqvist, J. 2013. Design as craft: performativity and interpellation in design history. Paper presented at 10th European Academy of Design Conference Crafting the Future,

Gothenburg. Proceedings 2013, published by EAD. Available at www.trippus.se/eventus/userfiles/67190.pdf (accessed 20 June 2016).

Rosenqvist, J. and Palmsköld, A. 2015. Att göra genus. In C. Hyltén-Cavallius, C. Zetterlund and J. Rosenqvist (eds) *Konsthantverk i Sverige del 1*. Botkyrka: Mångkulturellt centrum, pp. 33–44.

Sedgwick, E.K. 1993. Queer performativity: Henry James's *The Art of the Novel. GLQ* 1: 1–16.

Smith, L. 2006. *Uses of Heritage*. New York: Routledge.

Smith, L. 2008. Heritage, gender and identity. In P. Howard and B. Graham (eds) *The Ashgate Research Companion to Heritage and Identity*. Aldershot: Ashgate, pp. 159–178.

Stavenow-Hidemark, E. 1999a. 'Lilli Zickerman skrev många uppsatser'. In E. Stavenow-Hidemark (ed.) *Lilli Zickermans bästa: hemslöjdstankar från källan*. Umeå: Hemslöjden, pp. 10–19.

Stavenow-Hidemark, E. (ed.) 1999b. *Lilli Zickermans bästa: hemslöjdstankar från källan*, Umeå: Hemslöjden.

Svensson, B. and Waldén, L. (eds) 2005. *Den feminina textilen: makt och mönster*. Stockholm: Nordiska museets förlag.

UNESCO 2009. Implementing the Convention for the Safeguarding of Intangible Cultural Heritage. Available at http://unesdoc.unesco.org/images/0018/001891/189123e.pdf (accessed 20 June 2016).

Yafa, S. 2006. *Cotton: The Biography of a Revolutionary Fiber*. New York: Penguin.

Young, I.M. 1980/2005. Throwing like a girl: a phenomenology of feminine body comportment, motility, and spatiality. In I.M. Young (ed.) *On Female Body Experience, 'Throwing Like a Girl' and Other Essays*. New York: Oxford University Press, pp. 27–45.

Zetterlund, C., Hyltén-Cavallius, C. and Rosenqvist, J. 2015. *Konsthantverk i Sverige del 1*. Botkyrka: Mångkulturellt centrum. Available at: www.konsthantverkisverige.se (accessed 20 June 2016).

Zickerman, L. 1918. Den svenska hemslöjdens ortskaraktärer. In *Hemslöjdskommitténs betänkande*. Stockholm: Nordiska bokh, pp. 193–300.

Zickerman, L. 1937. *Sveriges folkliga textilkonst: utdrag ur Föreningens för svensk hemslöjd samlingsverk över svenska allmogetextilier. D. 1, Rölakan*. Stockholm: Svensk litteratur.

Zickerman, L. 1938/1999. 'Föreningens genombrottsår' Lilli Zickermans tal på 80-årsdagen 29 maj 1938 i Vittsjö. In E. Stavenow-Hidemark (ed.) *Lilli Zickermans bästa: hemslöjdstankar från källan*. Umeå: Hemslöjden, pp. 35–50.

Chapter 5

Naturing gender and gendering nature in museums

Smilla Ebeling

Introduction

"Who is the biggest conservationist?", asks a sign at the entrance of a local museum in Northern Germany. The question invites the visitors of the museum to lift a sailor's shirt next to the sign, which is prepared like a curtain. It is the first display the visitors meet when they enter a museum's section about the historical culture of the museum's region. Who may this "biggest conservationist" be? Who is being addressed? The sailor's shirt is blue with white stripes and part of the traditional clothing of male sailors. Also, in the German language the question is posed in the generic masculine that subsumes all sexes/gender under masculine pronouns. Issues of masculinity and androcentrism, which comes along with heteronormativity in a Western country like Germany, are immediately raised in this representation. But what appears when the shirt is lifted? The visitors face themselves in a mirror hidden behind the curtain-shirt. The mirror allows all visitors to see themselves as conservationists—regardless of their age, sexual orientation, gender identity, ancestry, or ethnic background; only the interest into nature conservation is needed for identification here. The curtain-shirt display, then, is an interactive display that allows for two conflicting readings at the same time: The generic language use and one object of the display—the shirt—present men as the norm (androcentrism), while it simultaneously diversifies with another object—the mirror (heterogeneity). Next to the sailor's shirt, a large diorama presents, among other animals, three padded seals lying next to each other on a beach. The seals in this display do not show obvious sexually dimorph features and according to biological descriptions they live in larger groups of males, females, and young ones. Yet the way in which this group of one small and two large seals is positioned invokes the idea of a middle-class nuclear family. The seal nuclear family is a museal fiction that fosters heteronormative ideals. So, how does the exhibit go on? Does it continue to represent heteronormative gender knowledge, androcentrism, and diversity? Or, does it focus and highlight only one of these aspects? This chapter asks if and in what way societal heteronormative gender discourses and gender theories of the last four decades inform museums. In particular, it focuses on displays that represent nature, as signified via animals.[1]

Background

Previous studies have shown that museums were established as places of male authority, shaped by male experts and representing ideas of male geniuses (cf. Schade and Wenk 2005). Women are often disadvantaged in their jobs, underrepresented or invisible in displays, or limited to object positions (cf. for instance Muttenthaler and Wonisch 2006; 2010; Porter 1988, 1996). According to Muttenthaler and Wonisch (2006), it is crucial to consider that museums started as projects invested with the authority of male, white and bourgeois citizens in the nineteenth century. Scholars, teachers, and academics dominated these institutions as actors with a high degree of symbolic capital (cf. Muttenthaler and Wonisch 2006: 14). Porter reflects how museums' practices, such as collecting, selecting, classification, and interpretation, contribute to women's invisibility in displays and to museal representations of women only in the contexts of housework and family. Since "housework is assumed to be familiar, unhistorical" (Porter 1988: 115) museums take this gender knowledge for granted and do not inform "about the particular features of domestic work in relation to period, locality, age, and class" (Porter 1988: 117) or about a broader spectrum of women's activities.

Moreover, museums tend to present their knowledge as given facts and veil the production process of this particular form of knowledge. Bal, for example, criticizes that museum curators remain invisible within the interaction between them and the visitors, so that the museum knowledge does not appear as something constructed by specific (male) persons, but as given (cf. Bal 1996: 3ff). Porter also evaluates the museums' epistemic position as problematic, i.e. she opposes the museums' perception of "their own work as factual, non-theoretical, working with the physical, the real" (Porter 1988: 120) and of themselves as "conveyors of 'truth' and 'reality'" (Porter 1988: 107). I perceive museums as places in which knowledge is constituted in the specific social, political, and cultural contexts of the museum actors—including curators, volunteers, displays, and visitors. Following Donna Haraway, I understand exhibits as representing situated knowledges (Haraway 1996) rather than factual knowledge—despite the museum's presentation of knowledge as *true*. In my analysis of museal representations of nature and gender, I take the processes of production into account, which combine the different situated knowledges of all museum actors. Meanings are produced by ongoing negotiations and interaction between the museum's protagonists, the displays, the museum's spaces and the visitors.

Museums have also been shown to implicitly communicate gender knowledge in their representations of nature: For example, Haraway (1989) pointed out gendered displays in the American Museum of Natural History in New York; Machin (2010) revealed heteronormative messages in the natural history galleries of the Manchester Museum in the UK, and Levin (2010) illustrated how museum displays on evolution rely on a heterosexist gender binary. By referring to biological knowledge about sex, museums tie in the authority and power of scientific knowledge with museum narrations—a seemingly positivistic knowledge that wants to tell *the truth* about nature. I follow a different notion of scientific knowledge about sex/gender, one that is developed in the area of gender and science studies. Particularly on the level of *science of gender* and *gender in science* (Keller 1995), it has been illustrated that biological-medical gender knowledge is a result of reciprocal actions between science on the one hand and societal factors as well as cultural values and norms on the other (cf. Fausto-Sterling 2000; Haraway 1990; Keller 1986; Schiebinger 1993; Schmitz and Ebeling 2006. Keller (1995) describes a third level of analysis, women in science, which is also interesting for investigating knowledge production in museums, but will play a minor role in this chapter).

Following gender and science studies, I regard knowledge about nature and about sex and gender not as a congruent description of given things, but as cultural products, which often present themselves as if nature was a given. Animals, also culturally constructed as part of nature and provided with symbolic functions, are a common and comfortable tool to negotiate social and political relations. Daston and Mitman (2005) termed those kinds of negotiations *thinking with animals*, and investigated various functions of anthropo- and zoomorphisms in the public as well as in academia. *Thinking with animals* means that humans use animals to express themselves, to think about society, and to clarify what it means to be human. According to them, *thinking with animals* is widespread and taken for granted not only in everyday life, but also in academia. Hence, *thinking with animals* is a valuable tool to analyze discursive negotiations of gender through animals (for negotiations of gender relations via animals see also Birke 1994; Ebeling 2011, 2002; Haraway 1995).

Popular as well as scientific depictions of animals suggest an animal kingdom with mainly sexually dimorphic and heterosexual animals. They stage animals in stereotypical gender roles such as pack-leading, guarding, and harem-owning males on the one hand, and nurturing and caring females on the other (for an analysis of heteronormative animal representations see Bagemihl 1999 and Roughgarden 2004). These descriptions also communicate—implicitly or explicitly—that only those gender relations found in the animal kingdom are *natural* and therefore the only legitimate gender models for human gender and sexuality. Homosexual activity, for example, counts for some people as objectionable, since they assume these practices would not exist in animals, i.e. in nature, and hence would be an *unnatural* form of sexuality. Others argue for the *natural* status of homo- und transsexualities by documenting these activities in the animal kingdom, and hence claim them as legitimate sexualities in human society as well (cf. Ebeling 2005). The biologist and sociologist Bruce Bagemihl (1999) and the biologist Joan Roughgarden (2004) provide insights into the variety of sex, gender, and sexuality in the animal kingdom). Thus, far from being innocent or neutral, animal representations in popular culture or science are means of gender politics.

My analysis focuses on the question of gender narrations in museal representations of nature. I will ask: How is nature charged with gender? And which (gender) identities are invited or discarded by the exhibits? Do the museums present descriptions beyond the heteronormative gender order? Do they narrate gender in their nature representations as a given truth and do the representations suggest dominant gender readings? Or, do the museums open their gender narrations for discussion and alternative readings and show them to be social constructions?

The four museums analyzed here are regional museums, formerly classified as *Heimatmuseums*. This type of museum is said to suffer from the reputation of being petty, bourgeois, and conservative (cf. Bollmann 2015; Korfkamp 2006; for the concept of *Heimat* in Germany see Bickle 2002). They aim to preserve a local cultural and natural heritage, to provide historical knowledge and to serve a regional identity formation. Since heteronormative gender relations and aesthetic concepts of nature served as two constitutional elements of the nineteenth-century bourgeoisie, and since regional museums follow this tradition, it is to be expected that they are bound to particular traditionalized narrations of nature and gender. However, the social and cultural contexts of museums are constantly changing and so do the regional museums. The museums in focus have all been founded or re-established since the 1980s. Also, they now exist in new contexts such as climate change, migration, globalization, and scapes—imagined worlds or communities that structure global spaces and that build transnational cultures that do not necessarily attach culture to material places, for example, ethnoscapes, technoscapes, financescapes, mediascapes, and ideoscapes (cf. Appadurai 1990, 1996 cited in Kaiser 2006).

All four museums are located in (very different) rural areas, i.e. at the North Sea, at the Baltic Sea, in a low mountain range called Thuringian Forest, and in the Swiss Alps. At first sight, they all fulfill stereotypical ideas of small local museums. They focus on the local culture of their regions and have been called *Heimatmuseum* but now reject this classification and I follow their new self-description as *regional museums*. The *Werratalmuseum Gerstungen* was founded in 1932 and is located in the German county Thüringen, next to the county Hessen. Before the German reunification, the little town Gerstungen was located on the Eastern side of the inner German border. In the course of political developments, the museum was closed and re-opened three times, the latest in 1990. The exhibits focus on the geology of the Werra valley, Werra pottery, rural handcraft, nineteenth- and twentieth-century regional bourgeoisie, and regional railway history. The *Nationalpark-Haus Museum Fedderwardersiel* is located in a small fishing village Fedderwardersiel, directly at the coast of the North Sea in Lower Saxony. It is housed in two historical buildings and exists since 1986 as a unique cooperation of a regional museum with a national park house. The local culture and the national park Wadden Sea are the central topics of display. The *Landschaftsmuseum Angeln/Unewatt* opened in 1993 in the northern part of Schleswig-Holstein in the village Unewatt. It is located close to the Baltic Sea and consists of five so-called museum islands that are spread over the whole village. A visit to the museum necessarily includes a walk around the village. All five historical museum buildings are restored and serve at the same time as both, display rooms and museal objects. The agriculture specific to the region and the rural country life are the main topics of the displays. The *Lötschental Museum* opened in 1982 in the remote Swiss village Kippel. It focuses on the regional history and the traditional customs of the valley.

Family pride: the stork

One prominent animal species on display in the *Werratalmuseum* is the stork. The stork is a large migrating bird that travels from Africa to northern Europe. For more than 300 years it has opted for the *Werratalmuseum* in the little town Gerstungen as a resting and nesting area. Since the stork is not domesticated and chooses to stay in Gerstungen on top of the museum's building on its own account, the stork stands for a commonly accepted feature of nature (Kühne 2013). Its presence makes Gerstungen and the *Werratalmuseum* a privileged place, chosen by a wild creature. This prestige grows by the fact that the stork uses the museum's building for breeding, which—from a biological perspective—is regarded as the sense of life. Since free-living or *wild* animals are said to stay only in undisturbed and untreated places and to successfully reproduce exclusively under the best possible conditions, the breeding stork represents an *intact natural world* and transfers this image to the museum. Moreover, for about 200 years the stork has symbolized *being blessed with children* (in pictures, the stork literally carries babies to their mothers) and good luck (this German fairy tale is of unknown origin; early references are Andersen 1900; Grimm and Grimm 1723). The stork has significance for the town Gerstungen: It has used a picture of a spindle-legged stork as an emblem in its coat of arms for 300 years and today features a live stream of a stork family on the town's homepage. The stork, it can be said, is central to the town's identity formation. The *Werratalmuseum* continues this symbolic function of the stork and uses a stylized strutting stork as its logo (Figure 5.1) (Einheitsgemeinde Gerstungen 2014). A picture of a stork family nesting on top of the museum's building with two adults and two hatchlings is shown on the town's homepage and connects museum and town. By using stork representations

Figure 5.1 Logo of the Werratalmuseum Gerstungen

66 Smilla Ebeling

as logos, the *Werratalmuseum* and the town Gerstungen allude to procreation, family, children, naturalness, and pride that are associated with the stork. They integrate these aspects in their identity formation. Although the sex of the individual animal represented is not identified, the stork representations evoke the structure of a middle-class nuclear family.

Aircraft performance: the red knot

Another migrating bird on display in the *Nationalpark-Haus Museum Fedderwardersiel* is the *red knot*. The *Nationalpark-Haus Museum Fedderwardersiel* represents these swarm birds in relation to their aircraft performance—a topos not mentioned in the representations of the stork in the *Werratalmuseum Gerstungen*. One display shows pictures of red knots, which migrate in huge flocks from Africa to the Arctic and rest in the Wadden Sea. A large poster explains their migration biology with pictures, sketches, and texts. They rationalize and mechanize the flock birds by giving a lot of numerical proportions, e.g. the percentage of body weight, food intake and flight distance, and by extensive use of metaphors. In two to three days of a "non-stop-flight" the birds lose a calculable weight and visit the mudflat as a "gas station." Another play with words sets the birds into the context of the train system: The headline of a poster, "Zugvögel in der Nordseeküste," translates

Figure 5.2 Poster in the Nationalpark-Haus Museum Fedderwardersiel, "Migrating birds at the coast of the North Sea"

Source: photograph by author.

to "migrating birds at the coast of the North Sea," but the German term "Zugvögel" ("migrating birds") also refers to the German concept for train ("Zug"). This headline titles an information board about the arrivals and departures and about the travel routes of migrating birds in the Wadden Sea. These information boards imitate the schedules of the German railway. Corresponding with this design, a silhouette of flying geese suggests the flight course of these birds on the visual level. A bench in front of the poster adds to or even mimics the situation in a train station (Figure 5.2). In the context of the conservative bourgeois institution of a regional museum, which entails heteronormative gender relations as a cultural heritage, this connection of aircraft performance, technology, and birds suggests associations with a particular masculinity. In accordance with the invoked masculinity, and in contrast to the museal depictions of the stork in the *Werratalmuseum*, this display does not allude to the issues of procreation or family. The latter would possibly disturb the idea of male-coded technology and physical peak performances.

Emotionalizing reproduction: seals

In the *Nationalpark-Haus Museum Fedderwardersiel* several prominent object groups with seals draw the visitor's attention, e.g. one diorama with three padded seals, various posters with pictures and texts in the museum's inner and outer area, a map with in-depth information, and diverse pictures. These seal displays explicitly assign a sexual dimorphism to the animals by focusing on females. The texts explain the seal's reproduction cycle in detail and since the texts and pictures focus on females with their offspring only and mostly ignore males, they connect procreation with femaleness. Moreover, procreation is emotionally charged by presenting seal cubs showing *babyfaceness* (*kindchenschema*), i.e. big-eyed seal pups looking into the camera. *Babyfaceness* is an ethological concept for the emotionally intensifying effect of facial features that make a creature appear cute. Emotional reactions by the visitors are also provoked by presenting single, individualized seals opposed to larger groups of animals. Repeated use of terms like "cub," "mother," and "howler" excite emotional responses, too, i.e. they emotionalize the relation of the mother animal and its young.

Another plate with texts and pictures visually highlights the pregnancy of the female seals by a drawing of females with small seals in their abdomen during the gestation period. Without any other biological explanations of the seal's life, the illustrated reproductive cycle is called the "circle of the year." This representation reduces the female's life to reproduction (Figure 5.3). Furthermore, the displays emphasize a sensitive relation of mother animal and young one, and present this relation as potentially threatened by high pollutions of the seal's milk, by maritime traffic, or by tourists.

The link between femininity, reproduction, raising pups, and emotionality is particularly emphasized in the anthropomorphized representation of seals, which belong to the mammalia—a group of all groups that humans also belong to. In addition, the displays give hardly any information about the male's contribution

Figure 5.3 Plate in the Nationalpark-Haus Museum Fedderwardersiel, "The seal—circle of the year"
Source: photograph by author.

to procreation, so that they seem not to be involved in the raising of the young animals. This resembles the structure of a bourgeois family with mostly absent fathers. As previous research has shown, without explicit alternative articulations, the viewers tend to interpret in accordance with an already dominating matrix (cf. Grahn 2011; Porter 1988, 1996). Here, the heterosexual matrix (Butler 1990) functions as a filter through which the past is easiest understood and the preferred meaning is constructed. In an already naturalized and self-evident context like this, alternative readings are unlikely to emerge. In total, the seal representations evoke heteronormative gender relations including the structure of the middle-class nuclear family.

Breeding and the order of the sexes: cattle and pigs

The *Landschaftsmuseum Angeln/Unewatt* dedicates comprehensive sections of their exhibition to regional breeds of cattle and pigs. These mammals also activate stereotypical ideas of gender as they are presented as sexually dimorphic individuals, e.g. in pictures and mock-up models of bulls, cows, boars, and sows. Moreover, they tend to be represented in the context of their function as farm animals, as livestock that produce meat and milk for commercial purposes. While the representations of reproduction in wild, undomesticated animals signal nature, the displayed reproduction of cattle and pigs marks successful breeding strategies and emphasizes the animals' position as cultural products. Whereas cows and sows are represented in close connection to milk, suckling, offspring, and good motherly features, bulls and boars appear as carriers of high-quality genetic material (for details see Ebeling 2016 and forthcoming). These entanglements of femininity and nature and of masculinity and culture are also established by representations of women and men in different relations to the animals. The cows, for example, are pictured in close connection to milkmaids, who physically bond with the cows. One historical advertisement shows a smiling milkmaid leaning against and embracing the cow (Figure 5.4). Another example is a historical picture of a woman who guides "her cow home"; the museum called this picture "atmospheric homeland." This picture seems to present the woman as the owner of the cow, but also puts woman and cow in an emotional context.

Bonding and physical contact between women and cows is also represented in another big picture showing several women milking cows on a fenced range. A male milk controller with writing utensil is standing outside the fenced area. In these pictures, women are positioned close to the cows and hence in proximity to nature, which follows a traditionalized representation of women within the dichotomous frame of masculinity and culture on the one side and femininity and

Figure 5.4 Poster in the Landschaftsmuseum Angeln (Unewatt milkmaid leaning against a cow on a historical advertisement)

Source: photograph by Karen Precht. © Landschaftsmuseum Angeln/Unewatt. Courtesy of the Landschaftsmuseum Angeln/Unewatt.

nature on the other (see, for example, Grosz 2005). Both women and cows are separated from men, who are represented in a different relation to the animals in the displays. Men are shown as breeders, owners, and prize winners for their pedigree cattle or pigs as well as during the shipping of pigs and the guiding of cows on auctions. They are barely in body contact with the cows, rather they demonstrate single bulls or cows on leashes. Also, men are represented as name-giving breeders and owners, who produce cattle and breed sows, i.e. they manufacture and manage cultural products. Here we see animals and humans with well-known sex characteristics: masculinity is combined with ownership, guidance, heritage, control, and culture; whereas femininity is connected to physicality, emotionality, caring, and offspring. Women are close to nature, men are disconnected with both nature and women. Both humans and animals are stereotypically differentiated into two sexes and positioned in a heteronormative frame.

Delicacy gone wild: the Pacific oyster

There is only one animal on display in the four museums that is not a sexually dimorphic species: the hermaphroditic Pacific oyster. An in-depth information map connected to a diorama with a blue mussel habitat in the *Nationalpark-Haus Museum Fedderwardersiel* explains its sex change, reproductive system, and breeding. After the Pacific oyster had been imported to and successfully cultivated around Sylt, an island in the North Sea known for its share of celebrity and nouveau riche tourists, the oyster left the designated oyster farmland and populated large areas of the North Sea. The information map describes the high reproduction rate of the oyster and invokes the idea of a dangerously overgrowing femininity: in its female stage, the oysters produce several times a year between 50 and 100 million eggs. Thereby, the oyster that "escaped" from its designated area around Sylt was able to "inexorably sprawl." Moreover, the information map highlights the supposedly negative impact of the oyster. Its growing population casts out native species of mussels and fish, lowers the food supply for birds, changes the element budget of the ocean water, and tourists enjoying a walk across the mudflats injure their bare feet on its sharp edges. A comment on the oysters' appearance—they are "ugly" and could never win a "beauty contest"—measures them with respect to particular feminine ideals and beauty norms. The Pacific oysters are hermaphrodites and there is no reason to refer to them in terms of females and males. Thus, the stereotypical female encodings impose the norm of sexual dimorphism onto hermaphroditic animals. Also, the text correlates the categories of sex and ethnicity in a xenophobic statement when it refers to the oysters' growing population as an "invasion [...] of foreign animals." In the case of the Pacific oyster, an animal species whose individuals are neither restricted to one sex nor to maintain one sex throughout their lives is pushed into a binary sexual order. Furthermore, cultural ideas of femininity, wilderness, ugliness, quantity, and foreignness are staged as a threat and femininity is degraded. At the same time, hermaphroditism is adjusted to the heteronormative sexual order. The oysters' capacities for adaption, reproduction, and survival are described as positive only in their use as a commercial product and as long as they live under human control. While the good breeding features and the oyster's status as a delicacy get a lot of attention in the information map, it is notable that both its ability to change sex and its high reproduction rate are only represented in a pejorative way.

The animal inside men: Tschägätta

The *Lötschentaler Museum* displays a gender-coded transgression of the human–animal dualism that belongs to a Lötschental custom called *Tschäggätta*. This transgression is also staged as a deviation from a norm. During a specific time of the year, male villagers wear masks and bodysuits that were carved by specialized (and traditionally male) woodcarvers. The custom *Tschäggätta* is displayed in a large display section with several masks and additional information about the historical development of the custom up to an internationally well-known hallmark. At the beginning of this section, an artistic picture of a mask—titled "larva"—points to a connection to an animal in the state of transition. In combination with wood, the title associates insects that produce larvae as part of their reproduction cycle: sexually mature bugs eclose from the larvae in order to dedicate the rest of their short lives to reproduction. According to a displayed video, several pictures, and texts about the *Tschäggätta*, only unmarried men of the village dress with the scary masks annually at Shrove Tuesday. They wear big wooden masks on their heads as well as bodysuits made of animal fur, teeth, blood, and horns. The participants then walk through the Lötschental villages and frighten the villagers. The exhibit mentions that the community of Lötschental valley assigns a high value to the rule that only unmarried men carry the masks and that they remain anonymous. The tradition also only allows men to carve the masks and today, only very few women adopt the carving. However, the proposed anonymity of *Tschägätta* participants leaves room behind the masks for all genders (Figure 5.5).

A local newspaper article (not exhibited in the museum) explicates *Tschägätta*'s crossing of the human–animal border. Accordingly, the mask carriers change their personality during the (strenuous) clothing procedure; the "wild guy [. . .] turns into an animal" (Schindler 2014: 34). This transmogrification includes a gender bending:

> Not woman, not men [. . .] Demon, forrest gnome, death ghost [. . .]? What the hell is the [feminine pronoun in the German language, S.E.] (yes: female, singular) Tschäggätta actually? [. . .] She is an intermediate being, neither man nor women [. . .]. Witch, goop, thief, something mystical-anima.
> (Schindler 2014: 42).

But the information about the sexual indifference of *Tschägätta* is precluded from the museum's presentation of the custom. The same applies to the women of the

Figure 5.5 Poster in the Lötschentaler Museum. Original picture of a group of *Tschäggätta* participants

Source: photograph by author. Courtesy of the Lötschentaler Museum.

village: what do they do during *Tschäggätta*? According to the museum's homepage, they come together for needlework in private homes. In the evening, they meet the mask carriers after they transformed back into human beings for dancing in the parish hall. Since the museum presents *Tschägätta* as a gendered practice (men carve the masks and men wear them, while women do needlework), the representation only shows the custom's link to masculinity in connection to the public as well as to wild and threatening animal-like creatures. However, the discussion in the local newspaper points out that *Tschägätta* presents participants with the possibility to bridge the gender binary and to comfortably evoke an in-between status. Nevertheless, the custom is restricted to a specific season and all members of the valley readjust to both, the human–animal and the man–woman binaries once the season is over. Hence, these bipolar orders remain ultimately untouched.

Heteronormativity with a view

Analyzing *thinking with animals* in museums reveals multiple processes of naturalization and of the production of gender knowledge. The representations of animals in the analyzed museums implicitly contribute to heteronormative gender narrations in different ways. They reproduce conventionalized ideas of femininity and close mother–child relations with absent fathers, or unregulated and all-devouring femininity. While females are associated with reproduction, males are connected to technology and aircraft performance. These patterns of representation match with human heteronormative ideals of the nuclear family. Yet, they do not necessarily correspond with animals described in biology. The Pacific oyster and the cultural practice *Tschägätta* offer the potential to describe non-heteronormative practices. Representations in the museums, however, do not explore this potential and relocate possibly unsettling aspects into the realm of heteronormativity: The hermaphrodite is feminized and controlled; *Tschägätta* is reduced to a male practice. All in all, only a few museal animal representations show a potential to unsettle heteronormative gender knowledge. And this potential can neither thrive in the displays nor contribute to ideas of multiple genders. Human representations communicate with these stereotypes: Women are often represented as being close to nature, which is associated with being loving and emotional. Men are usually separated from nature, yet they do show some *wild* and animal-like features. Masculinity is mostly represented in connection with technology, culture, economy, and ownership.

In sum, the individual museums reproduce heteronormativity. Yet, a comparison of the four museums points out that the representations of nature are coded by diverse and context-related gender ideas. Moreover, nature is shown to be remarkably flexible: Migrating birds reproduce the nuclear family or present long-distance flyers; femininity can be regarded as wild, unregulated, and threatening on the one hand, or it can be used to emphasize maternal qualities like caring and nurturing on the other hand. Wilderness does not necessarily go along with danger, but can, with the example of the stork, represent purity and naturalness. The topic of reproduction, again depending on the context, may stand for the well-being of animals, for intact nature, for animals as a threat, or as a cultural product like cattle. Nature, then, is represented as both female and male, and may be encoded with different, even opposing forms of femininity. This flexibility and respective ambiguity of nature provides spaces of possibilities, which have remained largely unexplored so far.

Sometimes, the representations reveal nature to being a social construction: The *Werratalmuseum*, for example, contrasts a narration of nature as a resource for human exploits and human progress with a narration of nature as part of one's homeland and worthy of protection for future generations. The nature as resource narration is dominant and developed in all exhibition rooms. Regional progress and societies are tied to the exploitation of nature's resources for their own development. In contrast to this narrative, the visitor is confronted with the narration on nature as worthy of protection in the museum's entrance hall—even before the official exhibition begins. The display in the entrance hall needs to be passed when entering the exhibition, a second time during the gallery tour, and a third time when leaving the exhibition. Thereby, the narration of nature preservation functions as a foreword, an interim remark, and an endnote. The presentation of nature as worthy of protection irritates the dominant narrative of nature as resource, and the pluralization of nature narrations shows that the museum does not present nature, but re-presents nature, i.e. the museal presentation is the product of a construction process and never nature as such.

Some displays in the *Nationalpark-Haus Museum Fedderwardersiel* reveal nature as constructed, and, literally, as man-made, and oppose the museum's otherwise positivistic epistemological understanding of nature: For example, the museum illustrates how coast dwellers construct new land for farming or herding sheep. Moreover, the museum places its representations of the local culture not only in terms of traditionalized homeland protection but also in the context of global nature conservation and thereby expands the scope of the regional museum. An interesting practice of the *Landschaftsmuseum Angeln/Unewatt* is its deconstruction of *landscape* as an unmediated, naturally given category. It repeatedly shows and highlights pictures of active landscape construction. At the same time, it displays its own processes of knowledge production and thereby highlights its museal knowledge as produced knowledge.

With regard to gender, however, alternative narratives or new display practices are hard to find. Hence, the heteronormative heritage proves to be very persistent in the exhibits of the analyzed regional museums. Although the museums may seem to be resistant to represent non-heteronormative aspects, I argue that they remain spaces, which are open for negotiations of gender. My cooperation with the staff members of the four analyzed museums revealed that they are interested in learning about museal gender investments or that they are open for a careful dialogue on gender representations. In workshops and in individual conversations, they asked for support in implementing deconstructive or reflexive elements of meta-narratives on gender. In order to meet this aim and to facilitate discussions on and changes in gender narratives represented in museums, I developed a guideline called *Museum and Gender* (Ebeling 2016) in collaboration with the museums' staff members.

The guideline: *Museum and Gender*

My complete study on gender knowledge in regional museums includes an analysis of representations of women and men (Ebeling forthcoming). These results do not only correspond with my findings on the museal presentations of nature in a heteronormative frame, but also support previous studies on museums and gender in Germany and also in Norway, Sweden, and the UK (cf. Krasny 2006; Muttenthaler and Wonisch 2006, 2010; Porter 1988; Unger 2008).[2] During the intense cooperation with the four regional museums under scrutiny, I had the opportunity to discuss representations of gender with the various actors in the museums such as curators and volunteers. The dialogue showed that most museum actors were neither aware of gender or ethnicity as socially constructed categories nor of nature as a means to tell stories about these and other social categories. But these museum actors proved to be open and interested in learning about possibilities to reflect these categories and to develop ideas to represent gender as a multidimensional category in their exhibits. On this basis and in close dialogue with the museums' staff members, I developed the guideline *Museum and Gender* (Ebeling 2016).

Museum and Gender aims at raising awareness for gender issues and provides basic information on theories of gender and on gender varieties as a lived reality in today's society. Moreover, the guideline serves to enable local museum actors to critically reflect on gender representations in their exhibits and to develop and exploit the potential of their displays as gendered interventions in the production of their local heritage. The guideline is designed for all types of museum and for all museums actors ranging from volunteering senior citizens to academic curators, who may or may not be familiar with gender and queer theories. One result of the dialogue with the museum actors is that the guideline needs to be understandable without prior knowledge about gender. It requires being written in an accessible style. Therefore, the guideline opens with a chapter that illustrates the necessity to actively explore the complex issue of gender relations in society and particularly in museums. A second chapter provides basic information about gender and queer theories in form of a "101 of gender theories." It is divided into parts for absolute beginners and parts for readers with basic knowledge. The third chapter uses examples from selected exhibits to illustrate how gender is explicitly and implicitly negotiated and addressed in German museums. A fourth chapter provides a questionnaire, which allows the museum actors to scrutinize their own displays from a gender perspective and to reflect about the gender narrations they represent. The questionnaire covers questions of explicit as well as implicit gender narrations, of individual, everyday and scientific gender knowledge, and about the individual and the structural level in museums. Since most museum actors reported a general lack of time as an impediment to serious reflections on gender in their exhibits, the guideline also provides a *Quick Start*: Readers with little time resources may scrutinize their exhibit by the means of only five gender-related questions. The *Quick Start* is aimed at provoking first thoughts and ideas about the complexity of gender in museums.

I regard the guideline as one step to reflect on gender in museums. It helps to raise awareness, to learn about the complexity of gender issues in museums, and to revise museal gender representations and gendered displays. However, the guideline refrains from giving advice on how to structure an exhibition, does not suggest any display designs, and leaves the museum actors alone with this task. The aim of the guideline is not to *streamline* the diversity in museums and to reduce the variety of museal representations. Rather, museums shall be enabled to critically reflect on their own practices, to explore gender as a complex category on the levels of organization, knowledge, exhibitions, and collections, and to engage productively with this category. Since the museum actors expressed the need for support for handling this and other guidelines, follow-up devices like workshops have to be developed. The current situation leaves a great amount of work to do. More elaborate research on gender in museums is one task (Hein 2010;

Porter 1996). Another challenge is to transfer the research results into applicable means for museums, particularly for museums with little financial and personal resources. Porter suggests directions for feminist exhibition-making and describes feminist exhibitions that do not only focus on adding women and femininity into displays and museum practices but that build "new ways which are more productive, diverse and open to re-reading" (Porter 1996: 110). Heteronormative narratives on gender preserved in various institutions of cultural heritage appear to be obdurate and persistent. However, neither museums nor gender are fixed and stable. Rather, they are changing over time and museums are particularly known to be "slow shifters" (Kos cited in Krasny 2006: 49). Altogether, I argue to closely cooperate with museums on the development of means to revise gender issues in museums on all levels.

Notes

1 The chapter presents some results of a study on gender narrations implicit in representations of nature in four regional German and Swiss museums. I conducted the study as a part of the research project *New Heimatmuseums as Institutions of Knowledge Production* at Oldenburg University (Germany), funded by the VolkswagenStiftung. I want to thank Daniela Döring, Jennifer Jones and Michaela Koch for their critical revisions of an earlier and different version of this chapter.
2 Concerning the display of gendered human individuals, my analysis illustrates in brief summary that the analyzed museums are bound to the heteronormative structure of two sexes sexually related to each other. They are far away from displaying a variety of genders and sexualities. On the level of texts, images, and figures the majority of displays are concerned with men and maleness. Women are underrepresented and restricted to marginal objects. Only one museum includes the everyday life of village women. Because the research project addressed gender as a relevant category, another museum recognized gender as an issue and chose to restructure a part of its exhibit: In addition to a *man's room*, they added a *women's room*, which represented—of all things—a kitchen. So it seems that, at the moment, representations of two sexes in stereotypical gender roles—without comments—are as good as it gets. Finally, the language used in museums is not gender sensitive, but strictly in the generic masculine. Interestingly, all five museums employ women as directors or scientific assistants and it seems that—at the level of staff—local museums are changing. This development is imbedded in a discourse of femininization of (local) museums and has to be scrutinized carefully. The complete results of my analysis will be published in *Durch die Blume. Geschlechternarrationen in musealen Naturdarstellungen. Münster: Waxmann* (in print).

Bibliography

Andersen, H.C. 1900. *Sämmtliche Märchen*. Translation Julius Reuscher, Illustration Ludwig Richter et al. 31st expanded edition. Leipzig: Abel & Müller.
Appadurai, A. 1990. Disjuncture and Difference in the Global Cultural Economy Theory. *Theory, Culture & Society* 7: 295–310.
Bagemihl, B. 1999. *Biological Exuberance, Animal Homosexuality and Natural Diversity*. New York: Profile Books.
Bal, M. 1996. *Double Exposures*. New York London: Routledge.

Bickle, P. 2002. *Heimat: A Critical Theory of the German Idea of Homeland*. Rochester, NY: Camdon House.
Birke, L. 1994. *Feminism, Animals and Biology. The Naming of the Shrew*. Buckingham, VA and Philadelphia, PA: Open University Press.
Bollmann, S. 2015. Heimat im Heimatenmuseum. Konzepte, Bilder, Vorurteile Neuer Heimatmuseen. Unpublished Dissertation. PhD Thesis. Carl von Ossietzky Universität Oldenburg.
Butler, J. 1990. *Gender Trouble: Feminism and the Subversion of Identity*. New York: Routledge.
Daston, L. and Mitman, G. (eds) 2005. *Thinking with Animals: New Perspectives on Anthropomorphism*. New York: Columbia University Press.
Deutscher Museumsbund. Homepage. Available at: www.museumsbund.de/en/home/aaa/0 (accessed August 17, 2015).
Ebeling, S. 2005. Das Sexualverhalten der Tiere als Legitimationsbasis menschlicher Sexualität. In S. Ebeling and V. Weiss (eds) *Homosexuell durch die Geburt? Biologische Theorien über Schwule und Lesben*. Göttingen: Waldschlösschen Verlag, pp. 70–80.
Ebeling, S. 2011. Tierisch menschliche Geschlechter. Mit Tieren Geschlechter bilden. In A. Qualbrink and M. Wischer (eds) *Geschlechter Bilden*. Gütersloh: Gütersloher Verlagshaus, pp. 50–61.
Ebeling, S. 2016. *Museum & Gender. Ein Leitfaden*. Münster: Waxmann.
Ebeling, S. (forthcoming). *Durch die Blume. Geschlechter- und Kollektivitätsnarrationen in musealen Naturrepräsentationen*. Münster: Waxmann.
Einheitsgemeinde Gerstungen, 2014. Available at: www.gerstungen.de/scripts/angebote/2017 (accessed September 16, 2014).
Fausto-Sterling, A. 2000. *Sexing the Body: Gender Politics and the Construction of Sexuality*. New York: Basic Books.
Grahn, W. 2011. Intersectionality and the Construction of Cultural Heritage Management. *Archaeologies: Journal of the World Archaeological Congress* 7(1): 222–250.
Grimm, J. and Grimm, W. 1723. *Deutsches Wörterbuch*. Available at: http://dwb.uni-trier.de/de/ (accessed May 22, 2016).
Grosz, E. 2005. *Time Travels: Feminism, Nature, Power*. Durham, NC: Duke University Press.
Haraway, D. 1989. *Primate Visions. Gender, Race, and Nature in the World of Modern Science*. New York: Routledge.
Haraway, D. 1990. *Simians, Cyborgs, and Women: The Reinvention of Nature*. London and New York: Routledge.
Haraway, D. 1995. Primatologie ist Politik mit anderen Mitteln. In B. Orland and E. Scheich (eds) *Das Geschlecht der Natur. Feministische Beiträge zur Geschichte und Theorie der Naturwissenschaften*. Frankfurt am Main: Suhrkamp, pp. 136–202.
Haraway, D. 1996. Situiertes Wissen. Die Wissenschaftsfrage im Feminismus und das Privileg einer partialen Perspektive'. In E. Scheich (ed.) *Vermittelte Weiblichkeit. Feministische Wissenschafts- und Gesellschaftstheorie*. Hamburg: Hamburger Edition, pp. 217–248.
Hein, H. 2010. Looking at Museums from a Feminist Perspective. In A.K. Levin (ed.) *Gender, Sexuality, and Museums*. London and New York: Routledge, pp. 53–64.
Kaiser, M. 2006. Die plurilokalen Lebensprojekte der Russlanddeutschen im Lichte neuerer Sozialwissenschaftlicher Konzepte. In S. Ipsen-Peitzmeier and M. Kaiser (eds) *Zuhause fremd: Russlanddeutsche zwischen Russland und Deutschland*. Bielefeld: Transcript, pp. 19–59.

Keller, E.F. 1986. *Liebe, Macht und Erkenntnis*. München: Carl Hanser.
Keller, E.F. 1995. Origin, History, and Politics of the Subject Called, Gender and Science—A First Person Account. In S. Jasanoff, G. Gerald, J. Peterson and T. Pinch (eds) *Handbook of Science and Technology Studies*. London, New Delhi, and Thousand Oaks, CA: Sage, pp. 80–94.
Korfkamp, J. 2006. *Die Erfindung der Heimat. Zu Geschichte, Gegenwart und politischen Implikaten einer gesellschaftlichen Konstruktion*. Berlin: Logos.
Krasny, E. 2006. Museum Macht Geschlecht. In V. Kittlausz and W. Pauleit (eds) *Kunst—Museum—Kontexte. Perspektiven der Kunst- und Kulturvermittlung*. Bielefeld: Transkript, pp. 37–54.
Kühne, O. 2013. *Landschaftstheorie und Landschaftspraxis. Eine Einführung aus sozial-konstruktivistischer Perspektive*. Wiesbaden: Springer VS.
Levin, A.K. 2010. Straight Talk: Evolution Exhibits and the Reproduction of Heterosexuality. In A.K. Levin (ed.) *Gender, Sexuality, and Museums*. London and New York: Routledge, pp. 201–212.
Lötschentaler Museum. 2015. Available at: www.loetschentalermuseum.ch/archiv-loetschental/braucharchiv/tschaeggaettae-die-loetschentaler-holzmasken (accessed February 27, 2015).
Machin, R. 2010. Gender Representation in the Natural History Galleries at the Manchester Museum. In A.K. Levin (ed.) *Gender, Sexuality, and Museums*. London and New York: Routledge, pp. 187–200.
Muttenthaler, R. and Wonisch, R. 2006. *Gesten des Zeigens: Zur Repräsentation von Gender und Race in Ausstellungen*. Bielefeld: Transcript.
Muttenthaler, R. and Wonisch, R. 2010. *Rollenbilder im Museum*. Schwalbach: Wochenschau-Verlag.
Porter, G. 1988. Putting Your House in Order: Representations of Women and Domestic Life. In R. Lumley (ed.) *The Museum Time-Machine*. London: Routledge, pp. 102–127.
Porter, G. 1996. Seeing Through Solidity: A Feminist Perspective on Museums. In S. Macdonald and G. Fyfe (eds) *Theorizing Museums. Representing Identity and Diversity in a Changing World*. Oxford: Blackwell, pp. 105–126.
Roughgarden, J. 2004. *Evolution's Rainbow. Diversity, Gender, and Sexuality in Nature and People*. Berkeley, CA: University of California Press.
Schade, S. and Wenk, S. 2005. Strategien des "Zu-Sehen-Gebens": Geschlechterpositionen in Kunst und Kunstgeschichte. In H. Bußmann and R. Hof (eds) *Genus. Geschlechterforschung—Gender Studies in den Kultur- und Sozialwissenschaften. Ein Handbuch*. Stuttgart Köln: Kröner, pp. 144–185.
Schindler, I. 2014. Brauchtum. Wilde Kerle, starke Frauen. *Schweizer LandLiebe* January/February, 30–43.
Schiebinger, L. 1993. *Nature's Body: Gender in the Making of Modern Science*. Boston, MA: Beacon Press.
Schmitz, S. and Ebeling, S. 2006. Geschlechterforschung und Naturwissenschaften. Eine notwendige Verbindung. In S. Ebeling and S. Schmitz (eds) *Geschlechterforschung und Naturwissenschaften. Einführung in ein komplexes Wechselspiel*. Wiesbaden: VS Verlag, pp. 7–32.
Unger, P. 2008. Gender im Museum. In I. Appiano-Kugler and T. Kogoj (eds) *Going Gender and Diversity*. Wien: facultas, pp. 83–89.
Verwaltungsgemeinschaft Gerstungen (ed.) (2005) *Gerstungen—Informationsbroschüre*, 4. Auflage.

Part III
Place

Chapter 6

It's a man's world. Or is it?

The 'Pilgrim Fathers', religion, patriarchy, nationalism and tourism

Anna Scott

Introduction

This chapter explores interactions of gendered representation focussing on the heritage of the 'Pilgrim Fathers' or '*Mayflower* Pilgrims', how this is associated with places in England, and how it has been mobilised for heritage tourism. In 1620, a ship called the *Mayflower* sailed from Plymouth, England, to Plymouth, Massachusetts where they established one of the earliest successful colonies in North America. Its passengers became known as the Pilgrim Fathers and came to symbolise a worthy and honest origin story for the early American state, rooted in a familial and patriarchal tradition exemplified by the 'Pilgrim Fathers' epithet. Recognised now as more than 'Fathers', accompanied as these men were by women, children, servants, and the ship's crew, a tendency towards the representation of a male-centric history remains in England. The story is rising to prominence once again as the 2020 quarter-centenary approaches, which is why it is important to analyse how and why the narrative has been represented.

Tourism agencies, local authorities, and heritage groups have been involved in negotiating their positions in the generation and development of a rejuvenated Pilgrims' heritage product in Britain. Much of this is being organised around the '*Mayflower 400*' heritage campaign led by Plymouth City Council, and partnered by organisations with a link to the story in the East Midlands, Yorkshire, London and the south coast in England, and Leiden in the Netherlands. The documentary sources that underpin the story are heavily gendered as masculinities, in terms of their male authorship, as diaries (principally colony governor William Bradford's seventeenth-century *Of Plimoth Plantation* 1898; see Anderson 2003), transatlantic correspondence (including Bradford's letters; Bowman 1906; Young 1841), and political narratives of the early colony (including Edward Winslow's *Good Newes from New England* 1624; Wisecup 2014). This is unsurprising in the wider context of English early modern period or American colonial period sources, but it has become an emotive, at times controversial and mythologised narrative (Deetz and Deetz 2000a, 2000b), with a complicated historiography attracting conscious and unconscious gendered interpretations linked to agendas of nationalism, faith, politics, and power. Ongoing use of the term 'Pilgrim Fathers' perpetuates male bias by failing to reflect the key role women played in the original history, and its uncritical use cannot continue without comment in light of contemporary debates within critical heritage studies (see Waterton and Watson 2015).

I will chart the use of the term 'Pilgrim Fathers' in representations of Pilgrims' history and the *Mayflower* voyage in heritage contexts in England. Exhibition texts, interpretation panels and commemorative material related to Pilgrims' heritage have been examined using a discourse analytical perspective. The approaches adopted by Smith (2006), using critical discourse analysis (CDA) and Foucauldian perspective, and Dicks (2000), exploring heritage and rhetoric, informed analysis used here. The work of Foucault has been key to understanding discourse, or, in other words, rules that govern our cultural world (history, economics, social practices, language, ancestral mythologies, and stories from childhood), which we are not conscious of; something that people can find difficult to recognise (Foucault 1972/2002: 232). Dicks (2000) used the concept of intertextuality, focusing on the presence within texts of other constituted texts and wider ideological discourse not formally in texts, after Fairclough's approach to CDA (1993, 2010) based on intertextuality and interdiscursivity, or how discourse conventions are configured that constitute a text. Representational analysis used here reveals affective uses of Pilgrims' discourse, which reinforces a particular set of gendered tropes. Pilgrims' heritage has been overlooked in trends for engendering representations of the past. Gender here is interpreted as socially and culturally constructed and is often intertwined in this narrative with constructions and representations of motherhood. Recognising the need to integrate critical gender perspectives into narratives of the past is nothing new (see e.g. Moore and Scott 1997; Reading 2015), but it continues to be an unfinished project.

Background

The principal primary source for Pilgrims' heritage is a journal written by William Bradford, a Separatist from South Yorkshire in England who became the governor of Plymouth colony in America. Bradford recorded his narrative retrospectively, from 1630 onwards, 10 years after arriving in America (Anderson 2003). His journal was published much later (Bradford 1898), having been lost for some years (see Bradford 1981; *In the Matter of the Log of the Mayflower* 1897). The basic story, represented at heritage sites in England and relying heavily on Bradford's narrative, can be summarised as follows.

A group living in the rural East Midlands in England, unhappy with the established Church, formed their own religious congregation in and around Scrooby, illegally separating (becoming 'Separatists') from the Church. Under pressure from Church authorities and their own communities, conviction in their beliefs led them to seek exile in Holland. After failing to escape from Boston, they escaped further north, arriving in Amsterdam in 1608. Moving later to Leiden, they lived in straitened circumstances, until some decided to emigrate as 'planters' to Virginia. After tortuous negotiations, they bought a ship called the *Speedwell*. In 1620, they set sail for

Southampton, England, to rendezvous with a second ship, the *Mayflower*. The ships set sail, but the *Speedwell* began to leak, returning to Dartmouth for repairs. Setting sail again, the *Speedwell* was still taking on water, so they returned to Plymouth where it was abandoned. Those dedicated to their cause boarded the *Mayflower* and departed. After a lengthy voyage, they arrived in November, not in Virginia as intended but on the shores of Cape Cod. A search party scouted the coast for a settlement site, eventually choosing a former Native American village, mapped previously and incidentally called Plymouth. After six weeks, the ship's passengers came ashore, facing sickness and starvation throughout that first New England winter; half of them died, despite so successfully surviving the voyage.

Popular American versions of the story often focus on the *Mayflower's* voyage and the development of Plymouth colony with few details of the European origins. Of primary significance for the United States' narrative is the signing of a document by the men on the ship now known as the *Mayflower* Compact (see Bradford 1898: 109–110). The need for a legal agreement arose because of the unplanned arrival in Massachusetts rather than Virginia (granted in their original agreement [patent]) and discord among the emigrants, particularly between Separatists and non-Separatists. Its signatories agreed to

> covenant & combine our selves togeather into a civill body politick, for our better ordering & preservation [. . .] to enacte, constitute, and frame such just & equall lawes, ordinances, acts, constitutions, & offices [. . .] for ye generall good of ye Colonie, unto which we promise all due submission and obedience.
>
> (Bradford 1898: 110)

Other key features of the narrative include colonists' negotiations and settlements with local indigenous people over land and access to resources, the 'first' Thanksgiving, and the 1620–1627 'communal' system and its perceived failure (as land was distributed to individual families after 1627 rather than worked communally).

The complete narrative as it is represented today, whether in whole or in part, from origins to colony foundation and development, is characterised by a series of themes or tropes that are heavily symbolic and emblematic of wider tropes of American identity and nationhood. These include the quest for religious freedom, tolerance, escape from persecution and democratic principles of governance. British and Anglo-American representations of the story evoke the 'special relationship' (including *Mayflower 400*), which also underlines many of these key tropes. The narrative is strongly gendered in favour of various portrayals of masculinity, frequently mediated by religious characterisation and the nature of faith, as either 'Saint', a Separatist from the original Scrooby or Leiden congregation, or 'Stranger', other passengers on the *Mayflower* not adhering to the strictures of the Separatists' congregational, covenant theology (see Willison 1983; Turley 1998: 7; cf. Bangs 2009: 277).

'Pilgrim Fathers' deconstructed

The term 'Pilgrim Fathers' continues to be commonly used in England in representations of the Pilgrims' history, although is not universally applied. Anecdotal evidence collected in the course of the author's research, through discussions and correspondence with American visitors to Britain and *Mayflower* descendants, suggests it is not widely used in modern America, where the terms 'Pilgrims' or 'Forefathers' (i.e. to the nation's 'Founding Fathers') tend to be more common. 'Pilgrim Fathers' is the traditional term that emerged in the nineteenth century as the history of this group of Separatist colonists linked to a transatlantic voyage of a single ship, the *Mayflower*, grew in prominence. It is a term more representative of the period approximately 200 years after the *Mayflower* passengers arrived in America than it is of any other period, making it a retrospective label falling short of modern sensibilities in two main respects. First, 'Pilgrim' refers implicitly to the religious Separatists on the *Mayflower*, who made up less than half of the total number of passengers. Second, 'Fathers' is indicative only of male, patriarchal roles, making no direct reference to other participants in the venture. These included women, servants and children, who are implicated (subordinately) by this epithet, indicative as 'Fathers' can be of the senior rank (in age, experience and wisdom) within a wider social, family unit.

The evocation of wisdom and seniority implies older men, even men of great age, which serves the purpose of imagining forefathers for the nation (for an extensive analysis of how the Pilgrims have been represented in art and culture in relation to this see Abrams 1999). The implication of great age distorts the reality of the group's age profile when they left England and their age when they made the voyage. William Bradford was 18, joining the 'elder' Brewster, who was in his early forties when they escaped England. Bradford was 30 years old when they left Holland, leaving behind a 3-year-old son, who his wife Dorothy would never see again (see Anderson 1995: 208; Stratton 1986: 251, 324). These men, and the women accompanying them some of whom were pregnant, were relatively young. This age dimension has been given little obvious attention in touristic discourses, particularly those emanating from the East Midlands. This is potentially evidence of a discourse that has emerged to cater largely for American audiences, or at least has drawn heavily on American representations of the narrative in art, where men are apparently much older. Pilgrim men would have of course been older during the American part of the story, many having grown old and died there – but their youth in England has never been priority for heritage interpretations; Figure 6.1, for example, shows how the story is portrayed in Bassetlaw Museum in Nottinghamshire, close to the original homes of the leading Separatist Pilgrims.

The term emerged in the context of religious and political discourse in the late eighteenth century, corresponding with sermonising agendas at that time, and was used throughout the nineteenth century (see Hunter 1849: 1–2; Matthews 1915: 351, 358). Matthews reflected on the 'momentous' period in the United States from 1769 to 1820, featuring the American Revolution, adoption of the Federal

Figure 6.1 Pilgrim Father Bassetlaw Museum
Source: photograph by author.

Constitution, problems with France, party shifts in government, the purchase of Louisiana, partial abolition of slavery, and the 1812 war with England. It was:

> a period when people took their politics very seriously, [. . .] that period saw the introduction of an American episcopate, the spread of Unitarianism, and many departures from the customs and manners of 'the fathers'. The feelings engendered by these great political, religious, and social changes are reflected in the discourses delivered on Forefathers' Day and even more in the newspaper accounts of the celebrations.
>
> (Matthews 1915: 296)

Writing in 1915, Albert Matthews (1915: 351) traced these developments in relation to the tradition of Forefathers' Day, identifying the appearance of 'Pilgrim' to 1798, with 'Pilgrim Fathers' coming into use a year later. Forefathers' Day was first celebrated in Plymouth, Massachusetts in 1769 and developed as a tradition to honour those who first established Plymouth colony – and who soon became commonly known as the Pilgrim Fathers (see Matthews 1915). Around this time, nuances in Pilgrim identity were emerging, as contrasts were made between Protestant 'Puritans' (seeking to purify the established Church from within) and 'Separatist' Pilgrims (separating from the established Church and forming their own congregations according to religious conscience). Matthews' review of the historical terminology dwelt on these religious aspects while leaving aside consideration of the nature and use of the 'Fathers' element.

The movement away from common usage, particularly in the United States, has arguably been reflected by the growing genealogical movement of Americans descended from *Mayflower* passengers. One of the principal societies for descendants is, after all, the General Society of *Mayflower* Descendants (GSMD), rather than a society of Pilgrim Fathers' descendants. The GSMD was founded in 1897, eschewing the term 'Pilgrim Father' over a century ago, and now consistently refers to the 'Pilgrims'. Specifically:

> Anyone who arrived in Plymouth as a passenger on the Mayflower is considered a Pilgrim, with no distinction being made on the basis of their original purposes for making the voyage. Proven lineage from a passenger, approved by a Historian General, qualifies one to be a member of the General Society of Mayflower Descendants.
>
> (GSMD 2014)

There is a disjuncture between the terms used in Britain and the United States; Britain has retained 'Pilgrim Fathers', while there was apparently a movement away from this narrow male-dominated characterisation in the United States over a century ago, as a 'Pilgrim Mothers' discourse emerged. This was memorialised around the time of the *Mayflower* tercentenary. In many ways, the point is not how problematic the 'Pilgrim Fathers' term is, but why people continue to want to use it, or not. Persistence in usage might be attributed to habit or traditional use, to 'brand' recognition in a marketing sense (an unwillingness to alter the 'brand'), or to a lack of critical awareness, and connected to this, apathy and disinterest related to disconnectedness from the story and lack of knowledge about it.

The Pilgrim element of the term, used in both spoken and written discourse, seems unlikely to change. It has multiple meanings – with religious connotations, representing the journey as an embodied spiritual endeavour, and as a broader term to describe travellers on the *Mayflower*, Separatist or not. The more specific use of '*Mayflower* Pilgrim' serves to distinguish the term in relation to other European contexts of pilgrimage, such as those travelling the Camino de Santiago in Spain, as well as sidelining the masculine connotations of 'Fathers'. It remains reflective of religious imaginings of the story as it became part of the popular consciousness during the nineteenth century, through its advocacy by religious scholars and the Separatists' own writings and biblical references. The 'Pilgrims' themselves used the term in their own discourse, in particular: 'But now we are all in all places strangers and pilgrims, travellers and sojourners, most properly having no dwelling but in this earthen tabernacle', attributed to Robert Cushman

(Heath 1963: 89), who was instrumental in planning the voyage, and William Bradford's history, which reflects on the spiritual journey as they embarked from Holland for America, as a metanarrative to their physical voyage:

> So they left that goodly and pleasant city [Leiden] which had been their resting place near twelve years; but they knew they were pilgrims, [Hebrews xi. 13–16 (Bradford's note)] and looked not much on those things, but lift up their eyes to the heavens, their dearest country, and quieted their spirits.
> (Bradford 1981: 50)

The 'Pilgrim' element is so embedded in what Parini has termed 'the American mythos', that in addition to representing national memory, a 'most potent' story in 'our treasure-house of tales' (Parini 2012: 53), as secular memory it represents the embedded and integrated religious memory that, while nominally separate, are fundamentally and inextricably intertwined in American social, political and economic life. It was partly through the advocacy of the story by politicians from John Quincy Adams onwards that this has been achieved (see Bangs 2009: vii).

Pilgrims' heritage tourism in England

Different terms are used to describe the Pilgrims in local histories and tourism literature. The core congregation of religious Separatists originated from the East Midlands of England; here, some local histories refer to *Mayflower* Pilgrims (Dolby 1991; Allan 2011) in line with current American usage, while heritage and tourism literature (including trail brochures) refer to the 'Pilgrim Fathers' (e.g. Bassetlaw District Council's *The Pilgrim Fathers' Story* n.d.; Board 2006; Cook 2013; Haden *et al.* 2007). The Pilgrims' heritage advocacy organisation for this region adopted the term in its own title, as the *Pilgrim Fathers UK Origins Association*, which formed prior to the 400th anniversary of the Separatists flight from Nottinghamshire, in 2007. Of the two main exhibitions in the area making reference to the history, both used the term as a title combined with texts and images, with Bassetlaw Museum's display 'The Pilgrim Fathers: Religious Rebels?' and the 'Gainsborough Old Hall Pilgrim Fathers Exhibition'. This preference for 'Pilgrim Fathers' is replicated in other regions claiming a connection with the story, both at the local level, in Boston and Plymouth for example (e.g. Almond and Lambourne 2011; Barber 1997; Cammack and Cammack n.d.; Cammack *et al.* 2002), and from a national perspective, through trails and landmark guides for example (e.g. Cheetham 2001; Dowsing n.d.).

Contrast can be made between local histories and more commodified, marketed, heritage tourism interpretive materials, which is where 'Pilgrim Fathers' is often used – a recognised brand for the narrative in many of its popular forms. In the East Midlands, it has been widely used in local media and in tourism initiatives. Pilgrims' heritage became more prominent in one particular area of the East Midlands due to the efforts of a clergyman, Rev. Edmund Jessup, whose church

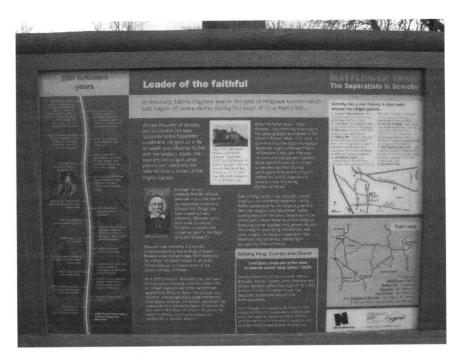

Figure 6.2 Scrooby Manor trail board
Source: photograph by author.

was attended by the Separatists before they left the established Church. Jessup's study of the subject replicated earlier histories' uses of the term Pilgrim Fathers, although he took a reflective view of the role of women in the story, complementing his *Mayflower Story* pamphlet (1977) with one on the *Pilgrim Mothers* (1976). This exception to the general pattern of usage of the term had little long-term impact in influencing how the story of the Pilgrims was presented in this region in subsequent decades. Local interpretation panels as part of the *Mayflower* Trail, and replaced in 2008, did, however, make a notable contrast to newer replacement boards. One panel in the village of Scrooby near the Manor, the home of the Pilgrims' 'elder' William Brewster, and since replaced, did not make use of the term Pilgrim Fathers, unlike the panels used in a rejuvenated trail launched to coincide with the 400th anniversary of the date the Separatists escaped England in 2008 (see Figure 6.2).

There was an interpretive shift in Nottinghamshire's representation of the story evident in these boards, which appears to be associated with stronger packaging of the 'product' – where the 'Pilgrim Fathers' are embraced as the brand in the most recent board but not referred to as such in the earlier board. The pre-2008 board does not name the Pilgrims explicitly and takes its lead from the historic building associated with Brewster, a leading Pilgrim/Separatist; featured images take a landscape/buildings perspective. The replacement board takes a very different narrative tone, focusing more on Brewster himself. This board (and others on the trail) feature images that reinforce masculine bias and represent old men. Figure 6.2 shows the image used on the board to illustrate Brewster – originally published in Burbank's story of the Pilgrims from 1904 (see Addison 1911) – despite there being no known illustration of him during his lifetime and being in his early forties when he left Nottinghamshire.

A more dramatic and affective tone characterises the replacement board. The text refers to the 'religious turmoil' of the period, and Brewster is described as a 'loyal' Separatist, implicative of unquestioned dedication, who 'gave up a life of wealth and influence to flee with the religious rebels'; his choices are presented in a dramatic way, emphasising rebellion. As 'rebels', the narrative creates a sense of law-breaking – making Brewster as much of an outlaw as Nottinghamshire's other famous mythologised son, Robin Hood. 'His path', as implied singular and one-way trajectory, 'led him to gaol, exile, poverty', a forced choice of loss of status, which is finally mediated by a rise in status to 'leader of the Pilgrim Fathers', or holder of power and influence and leader of men, and as a consequence, of all. The more sedate description of the replaced board referred to 'meetings of the Scrooby Separatist congregation' at the Manor House, but no more complicated reference to the religious situation or the term Pilgrim Fathers.

The tendency towards affective representations of the narrative combine in this case with use of artistic images from the nineteenth and early twentieth century, which often create romanticised and sentimentalised depictions of the story. The metanarrative here – the intertextuality – became more personal and dramatically evocative, coinciding as it did with a significant anniversary. Agnew (2007) observed the affective historical turn in relation to re-enactment, where historical representation is characterised by conjectural interpretations and emphasis on affect and individual experience, which can, to some degree, be seen in this example. The idea of 'Pilgrim Fathers' aligns closely with the American epithet of 'Forefathers', and perhaps this contributed to its re-introduction.

Attempts at commodifying the story by using 'Pilgrim Fathers' establishes consistency in the 'product'/'brand' – making it recognisable and differentiating it from other 'Pilgrim' narratives. On the other hand, its reuse can be seen as uncritical, disengaged, or ambivalent; there is no recognised need to 'update' the term or to consider any potential in broadening the frame of reference. Such an approach has been possible in the context of a lack of local knowledge (or interest) in the story in Nottinghamshire for example (Scott 2012; Thinking Place 2014). That the term is embedded locally contrasts with other representations in Plymouth, Devon, for example, at the Plymouth *Mayflower* Tourist Information Centre exhibition (visited in 2009; recently refurbished) sited adjacent to the *Mayflower* Steps. Plymouth's *Mayflower 400* project for 2020 is engaging with new approaches to the history that take a more critical view, mainly involving developing understanding of the indigenous narratives of encounter, co-operation and resistance in relation to the pre-eminent colonial narrative. The equally significant indigenous voice has been much less thoroughly integrated into public discourse in the UK, beyond tales of 'Squanto the interpreter', a weakly interrogated narrative motif. Despite this, the role of Native Americans often remains more clearly articulated than the role of women in these exhibited interpretations and in heritage tourism literature. Historical details of specific women's lives are little known, beyond occasional details of their births, marriages and deaths, their inheritance as widows or their roles as witnesses to others' marriages in formal records (as in Leiden; see Bangs 2009); their touristic representation usually only reflects their status as 'wife of . . . ', 'mother of . . . ', and 'widow of . . . '.

'Pilgrim Mothers' deconstructed

Historically, the term 'Fathers' is reflective of the contemporaneous attitude to women in the early modern/colonial period, as much as it is of the later period when the term came into currency. Crawford noted that:

> a good wife [. . .] was loving, obedient, subordinate and passive. Theologically, Calvin's concept of an active God, seeking to save his elect, emphasized the human being as a receiver of grace, and such a passive position again was associated with femaleness.
>
> (Crawford 1993: 13)

Religion was the fundamental core of people's social lives during the early modern period, and the Reformation and post-Reformation Christian ideology of the time reinforced the view of women's inferiority to men; and yet, women were able to accept this position of inferiority and sometimes transcend this in subtle ways (Crawford 1993). Rather than existing with passive and oppressed lives, they were 'making their history within a social structure which was not of their making'; women were thought to be inferior to men, but by accepting this inferiority they were able to transcend it, becoming active agents in their own lives (Crawford 1993: 1). The role of gender in the popular myth of the Separatists is, as already noted, easily overlooked. As Crawford notes, gender 'is specific to a society and is subject to historical change' (1993: 2), but the exclusion of the female experience from modern narratives serves to normalise and universalise the human experience of groups like the Separatists by concealing what Crawford terms 'the sexual politics of religion' (1993: 3) and what contemporary audiences would not recognise in relation to modern social standards. This idea of female experience includes perception, and relates to the female body and physiology (see Crawford 1981, 1990, 1993: 7).

The opportunity to promote or provoke reflection on the role of women in the Pilgrims' story is not commonly expressed in English contexts. This might be a largely evidence-based outcome, whereby narrators of the story rely on sources that overlook, ignore, or assume women's contributions, and where primary documentary evidence is sourced from leading male figures. Alternatively, it is possible that the role of women and their status as mothers is incorporated into narratives through uncritical assumptions or a certain lack of interest in female-gendered interpretations of the story. Where the 'Pilgrim Mothers' have been recognised (e.g. Jessup 1976), the universalising discourse of 'motherhood' as an unchanging concept characterised by nurturing within the private, domestic sphere of the home readily emerges. This conservative representation of motherhood, and a concomitant lack of exploration of gender, results in what Crawford might recognise as the 'perpetuation and legitimation of certain kinds of gender hierarchies' (1993: 3). An interesting example that springs from this concerns a particular period in the history of the Daughters of the American Revolution (see below).

The nature of masculinities, power, patriarchy and gendered roles in representations of the English origins element of the Pilgrims' narrative is implicit. Woodbridge, discussing the infancy of modern feminism during the Renaissance, pertinently asked 'Could the age that gave us the printing press, Protestantism, and gunpowder prove remiss where women are concerned?' (1984: 2). Bangs' (2009: 355–407) exploration of family life and the Pilgrims signposted sources that could contribute to more considered gendered interpretations and representations of the narrative that go beyond either the invisibility of women, or their two-dimensional presence as support to their husbands and families. He suggests Capp's exploration of patriarchal assumptions and disparities between these and actual social conditions (Capp 2003; see also Walzer 1973); Norton's exploration of gendered power is also significant (1996). Additionally, Prior (1985) and Cressy (1997) offer 'the most thorough and convincing study of English attitudes and customs that form the background from which the Pilgrims emerged' (Bangs 2009: 361), including their religious convictions, social and personal lives (see also Gowing 2012 on gender relations). The incorporation of research exploring these themes could serve to counter-balance the story, from one that projects the roles of leading men towards a narrative that incorporates women and other men, or actually moves away from binary representations of masculine power (religious and political) and feminised subordination, associated with domesticity and nurturing. This could potentially attract wider interest by effectively destabilising a narrative so embedded with patriarchal stereotypes, although it risks reinforcing an opposing matriarchal representation; the Pilgrim Mothers archetype emerging in response. Understanding how gender is socially and culturally constructed can help inform more nuanced representations of gender within Pilgrims' heritage. It is tempting to focus on domestic work and child-bearing roles of women – the personal, bodily, visceral and affective aspects of social life – while men can appear as detached, active, thoughtful and reasoned. Details from the history reveal the inaccuracy of such codifications, but these are lost where the narrative is given a solidly biased title and continues to be represented through art that was popular over a century ago.

Incorporating gender history into the Pilgrims' narrative requires more work, particularly in terms of wider dissemination and heritage tourism texts.

The religious Separatists on the *Mayflower* have been described as a 'small, renegade cult' (Abrams 1999: 24), in which case, applying more general studies of gender from the early modern/colonial period may be problematic. Local history researchers in the East Midlands perhaps offer some more specific insights into the gendered lives of the original Separatist congregation, as they begin to address the 'missing' women from the history. Rose Hickman, a supporter of the Separatists from Gainsborough, has been characterised in this way (Allan 2009), claimed as a supporter of the Separatist cause, as have the Wray sisters (Gray 2014), in the context of an emerging exploration of the Christian heritage of the story in this region. Genealogical (i.e. familial/descendants' history) and localised research here (micro-histories), as well as that conducted by the many genealogical societies in America (e.g. Stratton 1986), offer insights into individual's lives, and overlooked roles of other local people in the story, including women. The most well-known primary source narratives (including Bradford's diary, a journal known as *Mourt's Relation* (Heath 1963), and Winslow's *Good Newes*) present conscious re-telling/re-workings of an epic narrative. Bradford referred to himself in the third person according to his leading role in the community, as 'the Governor'. Winslow's narrative described friendly relations with the native population, while masking incidents of brutal violence against them as well as mutual mistrust; he sought to promote colonial travel with his ongoing diplomatic role in negotiations with supporters in England (Wisecup 2014). A large amount of propaganda was involved in the planning for and establishment of the early colony, following in the tradition of earlier sources. The Christian narrative and sermonising nature of the early sources set the tone for the Pilgrims' narrative in later periods.

Where some groups of women acquired more power in the post-World War I period they were able to change the Pilgrims' narrative (Wendt 2012), though not always in ways that modern feminists might expect, or agree with. This was significantly evident in the contradictions involved in the expressions of motherhood by the Daughters of the Revolution (DAR, an American genealogical society founded in 1890), during the early twentieth century (Wendt 2012). Evidence of DAR's commemorative activities demonstrated the 'paradoxical efforts of conservative white middle-class women's associations to emphasize female agency and patriotism while simultaneously opposing the various challenges to traditional notions of gender that characterized the first half of the twentieth century' (Wendt 2012: 32).

For the DAR, 'challenges such as feminism and the "New Woman" threatened the stability of both the family and the nation' (Wendt 2012: 32). Women, for the DAR, were important but ultimately 'merely auxiliary help-mates', while men were the 'real agents of historical change'; their 'cultural power' was impressive, but maintained a particular set of traditional family values in the United States (Wendt 2012: 33). Their views on the Pilgrims a century ago anticipated the pressures exerted by some in the emancipation of women, rejecting them wholeheartedly for the perpetuation of a conception of closely interconnected ideals of the family and the nation:

The Daughters believed that mothers had contributed to the process of American nation-building from the very first moment that European women set foot on the continent. Speaking at the Pilgrim Tercentenary of 1920 in Provincetown, Massachusetts, DAR President General Anne Rogers Minor exhorted her audience to cherish the character traits that the first European women had displayed in 1620. 'Like the Pilgrim Mothers,' she said, 'we must be filled with the same spirit of service to the common cause, the same faith, courage and unselfish devotion that led them into a strange world and enabled them to build the homes that they have transmitted to us to preserve.'
(Wendt 2012: 41, citing a quote from A.D. Campbell on The Pilgrim Tercentenary at Provincetown, Mass., 1620–1920, DAR Magazine, December 1920: 705)

Their recognition of the overshadowing of the women of the *Mayflower* by their male counterparts was at odds with their views of the women's roles in terms of modern sexual politics.

Wendt has associated the DAR with Carrigan, Connell and Lee's theory of 'hegemonic masculinity', described as 'how particular groups of men inhabit positions of power and wealth, and how they legitimate and reproduce the social relationships that generate their dominance' (Carrigan *et al.* 1985: 592). So too the Pilgrim story has come to represent patriarchy and power in the hands of men, through its retelling (sometimes by women), particularly through the explicit use of the term 'Pilgrim Fathers' and the heavily emphasised role of the leading men. These men, as signatories to the *Mayflower* Compact and authors of letters and journals, emerge unsurprisingly as the sole representatives of a diverse group by virtue of their contributions to the documentary record. A more inclusive and representative modern interpretation of the story would not fail to recognise and explore this diversity in a more systematic way, which looks beyond current representations of Pilgrim women as followers, protectors of their children (upon their separation from *their* men), believers and subordinates.

Even without complicated critical analyses of gendered roles and patriarchal power in the Pilgrims' history, there is enough evidence of women's lives to contribute more to touristic representations of the story and counterbalance embedded masculinities. While these masculinities are framed through different discourses of religion (represented by characterisations of 'Elder Brewster'), politics ('Governor Bradford'), military power ('Captain Standish') or economics (merchant, trader, non-Separatist, like Stephen Hopkins), female experience is present, framed through the lens of motherhood. Women were separated from men upon their escape from England, along with their children (Bradford 1981: 13–15), and somehow made their way to Amsterdam. Three women were pregnant on the *Mayflower*, two babies were born and one stillborn (Philbrick 2007). Bradford's own wife Dorothy fell to her death from the ship as it lay at anchor in Cape Cod, a narrative not without its own controversy having been subject to an imagined reworking as a suicide (summarised by Philbrick 2007: 377–378).

The first governor died in the first year, and his wife Catherine, 'being a weak woman, died within five or six weeks after him' (Bradford 1981: 95). These women and their children, on that same voyage as the men, are important valid sources of a rich variety of their own significant experiences shaped by gendered and biological subjectivities.

The lens of motherhood is clearly evident in later representations of Pilgrim women in art, particularly in the nineteenth century and around the 1920 tercentenary, and reflects the significant shifts in gender identity involved in appropriating a particular culturally gendered experience; art often represents tropes of motherhood evocative of the period when it was created. These images tend to depict women as mothers, nurturers and child-bearers, frequently seated, as supporting and subordinate characters (see Abrams 1999: 147, 161, 181, 183–184, 186, 189), feminised, romanticised, delicate and historically anachronistic (Seelye 1998: 361–395). For example, in Robert Weir's (1803–1889) famous painting, *Embarkation of the Pilgrims* (1843), today displayed in the US Capitol building, the most prominent and distinctively dressed woman is Edward Winslow's wife. Winslow played a leading role in the colony's development and created significant legacies (see Wisecup 2014). These images continue to be used in contemporary representations to illustrate the narrative, but without further critical insight or specific interrogation of the gendered roles that this art depicts. Weir's work was reproduced in Plymouth *Mayflower*'s Pilgrim Fathers exhibition until 2015 (part of the Tourist Information Centre in Plymouth, England).

There are contrasts to depictions of male leadership and female subordination, with for example, Jennie Brownscombe's 1920 depiction of *The Landing of the Pilgrim Fathers*, although this representation has not been observed at sites associated with the history in Britain. Brownscombe places a woman at the centre of a pyramidal arrangement, and, as Seelye observes, while the prayerful posture and composition continues in the tradition of the previous century, the gendered aspect has been reversed. A woman dominates the landing scene, as they had also come to be central to the idea of the 'First Thanksgiving' as symbols of home for this 'intensely domestic occasion'; 'it reminds us that by the tercentenary year women in America were gathering political strength' (Seelye 1998: 17–18, 362). Whether politically significant or romantically represented (as with Henry Wadsworth Longfellow's 1858 poem 'The Courtship of Miles Standish', a love story between John Alden and Priscilla Mullins; Seelye 1998: 378), this is a story with rich possibilities for exploring gendered interpretation with parallel, scalable stories: the intimate history of English colonists in the early seventeenth century, and the transatlantic history of England and America over the past four centuries.

Conclusion: en-gendering the Pilgrims

Is it possible to integrate gender more effectively and holistically into popular representations of Pilgrims' histories in heritage tourism contexts? Various representations of masculinities are commonly reproduced, like Bradford's self-styled leader,

Winslow's diplomat, Brewster's religious elder, Standish's captain and Hopkins' planter. These are strong, affective characterisations that represent leading men, and their motivations and actions. Other men, servants or the ship's crew can be less well articulated, and, like the women, fade into the background, particularly those who died within the first year at Plymouth. It would be inaccurate to say women were never there in past representations of the story. Women and their roles feature heavily in artistic depictions of the story, often in line with social and cultural assumptions and norms reflective of the period when these images were produced and that period's own retrospectives on the Pilgrims' history; their reuse as historical illustrations of the story often fails to contextualise this and creates/perpetuates gendered stereotypes.

There is literature that gives insight into gendered lives in this period, and into gendered interpretations of femininities and masculinities throughout the history's subsequent reuse (e.g. Norton 1996; Seelye 1998). Existing representations have frequently been framed around the family unit and its strength in religious terms, as a model for social life (based on patriarchy), a sound basis for the founding of the future nation and as a conservative tourism narrative of triumphalism and exceptionalism, appropriated both by Britain and the United States and framed as emblematic of the rhetoric of the Anglo-American special relationship. Countering these tropes is only really possible through what Launius has described as meaning, nuance and communication (2013): the past needs to be effectively communicated, its nuances embraced and its meanings related to the present, which includes, of course, visible representations of the complexities, subjectivities and experiences of gendered lives. Further research is required to explore and then integrate alternative gendered interpretations into Pilgrims' heritage, for different viewpoints to emerge; these have been overlooked in English contexts despite trends for gendered critiques of represented heritage (Reading 2015) and 2020 offers the ideal opportunity for this. There is an ongoing need to develop clearer dialogues between critical gendered histories and popularly represented heritage (at least in this case), not to impose the authority of the expert (see Smith 2006; cf. Holtorf's 'public intellectual' 2013) but to recognise the need for considered, equitable and nuanced interpretation.

Acknowledgements

I am grateful to Dr Kate Hill, Professor Heather Hughes and Professor Krista Cowman for their support and helpful comments in relation to this research.

Bibliography

Abrams, A.U. 1999. *The Pilgrims and Pocahontas: Rival Myths of American Origin*. Boulder, CO: Westview Press.

Addison, A.C. 1911. *The Romantic Story of the Mayflower Pilgrims and Its Place in the Life of Today*. Boston, MA: L.C. Page & Company, Project Gutenberg. Available from: www.gutenberg.org/files/36756/36756-h/36756-h.htm (accessed 12 March 2015).

Agnew, V. 2007. History's affective turn: historical reenactment and its work in the present. *Rethinking History: The Journal of Theory and Practice* 11(3): 299–312.
Allan, S. 2009. *Lady Rose Hickman: Her Life and Family*. s.l.: domtom.
Allan, S. 2011. *Steps Along the Mayflower Trail*. s.l.: domtom.
Almond, J. and Lambourne, D. 2011. *Boston St Mary's Guildhall: A History*. Boston, MA: Boston Borough Council.
Anderson, D. 2003. *William Bradford's Books: Of Plimmoth Plantation and the Printed Word*. Baltimore, MD: Johns Hopkins University Press.
Anderson, R.C. 1995. *The Great Migration Begins: Immigrants to New England, 1620–1633*. Vol. 1. Boston, MA: New England Historic Genealogical Society.
Bangs, J.D. 2009. *Strangers and Pilgrims, Travellers and Sojourners: Leiden and the foundations of Plymouth Plantation*. Plymouth, MA: General Society of Mayflower Descendants.
Barber, C. 1997. *The Great Little Plymouth Book*. Reprint edition. Exeter: Obelisk Publications.
Bassetlaw District Council (n.d.) *The Pilgrim Fathers' Story*. Bassetlaw: Bassetlaw District Council.
Board, J. 2006. *Pilgrim Country: An A to Z Guide*. Waltham Cross: John Merrill Foundation.
Bowman, G. 1906. *Governor William Bradford's Letter Book*. Boston, MA: Massachusetts Society of Mayflower Descendants. Available from: https://archive.org/details/governorwilliam00bradgoog (accessed 2 March 2015).
Bradford, W. 1898. *Bradford's History 'Of Plimoth Plantation': From The Original Manuscript: With a Report of the Proceedings Incident to the Return of the Manuscript to Massachusetts*. Boston, MA: Wright & Potter. Available from: https://archive.org/download/historyofplimoth00braduoft/historyofplimoth00braduoft.pdf (accessed 26 June 2014).
Bradford, W. 1981. *Of Plymouth Plantation 1620–1647: Introduction by Francis Murphy*. New York: Random House.
Cammack, J. and Cammack, J. (n.d.) *Boston 'Heritage and Influence': A Trail About Town*. Boston, MA: Boston Borough Council.
Cammack, J., Wright, N. and Holton, W. 2002. *Boston and (the Foundation of) the United States of America*. Boston, MA: Boston Borough Council; Historic Bostons' Partnership; Boston Preservation Trust; History of Boston Project; Cammack & Sons.
Capp, B. 2003. *When Gossips Meet: Women, Family, and Neighbourhood in Early Modern England*. Oxford: Oxford University Press.
Carrigan, T., Connell, R. and Lee, J. 1985. Toward a new sociology of masculinity. *Theory and Society* 14(5): 551–604.
Cheetham, J. 2001. *On the Trail of the Pilgrim Fathers*. Edinburgh: Luath Press.
Cook, D. 2013. The birth of the Pilgrim Fathers. *Retford Life* November: 50–51.
Crawford, P. 1981. Attitudes to menstruation in seventeenth-century England. *Past & Present* 91: 47–73.
Crawford, P. 1990. The construction and experience of maternity in seventeenth-century England. In V. Fildes (ed.) *Women as Mothers in Pre-Industrial England: Essays in Memory of Dorothy McLaren*. London: Routledge, pp. 3–38.
Crawford, P. 1993. *Women and Religion in England 1500–1720*. London: Routledge.
Cressy, D. 1997. *Birth, Marriage, and Death: Ritual, Religion, and the Life Cycle in Tudor and Stuart England*. Oxford: Oxford University Press.
Deetz, J. and Deetz, P.S. 2000a. Rocking the Plymouth myth. *Archaeology* 53(6): 16–18.

Deetz, J. and Deetz, P.S. 2000b. *The Times of Their Lives: Life, Love and Death in Plymouth Colony*. Basingstoke and New York: W.H. Freeman & Co.

Dicks, B. 2000. *Heritage, Place and Community*. Cardiff: University of Wales Press.

Dolby, M. 1991. *William Bradford of Austerfield: Mayflower Pilgrim 1589/90–1657: His Life & Work*. Doncaster: Doncaster Library & Information Services.

Dowsing, J. (n.d.) *Places of the Pilgrim Fathers: Landmarks in England (and the Netherlands)*. London: Sunrise Press.

Fairclough, N. 1993. *Discourse and Social Change*. Cambridge: Polity Press.

Fairclough, N. 2010. *Critical Discourse Analysis: The Critical Study of Language*. Second edition. Harlow: Longman.

Foucault, M. 1972/2002. *The Archaeology of Knowledge*. London: Routledge.

General Society of Mayflower Descendants. 2014. *General Society of Mayflower Descendants*. Available from: www.themayflowersociety.com/ (accessed 28 June 2014).

Gowing, L. 2012. *Gender Relations in Early Modern England*. London: Pearson.

Gray, A. 2014. *Two Sisters and the Puritan Revolution*. Available from: http://pilgrimsandprophets.co.uk/historical/two-sisters-and-the-puritan-revolution/ (accessed 30 August 2015).

Haden, J. and Pupils of Parish Church Primary School, Gainsborough, 2007. *William Brewster of the Pilgrim Fathers*. American Roots in English Soil (ARIES) Series. Grantham: Barny Books.

Heath, D.B. (ed.) 1963. *Mourt's Relation: A Journal of the Pilgrims at Plymouth*. 1622 Reprint edition. Bedford, MA: Applewood.

Holtorf, C. 2013. The need and potential for an archaeology orientated towards the present. *Archaeological Dialogues* 20(1): 12–18.

Hunter, J. 1849. *Collections Concerning the Early History of the Founders of New Plymouth: The First Colonists of New England*. London: John Russell Smith. Available from: https://archive.org/details/collectionsconce00hunt (accessed 30 June 2016)

In The Matter of the Log of the Mayflower 1897. Consistory Court of London, Probate Division (C.F.J.) 29 April, 208–222.

Jessup, E. 1976. *The Pilgrim Mothers*. Retford: Whartons.

Jessup, E. 1977. *The Mayflower Story*. Fourth edition. Retford: Whartons.

Launius, R.D. 2013. Public history wars, the 'One Nation/One People' consensus, and the continuing search for a usable past. *OAH Magazine of History* 27(1): 31–36.

Matthews, A. 1915. *The Term Pilgrim Fathers. Reprinted from the Publications of the Colonial Society of Massachusetts, Vol. XVII*. Cambridge: John Wilson & Son. Available from: https://archive.org/download/termpilgrimfathe00matt/termpilgrimfathe00matt.pdf (accessed 1 March 2010).

Mayflower 400. 2016. *Mayflower 400*. Available from: www.mayflower400uk.com (accessed 30 June 2016).

Moore, J. and Scott, E. (eds) 1997. *Invisible People and Processes: Writing Gender and Childhood into European Archaeology*. London: Leicester University Press.

Norton, M. 1996. *Founding Mothers and Fathers: Gendered Power and the Forming of American Society*. New York, NY: Alfred A. Knopf.

Reading, A. 2015. Making feminist heritage work: gender and heritage. In E. Waterton and S. Watson (eds) *The Palgrave Handbook of Contemporary Heritage Research*. Basingstoke: Palgrave Macmillan, pp. 397–413.

Parini, J. 2012. The American mythos. *Daedalus: Proceedings of the American Academy of Arts and Sciences* 141(1): 52–60.

Philbrick, N. 2007. *Mayflower: A Voyage to War*. London: Harper Perennial.
Pilgrim Fathers UK Origins Association, 2012. *News*. Available from: www.pilgrimfathersorigins.org/G_communitynews_2011.html (accessed 25 August 2015).
Prior, M. (ed.) 1985. *Women in English Society 1500–1800*. London: Methuen.
Scott, A. 2012. Publics versus professionals: agency and engagement with 'Robin Hood' and the 'Pilgrim Fathers' in Nottinghamshire. In L. Smith, E. Waterton and S. Watson (eds) *The Cultural Moment in Tourism*. London: Routledge, pp. 131–158.
Seelye, J. 1998. *Memory's Nation: The Place of Plymouth Rock*. Chapel Hill, NC: University of North Carolina Press.
Smith, L. 2006. *Uses of Heritage*. London: Routledge.
Stratton, E. 1986. *Plymouth Colony: Its History and People 1620–1691*. Salt Lake City, UT: Ancestry Publishing.
Thinking Place 2014. *Creating a New Story for Bassetlaw*. Preston: Thinking Place.
Turley, D. 1998. Introduction. In D. Turley (ed.) *American Religion: Literary Sources and Documents. Vol. I: From the Beginning of European Settlement to the Effects of Political Independence*. Mountfield: Helm Information, pp. 5–75.
Walzer, M. 1973. *The Revolution of the Saints: A Study in the Origins of Radical Politics*. New York: Atheneum.
Waterton, E. and Watson, S. (eds) 2015. *The Palgrave Handbook of Contemporary Heritage Research*. Basingstoke: Palgrave Macmillan.
Wendt, S. 2012. Nationalist middle-class women, memory, and conservative family values, 1890–1945. In I. Heinemann (ed.) *Inventing the Modern American Family: Family Values and Social Change in 20th-century United States*. Frankfurt-on-Main: Campus Verlag GmbH, pp. 31–58.
Willison, G. 1983. *Saints and Strangers: Being the Lives of the Pilgrim Fathers and Their Families, with Their Friends and Foes and an Account of Their Posthumous Wanderings in Limbo, Their Final Resurrection and Rise to Glory, and the Strange Pilgrimages of Plymouth Rock*. Reprinted Edition. Orleans, MA: Parnassus Imprints.
Winslow, E. 1624. *Good Newes from New England, or a True Relation of Things Truly Remarkable at the Plantation of Plimoth in New England*. Available from: https://archive.org/download/goodnewesfromnew00wins/goodnewesfromnew00wins.pdf (accessed 9 July 2014).
Wisecup, K. (ed.) 2014. *'Good News from New England' by Edward Winslow: A Scholarly Edition*. Amherst, MA: University of Massachusetts Press.
Woodbridge, L. 1984. *Women and the English Renaissance: Literature and the Nature of Womankind, 1540–1620*. Brighton: Harvester Press.
Young, A. (ed.) 1841. *Chronicles of the Pilgrim Fathers of the Colony of Plymouth, from 1602–1625*. Boston, MA: Little & Brown. Available from: https://archive.org/details/chroniclesofpilg00young (accessed 18 January 2015).

Chapter 7

The fleshyness of absence
The matter of absence in a feminist museology

Arndís Bergsdóttir and Sigurjón Baldur Hafsteinsson

Introduction

This chapter is in dialogue with a growing number of scholarly engagements with feminism and cultural heritage museums. It shares the concerns of such scholarly insights about an absence of women from exhibitions – if not a general absence from particular museum narratives, then an absence of aspects that do not fit stereotyped perceptions about women or established ideas about gendered roles. It is also concerned with how addressing the gender political aspects of presence and absence reiterates binaries where absence is reduced to a relationship of present men and absent women. Deconstructions of power relations where absence is viewed as a *result* of systematic subordinations of genders, and phenomenological approaches to the political aspects of *being missing* have yielded valuable contributions in elucidating the politics *inherent* in absences. But, the problem, we argue, with viewing absence as a part of causal relationships or as a pre-existing entity is that we miss the opportunity to view an absence of women in ways that it deserves: to address absence – not as an unagentic nothingness that is *symbiotic* with presence – but as *dynamic* agencies that entwine in mutual relationships. As always already entwined with presence, absence takes an agentic part in the world's materializations. Materializations, as Barad (2007) claims, emerge through intra-actions. As part of her agential realist onto-ethico-epistemology, intra-actions are dynamic relationships – that do not take place *between* individual entities – but *within* phenomena. Yet, intra-actions are not only about connections. They also involve separations where exclusions enact differentiations *within* materializations. Thus, iterative exclusions of women's absences in museums can be viewed as performances that create specific understandings. As such, they are enmeshed with ethics. In other words, responsibilities towards inclusions, exclusions and the ability to respond are always already entwined with matterings – it is only a question of attending to absences in ways they deserve. We propose a shift in critical lens to one capable of theorizing absence as a *whole*, instead of half of a binary; as entanglements of presence, absence and ethical accountability.

We approach the matter of absence through the study of a particular museum object – a hidden man's penis exhibited at The Phallological Museum of

Iceland – a museum that opened its doors in 1997 and in itself entwines notions of nature/culture, materiality/discourse and presence/absence. Containing a collection of more than 300 mammal penises native to Iceland (Hafsteinsson 2014), The Phallological Museum has been described as one of the most exotic, horrifying and *wackiest* museums in the world (Grossman 2014). Such descriptions mostly speak to the museum's exhibition where mammal penises are stacked on shelves in formalin-filled jars, larger (whale) specimens are positioned totem-like on the floor and taxidermied members are mounted on walls like hunting trophies. The museum's emphasis on mammal members does not exclude humans as the museum exhibits its first human male specimen: a penis and scrotum pledged by its owner before his death. Among animal/human specimens are things that display practicality and humor: lampshades made from tanned phallic skins hang from the ceiling and imitations of the Icelandic handball team's members stand erect in a glass case arranged like a team photo. Entwined with specimens of 'present' bodies the museum also displays objects connected to Icelandic folklore: among these are a penis of an adult Nicor (a horse-like water spirit), catafox (mixture of cat and fox), seahowler (an Icelandic sea monster), Christmas lad (one of the 13 Icelandic 'santa clauses') and – relevant to our case study – a hidden man. The hidden man's member is the only specimen in the museum's exhibition that is not 'there' – yet teeters on the verge of absence and presence.

Not many Icelanders still believe in hidden people. Yet, they believe that they believe. In fact, hidden people are not a question of belief or non-belief, but stories that are thoroughly woven into the fabric of humans and non-humans. They emerge through intra-actions; an ongoing flow 'through which "part" of the world makes itself differentially intelligible to another "part" of the world and through which local causal structures, boundaries, and properties are stabilized and destabilized' (Barad 2008: 135). In this museum exhibition, a hidden-man's penis that is neither present nor nothing gives us an opportunity to explore absence as always already differentially entwined with factors that make the world intelligible. The matter of hidden people – how hidden people *are* and *are known* – is threaded *through* and *with* our act of observation. Thus, our aim here is to create a new way of reading that enables us to engage with absence as an ontological entity intertwined with presence. We seek theoretical concreteness in new-materialism and post-human theories, including post-human feminism and feminist technoscience studies, where the politics of gender critically speak to agency, rationality, scientific knowledge production, practices of museum technologies and nature/culture dichotomies are central (see Åsberg and Lykke 2010). As we articulate absence as produced in mutually affected relationships *in* and *of* the world, we follow the work of Karen Barad (2007) on how the world comes into being through relationships that are not pre-existing, but intra-actively enact specific connections that always already entail different versions of ontologies, ethics and epistemologies: onto-ethico-epistemological entanglements.

Absence, women and museums

The matter of women's absence in cultural heritage museums may come in various constellations of absences and presences. Apart from elucidating the peripheral locations of women in grand narratives (Haraway 1984; Porter 1995), stereotypical bodily depictions (Summers 2000), restricted roles (Kavanagh 1994), and lack of intersectionality (Robert 2014), scholars attending to a feminist museology have presented compelling examples on how absence is built into the exclusionary practices of cultural heritage museums. Examining gendered corporealities in research and display of historical costumes Leigh Summers (2000) argues that exhibitions, in both Australian and English museums, may claim to include both men and women. Yet, value is placed on objects that visibly retain traces of men's bodies (sweat, blood, grime), while women's bodies are excluded from such depictions of active presence, by, for example, predominantly exhibiting (petite and immaculate) costumes that speak to passivity and stereotypical images of women. Wera Grahn has demonstrated with her study of the Nordic Museum in Sweden how the belongings of a home*less* woman were transformed by museum processes into versions where she 'devote[s] herself to traditionally female duties' (Grahn 2006: 446), thus attuning human and non-human beings to hegemonic gender ideals. In general, we may sense omissions, gaps and voids and understand that they are generated by depictions of women as passive configurations, peripheral to an active male presence. But what *is* absence?

Concerned with omissions of absence from the world's materialities, emerging theorizations, particularly within anthropology, elucidate the ubiquity of absence – and claim that while often forgotten and excluded, absence is inextricable from the world we inhabit. Severin Fowles argues, for example, that the world is filled with 'crowds of non-things, negative spaces, lost or forsaken objects, voids or gaps – absences, in other words, that also stand before us as entity-like presences with which we must contend' (2010: 25). Absences, as Morgan Meyer and Kate Woodthorpe (2008) argue, are performative entities that occupy spaces within environments filled with material presences and practiced through the 'paradoxal intersections of what is there and what is not' (Bille *et al.* 2010: 13). Such presences, Meyer (2012: 104) notes, reveal the agency of absence and its capacity to critically effect the social world. It is this effect on the social world – or more precisely on humans – that is the centre of the discussions mentioned above. As, Bille *et al.* (2010) also argue, absences come into the purview of humans as sensuous or cognitive disturbances that trouble their being in the world. In this sense, absences call for human engagement. As in the case of the hidden man's member at The Phallological Museum of Iceland, the *absence* of this specific object prompts visitors to respond much in the same way as the *present* mammal phalluses in the exhibition.

According to these approaches, absences cannot be dismissed as inert nothings. Rather, they trouble human lives, and can in some instances act – as Zoe

Crossland (2002) shows in her study of Argentina's disappeared – as *critical political objects*. Crossland's discussion implies, we suggest, that the absences generated by women's peripheral locations in narratives, stereotypical depictions – or plain obscurity – may have a critical stance that affects the social world. Yet, as argued by Meyer and Woodthorpe (2008), human engagements with absence can take the form of obstruction where humans act upon absence – using the presence of objects to occupy absence thus restricting their agency. Such discussions elucidate that despite the agency of absence, its (critical) nature and liveliness is seldom manifest within museums. They imply that absence – in the form of untold stories, disremembered lives and forgotten experiences – is subordinate to the presence of *man*.

Defending the agencies of absence and acknowledging the politics inherent in non-present entities is a valuable contribution to articulations of a feminist museology. Yet, focusing on such compensations for 'nothingness', we argue, shows indifference towards absence *as absence* and disregards the material entanglements that are part of the enactments and dynamic movements of agencies. In other words, articulating absence as independent from a human subject has allowed for engagements with the agency of absence. But, at the same time, focusing on humans and absence as pre-existing entities deflects the materiality of *doings and actions*. Agency, as Barad (2007) argues, is not a pre-existing prerogative of humans, but an enactment in the everyday relationality of human and non-human being in the world. Thus, portraying a home*less* woman as devoted to domestic duties, as discussed above by Grahn (2006), speaks to performances of presence and absence and the accountabilities of museums towards such enactments.

When it comes to reworking the entangled states of knowing, being and accountability into theorizations of absence that aim at contributing to a feminist museology, a shift in our critical lens toward absence as a relational entity, calls for theoretical precision.

New materialist cartographies include Barad's (2007) post-human feminist theorization of agential realism. It is an onto-ethico-epistomology that entangles humans and non-humans in enactments of being and knowing. The matter of absence is not inherently agentic, prepared for encounters and social interaction, but comes into being through the dynamic movements of intra-acting agencies. In Barad's (2007) post-human feminist theorization of agential realism, ethics cannot be separated from becomings of matter. The subject, according to Barad (2007), is still *there*, but is de-centred in relational entanglements. This means that we are not only responsible for ourselves. Responsibility, she argues, extends to the entangled other: who is excluded and who is not. In other words, engaging with a homeless woman (Grahn 2006) or historical costumes (Summers 2000) prompts museums to respond in ways that are demarcated by their practices – and what enactments these practices allow – not the possibilities inherent in these specific histories and heritage. Although prevailing discourses effect museums' engagements with women's histories, the matter of women in museum exhibitions is not merely shaped by (hegemonic) discourses. Rather, it emerges as material-discursive phenomena through intra-acting agencies that are ontologically inseparable (Barad 2007). Thus, in Barad's terms, accountability and ethics are always already entwined with certain practices of mattering. There is no innocence to such practices. Rather they are acts of iteratively summoning certain possibilities – to the exclusion of others, thus normalizing *specific* understanding of women's being in the world

Responsibility and accountability towards entangled others cannot, Barad (2007) claims, be substituted by scientific approaches – and their generally presumed inherent objectivity. As Haraway (1988) demonstrates in her detailed discussion on situated knowledges, the relationship between science and an objective, omniscient observer is a mythical one. Contrary to such notions, she argues, scientific practices inherently involve political and ethical aspects that call for accountability (see also Åsberg 2013). Technologies and science, in terms of Barad's (2007) onto-ethico-epistemology, demarcate meaning and matter. Such demarcations rest on the (simultaneously) material and ideological scientific instruments applied – and the possibilities (and impossibilities) they are able to bring about. In other words, understanding of the world is generated through the inclusions and exclusions inherent in apparatuses.

Sensing accountability for gendered absences

Subversions of absence in cultural heritage museum exhibitions not only refer to an absence of women's lives and experiences in narratives, but an absence that is already woven into the dynamic mesh of museum technologies and knowledge-making practices. Women are not just absent from historical accounts – as if the road to public depiction as participants in life is not theirs to take; their absence is also endorsed through museum technologies. Here we refer to the scientific and epistemological technologies applied within different realms of museums that unified produce certain knowledges within their exhibition spaces (Olsen and Svestadt 1994; Preziosi 2012). In paying critical attention to absence, we must, therefore, move beyond the approach that poses that an absence of women is a forgotten entity that may be retrieved, foregrounded and understood as an entanglement for which the practices and processes within museums must be held accountable. Cultural heritage museums are apparatuses, where claims of authenticity and authority have been thoroughly grounded in science (Haraway 1984; Olsen and Svestad 1994; Preziosi 2012). Apparatuses, Barad argues, 'provide the conditions for the possibility of determinate boundaries and properties of "objects" within phenomena' (2007: 127). In this sense, absence and its entanglements of being in and of the world, critically speaks to museums as apparatuses, thus involving them as entities that are politically and ethically accountable to women's absence in exhibition narratives.

Generally, museums aim to convey an account of a reality outside their walls that (although severely shorthanded to fit into a certain demarcated space situated in the present) claims to offer a truthful and correct depiction (Rekdal 2014).

After all, they are information produced by the *infallibility* of science for the benefit of museum's communities. It is science that produces the knowledge depicted in narratives on cultural heritage; museums are merely its humble servants. Feminist technoscience studies, however, trouble these uncontested, paternalistic and linear connections between *good science* and the general *good of society*:

> For researchers within the overlapping fields of science and technology studies (STS) and feminist technoscience studies, there is no such thing as a pure and politically innocent 'basic' science that can be transformed into technological applications to be 'applied' in 'good' or 'bad' ways at a comfortable distance from the 'clean' hands of the researcher engaged in the former. It is a shared assumption of researchers within the fields of STS and feminist technoscience studies that 'pure', 'basic' science is as entangled in societal interests, and can be held as politically and ethically accountable, as the technological practices and interventions to which it may give rise.
> (Åsberg and Lykke 2010: 299)

Ethics speak to intentional absence, that is power relations where absence is disregarded or even obscured to enhance the significance of presence. The performances of reciprocal intra-actions – the material-semiotic *companion species* also include power relations (Haraway 2008). Barad's articulation of the nothingness inherent in the materialization of matter, which as I elaborate later in this chapter, disrupts the presence/absence binaries and elucidates the possibilities always already inherent in matter. It speaks to relationality, and thus, accountability and shared obligations. These are not neccessarily human attributes that can be electively applied wherever and whenever humans see fit. They are 'crafted in intra-action through which entities, subjects, and objects come into being' (Haraway 2008: 71). Responsibility is a question of responses, not reactions – from all entities (human and non-human) that enter into relationalities. It also raises questions as to how practices – that do not rely on preexisting entities, but come into being through intra-acting agencies (Barad 2007) and *becoming with* (Haraway 2010) – are a practice of worldly intra-connections that 'make us responsible in unpredictable ways for which worlds take shape' (Haraway 2010: 36). Thus, as argued by Åsberg (2013), they entail ethics.

In this approach to ethics, responsibility does not entail the recovery or re-instatement of past events – as if all wrongs can be put right by reclamation and re-assemblage. As noted by Barad (Juleskjær and Schwennesen 2012), that which has come about in the past has not been frozen in time. We cannot re-present – make present again – something that has been absent. Barad explains the 'undoing of loss and the recovery of some prior state of existence' (Juleskjær and Schwennesen 2012: 21) in terms of the quantum eraser experiment, but as illustrated by the relationality of non/existence (through the mediated exchange of physical and virtual particles) absence cannot be the equivalence of erasure. The quantum eraser experiment shows that when information that has been gathered on certain entities – thus forming particular notions about their being and identity – is erased, this *erasure* rewinds shapes and configurations of entities back to the state they were in *before* the information was gathered. Moreover, the experiment implies that an entity's '*past identity, its ontology, is never fixed, it is always open to future reworkings*' (Barad 2010: 260, emphasis in original). Thus, according to classical physics the conception of *erasure* indicates that there is an inherent hope that wrongs can be put right and wrongdoings rectified by reassembling events to the point that nothing seems to have disbanded them in the first place. If we follow this interpretation of the quantum eraser experiment into feminist concerns in museums, then changes in museum practices that substitute presence for absence – for instance by adding objects and issues pertaining to women to exhibition narratives – may indeed be attempts to 'rectify' absences and unjust situations. The classical interpretation of quantum erasure, Barad (2007, 2010) argues, rests on the assumption that entities are distinct individuals that can be recovered in their 'original' states. The practices used to shape our understanding and the entities that form specific patterns or outcomes are not distinct but all part of the same phenomenon. Moreover, the state of entities – recovered after the gathering (forming) of information has been erased – is not an 'original' state, but has to be actively reworked so it contains traces of the practices that shaped the understandings we have rewinded from. Therefore, there is not 'going back' as there is no 'back' but rather enactments of entanglements where time and space are threaded in and through phenomena as they come to matter in the world. The non-fixity of temporality calls for attention to all matters, 'not just for what comes to matter, but what is constitutively excluded from mattering in order for particular materializations to occur' (Juleskjær and Schwennesen 2012: 21). Therefore, absence is not *erased* humans, non-humans, issues or events, but rather absence is *enacted* in and with specific practices that cannot be undone – only reworked in ways that are always already entwined with the notions that made them absent in the first place. In this framework, when we consider museums, with their knowledge production through presences and absences, this raises questions about the parts their processes have played in neglecting women's experiences and lived lives. In a feminist museological context, Barad's (2010) articulation of the quantum eraser experiment elucidates the responsiblities inherent in museum processes and prompts us to question how (despite efforts to increase institutional agility) museums have created and supported androcentric strategies of (his)tory-telling. It follows, then, to ask how museums intend to be accountable – not within their general attempts to recover women's lives and experiences as an effort of rescue – but by showing accountability toward understandings enacted by their practices, by 'being obligated to the bodies that are marked by these encounters' (Juleskjær and Schwennesen 2012: 20). The ethics inherent in museum work are not an elective attitude toward the performance of museum practices. Ethics and responsibilities do not reside outside of museums and, therefore, they cannot be *added* to performances as a conscious gesture toward the world. They are already an inseparable part of phenomena; the onto-ethico-epistemological entanglements of intra-acting agencies (Barad, 2010). Ethics, as argued by Åsberg (2013: 2), are not a concern for the good. Nor does it refer only to a Foucaultian meta-ethics or care for the self. Rather, the ethical turn in this field is in the materialist wake of poststructuralist theory an attempt to recognize the other.

Threading through nothingness and infinity – what does it entail?

> Nothingness is not absence, but the infinite plentitude of openness.
> (Barad 2012: 16)

We shall begin with Barad's (2012) distinction between nothingness and absence. Her articulation of absence – which she refers to as a vacuum or void – relates to the approach of classical physics to nothing in nothingness. She argues that absence (the vacuum) is the conditions of 'im/possiblity for non/existence' (Barad 2012: 12). It is impossible to determine if the conditions of absence do indeed hold nothing – or for that matter – something. Yet, it is the possiblity – of nothing. Seen through the lens of the quantum principle of ontological indeterminacy, nothingness is a space that is neither nothing nor something and comes into non/being through the dynamic movements of in/determinacy (indeterminacies-in-action). To explain this more carefully: if the dynamic movements of indeterminacy is grounds for the existence of virtual particles then the void 'is a spectral realm with a ghostly existence' (Barad 2012: 12). Virtual particles are not presence – but they are not absence either. They hover on the brink – on the *in-between-ity* – of non/existence where they engage in (virtual) intra-actions with physical particles. There, each virtual and physical particle can make multiple connections in a mediated exchange. A physical particle is never isolated from its own intra-actions with virtual particles, but always a sum of *itself* and *them*. It is a complete ontological insensibility, which destabilizes non/existance (non/being). Somethingness cannot stand alone; it cannot be stripped of nothingness as it is always engaged in intra-action. Thus there are no boundaries between matter as a materialized entity and possiblities that need to be eradicated.

For Barad, 'Infinity' (written with a capital 'I') does not refer to an unreachable countlessness, but the 'ongoing material reconfiguring of nothingness' (Barad 2012: 16). Infinitude, she argues, is infinitely threaded through nothingness, 'so that every infinitesimal bit of one always already contains the other' (Barad 2012: 17). In fact, Barad's articulation of nothingness is a detailed illustration of the interconnectedness of all that is in the world, and thus shared responsibilities. However, it is the part of absence, or the void, that is of particular interest to us. The inbetweenness of virtual particles troubles the presence/absence, there/not there binaries. Out of presence may be out of mind, but it is certainly not exempt from being in the world. Thus, absence is not a void in the sense of a passive element waiting to be filled, but an animate existence of indeterminancy. As physical particles interact with virtual particles of absence (or void), we are in fact inseperable from the void; the very conditions that make all possibilities possible. Absence and presence cannot be viewed as separate entities, but are interconnected – an *absencepresence*. In museums, an absence of women in narratives cannot be dismissed as a void without inherent possibilities – as a nothingness in the face of present stories. Rather, absences are *understandings* generated by the material and ideological apparatuses of museums – entangled *in and of* their responsibilities and ethics.

Hidden entanglements

The case of the *absent* artifact employed by The Phallological Museum of Iceland to depict the hidden people in Iceland reveals the entanglements of presence and absence, non/being and thereby disrupt the binaries where presence is noteworthy and absence is alternately irrelevant, nonexistent or subservient to humans. Informing our conceptual articulation are the antics of an artifact at The Icelandic Phallological Museum – the hidden man's penis. The 'hidden people' are a sporadically visible race of supernatural beings that bear a strong resemblance to European elves or fairies, and like their relatives on the mainland they circulate in folk stories. Hidden people, however, are human-like, a similar height and build to visible people, but usually, according to Icelandic folklore, superior in looks and demeanour. This particular artifact – the hidden man's penis that is displayed in its non-presence inside a glass accompanied by a museum label – is an entanglement of presence and absence. It speaks to hidden people – the others in Icelandic culture – as a virtuality that does not adhere to our constructions of time or space, but a beyond that seems ungraspable. Yet, it is *there*, knit into (all of) our 'being-in-the-world'. Hidden people materialize in present physical matter, such as swerves built into urban road systems to avoid destroying hidden people's habitats (rocks), exquisitely embroidered cloths that were given to humans in exchange for help, or human children that have come into being from hidden/non-hidden encounters (Hafsteinsson 2009). These are enactments of differences and similarities in becomings that cannot be split into humans and hidden people, but are always already entanglements of both.

The artifact's label explains hidden people as part of Icelandic culture. Around Iceland, some cultural heritage museums as well as The National Museum of Iceland exhibit one or two artifacts that were made by or belonged to hidden people (Hafsteinsson 2014). Among them are pots, silver chains and manteaux that have spoken to the bodies of hidden people. Yet, since the opening of the Phallological Museum, bodies of hidden people – the matter of their absence – has counted in a world of present phalluses. Hidden people are not a pre-existing entity, already fixed as non-relevant in the museum world of present entities, but '"scale-making"' of world-making kinds, in which re-opening what seemed closed remains possible' (Haraway 2003: 64). There is a significant otherness between the present world of humans and absent world of hidden people; they are within the figure of companion species and partners that come into being through intra-relations (Åsberg 2013; Haraway 2010, 2003). Tracing entanglements to elucidate matter and meaning (Barad 2007; Haraway and Goodeve 2000), the case of the hidden man's penis reveals dynamic becomings of partnerships (Åsberg 2013), where the matter of hidden people and unconcealed humans materializes through the eradicated boundaries of presence and absence. For Haraway (2008), companion species are not pre-existing realities, but come into being and knowing through intra-actions – the relationality that queers the agentic individuality inherent in our traditional notions of cause and effect (Barad in Kleinmann 2012) – of *fleshy* entities (Haraway 2010). The material turn has focused on all things physical. However, fleshyness is not the prerogative of entities that appear fully present. Indeed, that would assume that presence is stable and given. Rather, it always already entails both presence and absence

Materializations of absence

The hidden man's penis is (in its non/existence) in a jar filled with clear liquid. Visually, we detect a glass jar, similar to containers that can be found in kitchen cabinets. Inside the jar is clear liquid – and the absent/present matter of the hidden man's penis. Barad's description of absences/presences, nothings/somethings follows notions of intra-actions of physical and virtual particles. It speaks to material discursive practices where matter materializes as the undertaking of boundaries – boundaries that come into being through intra-acting agencies. According to the Phallological Museum's director and collector, this penis is only visible to those who are unusually perceptive (Hafsteinsson 2009). Perceptive humans are therefore part of the museum apparatus. The hidden man's penis does not become visually detectable through interaction such as staring at the jar, but through 'the co-constitution of determinately bounded and propertied entities results from specific *intra-actions*' (Barad 2010: 253). We can and cannot *see* absence, as

> the actual object referent is the phenomenon – the intra-action of what we call the electron and the apparatus. And so the fact that its ontology changes when we change the apparatus is therefore of no surprise, as we are investigating an entirely different phenomenon.
>
> (Dolphijn and Van der Tuin 2012: 61)

Detecting the penis, therefore, elucidates its boundaries and properties – but not as a fixed entity (either visible or not). Its properties – *what it is* – are determinate; yet, only in *these* particular circumstances – of the intra-action between the perceptive person and absent/present penis. As a material discursive apparatus, the Phallological Museum performs similar intra-actions – that allow the recognition of phenomena by elucidating its possibilities (Barad 2007) – between the observed hidden man's phallus and its agencies of observation. Apparatuses are material-discursive practices that produce phenomena, but in doing so, become part of their dynamic being in the world. This shifts our point of reference – the subject position – from that which is observing or that which is being observed to their intra-active co-creation of phenomena. Thus, positions of subject and object are inseparably entangled. It is not the hidden man's penis – a distinguishable material entity with clear boundaries between observer and observed – that is phenomena, as its ontology changes according to how it is measured or observed. Rather, phenomena is '*the ontological inseparability of intra-acting "agencies"*' (Barad 2007: 333, emphasis added). In this case, entangled becomings of the hidden man's member, a jar, the liquid that fills it, museum text and a perceptive human

As argued by Barad (2007), matter comes into being through a fluid process where agency, which emerges through the movements and entanglements of phenomena, is framed by ontic and semantic boundaries. Agency is 'not a matter of something somebody has but it's a doing, it's the very possibilities for reworking and opening up new possibilities' (Juleskjær and Schwennesen 2012: 17). In this post-humanist sense, it is not a trait reserved for humans, but an entanglement of thinking *and* being that allows for the construction of new arrangements while building on former insights. The limitations to the material-discursive boundaries are enacted through the dynamic process of discursive practices that are 'specific material configurings of the world through which determinations of boundaries, properties, and meanings are differentially enacted' (Barad 2007: 335). The absence of the hidden man's penis is not absence as this is generally understood, but always inherent in dynamic entanglements where matter comes to matter. Thus, it is also the dynamism of partnerships that are the possiblities of not only grasping the *fleshyness* of presence, but of absence as well. Absence cannot be complete. It, cannot *not be*, but is always the conditions for shared intra-actions of non/existence. Matter is, thus, the ontics and antics of indeterminacy: impossible to secure as a set entity as 'closure can't be secured when the conditions of im/possibilities and lived indeterminacies are integral, not supplementary, to what matter is' (Kleinmann 2012: 16).

Feminist absence

Absence challenges the binary structures of cultural heritage museum exhibitions, and furthermore, its agentic configuration with ethical and political implications (Barad 2007). Acknowledging absence as matter exposes the vulnerability of cultural heritage museum exhibitions. It destabilizes the perfect vision of the past presented (in an attempt to re-present), through the presence of contextualized objects. Reality, Barad argues, is not inherent in things; nor is it a hidden meaning, or an interpreted metaphor. Reality is *in* the primary ontological unit, the phenomenon, where things exist through their entanglement. Within this entanglement are apparatuses that are productive of, as well as part of, phenomena. As intra-acting agencies are inseparable, so are phenomenon and apparatus, the observer and observed. This is important to stress in a feminist museological context as it refers to the observers within museums; the scientific practices that cannot be untangled to the intra-activity of differential mattering. That is essential to the discursive-material reconfigurings of the hidden man's penis, which, like every present/absent artifact, is an ever-changing network of activities and materialization that is determined by structures and boundaries.

The case of the hidden man's penis allows us to encounter absence as material in a museum exhibition, this commonplace *matter* that has been severely undertheorized. This particular museum object elucidates that absence is not a forgotten pre-existing material entity, something that is out of sight and thus equally out of mind, but certain configurings *within* phenomena – the primary ontological unit – towards which we, as feminist museologists, have been critically inattentive. It also speaks to the absence of women in cultural heritage museums, where our indifferent attitude has left the gendered absences *within* museum materialities unattended, as we mention at the beginning of this chapter. The hidden man's penis speaks to the lived lives and experiences of humans and non-humans, to presence and absence. We can speak of the cloth, the swerve in the road or the children who have come about through the romantic encounters of hidden people and humans as yet other metonyms.

From a feminist museological point of view, the scientific processes that lie at the heart of cultural heritage museums and their more recent emphasis on exhibition practices that seek to represent certain social and historical realities, make for strange bedfellows. On the one hand, scientific practices in museum spaces are meant to present an objective view of the world, on the other, science is never politically innocent. It evades accountability (Åsberg and Lykke 2010: 299), which would make the very basis on which museums build their authoritative status incompatible with depictions of social and historical realities that are sensitive to feminist needs and requirements. With exceeding emphasis on technology as a way to, purify and perfect the past – either through elaborate investigative sciences or the technological fireworks used for dissemination, museums strive to become more perfect, and less vulnerable. This, as argued by Åsberg (2013: 4), 'is incompatible with feminist posthuman ethics'.

Conclusion

As mentioned at the beginning of this chapter, studies of the roles and depictions of women in cultural heritage museums reveal explicit absences. Discernable in many guises throughout museum narratives, the foundations for these absences have elicited valuable contributions to feminist research in museums. Yet, the heart of the matter – the presence of women's absence – has received less attention than it deserves. Thus, in this chapter, we have been concerned with addressing absence in terms of onto-ethico-epistemological entanglements, where absence is as a dynamic agency enmeshed in the world's materializations. To articulate, an otherwise elusive absence, the hidden man's penis at The Phallological Museum of Iceland provides a case where absence is palpable within the framework provided by the museum, display and surrounding folklore. Our claim is that such a contribution to conceptualizations of absence and presence as intra-active agencies – absencepresence – elucidates how an absence of women comes to matter in cultural heritage museum exhibitions. Absences, we argue, are everywhere. Yet, they cannot be dismissed as *nothings*, for absence and presence are entangled becomings: performances that emerge as understandings always already entwined with museums' responsibilities and ethics.

Bibliography

Åsberg, C. 2013. The timely ethics of posthumanist gender studies. *Feminisistische Studien* 1: 7–12.
Åsberg, C. and Lykke, N. 2010. Feminist technoscience studies. *European Journal of Women's Studies* 17(4): 299–305.
Barad, K. 2007. *Meeting the Universe Halfway: Quantum Physics and the Entanglement of Matter and Meaning.* Durham, NC: Duke University Press Books
Barad, K. 2008. Posthumanist performativity: toward an understanding of how matter comes to matter. In S. Alaimo and S. Hekman (eds) *Material Feminisms.* Bloomington, IN: Indiana University Press, pp. 73–98.
Barad, K. 2010. Quantum entanglements and hauntological relations of inheritance: dis/continuities, spacetime enfoldings, and justice-to-come. *Derrida Today* 3(2): 240–268.
Barad, K. 2012. What is the measure of nothingness? Infinity, virtuality, justice. In B. Funcke (ed.) *100 Notes – 100 Thoughts, No.099.* Ostfildern: dOCUMENTA and Hatje Cantz Verlag.
Bille, M., Hastrup, F. and Sørensen, T.F. (eds) 2010. *An Anthropology of Absence.* New York: Springer.
Colebrook, C. 2008. On not becoming man: the materialist politics of unactualized potential. In S. Alaimo and S. Hekman (eds) *Material Feminisms.* Bloomington, IN: Indiana University Press, pp. 52–84.
Crossland, Z. 2002. Violent spaces: conflict over the reappearance of Argentina's disappeared. In J. Schofield, W.G. Johnson and C. Beck (eds) *Matériel Culture: The Archaeology of Twentieth-Century Conflict.* London: Routledge, pp. 115–131.
Dolphijn, R. and Van der Tuin, I. 2012. *New Materialism: Interviews & Cartographies,* Ann Arbor, MI: Open Humanities Press.
Fowles, S. 2010. People without things. In M. Bille, F. Hastrup and T.F. Sørensen (eds) *An Anthropology of Absence.* New York: Springer, pp. 23–41.
Fuery, P. 1995. *The Theory of Absence: Subjectivity, Signification, and Desire.* Westport, CT: Greenwood Press.
Golding, V. 2013. Museums, poetics, affect. *Feminist Review* 104(1): 80–99.
Grahn, W. 2006. Känn dig själf: Genus, historiekonstruktion och kulturhistoriska museirepresentationer. Unpublished PhD thesis, Linköping: Linköpings universitet
Grossman, S. 2014. The 10 weirdest museums in the world. *Time,* 18 May. Available at: http://time.com/101851/weirdest-museums-in-the-world/ (accessed 18 May 2014).
Hafsteinsson, S.B. 2009. Huldumannstyppi og næmar konur. In: G.Þ. Jóhannesson and H. Björnsdóttir (eds) *Rannsóknir í Félagsvísindum X, Félagsvísindadeild. Erindi Flutt á RáÐstefnu í Október 2009.* Reykjavík: Félagsvísindastofnun Háskóla Íslands, pp. 517–527.
Hafsteinsson, S.B. 2014. *Phallological Museum.* Berlin, Münster: LIT Verlag.

Haraway, D.J. 1984. Teddy bear patriarchy: taxidermy in the Garden of Eden, New York City, 1908–1936. *Social Text* 11 (Winter): 20–64.

Haraway, D.J. 1988. Situated knowledges: the science question in feminism and the privilege of partial perspective. *Feminist Studies* 14(3): 575–599.

Haraway, D.J. 2003. *The Companion Species Manifesto: Dogs, People, and Significant Otherness*. Chicago, IL: Prickly Paradigm Press.

Haraway, D.J. 2008. *When Species Meet*. Minneapolis, MN and London: University of Minnesota Press.

Haraway, D.J. 2010. When species meet: staying with the trouble. *Environment and Planning D: Society and Space* 28(1): 53–55.

Haraway, D.J. and Goodeve, T.N. 2000. *How Like a Leaf: Donna J. Haraway – An Interview with Thyrza Nichols Goodeve*. New York and London: Routledge.

Juleskjær, M. and Schwennesen, N. 2012. Intra-active entanglements: an interview with Karen Barad. *Kvinder, Køn og Forskning* 1(2): 10–24.

Kavanagh, G. 1994. *Museum Provision and Professionalism*. London: Routledge.

Kleinmann, A. 2012. Intra-actions. Interview of Karen Barad. *Special dOCUMENTA, Mousse Magazine* 12: 76–81.

Meyer, M. 2012. Placing and tracing absence: a material culture of the immaterial. *Journal of Material Culture* 17(1): 103–110.

Meyer, M. and Woodthorpe, K. 2008. The material presence of absence: a dialogue between museums and cemeteries. *Sociological Research Online* 13(5). Available at: www.socresonline.org.uk/13/5/1.html (accessed 14 October 2016).

Olsen, B. and Svestad, A. 1994. Creating prehistory: archaeology museums and the discourse of modernism. *Nordisk Museologi* 1: 3–20.

Pétursdóttir, Þ. and Olsen, B. 2014. Imaging modern decay: the aesthetics of ruin photography. *Journal of Contemporary Archaeology* 1(1): 7–23.

Porter, G. 1995. Seeing through solidity: a feminist perspective on museums. *The Sociological Review* 43(S1): 105–126.

Preziosi, D. 2012. Narrativity and the museological myths of nationality. In B.M. Carbonell (ed.) *Museum Studies: An Anthology of Contexts*. Malden and Oxford: Blackwell, pp. 82–91.

Rekdal, P.B. 2014. Introduction: why a book on museums and truth? In A.B. Fromm, V. Golding and P.B. Rekdal (eds) *Museums and Truth*. Newcastle upon Tyne: Cambridge Scholars Publishing, pp. xix–xxv.

Robert, N. 2014. Getting intersectional in museums. *Museums & Social Issues* 9(1): 24–33.

Summers, L. 2000. Sanitising the female body: costume, corsetry and the case for corporeal feminism in social history museums. *Open Museum Journal* 1. Available at: http://hosting.collectionsaustralia.net/omj/vol1/summers.html (accessed 14 October 2016).

Van der Tuin, I. 2014. Diffraction as a methodology for feminist onto-epistemology: on encountering chantal chawaf and posthuman interpellation. *Parallax* 20(3): 231–244.

Chapter 8

Taller than the rest

The Three Dikgosi Monument, masculinity reloaded

Keletso G. Setlhabi

Introduction

In the Central Business District of Gaborone, Botswana, lies the gigantic Three Dikgosi Monument commemorating *Kgosi* (chief) Bathoen I of Bangwaketse, *Kgosi* Khama III of Bangwato and *Kgosi* Sebele I of Bakwena. The trio travelled to England in 1895 to protest against possible transfer of their land to the British South Africa Company. They are highly respected and regarded as national builders and heroes in the country for their negotiation, often even based on a distorted narrative that they went to England to ask for independence from the queen. How else could the Botswana government ensure their continuous presence in the memory of its people except through a highly visible national monument in the centre of the capital city? In this chapter, I look further than the national value of the monument and dwell on how it praises the masculinity of men in Tswana culture. The conceptual framework of the study is based on gender archaeology, which is applied to the ethnography of gender roles in Tswana communities. It is guided by gender archaeology's question of 'Were they all male?' I rephrase the question and ask 'What if the three Dikgosi (chiefs) were women?' The accepted relegation of female roles into private spaces behind the scenes is interrogated through the masculine posture of males on this public monument. In conclusion, I argue that the Three Dikgosi Monument is an appropriation of the power of men in the patriarchal Tswana culture depicted through gendered national heritage.

Gender and heritage framework in Botswana

The conceptual framework of this chapter is based on gender archaeology that emerged during the postprocessual era during the 1980s (Engelstad 2007; Sorensen 2004). Its contestation was the invisibility of women in the interpretation of the archaeological record as depicted in the discipline, which translates to the male bias in archaeology (Johnson 2010). Gender archaeology addresses the roles of women and men in the archaeological record using contexts such as settlements, household organizations, status, labour division and material culture creation, use or ownership. Feminist archaeology, on the other hand, arose through questioning the dominance of men and the absence of women in the archaeological record. It argued that perhaps women used perishable material that did not leave any material evidence and that this should not result in their exclusion from the interpretation of the past. When turning to the general gender framework in Botswana first, the 1980s saw a period in which gender activism was vocal as seen through establishments of civil society movements like Emang Basadi (Balozwi 2014). Specifically established in 1986 as a reaction tool against the Botswana 1982 Citizenship Act and the 1984 Citizenship (Amendment) Act, through which children of Batswana women who were married to foreigners were denied citizenship. The movement led by Dr Athalia Molokomme, a law academic at the University of Botswana then and currently the first female attorney general in Botswana, sought to sensitize women on their discrimination in Botswana (Selolwane 2004). In this case, Unity Dow challenged the law that discriminated her two children born after her marriage to an American citizen, Peter Dow, from acquiring Botswana citizenship. Her successful challenge resulted in her children and all others of foreign fathers to automatically attain Botswana citizenship (Government of Botswana 1992).

The landscape of gender imbalance shook and the reluctance of the Botswana government to initially implement the judgment of the case was caught by international watchdogs such the Human Rights Watch/Africa Human Rights Watch Women's Rights Project (1994). It raised concerns about the continued discrimination against women in Botswana despite the judgement. Eventually the government took steps such as upgrading the Women's Unit established in 1978 to a Department of Women's Affairs in 1996 (Morna and Tolmay 2006). It also ratified the Convention on the Elimination of Discrimination against Women (CEDAW) in 1996 (Bauer 2011). However, gender imbalance in Botswana is still visible in other sectors such as politics and education. This also includes the subject of this chapter, the masculine gender presentation in Botswana's heritage. The androcentric presentation of heritage in Botswana is briefly highlighted by Keitumetse (2011) through examples such as the male-oriented socio-cultural spaces such as the *kgotla* (village meeting space) where women have always had a lesser voice. This demonstrates a gendered space in past Tswana settlement patterns known as the *kgotla*, was a public space for only men and the female space (*malwapa*) was reserved for female-oriented activities and constructed in front of their houses with the boundaries of the homestead (Reid *et al.* 1997).

The erection of other monuments within Botswana like the Livingstone Memorial in Kolobeng tend to mainly focus on the role of the missionary and not his wife Mary (Keitumetse 2011). The documentation of heritage reflects patriarchy bias of male roles in Tswana societies. Further examples are the statues of the first president of Botswana, Sir Seretse Khama, the war memorials in front of the National Parliament and North East and Dimawe where Bakwena defeated the Boers in 1852. The monuments and sites honour men and their masculine roles in society, such as leadership, chieftaincy, war, cattle herding and hunting. The absence of feminine roles is a depiction of the accepted 'norm' that these roles are less important. The gender representation of national monuments (statues) in Botswana that is depicted on the Botswana National Museum's site register also reflects the masculinity of Botswana heritage.

The only female statue I know of in Botswana is erected in the University of Botswana where a woman is portrayed inducting a child on a laptop. Even where an opportunity avails itself to depict equality in education among all genders, the motherly role of women is given most preference. The little-known statue is only part of the university landscape and not a national monument. This is contrast to the most popular statue on campus, 'Motho le Motho Kgomo', which depicts the masculinity of cattle in Botswana. It is a symbol of how the national university was built through donation of a cow by families in Botswana. The portrayed man herding a cow is a masculine role in Tswana societies. What is excluded, as with other, statues, is the role of women in the cattle donation process (HATAB 2015; Seretse 2008). The woman's role remains invisible even though she was part of the decision-making process and practically assisted in the donation through tasks such as preparing for the journey. The value of this statue is mostly celebrated during the university graduation ceremonies. The bias can also be linked to insufficient archaeology and cultural education in Botswana. Heritage education could be used as a tool in the heritage preservation and presentation (Kiyaga-Mulindwa and Segobye 1994). The Archaeology Unit in the History Department of the University of Botswana is still the only place that offers formal training in archaeology, which was introduced as a single major in the History Department in 1992 (Campbell 1998). It is through formal education structures that gender imbalance in Botswana's heritage can be corrected through gender archaeology modules currently offered as part of archaeological theory.

Masculinity and the role of a chief in Tswana culture

The central theme of this chapter, masculinity and heritage, will be discussed within the context of Tswana society – patriarchal in nature and patriarchy that includes a key element of hegemonic masculinity, that is, where men are socially dominant over women (Jewkes *et al.* 2015). This type can be further classified as African masculinity traced back to the pre-colonial period (Morrell 1998). The Tswana people, also identified as South-Tswana, are part of the Bantu with a patriarchal societal structure in which a male chief is the overall ruler of the *morafhe* (community) (Mannathoko 1999; Ngcongco 1979). He is guided by his paternal uncles during his reign. According to tradition, a chief is always the eldest son of the family and where polygamy was practised in the past, he was the eldest son of the first wife, who is the queen (*Mohumagadi*). This indicates a patrilineal system of inheritance as the male child is expected to pass on the family's name to his heirs. There are documented cases in which the eldest child, a woman, sought to rule but often led to breakaways based on the Setswana language expression '*ga di ke di etelelwa ke manamagadi*', which translates to 'males cannot be led by females'. For example, some oral traditions state that Bakgatla-ba-Kgafela broke away from the rest of Bakgatla under the leadership of the younger male Kgafela. This was after the eldest child of *Kgosi* Matshego, a woman named Mosetlha, took over the reign of her father (Schapera 1942). The patriarchal type of governance by chiefs was the only one that imperialists and missionaries found during the pre-colonial period. The rulers were in control of all vital resources such as the distribution of land, an indication of their importance in Tswana societies (Holm and Botlhale 2008; Samatar, 1999). The role changed slowly from independence when Botswana turned into a Republic in 1966.

The head of the state has since been an elected president and chiefs are customary leaders of their ethnic groups. Their power was reduced significantly as they report to a government minister and operate under Bogosi ACT of 2008 (Government of Botswana 2008). However, the chiefs are still respected by their communities and hence the constant engagement by government. Communities in the past tended to follow their chief in religious choices and this is why conversions into Christianity often began with him, which assured the conversion of the whole community into similar faith (Matemba 2010). The same continues post-independence as shown by how communities tend to support their chief's political party as demonstrated by how *Kgosi* Bathoen II of Bangwaketse stood for Botswana National Front (BNF) parliamentary seat and won in 1969 (Maundeni 2005). Other examples are those of *Kgosi* Moremi Tawana of Batawana who first became a Member of Parliament under the ruling Botswana Democratic Party (BDP) in 2010. He later defected to a breakaway party of the ruling Party, the Botswana Movement for Democracy (BMD) in 2012 and went on to win the parliamentary seat under the BMD during the national elections in 2014 (Moloi 2015). His people easily switched allegiance to him politically. The role of the chief should be understood within the patriarchal system of Tswana societies where the male is dominant and powerful. This is an instance that can be collectively identified under 'chiefly or tribal' patriarchy of the African homestead because of its presence in African settlements (Bozzoli 1983; Morrell 1998).

Three Dikgosi Monument, a national monument and public heritage

When Botswana was declared a British Protectorate in 1885, chiefs remained with their power and worked closely with the Colonial Administrator based in the then capital, Mafikeng (Tlou and Campbell 1984). Among those in power were the Three Dikgosi, who are the main figures of the Three Dikgosi Monument (see Figure 8.1). Traditionally, nationalist history and cultural memory portrays these chiefs as initially against the establishment of the British Protectorate (Mogalakwe 2003; Ramsay 2015). However, in 1895, the British were ready to relinquish their power but this is when the Three Dikgosi travelled to England to meet Queen Victoria in order to protest against the threat of expansion by the British South Africa Company under Cecil John Rodes (Kutlwano Magazine 2013). Their request was granted, which extended the British protection until independence in 1966. Their travel journey is popular in Botswana with its history is taught from early childhood. The Three Dikgosi are celebrated for their bravery and nationalistic endeavour, which it believed led the country to independence, hence they are perceived as the 'Founders of the Nation' (Parsons 2006: 679). Sir Seretse Khama, an heir to the Bangwato chieftaincy and the grandson of Khama III, was inaugurated as the first president of post-independent Botswana. His philosophy was geared towards nationality rather than tribal identity as portrayed by the choice of Setswana as a national language for all (Werbner 2004).

The Three Dikgosi Monument is composed of three 5.4m high bronze statues depicting the three chiefs as in Figure 8.1. It was funded by the state and erected as a national monument in the Central Business District of the capital city, Gaborone, in 2005 to celebrate their roles. In order to emphasize its national value, it was unveiled by the President of Botswana, H.E. Festus Mogae, who praised the role of the chiefs for seeking protection against a greater enemy, Cecil John Rhodes (Parsons 2006). It is often echoed that, if it was not for their journey, the current nation-state would be non-existent and this is why the monument is national, meant for the whole people of Botswana. As with other gazetted monuments, it is under the custodianship of the National Museum and Monuments (then known as the National Museum, Monuments and Art Gallery). As an elevated national

Figure 8.1 The Three Dikgosi Monument, Gaborone, Botswana
Source: photograph by author.

identity symbol, the Three Dikgosi Monument is engraved with a national symbol, the Botswana's coat of arms just below the three chiefs (Figure 8.2). The symbol is strictly reserved for highly honoured matters of national significance like the country's currency, Pula and Thebe. Pula, which means rain, is also a national slogan that is echoed at the end of the national anthem. As expected, non-Tswana ethnic groups have raised their voices in protest against Tswana dominance from independence to the present period. The imagined role of the monument as a unifying factor in Botswana is contested because as Becker (2011) argues, the rationale for the creation and memory of monuments represent the creators, in this case the Botswana Government, rather than all the people of Botswana.

The erection of the Three Dikgosi Monument reflects the trend in postcolonial Africa where national monuments were erected to symbolize national identity (Becker 2011; Chirambo 2010). This was part of the establishment heritage institutions such as national museums, which were used by the new independent states to tell their own stories. Some countries were also named after monuments post-independence. For example, the change of the name Southern Rhodesia to Zimbabwe is a classic example of a national identity framed around built heritage or architecture (Vale 1999). The ruins of Great Zimbabwe whose origins were at one point the centre of contestation, symbolize many centuries of history of the country and it is used to unite and identify its people around a common cause. Another African example is that of post-independent Kenya where the statue of the first president, Jomo Kenyatta, was erected in the centre of Nairobi in 1963. Its importance was to celebrate his role in the country's independence and it was also meant to establish Kenyan national identity (Larsen 2011).

Three Dikgosi monument and celebrated masculinity

> Heritage is gendered, in that it is often too 'masculine', and tells a predominantly male-centred story.
>
> (Smith 2008: 159)

The above quote affirms what is often ignored in the interpretation of heritage, which is gender of the represented or the voice of the representer. This exclusion in itself results in misinterpretation of heritage because societies that are represented by the monuments are gendered. What is instead shown as gender is based on the biological differences of male and female but as always emphasized, gender even though linked to men and women is more than the physical body, it is a social construct of roles (Smith 2008). In this chapter, the Three Dikgosi commemorated at the Three Dikgosi Monument lived within a patriarchal Tswana society where the male masculinity is dominant. The three chiefs were powerful and glorified and hence not a mere coincidence that it was the men who were brave and travelled to unknown lands seeking extended protection for their people. The same have become the main symbol of national identity in Botswana, the constructed identity that the politicians of the time, equally masculine, wanted to voice out. The people of Botswana are supposed not to only remember the enormous roles of the chiefs in building up their nation, but they have to collectively identify with them. This is why after many years of debating the strategic location of the monument, the Central Business District was chosen to cement their importance (Parsons 2006). The gigantic statues in Figure 8.1 are compelling and one cannot miss their presence. Their posture seems to invite worship because visitors stand in awe and it is hoped that this experience can be translated to their national value.

The excluded past: the role of women

Some sources bring to light the political role of the regency of women in Tswana societies during the pre-colonial and colonial periods. Matemba (2005) notes instances where royal women became regents. In the early 1830s, Bobjwale, *Kgosi* Kgari's second wife, became a regent due to the absence of children from his first wife Mmapolao and the death of her (Bobjwale's) eldest son Khama II in 1834. As expected, this was not accepted by Sekgoma I, who was *Kgosi* Kgari's son from the third wife, and the rift led Bobjwale to flee from Bangwato to Bakwena (Matema 2005; Mooko 1999). Another example is that when Sekgoma II of Batawana died, his sister became a regent between 1927 and 1930. A few decades later still among Batawana, *Mohumagadi* Pulane (1912–1994) was installed as a regent between 1947 and 1956 after the death of her husband *Kgosi* Moremi III. The heir to the throne, *Kgosi* Letsholathebe II was still a minor. Mooko (1999) discusses the role of royal women among Bangwato and also shows that there were similar instances elsewhere. For example, Gaogangwe (1845–1924) who was the wife of Bathoen I, was appointed as a regent from 1923–1924 and her daughter Ntebogang (1882–1975) took over from 1924–1928 after her death. Of importance to note is that the women could only be installed as regents and not into full chieftaincy. They were guided by a council of men because they were still barred from the *kgotla*, which was designated for males only (Mooko 1999). Even in modern times after the installation of women as chiefs in Botswana, some women continue to be regents instead of assuming chieftaincy in the absence of men. The appointment of *Kgosi* Kealetile Moremi as Batawana regent in 2003 after the resignation of the paramount chief *Kgosi* Tawana II serves as an example (Matemba 2005). Her appointment into regency followed her uncle's appointment and consultation with the community. As expected, there were sections of the community who were against the appointment of a woman onto the throne. She continues to be the regent for the young heir to the throne, *Kgosi* Tawana II's son, Leatile Tawana Moremi.

Exclusion of the wives of the Three Dikgosi

The conceptual framework of this section is derived from the ethnography of Tswana women who as in other African cultures and most parts of the world are the backbones of their families and marriages. Traditionally their tasks were both public- and private-domain oriented, an important aspect that does not fall within the gendered activities (Mafela 1997) or structuralism's binary opposites used to categorize roles of women in archaeology (Gilchrist 1999). The tasks included ploughing in the fields (*masimo*), building and repairing houses and courtyards (*lolwapa*), fetching firewood and food preparation. Once married, women acquired a status in which they were expected to run the affairs of their home diligently. She first becomes the caretaker of her husband and is eventually expected to bear him children who will become heirs. This is even more important in royalty as chieftaincy is passed down from father to the eldest son. The chores were much heavier when compared to those of men, which were hunting, herding cattle, milking cows and preparation of animal skins (Moffat 1842). Morally too, a woman was expected to upkeep moral standards of the family (Mannathoko 1999). As much as she was expected to run her household diligently, a woman in Tswana communities was placed below a man and her role viewed as inferior with lesser capabilities (Nkomazana 2008).

Based on these arguments, a hypothesis of the roles of each of the three wives of the chiefs is hence formulated. A queen (*mohumagadi*) was holistically responsible for the well-being of the chief, which included his image in the public. One of her main requirements was to bear a male heir to continue the royal lineage. Failure to conceive or have a male child resulted in the lineage moving down to the second or third wife's family. It could even change to the chief's brother in extreme scenarios. When one applies the roles to the importance of the mission to England in 1895, the wives must have prepared for the trip well in advance. I imagine how the three wives, *Mohumagadi* Sefakwana, the wife of *Kgosi* Khama III, *Mohumagadi* Ikanyeng, the wife of *Kgosi* Sebele I and *Mohumagadi* Gagoangwe, the wife of *Kgosi* Bathoen I, must have started the preparations after being told about the imminent journey abroad in those days when travel took longer by sea. First, the mental preparation would consist of continuous reminders of the importance of the chiefs' mission abroad to ensure the protection of their land, which was then demarcated into reserves. The magnitude of their roles as chiefs to save their people would be echoed. Second, the wives would have packed all the administrative aspects of the trip at home including all types of letters and other paperwork needed to present their case would be neatly packed and rechecked by the wives. For example, petitions sent to Chamberlain (Schmitt 2006). The public image of Dikgosi in a 'white' man's land would have pre-occupied *bahumagadi* even more. Utmost preparation of clothes was done to ensure that their husbands were dressed appropriately, if not to impress. The iconic images of the chiefs in Figure 8.1 speak silently about the women behind the scenes. The last important messages must have been relayed on the eve of the departure to Capetown on 6 August 1895 and lastly summarised on the departure day. The roles of wives were therefore holistic, including ruling with their husbands, but they are sorely celebrated in Three Dikgosi Monument. Upon returning home, the chiefs would have first gone home to share their amazing journey with the anxiously waiting wives before the rest of their communities. As Bowser and Patton (2004) explain, the house is a space where political decisions are made and therefore a political space where important decisions are made. Therefore, the political role of the wives cannot remain invisible and less important because they, together with their husbands, made political decisions. Hence they deserve to be also celebrated in Botswana's national heritage.

Perhaps the fact that the monument's project team was all male was a coincidence, but one wonders if the presence of a woman might have had an impact. When interviewed and asked why the chief's wives were not included on the monument, the project team leader's response was that they did not think about gender then, but the museum currently would like to be inclusive of women. He was quick to mention that the women are included on the surrounding pillars and this means there was gender consideration. The women are portrayed under pillars of Endurance and Independence but there is no direct link with the roles of chiefs in 1895 (Figure 8.2). The other three pillars at the monument depict men with captions of Tshireletso (Protection), Bogaka (Heroism) and Botshabelo (Refuge).

Figure 8.2 Boitshoko pillar at the Three Dikgosi Monument
Source: photograph by author.

The three terms are self-explanatory and reflects what the three chiefs are perceived to be in Botswana. Cementing why the government decided to celebrate them through a national monument.

Analysis of informants' responses

In order to obtain other perspectives on this topic, I sought feedback from the Monument's visitors through questionnaires and direct observations between May 2015 and October 2015. The questionnaires were distributed through the Monument's and National Museum's front officers. Out of the 100 questionnaires distributed, only 48 responded. Out of these, 25 were males while 23 were females. I first wanted to know the sex and gender of the respondents and all the informants' sex matched the common knowledge of gender. That is, female is feminine and male is masculine, as one respondent answered:

> 3DM5: Male is masculine, biological. Please review your knowledge on this.

Clearly the respondent was unhappy with my study as captured further below.

> Question: Would the Three Dikgosi Monument have the same meaning if the wives of the three Dikgosi were included as part of the monument? Why or Why not?
>
> 3DM5: 'I disagree with this suggestion. This is not family. They should not become part of this.'

The other male respondents stated that the wives did not go to England and including them would change the monument's meaning. On the other hand, the responses from the women were open to the inclusion of the wives of the Dikgosi on the monument. Another respondent answered the same question with:

> 3DM4: It would still have the same meaning because for the three chiefs to be looking that smart a wife packed clean clothes for her husband, she made sure he was well fed and looked after him to negotiate such a task.

When asked if the monument would still have the same meaning if the chiefs were women, she argues that the meaning would not change but the challenge is that men command more respect in Africa than women unlike in other countries such as the United Kingdom where democracy and freedom (liberation) have made some progress in addressing gender bias when compared to developing countries. What the answers reflect is how patriarchy was handed down from one generation to the other and the inequality of gender roles is an accepted stereotype. The application to the Three Dikgosi Monument shows how patriarchy in Tswana culture has been passed on and shaped the interpretation of heritage. This is why gender has to be understood within the context of the broader social relations of communities (Blake 2014). It is easy for the local visitors to appreciate the role of the three chiefs and view them as national icons because men were doing what they had to do, that is, protect their people as they would protect their families. It was not a woman's job to seek protection. This idolizes men and this is why most locals visit the monument to see the great men who rescued their people. As expected, the monument is very popular and is used and visited for various reasons. It is documented as the most visited place in Gaborone (HATAB 2015; Seretse 2008). It is now the most popular meeting place for public events such as non-governmental organizations. School group visits from within and outside Gaborone are very common especially during school vacations. The Monument's guides are passionate in their interpretation because of its national importance. They seem to want to ensure that no visitor leaves the monument without appreciating the role of the Three Dikgosi.

Direct observations of visitors during the already mentioned research period revealed a trend in which members of the public from offices in the neighbourhood had their lunch on the monument's garden benches. These were mostly daily users who seemed not to notice the three figures because of their frequent use of the space. They tended to head straight to the rest benches for their meals and leave without any observable interaction with the figures compared to perhaps their first visit to the site. Some of the sitting postures was facing opposite the

Figure 8.3 A group of friends at the Three Dikgosi Monument
Source: photograph by author

statues and leaving without any facing them. The observation also showed that of all the uses of the monument, photography was the most common because of its aesthetic value. The monument is very attractive and its gigantic posture becomes a beautiful background for photographs. What I observed was a balanced use by both males and females in taking photographs of themselves. For example, the friends in Figure 8.3 were on a girls' day out and went to the monument to take beautiful pictures. When informally asked about why they chose the Monument, their response was that they did not think deeply about its historic value.

When asked about how the chiefs' wives could be positioned if included on the monument, 3DM4 suggests a family setting around the fire to reflect how the chiefs and their families relaxed at home. The ladies' posture and dress in Figure 8.3 could not be an acceptable image of the wives of the three chiefs around their husbands if they were to be incorporated onto the statues. This is because in Tswana social settings, a woman does not wear trousers during social ceremonies such as funerals, wedding negotiations or *kgotla* meetings. *Bahumagadi* would, in fact, be criticized if they wore trousers, especially with their husbands in public, as it would be a symbol of dishonour and disrespect. A befitting posture could have been women wearing dresses and covering themselves with a *mogagolwane* (shoulder blanket). They could be sited near their husbands to show them respect and submission.

Conclusion

It is possible that this chapter may be perceived to be by a feminist scholar who probably does not respect her culture and chiefs but unless heritage interpretation is gendered to include all roles, values and performances of all genders then all aspects of the past will be biased (Levy 2013). The exclusion of women in heritage representations is visible in disciplines such as archaeology, art history and museums (Machin 2008). Positive results have emerged globally from the gender archaeology debates such as the construction of women's museums in the 1980s beginning with the Bonn Women's Museum/Frauenmuseum Bonn in 1981 (Krasny and Women's Museum Merano 2013). In Botswana, it can begin with honouring numerous women and their roles through heritage. Monuments of the first female chiefs, *Kgosi* Rebecca Banika and *Kgosi* Mosadi Seboko should be erected as national heritage as they signify major paradigm shifts in Tswana customs. This occurrence can be a public display of the inclusiveness of all gender in the country's sociocultural landscape. The roles of the female chiefs is also equivalent to that of males. For example, the recent call for initiation by *Kgosi* Seboko and the naming of *mephato* (regiments) was in the past only expected to be carried out by male chiefs (Setlhabi 2014). The female chiefs also wear leopard's skin that symbolizes royalty, as was seen during the coronation of *Kgosi* Mosadi Seboko as the first female paramount chief in Botswana.

This should be celebrated even though critiques could argue that women should hunt and kill their own leopard as male chiefs. Chiefs are draped with the leopard skin of their own kill. The complete hunting process for a leopard is an example of women's exclusion. What is celebrated is the final process, that is, the actual hunt and omitting the preparation, which includes their wives at home. The send-off at the *kgotla* always includes women. The symbolism of wearing a leopard's skin has royal value despite the person who hunted the animal. I argue that the Three Dikgosi Monument is a celebration of masculinity of Tswana communities combined with a national value. The roles of their wives are invisible, as they are not captured through their statues, publications or interpretations of the monument. *Bahumagadi* also deserve national honour similar to their husbands. I recommend their inclusion on the Three Dikgosi Monument to enhance its meaning. They can be mounted next to their husbands because of the earlier arguments that they were the powers behind their husbands. Their posture once included on the monument could be either standing next to their husbands or seated in front of them. The monument's central space can be regularly changed with rotating exhibitions of Dikgosi without any gender discrimination based on sex or sexual orientation. The celebration of citizens through national monuments should encompass non-royalty, for example, prominent women such as Dr Gaositwe Chiepe, one of the longest Member of Parliament and the first woman in Botswana to acquire a PhD. Unity Dow, the first woman judge with a documented citizenship landmark. Their roles have been equally important as that of the celebrated males.

One of the few symbolic importances of *bahumagadi* is in Tswana burials where they are honoured like men and their roles during their lives are also honoured. For example, *Mohumagadi* Seingwaeng, who is known for being a peace broker during the conflict between the colonial administration and her son *Kgosi* Molefi, is honoured at the Bakgatla Royal Cemetery in Mochudi (Legodimo 2012). The graveyard is part of the village heritage trail where the public is informed about the history and Bakgatla-ba-Kgafela heritage. The same applies to the Bangwato Royal Cemetery where the first president of Botswana, Sir Seretse Khama, a chief-turned politician, was buried. His wife, Ruth Khama was also buried at the Bangwato Royal Cemetery next to her husband 1992 (Akyeampong and Gates 2012).

As I conclude, I ponder on the question 'What if the Three Dikgosi were women?' The answer is found in the whole discussion through the demonstration of how heritage in Botswana celebrates masculinity over roles of women. Sarcastically one can argue that it was impossible to have female paramount chiefs then but if they were there could they be presently celebrated the same way as their male counterparts? My answer is NO, they would not be celebrated nationally the same way as the men through the Three Dikgosi Monument due to the persistent presentation of masculinity in heritage. Perhaps they would equally be labelled 'Mothers of the Nation' and celebrated individually in their villages. It is hoped that by highlighting in this chapter the important roles that women have played in Botswana and specifically the exclusion of the wives of the Three Dikgosi, the bias towards masculine presentation of heritage will lead to a balanced gendered landscape where both male and female roles are celebrated.

References

Akyeampong, E.K. and Gates, H.L. (eds) 2012. *Dictionary of African Biography*. Oxford: Oxford University Press.

Balozwi, B. 2014. Grey and shrinking – the state of Botswana's feminist movement. *Sunday Standard Online*, 2 March. Available at: www.sundaystandard.info/grey-and-shrinking-%E2%80%93-state-botswana%E2%80%99s-feminist-movement (accessed 25 May 2016).

Bauer, G. 2011. Update on the women's movement in Botswana: have women stopped talking? *African Studies Review*, 54(2): 23–46.

Becker, H. 2011. Commemorating heroes in Windhoek and Eenhana: memory, culture and nationalism in Namibia, 1990–2010. *Africa*, 81(4): 519–543.

Blake, J. 2014. Gender and intangible cultural heritage. In P. Keenan, K. Nowacka and L. Patchett (eds), *Gender Equality Heritage and Creativity*. Paris: UNESCO, pp. 49–59.

Bowser, B.J. and Patton, J.Q. 2004. Domestic spaces as public places: an ethnoarchaeological case study of houses, gender, and politics in the Ecuadorian Amazon. *Journal of Archaeological Method and Theory*, 11(2): 157–180.

Bozzolli, B. 1983. Marxism, feminism and Southern African Studies. *Journal of Southern African Studies*, 9(2): 139–171.

Campbell, A. 1998. The present status of archaeology in Botswana. In P. Lane, A. Reid and A.K. Segobye (eds), *Ditswammung The Archaeology of Botswana*. Gaborone: Pula Press and the Botswana Society, pp. 249–259.

Chirambo, R.M. 2010. A monument to a tyrant, or reconstructed nationalist memories of the father and founder of the Malawi nation, Dr. H.K. Banda. *Africa Today*, 56(4): 2–21.

Engelstad, E. 2007. Much more than gender. *Journal of Archaeological Method and Theory*, 14(3): 217–234.

Gilchrist, R. 1999. *Gender and Archaeology: Contesting the Past*. London: Routledge.

Government of Botswana. 1992. *Attorney-General v. DOW 1992 BLR 119* (CA). Gaborone: Government Printers.

Government of Botswana. 2008. *Bogosi ACT*. Gaborone: Government Printers.

HATAB. 2015. Botswana Pride. *HATAB (Hospitality and Tourism Association of Botswana)*. Available: www.this-is-botswana.com/index.php/component/content/category/21-botswana.html (accessed 19 September 2015).

Holm, J.D. and Botlhale, E. 2008. Persistence and decline of traditional authority in modern Botswana politics. *Botswana Notes and Records*, 40: 74–87.

Human Rights Watch/Africa Human Rights Watch Women's Rights Project. 1994. *Botswana: Second-Class Citizens: Discrimination Against Women Under Botswana's Citizenship Act*, vol. 6, No. 7. Available: www.hrw.org/sites/default/files/reports/BOTSWANA0994.pdf (accessed 23 January 2017).

Jewkes, R., Morrell, R., Hearn, J., Lundqvist, E., Blackbeard, D., Lindegger, G., Quayle, M., Sikweyiya, Y. and Gottzén, L. 2015. Hegemonic masculinity: combining theory and practice in gender interventions. *Culture, Health & Sexuality*, 17(2): 112–127.

Johnson, M. 2010. *Archaeological Theory: An Introduction*. Second edition. Oxford: Wiley-Blackwell.

Keitumetse, S.O. 2011. Sustainable development and cultural heritage management in Botswana: Towards sustainable communities. *Sustainable Development*, 19(1): 49–59.

Kiyaga-Mulindwa, D. and Segobye, A.K. 1994. Archaeology and education in Botswana. In P.G. Stone and B.L. Molyneaux (eds), *The Presented Past Heritage, Museums and Education*. London: Routledge, pp. 46–59.

Krasny, E. and Women's Museum Merano, 2013. *Women's: Museum Curatorial Politics in Feminism, Education, History, and Art*. Vienna: Löcker Verlag.

Kutlwano Magazine, 2013. *Kutlwano Magazine*, 51(6). Gaborone: Government Printing Press.

Larsen, L. 2011. Notions of nation in Nairobi's Nyayo-Era Monuments. *African Studies*, 70(2): 264–283.

Legodimo, C. 2012. The iconic Bakgatla royal graveyard. *Mmegi*, 21 September. Available: www.mmegi.bw/index.php?sid=7&aid=1404&dir=2012/September/Friday21 (accessed 5 July 2015).

Levy, J.E. 2013. Gender feminism and heritage. In P.F. Biehl and C. Prescott (eds), *Heritage in the Context of Globalization Europe and the Americas*. New York: Springer, pp. 85–95.

Machin, R. 2008. Gender representation in the natural history galleries at the Manchester Museum. *Museum and Society*, 6(1): 54–67.

Mafela, L. 1997. Competing gender ideologies a conceptual framework for the analysis among Batswana women of Botswana. c.1840–c.1994. *Pula: Botswana Journal of African Studies*, 11(2): 155–165.

Mannathoko, C. 1999. What does it mean to be a middle-class woman in Botswana? In C. Zmroczek and P. Mahony (eds), *Women and Social Class: International Feminist Perspectives*. London: University College London Press, pp. 9–24.

Matemba, Y. 2005. A chief called 'woman': historical perspectives on the changing face of bogosi (chieftainship) in Botswana 1834–2004. *JENdA: A Journal of Culture and African Women Studies*, 7: 18–29.

Matemba, Y. 2010. Continuity and change in the development of moral education in Botswana. *Journal of Moral Education*, 39(3): 329–343.

Maundeni, Z. 2005. Succession to high office: Tswana culture and modern Botswana politics. In Z. Maundeni (ed.), *40 Years of Democracy in Botswana: 1965–2005*. Gaborone: Mmegi Publishing, pp. 80–93.

Moffat, R. 1842. *Missionary Labours in Southern Africa*. London: John Shaw.

Mogalakwe, M.M. 2003. Botswana: an African miracle or a case of mistaken identity? *Pula: Botswana Journal of African Studies*, 17(1): 85–94.

Moloi, E. 2015. Chiefs and politics: time will tell. *Botswana Guardian*, 14 September. Available: http://botswanaguardian.co.bw/news/item/1500-chiefs-and-politics-time-will-tell.html (accessed 15 September 2015).

Mooko, T. 1999. The role of royal women in Bangwato politics under the regency of Tshekedi Khama, 1926–1949. *Pula: Journal of African Studies*, 3(1/2): 46–60.

Morna, L.C. and Tolmay, S. (eds), 2006. *At the Coalface: Gender and Local Government in Botswana*. Johannesburg: Gender Links.

Morrell, R. 1998. Of boys and men: masculinity and gender studies in Southern African Studies. *Journal of Southern African Studies*, 24(4): 605–630.

Ngcongco, L. 1979. The origins of the Tswana. *Pula: Botswana Journal of African Studies*, 1(2): 21–46.

Nkomazana, F. 2008. The experiences of women within Tswana cultural history and its implications for the history of the church in Botswana. *Studia Historiaesticae*, 34(2): 83–116.

Parsons, N. 2006. Unravelling history and cultural heritage in Botswana. *Journal of Southern African Studies: Special Issue Heritage in Southern Africa*, 32(4): 67–82.

Ramsay, J. 2015. The establishment of the protectorate (part 4) – 'Warren at Molepolole'. *Mmegi*, 23 June. Available: www.mmegi.bw/index.php?aid=51909&dir=2015/june/15#sthash.L0T0pWJZ.dpuf (accessed 7 July 2015).

Reid, A., Lane, P., Segobye, A., Borjeson, L., Mathibidi, N. and Sekgarametso, P. 1997. Tswana architecture and responses to colonialism. *World Archaeology, Special Issue Culture Contact and Colonialism*, 28(3): 370–392.

Samatar, A.I. 1999. *An African Miracle: State and Class Leadership and Colonial Legacy in Botswana Development*. Portsmouth, NH: Heinemann.

Schapera, I. 1942. *A Short History of the Bakgatla-baga-Kgafêla of the Bechuanaland Protectorate*. Capetown: University of Cape Town Press.

Schmitt, D.A. 2006. *The Bechuanaland Pioneers and Gunners*. Westport, CT: Praeger.

Selolwane, O. 2004. Profile: The Emang Basadi Association. *Feminist Africa*, 3.

Seretse, G. 2008. Monuments worth visiting. *Mmegi*, 17 October. Available: www.mmegi.bw/index.php?sid=7&aid=14&dir=2008/October/Friday17 (accessed 21 September 2015).

Setlhabi, K.G. 2014. The politics of culture and the transient culture of *bojale*: Bakgatla-Baga-Kgafela women's initiation in Botswana. *Journal of Southern African Studies*, 40(3): 459–477.

Smith, L. 2008. Heritage, gender and identity. In B. Graham and H. Peter (eds), *The Ashgate Research Companion to Heritage and Identity*. Aldershot: Ashgate, pp. 159–178.

Sorensen, M.L.S. 2004. The archaeology of gender. In J. Bintliff (ed.), *A Companion to Archaeology*. Oxford: Blackwell, pp. 75–91.

Tlou, T. and Campbell, A. 1984. *History of Botswana*. Gaborone: Macmillan Botswana.

Vale, L.J. 1999. Mediated monuments and national identity. *The Journal of Architecture*, 4: 391–408.

Werbner, R. 2004. *Reasonable Radicals and Citizenship in Botswana: The Public Anthropology of Kalanga Elites*. Bloomington, IN: Indiana University Press.

Chapter 9

Exploring identities through feminist pedagogy

Viv Golding

Introduction

This chapter reflects on the power of collaborative feminist praxis at a range of heritage sites, including museums, around the world. It references numerous case studies, notably an Arts and Humanities Research Council funded project (AHRC 2011–2013) entitled 'Behind the Looking-Glass: "Other"-Cultures-Within Translating Cultures', which was part of the AHRC's 'translating cultures' theme. This networking project brought together academics from 10 universities in the UK, Europe, USA and the Caribbean to consider how interdisciplinary challenges and affective multisensory experiences can productively address the historical and political contexts within which heritage is located. AHRC participants shared their distinct perspectives from the disciplinary fields of literature, museum studies, history, sociology and anthropology at regular skype and face-to-face meetings, which enabled wider dissemination through academic publication and conference: 'Other Cultures Within: Beyond the Naming of Things' (2012) at the Kluge Center, Library of Congress in Washington and 'Perspectives from "Other" Cultures Translating Cultures' (2013) at Goldsmiths College in London (Golding 2013a, 2013b). In addition, network colleagues engaged in seminar workshops with each other's students in Leicester, Grenada and Oxford. This chapter considers one project conducted at the Pitt Rivers Museum in Oxford with Dr Maria Lima and her graduate students from Geneseo, the State University of New York – a public liberal arts college in the USA. Geneseo students, from a range of disciplinary backgrounds, examined the construction of cultural identity and the possibilities for collaborative and creative sharing of knowledge(s) to facilitate fresh acts of translation at this site (Golding and Lima 2015).

The AHRC project also draws on 15 years teaching experience with international post-graduate students of museum studies at the University of Leicester UK (2002–) and 10 years teaching schoolteachers and pupils at the Horniman Museum in London (1992–2002). Overall, the chapter observes collaborative academic praxis that aims to counter the misrepresentation and silencing of certain communities, too often the poor, Black, women, at heritage sites around the world. While the chapter discusses work with university students and not a range of audiences, it outlines a number of creative resistances to subjection over time and space, which point to new ways of working that might open our field to fresh interpretations and more diverse visitors.

Theoretically drawing on Black feminist thought, philosophical hermeneutics, bricolage and creolisation theories, the chapter addresses key questions such as: what counts as heritage, for whom, who writes historical accounts, who listens and why? These are key questions that have been considered in the heritage and gender literature, for example, by Jo Littler and Roshi Naidoo (2005) in their edited volume focusing on 'race' and the global politics of representation. In Sweden Casja Lagerkvist (2006) observes the contested histories and lingering power politics undermining attempts to empower African voices while in the UK Sam Alberti and Bernadette Lynch (2010) note similar attempts to share ownership of museum discourse.

Laurajane Smith (2006), whose notion of Authorised Heritage Discourse (AHD) helps account for the widespread Eurocentric, white, privileged male focus that dominates and hampers alternative views of heritage and history. Smith and Campbell (2015) present a strong challenge to the received legitimacy of the AHD at British manor houses and draw attention to the multiple perspectives required in interpretation and programming at heritage sites for 'transformative' learning to occur (Mezirow *et al.* 2000). This requires the profession to engage visitors emotionally and not simply cognitively in the face of 'difficult' histories such as transatlantic enslavement, where high degrees of imagination and emotional intelligence proved helpful to counter the authoritative nature of museum institutions as conveyors of absolute and accurate scientific truths (Fouseki and Smith 2013).

Specifically, the chapter argues for a creolised, responsible feminist pedagogy, which like the heritage literature noted above is at heart dialogical. In other words, the chapter outlines a conversational model of heritage pedagogy, which highlights careful listening and speaking among all participants – heritage professionals and audiences – to raise diverse voices and visibilities at a region theorised as the frontiers. This is the site of affective relation, a zone of danger and imaginative effort – a productive 'both-and' location of new situated knowledge and identity construction for glocal communities – which lays beyond negative 'either/or' binaries to progress embodied learning and enrich intercultural understandings (Golding 2009, 2013a, 2013b).

The pedagogic practice discussed in this chapter that has been developed with graduate and post-graduate students aims to progress social justice and human rights in the museum and ambitiously in the wider world. It is innovatively rooted in the seemingly diverse fields of hermeneutic philosophy (Gadamer 1981) and feminism, drawn especially from Black women writers (Hill-Collins 1991; Lorde 1996). The chapter outlines museum pedagogy developed in the manner of the bricoleur, which as Claude Levi-Strauss explains

uses devious means ... a heterogeneous repertoire which, even if extensive is nevertheless limited. [Bricolage] has to use this repertoire, however, whatever the task in hand because it has nothing else at its disposal ... to 'make do with whatever is at hand' ... to bring out differences and similarities ... to engage in a sort of dialogue ... [put] something of himself [/herself] into it.
(Levi-Strauss 1989: 16–21)

Jaques Derrida reinforces this notion, writing of the bricoleur using the instruments she finds around her, adapting and changing them when necessary, or trying 'several of them at once, even if their form and their origin are heterogeneous' (Derrida 1995: 285). In other words, the chapter and bricolage structure mark a number of border-crossings, which have been found helpful, to address the limitations inherent in any single system, theory or method, at institutions such as the museum here. Bricolage helps me present a challenge to the traditional museum discourse, which erases the multifaceted identities of 'others' – Black people, women, working-class, young or disabled people.

Writing from the field of higher education and teacher training, Shirley Steinberg and Joe Kincheloe (2010) employ the concept of bricolage to reconceptualise the critical pedagogy of Paolo Freire (1970/1996) in ways that are useful to the museum context I outline, since they also take ideas from feminism, post-colonialism and hermeneutics to progress moral social relations. Bricolage in their hands frees theorists from the single-point perspective and enables looking through a more complex lens with the aim of progressing 'emancipatory democracy' that vitally involves dialogue and action. If we apply their argument in the museum context, individuals can develop a new critical consciousness and abilities to analyse and contest established power structures, which in turn may empower movement beyond accepted notions shaped by dominant discourses.

Research background

It is important to note here at the outset that collaborative praxis was initiated with Joan Anim-Addo and the Caribbean Women Writers Alliance (CWWA) in the early 1990s, at the borderlands or frontiers between the Horniman Museum and The Caribbean Centre of Goldsmiths College London (Golding 2009, 2013a, 2013b). Our collaboration regards museum visitors as essentially active individuals and members of social groups constructing personal meaning(s) and identities in museums, rather than acting as passive receptacles for taken-for-granted knowledge (Rounds 2010). Notably, our original collaborative research team of school and university colleagues continues to develop 'situated' practice and 'standpoint' epistemology (Haraway 1991; Hill-Collins 1991), most recently during AHRC research that built on almost two decades of activity around increasing plurivocality at the museum and university frontiers. Collaboration is not 'one-off' or tokenistic, but sustained.

In our AHRC research plurivocality aims ultimately to empower individuals and communities to interrogate existing interpretations both inside and outside the museum. These existing structures, too often negatively locate certain 'others', such as Black people, against 'us' white folk, through stereotypical framing of cultural objects. But, as this chapter highlights, museums need not continue to do so. Specifically, the chapter outlines how fresh uses of ethnographic collections and Black women's writing in the museum and university, can promote these institutional spaces as sites for active reflection and reinterpretation, highlighting the complexity of cultural identities to challenge essentialism and broaden future lives.

AHRC funding enabled us as academics to work collaboratively with each other's graduate and post-graduate students at our different university and museum sites and progress a diversity of voices among our student bodies. Despite the elite nature of higher education in general, the student groups we worked with were ethnically diverse, Howard University in Washington, DC, for example, is a historically 'black' institution. We note this point here as while our students had already made a giant leap across the borders of low expectations and academic achievement, the socio-economically 'uneven world' in which we live demands consistent efforts to spotlight and challenge injustice that presents barriers to the most prestigious jobs following university (Rhadakrishnan 2003). To emphasise this point, we note there is only one Black Professor of English in any UK University, Joan Anim-Addo, which seems to speak of institutional racism. Shepherd (2011), drawing on data from The Higher Education Statistics Agency (HESA) highlights that out of 14,000 British professors only 50 are black and only 10 of these are women.

One 'Translating Cultures' collaboration with Dr Maria Lima from Geneseo University in the USA at the Pitt Rivers Museum in Oxford in 2013 will help unpack these ideas. Lima and a group of 18 international graduate students were taking a course on the politics and affective power of texts and contexts, which included Joan Anim-Addo's *Imoinda* (2003/2008). We wanted the students to explore the potential for *Imoinda* within the museum to prompt productive moments of 'Relation' (Glissant 1997) through 'bricolage' or critical thinking. Pitt Rivers offered a site for individuals and their social groups to explore 'difficult' (Macdonald 2009) colonial histories and find a connection to each other. Drawing on Audre Lorde we envisaged the museum and the university examining our commonalities 'through our differences and making them strengths' (Lorde 1996: 159). Our project work involved a series of collaborative teaching workshops designed with the Pitt Rivers education team, notably Head of Education Andy McLellan and his colleague Salma Caller, who creatively engaged our students with ways in which the museum's tangible and intangible global heritage resonate in the transnational space inherent in *Imoinda*. Lima and I argue that studying Anim-Addo's work at a frontier site between the university and the museum enhanced student understandings of the text and the context from which it arises. Specifically, we note the value of our frontier work in progressing the critical thinking of the students, university lecturers and museum staff through establishing cognitive, emotional and sensory re-connections – relation – with material culture from around the globe to enrich intercultural knowledge.

Bricolage and creolising feminist pedagogy at the Pitt Rivers Museum

At the Pitt Rivers Museum Steinberg and Kincheloe's (2010) bricolage concept was useful. Their dialogical framework demands thinking about the historical operation of power, not simply nihilistically, but to explore ways in which people, previously excluded by race, class, gender, sexuality or geographical place, might be included (Aronowitz and Giroux 1991; Kincheloe 2001, 2008; Steinberg 2011). I argue that dialogue is central to critical museum education since it promotes connection and relation that is vital to creolisation theory, which I draw on here in the manner of the bricoleur.

Dialogue assumes a common language and during transatlantic enslavement as Éduoard Glissant (1990/2006: 34) notes, creolisation was attached to linguistics, 'limitless *Metissage*', which led to 'the adventure of multilinguism'. Bricolage is seen here to challenge notions of universalism, monolinguism and purity, building 'composite cultures' and community in the margins of power from all kinds of materials (Glissant 1997: 91). The concepts of bricolage and creolisation are connected here in preference to the more widespread term 'hybridity', which has a biological tone and problematic link with 'nature' where mixing two pure elements can weaken and lead to extinction.

Glissant's notion of relation is a vital part of creolisation theory that underpins the feminist pedagogy developed at the museum/university frontiers. Creolisation as Glissant (1997: 34) observes is 'not merely an encounter' but 'a new and original dimension' involved in creating something new. Relation points to the terrible colonial histories of enslavement and, most importantly, to the creative building of new community by displaced African people in Caribbean lands (Golding 2013a, 2013b). In the museum, creolising praxis is dialogical in essence. Like bricolage in critical theory it draws on feminism and philosophical hermeneutics to promote careful listening and speaking among teachers, students and museum specialists, striving to raise diverse voices especially of those silenced by the traditional museum framing of knowledge, through multisensory activities with museum objects that facilitate embodied learning.

Creolising museum pedagogy is most relevant to ethnographic museums. It shines a critical light on colonial histories, to better understand contemporary contexts, notably social inequalities, stereotype and racism that have historical roots and a stubborn persistence. The Pitt Rivers Museum in Oxford houses 22,092 ethnographic objects collected by Augustus Henry Pitt Rivers within a racial framework dominant in the nineteenth century and donated by him on 30 May 1882 (Chapman 1988). His typologically arranged displays, from the technologically 'simple' to the technologically 'complex', were designed to present visitors with Darwinian inspired theories on the evolution of human cultures.

These methodologically unsound, Eurocentric and prejudiced ideas were widely discredited in the early twentieth century and the museum website states, it 'does not (and could not) show the supposed evolution of objects', although it keeps the original exhibitionary organisation (Pitt Rivers Museum 2016).

Andy McClellan Head of Education at the Pitt Rivers Museum and his colleague Salma Caller wanted to work with our Geneseo students in the museum space, with the displays and handling collection of original objects from all over the world. Their 13 years of experience resonates in my 10 years (1992–2002) at the Horniman Museum. Our educational work shows diverse audiences can be engaged in dialogue on the museum and the politics of display evident in the organisation of the collections. At Pitt Rivers each case holds the original displays, so tightly packed with extraordinary objects of religious and cultural significance as well as items of daily life that audiences can easily become confused and disorientated. Perhaps this spatial dis-ease helps to shake us out of our theoretical comfort zones and established ways of thinking. Certainly, under the guidance of McClellan and Caller the whole museum becomes a space of experiential learning and the collections operate as pedagogical tools in dialogical praxis, which exemplifies the creolising feminist pedagogy we developed during the Translating Cultures project. The wide-ranging conversations McClellan and Caller lead in the museum are central to pedagogic practice, and vitally based on previous engagement with the project leaders.

McClellan and I have taught together at the University of Leicester on the MA in Museum Studies programme for some five years now and we know the importance of engaging each other in detail on the joint programme prior to the teaching events. We initiated an extensive email dialogue with Lima four months before the Geneseo students would start their 'Western Humanities II' course in Oxford (July 2013) to ensure our project would address their curricular needs. Western Humanities I and II are mandatory general education courses at Lima's institution, which endorses the Western thought of primarily male and white scholars (including Marx, Freud, Descartes, Locke and Rousseau) Lima locates the Triangular Trade at the centre of her curriculum in the single open category, 'a work from the twentieth (or twenty-first) century', to interrogate ideas of who counts as human today.

The 18 Geneseo students in Lima's Oxford group had explored theoretical notions of human nature and society from the seventeenth century to the present. They were beginning to perceive how the institution of slavery depended upon white colonists establishing dominance over Black bodies, minds and histories throughout the Americas, with racism as a lingering legacy of enslavement and colonial oppression long after the abolishment of slavery. With Lima the students were starting to reflect on the enduring hold of racism, ingrained in people's minds to the point of totally erasing the humanity of other-than-white-human beings. Audre Lorde helpfully reinforces the importance of addressing this aspect of oppression in our feminist pedagogy. Bringing her ideas to the museum, alongside our academic and institutional work, we note the need to recognise an outer world, where the real conditions of lived experiences can be investigated as that internalised 'piece of the oppressor planted deep inside each of us' (Lorde 1996: 170).

Lorde, a Black, Lesbian, poet, writes on contemporary identity as complex and rooted in history. She also highlights how racism and sexism are endemic to the racist legacy of historical oppression and need to be seen as intertwined for critical attention in our pedagogic praxis. Similarly, as will be obvious now, we are not separatist in our feminist positioning and take a creolising approach to the composition of our Oxford project's team leaders, three women and one man. We contend that it is not the sole responsibility of Black people to challenge racism nor women alone to challenge sexism, rather, it is by fighting together across race, gender and class lines that we can positively impact on injustice. Linked to our anti-separatist stance we also argue against essentialism and consider socio-political identities to be multi-faceted and dynamic. For example, while I was born into a very poor working-class family of mixed ethnicity, today I am part of the higher educational establishment and 'pass' as white, Lima also observes that while her students are of diverse ethnicities they are from middle-class families wealthy enough to afford the trip to the UK.

In Oxford Lima engaged the Geneseo group in a study of historical and personal identity focusing on Anim-Addo's (2003/2008) *Imoinda: Or She Who Will Lose Her Name*, which is the libretto of an opera that rewrites Apha Behn's (1688/2003) *Oroonoko*. Behn's prose fiction narrates the tragic love story of an enslaved African prince *Oroonoko* and an African princess *Imoinda* during the appalling Transatlantic Slave Trade. While in Behn's text Princess *Imoinda* is silent and eventually killed by Prince Oko,

Anim-Addo's *Imoinda* creatively 'counter-writes' a herstory from the perspective of the princess and a supportive new community of women who sing together in a chorus at intervals throughout the opera. Anim-Addo's 'counter-writing' gives the previously enslaved 'mute witness' voice and agency, as a 'subject in history'. We highlight Act 2 Scene 1 where aboard the 'Nightmare Canoe', which stands for the terrible historical time of the Middle Passage that reduced the African subject to c(h)attle or commodity, the women make a 'new family in sorrow' and develop strategies for survival (Anim-Addo 2003/2008: 57). This family is seen in the chorus of women and their 'affective solidarity' that represents community resistance. The final scene of *Imoinda* demonstrates community care when *Imoinda* chooses life for her baby, born of rape by the white master, rather than the choice of death in Toni Morrison's (1987) *Beloved. Imoinda*'s decision 'life', made with supportive calls from the chorus led by the maid *Esteizme*, points to the enslaved Black woman as organ of reproduction but also as mother and care-giver who determines the survival of the new nation.

Email exchange prior to the Geneseo museum visit helped us explore diverse ways that the museum workshops might support the student's *Imoinda* assignment and at our face-to-face meeting the week before the project we decided more precisely which parts of the collection might best resonate and fit Anim-Addo's text. The task of the museum collaboration was to work with objects and draw out connections between the imaginative contemporary work of *Imoinda* and the colonial histories on which it was based. In addition to the university/museum curriculum focusing on material culture and intangible heritage, Lima wanted the student assessment to be centrally considered in the museum work. It was eventually decided that the assessment would take two parts. First, the students would write a reflexive account of their learning, including their close reading of *Imoinda*, and the extent to which, if at all, the museum experience enhanced their understanding and appreciation of the text. In the second part of the assessment, the students would be required to design and produce a museum trail sheet, to engage a specific target audience with the *Imoinda* text and the museum's historical context. This dual aspect was intended to facilitate critical thinking on positioning, where we speak from and how we can connect with each other as humans across the divides of disciplines, time, space and age (Haraway 1991; Hill-Collins 1991).

Lima bravely entered this project as someone who did not visit museums, but she trusted my earlier collaborative work with Anim-Addo and McClellan. She was also impressed with the range of activities and events I conducted with Anim-Addo at the Horniman Museum, notably organising the first performance of the *Imoinda* opera (Act 1) with an original score by Junwon Ogungbe at the Horniman Museum in 1999. This *Imoinda* event was designed for families to mark 16 decades since the passage of the British Emancipation Bill and became part of annual programming with the handling collection of original objects (Golding 2009: 57). Our first-hand Horniman experience demonstrates the productiveness of transcultural interdisciplinarity for museum audiences, specifically that at the museum/university frontiers, stereotypical and biased ideas could be raised and questioned, in the course of dialogical exchange. It is through dialogical exchange and careful in-depth attention to real objects, their makers and users, that collaboration can present a broader and more positive view of African peoples and cultures, who are too often disparaged as a result of media representations of a starving and helpless populace (Amin-Addo 1999; Golding 2009).

The Horniman educational ethos resonates at Pitt Rivers where objects also inspire critical dialogue, as we will show. Similarly, in bricolage theory dialogue helps individuals develop a new critical consciousness and abilities to analyse and contest established power structures, which in turn may empower movement beyond accepted notions shaped by dominant discourses (Steinberg and Kincheloe 2010). Most importantly, dialogue or conversation that is not idle chatter but premised on a 'productive attitude' (Gadamer 1981: 264) is central to feminist pedagogy and it is to this special stance, embedded in philosophical hermeneutics that I now turn.

Philosophical hermeneutics: language, interpretation and dialogue

Today the term hermeneutics describes different theories of interpretation; all of which are premised on the employment of language to grasp and convey meaning.

As a university professor of English and a creative writer, Anim-Addo (2007) finds Gadamer's thought on language appealing and I have found it useful to progress literacy in the museum context (Golding 2009).

Pedagogically, we draw on Gadamer who recognises the central role of the knower, their background and their prior experience at the outset of the shaping of knowledge. His position aligns with Freire's (1970/1996: 50), which supports the learners' agency and opposes picturing people as passive objects because 'they cannot later become subjects'. Both theorists privilege language and Gadamer's notion of language 'living' in conversation. This can be seen as an art of 'philosophical midwifery' in 'Socratic dialogue', which is useful to feminist pedagogy (Corradi Fuimara 1995: 82, 143–168; Gadamer 1981: 432). The metaphor of birthing appeals to the feminist lens we employ as museum/university team leaders, we appreciate seeing dialogue as giving birth to new thought, which is communicated in 'dialogue' that is a 'discipline of questioning [responsiveness] . . . that guarantees truth' and is importantly distinct from manipulative or technical thinking (Gadamer 1981: 447).

At the Pitt Rivers Museum the student visitors, of whatever age and ability, spend a part of their visit engaged in face-to-face dialogue, which encourages posing questions about museum objects, working collaboratively with their teachers and the museum professionals. Importantly, posing questions leads to more questioning, which is a helpful idea for museum visitors since dialogue is never completed but 'adjourned' to be picked up again and again throughout our lives. Questioning is vital from pre-visit discussion to establish the knowledge base of the students and help them make connections between the new museum object and something familiar so that they can engage with the issues. To facilitate a flow of meaningful conversation in the museum we need to build on and extend the knowledge and interests of student visitors. Museum educators have object knowledge and working together with teachers' knowledge of students can best progress successful museum dialogue. Ideally, dialogue leads to further in-depth conversation and questioning after the visit rather than a single 'correct' answer.

Nina Simon offers helpful advice on posing questions in museums. She warns against asking questions that 'are too earnest, too leading, or too obvious to spark interest, let alone engagement'. Questions should not resemble 'nagging parents' or 'teachers who want parroted answers'. Nor should questions 'pander facetiously'. Most importantly Simon points to the 'intent on the part of the question-asker to listen to the answer' (Simon 2010: 139). Les Back (2007: 1) helpfully writes of active listening as an, 'art', which, if we employ his ideas in the ethnographic museum, requires us to 'pay serious attention' to the fragments, voices and stories that are passed over or ignored, since they challenge the meaning of events past and present. Such listening is a 'form of openness to others', not only 'one specific voice' but to the 'background and half muted' (Back 2007: 8). Careful listening then is part of the pedagogical responsibility of dialogue.

Notably, dialogue here challenges essentialist notions of value, of self and others. As Simone de Beauvoir (1973: 301) observes 'One is not born, but rather becomes, a woman', in other words she is constructed and subject to social limitations in cultural contexts, such as the museum. Our bricolage position is postmodern but not one of extreme relativism, since dialogical work aims to reach a 'common' understanding and like de Beauvoir's is deeply grounded in the analysis of established texts. Understanding is possible then. We are not trapped in the separate worlds of the relativist. On the contrary, dialogue in the museum can progress understanding, but, only if we examine our pre-conceived ideas or the prejudices that arise from our histories or traditions.

Prejudice, tradition and the circle of understanding where horizons fuse

We want to develop an optimistic thesis on understanding and sharing meaning as part of our human potential as creative language users in a shared world. Gadamer (1981: 239) does not write about the museum but his contention that 'prejudices' or preconceptions are an inescapable part of our lived experience is vital to museum pedagogy. Prejudices can hinder or help the hermeneutic task of understanding objects and other people and 'listening' with 'openness' to our partner (object or human) is critical for the positive power of prejudices to progress a sense of belonging together.

The notion that personal prejudices inevitably arise out of 'tradition' can also pertinently be applied to feminist pedagogy in museums. Gadamer's idea of tradition represents both the present-day 'horizon' of the interpreter, and the distant 'horizon' from which the object of interpretation or other person originates. The museum interpreters (staff working with teachers and students) are positioned in a socio-cultural world but they can come to understand another tradition or person by connecting with its contemporaneity, its meaning today. Tradition is a part of who we are then, but it does not fix us. In dialogue, we are capable of growth if we put the beliefs of our tradition 'at risk', in a 'fusion of horizons' with another tradition (Gadamer 1981: 239).

In the museum, interpreters need to approach the other tradition or person respectfully as a partner in communication. This respectful stance, in fellowship, is described as an 'I–Thou' relation by Gadamer (1981: 321) and echoes in Rastafarianism's idea of 'I and I' rather than 'me and you' in standard English. In successful 'I–Thou' dialogue our horizons fuse we can change our views. Ethnographic museums in particular, as a location of multiple traditions seem to offer places where a 'fusion of horizons' might be negotiated. While the ethnographic work of art has 'suffered an injury', becoming a museum object, possibly with a difficult history of colonial oppression, even looted, I-Thou dialogue 'protests' this injustice and bridges the gulf between past and present horizons, which fuse in new understandings (Gadamer 1981: 133).

The concept of the 'hermeneutic circle' further illuminates the fusion of horizons, describing understanding as a state of perpetual motion between 'the whole and the parts and back to the whole' (Gadamer 1981: 259). This circle of understanding is not a 'vicious circle' but one of 'positive possibility ... of knowing', which promises change and transformation from different starting points (Gadamer 1981: 235–236). It is borderland in-between location, a 'place between strangeness and familiarity' (Gadamer 1981: 262–263).

Gadamer's ideas usefully oppose binary thinking and break down the perceived barriers between theory and practice. His thought presents a model of learning as dialogue or conversation, which is valuable to bricolage and creolising feminist pedagogy, but there are serious weaknesses. Gadamer presumes a straightforward easy access to the dialogue and the questioning process but he neglects the difficulty of economically disadvantaged students or young people entering the museum conversation. He suggests that objects and people pose 'questions' for interpreters equally (Gadamer 1986: 59). Here Gadamer echoes Freire's pedagogy, which regards students not simply as docile listeners but as 'co-investigators' alongside their teachers (Freire 1970/1996: 98f), but Friere's ideal non-hierarchical positioning of teacher and student cannot be taken for granted in the museum. Feminist writers benefit museum pedagogy by addressing the socio-political weaknesses in philosophical hermeneutics.

Feminist-hermeneutic thought: situated knowledge(s) and standpoint texts

Feminist-hermeneutic dialogue vitally takes account of the social inequalities – the 'unsaid' – in past and present life-worlds, and centrally involves activist play with future possibilities. The 'unsaid' refers to the complexity of identity and social positioning that discriminates against Black women, for example, whose voices are ignored or erased in traditional museum collections. Mae Gwendolyn Henderson is helpful to the project of raising new voices in museums, she speaks of a 'multiple dialogic of differences' alongside a 'dialogic of identity' (Henderson 1993: 258) that might permit exploration of differences and similarities between as well as within individuals and social groups in the museum context.

Audre Lorde also deals with the 'unsaid', as the 'external manifestations of racism and sexism', which we internalise and that 'distort' our ideas of ourselves and others (Lorde 1996: 259). Lorde's thought breaks down hierarchical barriers between peoples and offers a tool for understanding and empowering all oppressed visitors to the museum, by recognising 'the other in ourselves' and using difference as a means of 'conducting creative dialogue' (Henderson 1993: 259–260).

These ideas resonate in Donna Haraway's feminist situated positioning. Haraway, like David Fleming (2015) notes we do not stand on a neutral ground, we all speak from somewhere. Haraway is suspicious of 'doctrines of scientific objectivity' that view 'objects of knowledge' as passive and inert things within 'a fixed and determined world', since these can serve 'the instrumentalist projects of destructive Western societies' and mask 'dominating interests' (Haraway 1991: 197). Patricia Hill-Collins (1991) is a key exponent of 'standpoint' theory, which reinforces Haraway's 'situated' theorising of multiple perspectives and knowledge(s). Standpoint theory foregrounds the 'texts' or work of black women intellectuals, writers and musicians without distinction, in a positive effort to erase dividing lines between discourse. The Black women's voices are the kernels of her epistemology since they articulate a complex standpoint about 'racism, sexism, violence, economic exploitation and cultural denigration' that has been suppressed by dominant discourses (Hill-Collins 1991: 22). 'Standpoint' texts do not make a claim to universal 'truth' but aim to provide 'a partial perspective on domination' (Hill-Collins 1991: 236). Most importantly for bricolage and the development of creolising museum pedagogy, the partial perspectives of these texts are not closed within the Black community, but are accessible to all readers who adopt the appropriate 'I–Thou' active listening attitude.

I cite Anim-Addo's *Imoinda* as a 'standpoint' text. Anim-Addo draws on Lorde, who describes herself as a warrior woman making 'common cause with others' throughout her life. Lorde argues for collaborative 'struggle', which recognises and builds on combinations of 'differences' as possible sources of increased power for oppressed people and both writers appeal to a concept of 'community', which presents a distinct possibility of building positive bridges between very disparate individuals. They offer no simple solutions or tools to aid bridge building and community but advise women to avoid the 'either or' dualist thinking that hinders mutual understanding. Their 'both-and' alternative is creativity, demonstrated in poetry, which helps break the chains that silence us and that featured in the Geneseo student experience at Pitt Rivers.

Geneseo student's engagement, reflection and *Imoinda* trails at Pitt Rivers

On the morning of the first workshop in Oxford, Geneseo students were shown a DVD performance of *Imoinda* at their Oxford College. Lima had facilitated this production in New York in 2008 at School of the Arts (SOTA), Rochester, New York. Seeing students of their age bring the text to life and discussing this 'translation' of the author's words provided an excellent introduction to the two-day event in the museum. The live voice and the Black characters taking centre stage in an opera production that challenged the traditional European art form, privileging African percussion, for example, and speaking creole, affected the students. The importance of questioning the truth-value of 'history' and the complex roles of individuals and communities from different walks of daily life was demonstrated. The performance also set the scene for the respectful 'dialogical' method that would engage them with objects, histories and the politics of display in the museum. At Pitt Rivers we wanted to bring new voices to consider the silenced issues of vital importance to all of us such as racism, prejudice, discrimination and stereotyping.

Andy McClellan welcomed us at the museum entrance with a warm smile and led us to a work-station that he had set up in the ground-floor gallery where he explained there would be four different activities of 30 to 60 minutes each, two sessions would be led by education staff, first him, then Salma, me and conservation staff. Andy started his session by outlining the history of the museum and then began showing us objects in his handling collection. His dialogical method exemplifies the feminist-hermeneutic practice I employed at Horniman with diverse audiences and illustrates how there is no feminist orthodoxy in the museum, men and women most effectively fight sexism together just as Black and white people challenge racism. For around 60 minutes Andy would hold up an object and start a conversation asking 'what do you think this is . . . have a good look . . . what is it made from . . . hold it . . . use your senses . . . what does the surface texture feel like . . . what sound does it make . . . does it have a smell . . .?'

Engaging physically and intellectually in conversation students are intrigued and come to understand, for example, that the gourd bottle made by Masai peoples in Kenya was used to contain a drink made from milk mixed with small amounts of cattle blood, which left an acrid smell behind. They were pleased to hear the cattle did not die as a result of bloodletting and began to appreciate the importance of research alongside handling and discussion to further knowledge. In discussion it became clear that the materials of the rattle made by Haida People from the north-west coast of Canada showed evidence of a life by the sea and forest. It also emphasised the importance of ceremony and the construction showed a strong aesthetic sense with skillful carving. Looking up from the table the Haida totem pole that dominated the end of the hall clearly exhibited similarly carved forms with the distinctive tapering lines and richly decorated surfaces. A Haida canoe was spotted hanging from the balcony and a paddle, not an oar that would be bigger with no rounded top, noted on the table.

Following this whole-group activity, Andy gave smaller groups of four students an object and a map of where similar ones could be found. The handling objects included small painted masks from Indonesia, wooden toys from Russia, shadow puppets from India, thumb pianos from Kenya, beaded necklaces from South Africa, Chinese shoes for children decorated with scary tigers to frighten demons who wanted to take the child's life, pieces of intricately woven kente textiles from Ghana and indigo printed cloth from Nigeria. Overall Andy's session pointed to what Glissant terms relation. Peoples around the world have common needs, for example, food, transport and shelter. We all want to mark special events in our lives and we do this in different ways with different objects according to our physical environment. Most importantly human beings do not stay in one place, we travel, intermarry, engage in warfare, and influence each other's cultural practices, not always for our mutual benefit.

Salma's session neatly expanded upon how people and objects travel to museums with complex biographies of entanglements. She began her session asking the students about their family backgrounds and cultural heritage. It transpired that only one student called herself 'pure' Chinese. Salma guided us around the museum highlighting objects from West and Central Africa that specifically related to the *Imoinda* text. Of special note are the Benin bronzes, which so impressively show the sophisticated culture and history of Benin City in Nigeria from the sixteenth century. Salma showed us photographs revealing the destruction of the Nigerian city and the looting by the British army in 1897 of the thousand plaques that covered the ruling Oba's palace. The impressively realistic and highly detailed plaques were made by the lost wax technique and sold to museums around the world, where they sit as testimony to the oppression of 'Others' during colonial times for selfish ends. From Central Africa, Salma showed us the display of Nkisi nail sculptures, which also strikingly pointed to hierarchies of power and control. Nkisi were traditionally used by shaman to seal contracts or settle disputes between parties, by banging a nail into the wooden figure the law is activated. Catholic missionaries who failed to notice the similarities of Christian imagery when Christ was nailed to the cross in Calvary deemed these incredible objects 'fetishes' and a mark of savagery. Musical instruments, masks and objects of daily life such as the beautiful beaded necklaces, ostrich egg beaded skirt panels and the cookware from Southern Africa gave some idea of the rich society that *Imoinda* would have experienced before enslavement.

A behind-the-scenes tour of the conservation centre and discussion with the conservators showed the students how the objects are cared for and why visitors cannot touch everything. We were especially fortunate to see the wonderful masks of Mende-speaking people from Sierra Leone. These are traditionally worn by elder women and show signs of female beauty in that part of the world – rings of fat around the necks – in marked contrast with the skinny models of the West. The conservators also showed us Gelede masks from the Yoruba-speaking peoples of Nigeria, which have symbols of power and strength – a tiger eating, a bird, or a motorbike – on top of a serene face. These masks were are traditionally worn by men to celebrate the elder women in their group who are thought to have a special power of flight and an ability to cause terrible mischief if not appeased.

My final powerpoint session drew attention back to the key theorists, notably Anim-Addo, and asked students to imagine the *Imoinda* performance on a loop display in the museum, how might they connect this production with the collection for diverse audiences. One slide included an audio clip of Anin-Addo reading a poem inspired by a 'maternity figure' made in the nineteenth century by Eloi Peoples from Nigeria housed in the Horniman. The poem, which was created during a series of 'Rewriting the Museum' adult workshops at Horniman, also referenced an enslaved woman *Sethe* from Toni Morrison's *Beloved*, pointing to the way the interpreter moves back and forth between historical and present-day times in making meaning or relation. Poetry was a vital way to empower audiences from four years old to elders in the Horniman and the acrostic and frame techniques we employed were outlined for the Geneseo students as possible features for assignment, to design their own trail for a specific target audience. Finally, some examples of museum trails from around the world were discussed and the student trail task clarified.

Student trails and their reflective statements

The student trails made empathetic connections between the historical times of *Imoinda* and contemporary time through questioning techniques. Nicole Curtis's museum trail connects 'good health and prosperity' as one of the diverse purposes underpinning African masks and masquerade, before asking her visitors: 'Draw your own mask. What would you use it for?' She maintains a friendly voice in her trail to reinforce relation or connection, asking 'How old are you? What do you like to do? What do you think Imoinda liked to do when she was your age?' Her 'I spy' gaming approach, directs visitors' attention: 'I spy something to sit on, . . . fight with, . . . wear on your head, . . . What am I?' Notably she carefully encourages visitors to reflect on enslavement and freedom, stating 'I became a slave. That means I was separated from my home and family, I couldn't eat sleep or play when I wanted to' before she asks 'What does freedom mean to you?' Additionally, Nicole offered her visitors an acrostic poem (writing the word down the page and using each letter to start a line of poetry) in her trail. She writes of Imoinda's enduring strength and identity despite enslavement.

> **I**moinda is a strong
> **M**atriarchal figure
> **O**f the Caribbean
> **I**nhabiting culture and society
> **N**ot even the slave owner and
> **D**river could take
> **A**way her strength, past and identity
> (Curtis 2013)

Poetry, as Lorde (1996: 95–96) notes 'is not a luxury' but can be part of a personal political activism. Asking visitors to write an acrostic poem on the *Imoinda* text can help creolise the museum, by affectively engaging visitors' creativity in the construction of something new.

Simone Grey highlighted the focus of her trail on the negative impacts of colonialism and affective understanding. She spoke of explaining to her audience that colonisers looted museum objects from Benin and to help them 'express how they felt about that', she 'connected the objects in the palace to objects in the White House with the purpose of getting them to empathise with what people of that time must have felt to get things from their culture stolen' or 'looted'. She wanted her trail to affectively direct 'our audience to see the humanity in Imoinda and Oroonoko, and to get them to empathise with their situation . . . to see the humanity of all the people it has on display, to make cross-cultural connections and understand we are all similar'.

Connection is discussed in terms of 'guided questioning dialogue on the objects' by Erin Rozewicz who relates male and female objects with the Imoinda text.

Erin writes of museum work that permits students 'to imagine ... explore and understand life as Oroonoko and Imoinda knew it'. She links the weaponry displays with masculinity across cultures, times and disciplines, noting Imoinda's father, 'A triumph of manhood, one who fights like the fiercest lion' (Anim-Addo 2003/2008: 10). For her trail she also sought 'a pendant that would resemble the pendants that Oroonoko and exchanged as a sign of their betrothal', specifically searching for carvings 'Imoinda references'. Erin recalls how in conversation on the objects the students were 'often able tell where a group came from, what their climate was like, what they were skilled in, what they valued, and several other details about their lives and surroundings, all from a simple object such as an oar'. In her trail Erin questions 'As a beautiful and respected woman what might Imoinda have worn?' She recalls 'Jewellery as a sign of betrothal' in Imoinda and to draw contemporary relation she asks 'How does jewellery symbolise affection today?'

Student trails strive to engage visitors with objects related to the history of enslavement that Anim-Addo imaginatively writes of in *Imoinda* and they creatively relate these to ideas and issues in the present day lives of the visitors. Ashley Jones focuses on the looted Benin 'ivory tusks' in her trail because she wanted 'to convey that the expensive materials represented higher status in African society, which is true in societies all over the world'. She observes: 'This is an example of the idea that all cultures, regardless of skin tone, share common values.' Ashley's trail expands on this point for her young audience, noting that

> in the United States, we view the Declaration of Independence as one of the most powerful documents in our society. If this was taken from us we would feel unjustly treated, and we would likely seek to retaliate against the group of people that tried to take our freedom away from us.

I have offered, because of space restriction, just a few glimpses into the student's work here. All of the student trails and their reflective statements on this project, in accordance with the AHRC funding, are available at the project website in a special journal edition (Golding and Lima 2015).

Conclusion

In this chapter, I discussed a dialogical or conversational model of learning employed at the Pitt Rivers Museum to engage a group of graduate students and their teacher Maria Lima from Geneseo University in the United States. Working collaboratively at the museum/university frontiers with the museum educators Andy McClellan and Salma Caller we shared our skills and knowledge to raise the student voices specifically with reference to issues of material culture, colonial history, identity and power that arise in Joan Anim-Addo's text *Imoinda*.

We employed a creolising feminist pedagogy, taking ideas from creolisation theory, philosophical hermeneutics and Black feminist thought. All humans have language and when we take turns to respectfully speak and listen in an I–Thou dialogue, bringing prejudices that come from our traditions or histories into the conversation, our horizons can fuse in mutual understanding. The fusion of horizons occurs within a circle of understanding when we bring the past into the present for the sake of a better future. Such fusion requires we risk our taken-for-granted ideas and widen our horizons, in other words we change our future lives.

In the museum context, objects of world art were seen to be vital for 'both-and' embodied learning across disciplinary frontiers. Students engaged with minds, bodies and emotions in understanding colonial histories and Anim-Addo's contemporary text. Their work impressively emphasises the points of contact that we can find to understand our similarities and make our differences strengths, as Lorde counsels. In an age of migration and rising prejudice there is an urgency to activist projects such as developing creolising feminist pedagogies in museums and we call on our readers to work collaboratively and creatively for the sake of all our futures.

Bibliography

Anim-Addo, J. (ed.) 1999 *Another Doorway: Visible in the Museum*. London: Mango.
Anim-Addo, J. 2003/2008. *Imoinda: Or She Who Will Lose Her Name: A Play for Twelve Voices in Three Acts*. London: Mango.
Anim-Addo, J. 2007. *Touching the Body: History, Language and African-Caribbean Women's Writing*. London: Mango.
Aronowitz, S. and Giroux, H. 1991. *Post-Modern Education: Politics, Culture, and Social Criticism*. Minneapolis, MN: University of Minnesota Press.
Back, L. 2007. *The Art of Listening*. Oxford: Berg.
Behn, A. 1688/2003. *Oroonoko, Or The Royal Slave: A True History*, edited by Janet Todd. London: Penguin Classics.
Chapman, W.R. 1988. Arranging Ethnology: A.H.L.F Pitt Rivers and the Typological Tradition. In G. Stocking (ed.) *Objects and Others: Essays on Museums and Material Culture*, Vol. 3, History of Anthropology. Madison: University of Wisconsin Press, pp. 14–48.
Corradi Fuimara, G. 1995. *The Other Side of Language: A Philosophy of Listening*. London: Routledge.
Curtis, N. 2013. Reclaiming the Human: Creolizing Feminist Pedagogy at Museum Frontiers. In J. Anim-Addo, G. Covi and L. Marchi (eds), *Synthesis: Perspectives from the Radical Other*. Available: http://synthesis.enl.uoa.gr/perspectives-from-the-radical-other-7-2015/viv-golding-and-maria-helena-lima.html (accessed 15 October 2016).
de Beauvoir, S. 1973. *The Second Sex*. London: Vintage.
Derrida, J. 1995. *Writing and Difference*. London: Routledge.
Fleming, D. 2015. A Sense of Justice: Museums as Human Rights Actors. *ICOM News*, 1: 8–9.
Fouseki, K. and Smith, L. 2013. Community Consultation in the Museum: The 2007 Bicentenary of Britain's Abolition of the Slave Trade. In V. Golding and W. Modest (eds) *Museums and Communities: Curators, Collections, Collaboration*. Oxford: Berg, pp. 232–245.
Freire, P. 1970/1996. *Pedagogy of the Oppressed*. London: Penguin.
Gadamer, H.G. 1981. *Truth and Method*. London: Sheed & Ward.

Gadamer, H.G. 1986. *Dialogue and Dialectic: Eight Hermeneutical Studies on Plato*. New Haven, CT: Yale University Press.

Glissant, E. 1990/2006. *Poetics of Relation*. Second edition. Trans. by B. Wing. Ann Arbor, MI: University of Michigan Press.

Glissant, E. 1997. *Poetics of Relation*. Trans. by B. Wing. Ann Arbor, MI: University of Michigan Press.

Golding, V. 2009. *Learning at the Museum Frontiers: Identity Race and Power*. Farnham: Ashgate.

Golding, V. 2013a. Creolising the Museum: Art, Humour, Young Audiences. In V. Golding and W. Modest (eds) *Museums and Communities: Curators, Collections, Collaboration*. Oxford: Berg, pp. 195–216.

Golding, V. 2013b. Museums, Poetics, Affect. *Feminist Review* 104(1): 80–99.

Golding, V. 2013c. Imoinda at Pitt Rivers Museum, Oxford. PowerPoint presentation.

Golding, V. and Lima, M. 2015. Creolising Feminist Pedagogy at the Museum Frontiers. In J. Anim-Addo, G. Covi and L. Marchi (eds), *Synthesis: Perspectives from the Radical Other*. Available: http://synthesis.enl.uoa.gr/perspectives-from-the-radical-other-7-2015/viv-golding-and-maria-helena-lima.html (accessed 15 October 2016)

Hannerz, U. 1996. *Transnational Connections: Culture, People, Places*. London: Routledge.

Haraway, D. 1991. *Simians, Cyborgs and Women: The Reinvention of Nature*. London: Free Association.

Henderson, G.M. 1993. Speaking in Tongues. In P. Williams and L. Chrisman (eds) *Colonial Discourses and Post-Colonial Theory*. Hemel Hempstead: Harvester Wheatsheaf, pp. 257–267.

Hill-Collins, P. 1991. *Black Feminist Thought Knowledge, Consciousness and the Politics of Empowerment*. London: Routledge.

Kincheloe, J. 2001. *Getting Beyond the Facts: Teaching Social Studies/Social Science in the Twenty-First Century*. New York: Peter Lang.

Kincheloe, J. 2008. *Knowledge and Critical Pedagogy*. Dordrecht: Springer.

Lagerkvist, C. 2006. Empowerment and Anger: Learning How to Share Ownership of the Museum. *Museum and Society* 4(2): 52–68.

Levi-Strauss, C. 1989. *The Savage Mind*. London: Weidenfeld & Nicolson.

Littler, J. and Naidoo, R. (eds) 2005. *The Politics of Heritage: The Legacies of 'Race'*. London: Routledge.

Lorde, A. 1996. *The Audrey Lorde Compendium: Essays, Speeches and Journals. The Cancer Journals. Sister Outsider*. London: A Burst of Light, Pandora.

Lynch, B. and Alberti, S. 2010. Legacies of Prejudice: Racism, Co-Production and Radical Trust in the Museum. *Museum Management and Curatorship* 25(1): 13–35.

Macdonald, S. 2009. *Difficult Heritage: Negotiating the Nazi Past in Nuremberg and Beyond*. Abingdon: Routledge.

Mezirow, J. and associates, 2000. *Learning as Transformation: Critical Perspectives on a Theory in Progress*. San Francisco, CA: Jossey Bass.

Morrison, T. 1987 *Beloved*. London: Chatto & Windus.

Pitt Rivers Museum, 2016. Augustus Henry Lane Fox Pitt Rivers. Available: http://history.prm.ox.ac.uk/collector_pittrivers.html (accessed 15 October 2016).

Rhadakrishnan, K. 2003. *Theory in an Uneven World*. Oxford: Blackwell.

Rounds, J. 2010. Doing Identity Work in Museums. *Curator: The Museum Journal* 49(2): 133–150.

Shepherd, J. 2011. 14,000 British Professors – But Only 50 Are Black. *Guardian*, 27 May. Available at: www.theguardian.com/education/2011/may/27/only-50-black-british-professors (accessed 23 May 2017).

Simon, N. 2010. *The Participatory Museum*. Santa Cruz, CA: Museum 2.0.

Smith, L. 2006. *The Uses of Heritage*. London: Routledge.

Smith, L. and Campbell, G. 2015. The Elephant in the Room, Heritage, Affect and Emotion. In W. Logan, M.N. Craith and U. Kockel (eds) *A Companion to Heritage Studies*. Malden, MA and Oxford: Wiley-Blackwell, pp. 443–460.

Steinberg, S. 2011. Employing the Bricolage as Critical Research in Science Education. In B.J. Fraser, K. Tobin and C.J. McRobbie (eds) *The International Handbook of Research in Science Education*. Second edition. Dordrecht: Springer, pp. 1485–1500.

Steinberg, S. and Kincheloe, J. 2010. Power, Emancipation, and Complexity: Employing Critical Theory. *Power and Education* 2(2): 140–151.

Chapter 10

Impasse or productive intersection?
Learning to 'mess with genies' in collaborative heritage research relationships

Joni Lariat

> We must strive, in the face of the here and now's totalizing rendering of reality, to think and feel a *then and there*.
>
> (Muñoz 2009: 1)

Introduction

In recent years heritage studies has increasingly turned its attention to its own discursive production. The utilisation of critical theory to facilitate this reflexive turn has only just begun, with numerous theoretical avenues yet to be explored. By applying existing theoretical contributions to empirically and contextually driven heritage projects, I suggest that critical heritage studies practitioners and academics can engage in cross-disciplinary discussions, pushing both heritage studies and critical theory in productive directions. This chapter opens up one such avenue for discussion. Working within the intersections of anthropology, queer theory and feminist studies, my analysis incorporates ethnographic, anti-racist feminist and queer methodologies to reflexively interrogate issues of positionality within collaborative research relationships. Guided by Haraway's (1988: 590) proposition that the partiality of situated knowledges allows "connections and unexpected openings" I argue that ontological and epistemological differences can be engaged in research relationships as productive intersections rather than prohibitive impasses.

My reflections emerge from an ongoing collaborative partnership with an independent female heritage practitioner named Trisnani Murnilawati (Nani). Nani and I met in Sabang, an island regency in Aceh, Indonesia, where she lives and works and where I have been engaged in ethnographic fieldwork. Increasingly, over the past three years, our conversations have become instrumental in provoking and maintaining a critical and questioning voice within my research. From our dialogue emerged a reflexive methodology that was adaptable and responsive to the contexts within which we worked; a methodology that became a pragmatic way to navigate the curious divergences in our interpretations of stories shared by interviewees, thus expanding the scope for the ways we imagined heritage as a lived experience of remembering. In this chapter, I explore the emergence of this reflexive methodology by tracing the effect of a single utterance in one of our early conversations. As I will describe in greater detail in the pages to come, the utterance referenced the role that genies (spiritual presences) play in research; disruptive presences that I began to see as synonymous with the frames that we all bring to research.

As heritage work is often a collaborative enterprise involving multiple differentially positioned practitioners, anti-racist feminist methodologies offer ways in which to engage critically with intersubjective power. Additionally, more recent continuations of critical feminist perspectives by queer practitioners, particularly those working empirically, offer further methodological considerations for social researchers, including those working from a cultural heritage perspective. In my reflexive engagement I have drawn on discussions of methodology by standpoint feminists such as Crenshaw (1991) and Harding (1997, 2004), specifically developments of intersectionality theory (McCall 2005; Yuval-Davis 2006) and transversal politics (Yuval-Davis 1999), to engage critically with the networks of power that shape access to knowledge production. Extensions of these formative feminist articulations of power by queer theorists, particularly Butler's (1990, 1993, 2004) extensive theorisation of identity and performance, facilitate a recognition of the very real effects of social location while unhinging identity from the static effects of essentialism. As I became increasingly cognisant of the ways social location produced positionality within our collaborative partnership, I also began to see heritage evidence in a new light: the places and voices from which heritage knowledge might emerge broadened. As I reflected on our ways of seeing (and not seeing) evidence, lived heritage suddenly became evident everywhere I looked, particularly in the ways people recalled otherwise hidden histories as performative moments within their everyday interactions. Such a shift in thinking beckons a questioning of what other kinds of evidence we might expect to fall within the bounds of a critical heritage studies, inclusive of a diversity of voices and experiences absent from hegemonic representations. This chapter then is both a reflection on collaborative research relationships and a case for everyday performance as uncharted territory for critical heritage studies.

Lived heritage, of the kind I am proposing here, is a dynamic field of inquiry insufficiently theorised in contemporary heritage studies. Performance is marked by its absence, where its conceptualisation has been limited to analyses of visitor engagements with recognised heritage sites (Bagnall 2015) and re-enactments of historical moments by professional actors as a mode of producing heritage for public consumption (Tivers 2002). Post-structuralist queer articulations of performance and performativity offer ways in which to envisage heritage acts in everyday life. Butler's (1990) theorisation of the discursive production of gender through the iterative process of performativity has created alternate ways in which to envisage the critical capacity of identity and performance from a range of academic perspectives (Muñoz 1999; Tate 2005). If we proceed from definitions by critical heritage studies theorists that heritage is a representation of the past produced in and through the lens of the present (Harrison 2013; Lowenthal

2004; Smith 2006), where "inherited and current concerns about the past" are negotiated (Harrison 2013: 14), then doesn't performance and performativity capture the very essence of heritage-making? With this focus on the interconnectivity of past and present and the active role that participants play in articulating this exchange, how can we overlook the significance of everyday performance as a key site of heritage production?

Performances of lived heritage also expand recent critical heritage discussions (Harrison 2013; Pétursdóttir 2013; Smith and Akagawa 2008), which complicate and call into question the false dichotomy of tangible and intangible heritage used within dominant conservation discourse to differentiate between material and immaterial heritage. Performance is fleeting and impermanent, yet is simultaneously embedded within the materiality of living bodies. The broadening of definitions of heritage to encapsulate relationships between place and identity as embodied dramatically redefines the ways we imagine heritage sites. In this theorisation, heritage sites become mobile, reflective of and responsive to, the nuanced complexity of everyday life. A more explicit connection between performance and heritage then is an important accompaniment to critical heritage studies, where practitioners can begin to see alternate perspectives and relationships with the ways histories are reproduced.

Gender is another obvious omission in many heritage representations. The contributions to this collection are evidence of how gendered experience has been lacking in both mainstream cultural heritage representations and heritage studies' theoretical engagements. As has been demonstrated exhaustively by feminists of colour, a focus on gender as a single analytical category does not constitute a comprehensive approach to rendering visible the diversity of lived experiences of oppression. Critical race applications of feminist standpoint theory, expounded by third-wave feminists such as Crenshaw (1991) and Harding (2004), drew attention to the complexity of lived experience and the ways in which research and representation effectively reproduced the hegemonic order in society. Indeed, as has been further emphasised by queer practitioners, the term 'gender' and the contextually specific meanings associated with its performative articulations in social life need to be interrogated before such a contested term can be put to use as a critical agitator. Gender intersects with other identity vectors in complex ways to shape our negotiation with context and evidence (Harding 1987). Context, in turn, shapes the ways identity is performed and managed within the social relationships that compose the fields within which we work. These dynamics not only exist 'out there' in the worlds with which we engage; they also permeate our research relationships and shape the kinds of knowledge we produce. For example, tangible barriers such as access to the recorded accounts of colonial administrations more profoundly inhibit the local independent female heritage worker than they do the visiting female academic; a stark difference invisible to a single-lens analysis.

To engage critically with such complex intersections requires a methodological approach with the capacity to reflect the nuances of lived experience and individual engagements with local histories. Intersectionality theory, and its various applications and permutations within contemporary critical theory, offer interrogative approaches for analysing the effects of differential social positioning in a range of contexts (Collins 1997; Crenshaw 1991; McCall 2005). These strategies not only provide a means for exploring the ways in which multiple categories of identity might shape a person's experiences but offer research practitioners a framework for interrogating the complex networks of power that permeate the relationships within which they work.

By focusing on these differences in positioning and understanding their influence on how and where we access evidence we can take account of how heritage knowledge is reproduced from within hegemonic discursive frameworks, thus disrupting those cycles of epistemic violence. By asking who can speak (Spivak 1988) and what can be asked, we can trace the silences and omissions within "authorized heritage discourse" (Smith 2006: 4). Approaching difference within research relationships reflexively enables alternate ways of imagining heritage within the contexts we seek to understand. If we delve beneath and between those bodies of evidence usually engaged by heritage practitioners, performances of lived heritage emerge as a series of counter-narratives, pushing heritage studies to account for a diversity of relationships with the past that may not sit comfortably with dominant historical representations. Such accounts are representative of everyday negotiations with the past and can become accessible and vibrant sites of community engagement.

Muñoz's (2009) conceptualisation of a queer futurity lends itself to a reimagining of the possibilities that could be engaged by such a dynamic approach to heritage studies. In keeping with current definitions of critical heritage studies, such a perspective recalls a "then and there" (Muñoz 2009: 1) of the past as it is performed through the contexts of the present, thereby opening up hegemonic representations for critical revision by those embedded in its citational reproduction. An expansion of heritage to include contemporary everyday performances allows a broader reflective imagining of alternate futurities while repositioning the inheritors of history as its producers. The following section explores the moment between Nani and I where a simple utterance highlighted for me key differences in our approaches to evidence. While my initial reaction was to attribute this disconnect to a fundamental and incommensurate difference between us, I argue here as a result of my own reflexive engagements, that such a moment rather provides an opportunity for critical exploration.

The genie

> The genie doesn't just mess with you in everyday life; they can mess with the past, they can mess with your research.
> (Field-note, October 2014, in conversation with Nani)

This was not the first time I had heard about genies or perceived their traces. Genies (Jinn, genii) are spirits in Islamic mythology who exist alongside humankind but form a parallel world. Diverse accounts of how these spirits interact with humankind abound throughout the Islamic world. Generally speaking, they can take the form of any living or non-living entity and can be either good or evil in their actions (Khalifa and Hardie 2005). In Sabang, genies are often described as untrustworthy and manipulative presences who occupy abandoned or uninhabited spaces. On several occasions during my fieldwork these figures were invoked to explain the unexplainable; to account for a reluctance to travel at night; or, to dissuade me from attempting to visit heritage sites abandoned to the jungle. I assumed they were stories embedded in the psyche of people at a young age aimed at curtailing their movements to the safety of the village. While I had thought about how human movement might be influenced by these presences, I had not realised the impact that a belief in them might have on the practices of local researchers. During the conversation I refer to in the field-note above, Nani had warned me against believing too easily the stories I heard from local people, as it was possible the stories had been manipulated by genies. She suggested a degree of scepticism when engaging with local stories and a process of verification between these histories and the factual accounts of the archives. It seemed to me at the time that Nani's belief in the genies and her assertion that they were able to influence research were intimately connected to the tensions I had felt during our discussions of methodology. It did not occur to me immediately that Nani likely felt the same frustration with my constant manoeuvring away from the recorded histories in the archives towards ethnographic interview as a principle method. My initial dismissal of the genies as superstition and my uncompromising privileging of people's testimony was perhaps a curious contradiction for Nani.

Subsequent conversations throughout our collaboration destabilised my initial response that the genies could only be understood as symptomatic of deeply rooted differences in ontology. From her description of personal encounters with them in various research contexts, from the reading room of the national archives to heritage sites in the jungle, I began to imagine them as presences that guided and shaped our ways of seeing. I could imagine them as both figurative and metaphorical presences, and began to see them in my own ways of seeing, and not seeing, evidence. Genies became, for me, an invitation to reposition my expectations in relation to the particular ontologies of the spaces in which I was both living and working. They became a point about which I was able to re-evaluate the assumptive voice in my own practice, and to read the contexts alongside, rather than from above, those around me. Finally, the genies came to represent the impossibility of knowing beyond the boundaries of the cultural frameworks that construct our realms of experience and understanding.

I will return to the seemingly paradoxical relationships to evidence exemplified by these 'strange presences' in the coming pages as I explore the ways a feminist standpoint approach can facilitate fruitful collaborations across difference.

Sabang: public silences, private memories

My ethnographic research and subsequent collaborations with Nani are centred on the ways colonisation is remembered and imagined in the various communities residing in Sabang. Sabang is the name of both a collection of islands on the north coast of Aceh and the town on the largest of these islands, Pulau Weh. Located at the intersection of the Andaman Sea and Indian Ocean, the islands of Sabang mark the entrance to the Malacca Straight, which separates the Malaysian Peninsula from the Indonesian island of Sumatra.

Sabang occupies an uncomfortable space in the dominant narrative of Acehnese resistance to colonial occupation. A persistent narrative within Sabang's recently emerging heritage discourse is that Sabang was an uninhabited island prior to the arrival of the Dutch and therefore existed somewhat outside the boundaries of an impervious Acehnese state. Prior to and throughout Aceh's resistance to Dutch occupation, Sabang was utilised as a centre for Dutch economic expansion. It was also a strategically important site due to its proximity to the Acehnese mainland and British-ruled Malaya. Oral histories and excavations of the archives of the Dutch East Indies reveal uses of Sabang that deviate significantly from its well-documented history centring on Sabang Free Port. Pulau Rubiah, a small fringing island on the northern extremity of Pulau Weh, was used as a quarantine station to house the continuous flow of *haji* (pilgrims) returning from Mecca. Built in the early 1930s Rubiah Quarantine Station facilitated the monitoring and regulation of the pilgrim's health prior to their re-entry into the general population. Whether there were other reasons for such management is open to speculation, indeed there is archival evidence to suggest that fears of pan-Islam were a key motivation behind increased surveillance systems, as Alexanderson (2014) discussed in a broader examination of the appropriation of Hajj networks by colonial occupiers.

Contradictory to the popular narrative that Sabang was an uninhabited island prior to colonial ingenuity, references in early merchant's travelogues written in the late seventeenth and early eighteenth centuries suggest that the Sultanate of Aceh sent prisoners to Pulau Weh as punishment, after their hands and feet had been amputated (Bowrey 1905; Lockyer 1711). The utilisation of Sabang as a site of forced removal continued under Dutch rule. Archival evidence strongly suggests that the decision to establish the region's largest mental asylum in Sabang was a response to a perceived increase in mental instability within the indigenous population. As many as 1,200 patients, sent from over-crowded facilities throughout the archipelago, were consistently housed in *Krankzinnigengesticht* Sabang (Sabang Mental Asylum) from 1927 until Japanese occupation forced its closure in 1942.

The sudden decision to overturn an earlier ruling that the facility was unnecessary in Aceh suggests that the administration perceived that a new demand had emerged. Kloos (2014) links the asylum in Sabang to the administration's growing fear that the resistance they faced on the mainland was rooted in religious fanaticism and that such a movement could have dire consequences if it was not controlled. As seen from a colonialist perspective, resistance to occupation and the prolonged effects of decades of war and domination culminated in what the Dutch called *Atjeh Moorden* (typical Aceh murder): multiple, seemingly random violent attacks on Dutch officials by lone individuals (Kloos 2014). Whether these attacks were symptomatic of mental health issues due to decades of war or were acts of defiant resistance depends upon which side of history one is located and what political ends particular versions of history serve.

My enquiries within local communities and the national archives revealed little as to the identity, origin and fate of the hospital's patients. However, over an extended period of time, I began to recognise traces of these stories in the ways people related to one another. People would often joke about the connection between contemporary inhabitants and this lost generation by suggesting that community members might be the descendants of the patients. I observed such during my first visit in 2004, when a group of children mocked the behaviour of an eccentric elderly woman from their village. They drew a line across their foreheads, a common gesture used to jokingly infer another's 'madness'. Upon further enquiry with the children's families, I found that this was a common game, played by adults and children alike; a jesting, playful prod at the past and its absences. The story of the mental hospital had led them to question the traces of those long lost patients, who may or may not have been their ancestors, within their community. The ambiguity surrounding their confinement allowed a space within which to renegotiate contemporary identity and to also engage critically with colonialist practices that sought to demonise and then control indigenous populations.

My subsequent ethnographic practice allowed me to follow these intriguing narrative threads, permitting me to recognise further performative moments connecting the fragmented stories of the past with contemporary identity performances. One particularly intriguing story references a therapeutic practice employed by Dutch over-seers of the mental hospital. It is recalled locally, as a result of a repetition of first-hand accounts within familial retellings, that patients were required to draw water from wells and lakes with a basket of woven rattan. Ideas as to whether this was conceived as a therapeutic approach to treatment; a strategy for ascertaining the patient's grasp on reality (the patient would presumably refuse to perform such a futile task as drawing water with a leaking basket when their mental affliction had passed); or a form of social control, varied among local narrators. These understandings depended upon what stories had been passed on by relatives with lived experience of these times and the narrator's own positioning within contemporary society.

Despite finding no mention of this practice in the available archives, this story is often recalled by mainland Acehnese when meeting a person, whether friend or new acquaintance, from Sabang. In mocking jest the phrase *cröeng ié lam raga* (taking water with the basket) is pronounced by the mainlander. The phrase is offered both in recognition of this history and perhaps to infer a fundamental difference between mainlanders and islanders: that this aspect of Sabang's history lives on in the character of people from the island. This performative moment connects the silenced histories of Dutch co-optation to a critical engagement with contemporary identity. I was intrigued by these moments and started to see them as important transactions where locals engaged and produced alternate histories.

Despite its seemingly uni-directional denigration of islander by mainlander, this performative moment also creates an ambiguous space for contestation and disruption to hegemonic representations of colonial presence in Sabang. The dominant representation suggests that while war was waged on the mainland the Dutch Administration had a benevolent relationship with Sabang residents, as demonstrated by the popular narrative I heard during my fieldwork that the practice involving the rattan basket was therapeutic in its intention. The momentary suspension of this narrative creates an ambiguous and rich space where multiple interpretations and relationships to the past can be critically engaged. As this otherwise hidden dynamic between mainlander and islander surfaces, the Sabang resident has an opportunity to enact a performance of identity that either refutes or accepts both its implied essentialism and associated narratives of Dutch beneficence. It provokes a contestation of the relationship between colonised and coloniser upon which Sabang identity is at least partially constructed. These performative contestations of 'historical truth' elicit 'a decolonial imaginary', defined by Pérez (2004: 123) as "a rupturing space, the alternative to that which is written in history". In my interpretation, this space, albeit temporary, is seized upon to critically engage hegemonic representations through subversive play and revision.

Such moments emerge from the gaps: they coagulate around deeply held questions of identity. They give voice to questions that cannot perhaps be easily asked. They are moments of criticality, which emit through the body what cannot be conveyed explicitly with words. Yet these moments were absent from local representations of heritage and the approaches Nani and I were forging together to understand local heritage narratives did not yet have the scope to accommodate such complexity. Our approaches to knowledge production did not have the capacity to see these performances as moments of living heritage. During our conversations, which seemed to pit archival and oral histories against one another, I wondered whether these performative moments might represent a third thread that worked dialogically between archival silences and oral histories.

Contemporary Sabang has seen a resurgence in interest in the precolonial and colonial periods in recent years. In comparison with my first visit to the island in 2004, in the last three years I have noticed an increase in open public conversations about the past and a willingness to share familial narratives once confined to the privacy of the home. This renewed interest and openness can be attributed to the conclusion of decades of fear imposed on the Acehnese population, both by the insurgents of the separatist movement, *Gerakan Aceh Merdeka* (Free Aceh Movement), and the Indonesian military. During the insurgency public discussion was avoided: stories of the colonial period were not necessarily of high importance to a population whose main concerns were avoiding drawing attention and staying alive. The insularity and decades of silence in Aceh were broken in the aftermath of the 2004 earthquakes and tsunami that acted as a catalyst to the Helsinki Peace Agreement in 2005 that ended the conflict. The devastation to the region demanded resolution of the conflict and the opening of Aceh to foreign aid workers. Rapid social change has ensued with huge increases in local and international tourists visiting Sabang. Simultaneously, politically motivated religious conservatism has reshaped the ways Acehnese society seeks to define itself amidst these changes.

This period of rapid change offers an opportunity to engage critically with Sabang's pasts, particularly as very little of these pasts has been mentioned beyond local engagements. As public discussion emerges, heritage practitioners are faced with the task of creating heritage narratives that make space for divergent and at times incoherent pasts. While the buildings of the Dutch Administration and the bunkers and tunnels of the Japanese have been methodically documented and displayed for public engagement by groups such as Sabang Heritage Society, they represent a popular, predictable and fairly safe narrative of foreign occupation. Hidden beneath these representations are the intricate and nuanced lived experiences of local populations as they are being continually negotiated in contemporary life.

Feminist standpoint theory and queer methodologies

Questions of methodology arise at such a juncture. If we posit that heritage can act as a site of critical engagement, how and where might we look for the evidence of such engagements? How can we grasp incoherent non-normative narrative threads to guide us towards peripheral voices so as to expand upon hegemonic heritage narratives? As Pérez (2004: 123) argues: "We must uncover the voices from the past that honor multiple experiences, instead of falling prey to that which is easy – allowing the white heteronormative gaze to reconstruct and reinterpret our past." Specifically, in the case of collaborative heritage research, how might practitioners see in their differences the reflections of diversity to be found within the communities they are engaging?

A deeper set of epistemological questions also require acknowledgement here. How can we challenge our own assumptions outside of the bodies of theory that constitute our intellectual histories and our personal and political relationships with the worlds that we inhabit and seek to understand? Our critiques are always already positioned. As someone who identifies as queer, and having grown up and gained an education in a middle-class Anglo-Australian context (with all that such a positioning infers) I am personally, politically and professionally attuned to particular ways of intellectualising the worlds I encounter. In terms of my experiences of self and community, I have found liberation from the confines of binary essentialism in queer theory while intersectionality offers a vital balance by refocusing on lived experience. It was to these bodies of knowledge that I reached in order to engage with the issues arising in my research.

In addressing these questions and connecting with a broader politics of inclusion, feminist standpoint theory and anti-racist queer methodologies offered me ways in which to frame a reflexive engagement with the dynamics of collaborative research. Such an approach has the capacity to unleash an imaginative relationship with heritage knowledge where multi-vocality and ambiguity can resurface within the gaps and silences of established heritage narratives. I found it particularly illuminating to reflect on the ways my queer sensibility worked as a lens for seeking out subordinate narratives and performative moments.

Collaboration, a common feature of heritage work, inevitably involves intersubjective power relations that influence both the working relationship and the types of knowledge produced. The inter-connected analytical strategies of intersectionality, reflexive positionality and transversal dialogue were useful in critically reflecting on such dynamics as they surfaced within the various contexts in which Nani and I worked. Dynamics between narrators and researchers created yet further intersecting and at times unsettling cultural transactions that inevitably shaped the ways we engaged with communities. These intersections offered vitally important sites of enquiry as they not only told us about the negotiations made in research partnerships but showed us how knowledge is produced and reproduced in accordance with existing political dynamics and assumptions.

As I suggested above, the catalyst for this reflection came from a seeming impasse in the ways Nani and I approached a project of resurfacing local cultural heritage in Sabang. Rather than dismissing the baggage we each brought to the research, I wanted to explore how we might work across and within our differences, to develop a shared platform from which to conduct research appropriate to the contexts of Sabang. I was struck by the irony of our hugely divergent perspectives: it seemed that while Nani privileged archival evidence over local knowledge, I wanted to challenge the narratives in the archives by accessing stories reproduced orally within local communities. Did Nani expect that I would privilege recorded history and so positioned herself accordingly? Or was this an example of what Linda Tuhiwai Smith (1999) argues is a legacy of colonialism: the delegitimising of traditional systems of knowledge? What about my privileging of local stories: was I being as critical of their production as I was of the colonial representations in the archives? How was my 'intellectual history' (Goslinga 2012) influencing the ways I was pursuing evidence? Was I privileging and romanticising certain perspectives over others?

Reading Nani's relationship to evidence meant shifting myself to understand something of her position beyond my own reactive assumptions. This shift was initiated by a later conversation when, after she had read the first draft of this chapter, Nani sought to clarify the contexts that shaped her reluctance to engage local stories with blind faith. Her deeper understandings of the social contexts within which we were working didn't afford her the same naivety in relation to the stories we heard; she had a far more attuned critical ear towards the various perspectives, born out of a deep understanding of the politics of place to which I was a distant bystander. My understandings of her complex and shifting positionality in the contexts within which she lived and worked added a necessary dimensionality to the ways I thought about how Nani engaged the social landscapes of Sabang and allowed me a vantage point from which to reflect on my own positionality.

Nani described her encounters with genies in the reading room at the National Archives. They had playfully attempted to distract her and lead her away from particular documents. The genies reminded me of the multitude of pathways we can take through a field-site, an archive collection, or a physical or social landscape and the ways individuals with specific yet shifting positionalities are drawn to or away from evidence. Nani's experience of working in the midst of genies is an example of a reflexive engagement: that pause of reflection on what it is that mediates our decisions, our attractions to particular evidence, to particular ethnographic experiences. It also beckons consideration of what types of evidence we are led towards as a result of a 'politics of access', depending on the particular contexts and relationships we encounter in the field.

What might these realisations mean in terms of my own reflexive practice within the context of our collaborative relationship? It meant, as Goslinga (2012) demonstrates in her reading of Crapanzano's (1980) explication of 'epistemological vertigo', being aware of the impulse to deconstruct Nani's ontology by relativising her genies within my own frames of intelligibility. To argue for a resistance to this urge to relativise is to ignore the productive potential of such destabilising moments and to deny that we are always already entwined in a process of sense-making in relation to others' world views. It meant, then, understanding the significance of the genies for her by reading evidence alongside her. It also meant grounding myself within my own positionality and learning to see the 'genies' in my own privileging and dismissal of evidence. Nani's genies provoked a more keenly tuned critical reflexivity in my engagement with oral histories. I began to see in these performances a broader social politics and it was in this negotiated space that a lived heritage emerged, where the past is continually negotiated in and through the politics of the present.

Further discussions with Nani suggested that fundamentally we both cared deeply about broadening the scope of existing heritage representations to include diverse perspectives, particularly the stories of women clearly absent within masculinist representations. Despite our differences in gender identity, sexuality and religious belief, as well as our academic and cultural backgrounds, we shared strong political commonalities. A criticality towards dominant representations, which grew from our own experiences and positionality, and the desire to expand existing heritage representations to include women's voices and memories, allowed us to work towards a common purpose.

It was within those conversations that a dialogical approach permitted recognition of a shared politics. The premise of a dialogical reading is that identification is co-produced through the exchanges that take place between self and culture. Such relationality and ongoing dialogical exchange creates an endless 'polyphony' of variant contextually produced responses (Bakhtin 1984). Within the context of collaborative research relationships, such a process encompasses the reflective and responsive exchange of perspectives that occurs between individuals and the cultural contexts within which they are embedded. In the case of my working relationship with Nani, this manifested in a realisation of the importance of discussions that moved beyond the confines of the immediate research context by exploring the ways our positionings affected our access and relationship with evidence.

In between interviews and during trips to the archives in Jakarta we shared our experiences of working and living within our own respective intellectual and social contexts. We shared our experiences and observations of gender inequality in social, academic and professional spaces. On one occasion we shared a joke about a fellow researcher in the reading room of the archive centre. He strode about, demanding attention and preference. His masculinity, whiteness and pensive furrowed brow collided to produce an impressive professorial habitus that filled the space. His performance had clearly corralled the reading room assistants so that they were at his beck and call, leaving little space for others needing guidance. In particular, the male English-speaking assistant was keen to assist this male academic. Nani had been blatantly dismissed by this same assistant the previous day, while I had been welcomed and assisted when I asked for advice. As we both noted this performance of self-importance, Nani leaned over to me and whispered, "When women do this kind of work, it is seen as a hobby. When men do it, it is work." We could see in this moment the intersections of gender, academic status and cultural background; the ways privilege worked to create three very different experiences. While my persona as a visiting white academic granted me a warm welcome, my perceived, but ambiguous, female gender identity clearly did not elicit the same eager response from the male staff member as it did my foreign male colleague. So while the attendants certainly didn't see me as partaking in a hobby, they did not take my work as seriously as my male colleague. Nani's position within the culture in which we were working and her gender identity, was a hindrance to her participation in this academic setting. Later conversations revealed the persistence of this issue for Nani within the male-dominated heritage organisations in Sabang, which are often deeply ideologically and financially connected to government. Evidence is as much shaped by access as it is by the ways we engage and interpret it. The everyday negotiations with power structures that either permit or restrict access to evidence, particularly those repositories housing documents of colonial administrations, have significant effects on how marginal voices might contest the linearity and homogeneity of dominant narratives.

We also shared a similarly critical perspective in relation to how power can be read within historical representations. This became apparent when we read imaginatively 'between' archival evidence, formulating alternative narratives for those exiled to Sabang Mental Hospital. For us, these individuals lost within the silences of the archives became resistance fighters; this reinterpretation dramatically shifted both the colonial representation of the island's pasts and the present day performative articulations of 'the story of the rattan basket'.

We spoke about our own independent research and the difficulties we had each experienced negotiating the politics of local communities in which we were both positioned as outsiders, whether that be an obvious straightforward case of being from a different country, as in my case, or being of a different social class and position in relation to systems of authority and government, as was the case between Nani and some of our interviewees. For example, immediately following one interview we discussed the tension we had both recognised during the interview.

Nani explained that existing tensions between residents and local government representatives due to a recent botched land agreement had likely caused the suspicion in the elderly woman and her family. The original representatives who were now perceived to have lied in similar face-to-face encounters were of a similar social class to Nani and so her presence at their door had set off immediate alarm bells. In this example, we can see the ways present-day politics shape the ways people interact with researchers, who, for the everyday person are synonymous with the government. Nani was more keenly aware that what people share with you, how they share and indeed whether they will at all is profoundly shaped by the various socio-political contexts within which they are located. From these insights, we were co-producing a reading of the contexts within which we were working. Rather than pushing our differences to the side, such exchanges utilised them to engage critically with privileged epistemologies and evidence, allowing the silences within our own practices to surface, forging paths into more critical discussions of methodology. Most importantly, it prompted us to see that a critical feminist perspective was fundamental to engaging with silences and guided us towards a deliberate privileging of women's voices in the heritage representations we sought, thus shifting the narrative away from the masculinist colonial impressions of Sabang towards a more nuanced discussion of the effects of colonialism, particularly the ways silence has persevered in contemporary contexts leaving a shadow over local capacities to connect with the past. This emergence of a shared politics can be seen as an example of an "epistemic community", as described by Assiter (2000: 333). Members of an epistemic community align behind common political values rather than their identification within identity-based communities. A dialogical process permits the sharing of values as they relate to shifting contextual factors, allowing individuals to "establish common narratives" in their political stances, and I would add in this context, in their research methodologies (Stoetzler and Yuval-Davis 2002: 320).

Feminist standpoint theory allows an interrogation of these complex and contextual weavings of power. The perspective encompasses various analytical strategies that strive for a nuanced consideration of how identification with, or perceived belonging to, categories of identity shape one's experience of the world, in particular, negotiations with systems of power that structure social, economic and political life (Collins 1997; Harding 2004). Articulations of feminist standpoint theory by women of colour emerged in response to omissions within the identity politics of feminist academia and activism during the 1970s and 1980s. Black feminist standpoint theory recognised the complex interconnectedness of race, class and gender in the reproduction of inequalities that exposed women of colour to specific experiences of disadvantage. The single-axis approach used by early feminists to analyse issues of gender inequality marginalised the experiences of women of colour because it did not take account of the ways race and class affected experiences of gender discrimination for non-white populations (Crenshaw 1991). Such omissions demanded a rethinking of methodological approaches to researching the diversity existing within and between categories of identity.

Cho *et al.* (2013) avoid a reductive definition or standardised methodology when describing the potentiality of an intersectional approach, preferring rather to see it as "an analytical sensibility" (Cho *et al.* 2013: 788), which imbues practitioners with a "way of thinking about the problem of sameness and difference and its relation to power" (Cho *et al.* 2013: 795). Importantly, an intersectional sensibility is not confined to that which it studies; our own praxis is embedded within dynamics of power and therefore demands attention and critical reflexivity. Intersectionality as an approach to interrogating the interstices of socio-cultural categories and their impact upon experience can benefit analyses of research relationships in transnational contexts. To turn this critical gaze back upon research relationships allows focus on how heritage representations are constructed through the positionalities of those involved in its construction. The implicit power dynamics within these relationships hugely influences which stories are told and how they are (or can be) told. Such a sensibility, when directed towards research relationships has the capacity to see difference and sameness in ways that create the kinds of "connections and unexpected openings" (Haraway, 1988: 590) that can expand the scope of heritage studies. Discussions with Nani throughout our collaboration illuminated, for me, not only a clearer understanding of her situated experiences but opened up a capacity to see the limits my location placed on understanding the complex relationships and politics operating around me. To observe Nani navigating her own interests alongside mainstream reproductions of existing historical narratives allowed me to understand, in a broader sense, the reproduction of identity in and through historical reproduction.

It would be an easy academic move to make to see Nani's preference for the concrete as a foundational positivism. But if I see her perspective in relation to her positionality I can begin to understand what factors influence and produce her relationships with evidence. Nani's limited access to archival documents and endless fight for recognition as more than a part-time hobbyist, combined with her position as a woman working within a typically patriarchal society, with its own history of imposed colonialist masculinist heteronormativity, shape her ability to be taken seriously outside the confines of accepted heritage practices. This denial of full participation and the delegitimising of marginally located voices echoes colonial practices of social control exacted through the tight regulation of public knowledge. Recognising that these practices are replicated within research contexts goes somewhere towards understanding the processes of hegemonic reproduction in contemporary heritage work.

Our shifting approach, 'from margin to centre' (hooks 1984), meant both hearing marginal voices as legitimate repositories of local knowledge and redefining the position from which to speak and think alternative modes of heritage representation. My assumptions about the clear boundaries between insider and outsider positions were shown to be incapable of accounting for the ways in which Nani and I were received by different members of the community. Depending on where we were working, people engaged with us differently and I came to understand that while I felt like an outsider and presumed Nani to occupy a clear and uncomplicated position inside the local culture, these positions were not so static or straightforward. This became particularly salient during our interviews with elderly female community members. I was able to see how our constellation of identity vectors reconfigured in different contexts to shape our interactions with participants. Simply stating that we were two women interviewing elderly women did not provide a nuanced understanding of the intensely complex effect of our presence in these women's houses. While Nani clearly occupied an insider position as a local resident, her affiliation with a group connected to the local government made the women wary of her presence in their private spaces. The legacy of silence surrounding the colonial period and the continuing disconnect between local communities and overarching government structures contributed to this distrust. My clumsy execution of normative social practices and my need for clarification of my understandings throughout the interviews positioned me clearly as an outsider, yet my presence and curiosity was more often than not presumed to be relatively benign. Thus, whereas my explanations of my interest as a foreign anthropology student elicited interested murmurs, Nani was met with suspicion. What the women shared with us was clearly influenced by this interplay of our shifting positionalities. Understanding the women's reservations, which shifted from individual to individual and sometimes shifted during the course of our conversations, required constant reflexive dialogue.

More recent critiques within queer theory by trans and antiracist scholars have highlighted the ongoing need for reflexive engagement within critical approaches, particularly in the ways research methodologies continue to limit inclusion (Browne and Nash 2010; Erel *et al.* 2010; Haritaworn 2008). Complexity, when met with inadequate methodologies, inhabits a space that "resists telling" (Crenshaw 1991: 1242), rendering unintelligible the lives of those who do not fit neatly within normative identity categories. Challenging accepted disciplinary practices shifts methodologies to account for diversity, an essential step for a burgeoning criticality within heritage studies. As Rooke (2009) and Fotopoulou (2013) have argued in relation to ethnographic practice, the value of a queer ethnographic approach is not only its capacity to render queer lives visible, it is also in the disruption it can provide to traditional ethnographic approaches. Such reflexive priorities can equally be applied to heritage research contexts where the textures of diversity as reflected in oral and performative systems of engaging and producing the past might not be recognisable to traditional approaches.

Guided by Erel *et al.* (2010) who suggest that a radical queer project ought to aim for multiple inclusions, my approach seeks voices beyond limiting categories of gender and sex and calls for the pursuit of more subtle intersections of difference, which are read in and through context. To render such intersections visible we need to foster an evolving relationship with context that has a capacity to see heritage as an endless reproduction of contradictory and often incoherent fragmented pasts. Fotopoulou (2013: 27) argues that "queer approaches could demonstrate how differences and identities are contextual and always 'becoming' according to what is socially acceptable within a given geography". Such a sensibility seeks disruptive performative moments as sites of dynamic heritage production. A queer perspective allows space for an ambiguity and subversive performativity, both in the imagining of what is communicated in the actions executed by people in their everyday lives and in the playful reflexivity of the researcher.

Particularly in postcolonial contexts, where meanings associated with categories of identity are often at odds with the ways they have been conceptualised in their largely Anglo-American origins, a queer approach begins with a deconstruction of terms and their contextual meanings, arguing fundamentally for an emplaced analysis of how such intuitive understandings become ways of knowing and being in the world. This means reframing narratives of the past within interview contexts to make space for alternate ways of remembering. By evoking the imagery of the rattan basket from the very beginning of some of our interviews, Nani and I deliberately disrupted the deeply ingrained repetition of hegemonic narratives. It also created spaces from which women could recall memories they might otherwise have thought irrelevant and opened up contemporary performances of this story as another layer within which to recognise lived heritage.

Recent discussions between queer methodologists cite reflexive positionality as a key consideration for researchers working in transnational postcolonial contexts (Erel *et al.* 2010; Haritaworn 2008) so as to mitigate the dangers of recolonising or "queering from above" (Haritaworn 2008) posed by reading Western ideations of identity and difference in non-Western contexts. This reflexive process is fundamentally concerned with contesting accepted methodological approaches within a range of empirically driven disciplines while addressing intersubjective power relations within research relationships. It also has the potential to change the direction of the research by being open and responsive to the 'unexpected openings' that inevitably arise in all research. Transversal politics is a valuable interconnection between intersectionality, reflexive positionality and ethnographic practice in that it demonstrates the movement or re-positioning required to conduct critical social research. Yuval-Davis (1999: 96) proposes:

> The idea is that each such 'messenger', and each participant in a political dialogue, would bring with them the reflexive knowledge of their own positioning and identity. This is the 'rooting'. At the same time, they should also try to 'shift' – to put themselves in the situation of those with whom they are in dialogue and who are different.

Transversal politics beckons a dialogical process of exchange between collaborative partners that is so necessary for visualising and enacting the 'shift' in perspective instigated are located. From these insights by a reflexive positionality. To use a Bakhtinian (1984) articulation, it is to see more of the other's location than they can see themselves and that we, therefore, can see of our own positionality. Such a strategy also has the scope to handle the fluid dynamics of social life, where shifting contexts require a theoretical approach that can 'move with' the research as it permeates multiple cultural contexts consecutively and indeed, simultaneously.

It was through this developing and situationally responsive reflexive process that a refocusing on the everyday took shape in the ways Nani and I approached research interviews and community engagement. In these spaces, contestation and ambiguity emerged as a series of alternative heritage narratives of Sabang that could then be engaged to provoke ongoing dialogue amongst participants. The seemingly oppositional repositories of the oral and the archival opened up to permit a third critical voice (in all its multiplicity) to be heard and observed. Seemingly insignificant everyday interactions and performances became imbued with significance. A child drawing a diagonal line across their forehead and a story about a rattan basket became significant indicators of the ongoing relationship between silenced histories and contemporary understandings of identity.

Conclusion

If we are to open heritage up to allow for broader and more inclusive representations, contextually appropriate methodologies that challenge the limiting effect of existing heritage narratives are needed. As I have shown through my reflections of working collaboratively in Sabang, this is particularly salient in postcolonial contexts where histories have been imposed by imperial occupiers, while local narratives have been delegitimised and silenced. Rather than setting my sights on omissions of gendered experience in existing heritage representations, I have reflected here on the mechanics of collaborative heritage research so as to critically engage with the ways different positioning systems and performances produce diverse relationships with heritage knowledge. Feminist standpoint theory offers deeply insightful analytical strategies, which provide the tools for a reflexive engagement with the ways we as researchers can work fruitfully within the interstices of difference, rather than bypassing opportunities for critical engagement.

A critical heritage studies can benefit from the reflexive gaze and dialogical approach promoted by epistemological perspectives such as feminist standpoint theory and anti-racist queer studies. If we are to take seriously the objective of a critical turn in heritage studies, we need to harness these conceptual tools to interrupt the re-inscription of hegemonic narratives. By expanding the scope of heritage studies to account for contemporary everyday performances, the possibility for a more nuanced public engagement with local heritage might be realised. From such performative articulations of the past and its legacies, alternative futurities are created by those who have inherited the silences and incoherencies of the past.

Bibliography

Alexanderson, K. 2014. A dark state of affairs: Hajj networks, pan-Islamism, and Dutch colonial surveillance during the interwar period. *Journal of Social History*, 47(4): 1021–1041.

Assiter, A. 2000. Feminist epistemology and value. *Feminist Theory*, 1(3): 329–345.
Bagnall, G. 2015. Performance and performativity at heritage sites. *Museum and Society*, 1(2): 87–103.
Bakhtin, M.M. 1984. *Problems of Dostoevsky's Poetics*. Minneapolis, MN: University of Minnesota Press.
Bowrey, T. 1905. *A Geographical Account of Countries Round the Bay of Bengal, 1669 to 1679*. Cambridge: The Hakluyt Society.
Browne, K. and Nash, C.J. 2010. Queer methods and methodologies: an introduction. In K. Browne and C.J. Nash (eds) *Queer Methods and Methodologies*. Farnham: Ashgate, pp. 1–25.
Butler, J. 1990. *Gender Trouble: Feminism and the Subversion of Identity*. New York: Routledge.
Butler, J. 1993. *Bodies that Matter: On the Discursive Limits of 'Sex'*. New York: Routledge.
Butler, J. 2004. *Undoing Gender*. New York: Routledge.
Cho, S., Crenshaw, K.W. and McCall, L. 2013. Toward a field of intersectionality studies: theory, applications, and praxis. *Signs*, 38(4): 785–810.
Collins, P.H. 1997. Comment on Hekman's 'Truth and method: feminist standpoint theory revisited': Where's the power? *Signs*, 22(2): 375–381.
Crapanzano, V. 1980. *Tuhami: Portrait of a Moroccan*. Chicago, IL: University of Chicago Press.
Crenshaw, K. 1991. Mapping the margins: intersectionality, identity politics, and violence against women of color. *Stanford Law Review* 43(6): 1241–1299.
Erel, U., Haritaworn, J., Rodríguez, E.G. and Klesse, C. 2010. On the depoliticisation of intersectionality talk: conceptualising multiple oppressions in critical sexuality studies. In Y. Taylor, S. Hines and M. Casey (eds) *Theorizing Intersectionality and Sexuality*. Basingstoke: Palgrave Macmillan, pp. 271–298.
Fotopoulou, A. 2013. Intersectionality, queer studies and hybridity: methodological frameworks for social research. *Journal of International Women's Studies*, 13(2): 19–32.
Goslinga, G. 2012. Spirited encounters: notes on the politics and poetics of representing the uncanny in anthropology. *Anthropological Theory*, 12(4): 386–406.
Haraway, D. 1988. Situated knowledges: the science question in feminism and the privilege of partial perspective. *Feminist Studies*, 14(3): 575–599.
Harding, S. 1987. Introduction: is there a feminist method? In S. Harding (ed.) *Feminism and Methodology: Social Science Issues*. Bloomington, IN: Indiana University Press, pp. 1–14.
Harding, S. 1997. Comment on Hekman's 'Truth and method: feminist standpoint theory revisited': whose standpoint needs the regimes of truth and reality? *Signs*, 22(2): 382–391.
Harding, S. 2004. Introduction: standpoint theory as a site of political, philosophic and scientific debate. In S. Harding (ed.) *The Feminist Standpoint Theory Reader: Intellectual and Political Controversies*. New York and London: Routledge, pp. 1–16.
Haritaworn, J. 2008. Shifting positionalities: empirical reflections on a queer/trans of colour methodology. *Sociological Research Online*, 13. Available at: www.socresonline.org. uk/13/1/13.html (accessed 15 August 2012).
Harrison, R. 2013. *Heritage: Critical Approaches*. Abingdon: Routledge.
hooks, b. 1984. *Feminist Theory: From Margin to Center*. Cambridge: South End Press.
Khalifa, N. and Hardie, T. 2005. Possession and jinn. *Journal of the Royal Society of Medicine*, 98(8): 351–353.

Kloos, D. 2014. A crazy state. *Journal of the Humanities and Social Sciences of Southeast Asia*, 170(1): 25–65.
Lockyer, C. 1711. *An Account of the Trade in India*. London: Samuel Crouch.
Lowenthal, D. 2004. The heritage crusade and its contradictions. In M. Page and M. Randall (eds) *Giving Preservation a History: Histories of Historic Preservation in the United States*. London and New York: Routledge, pp. 19–44.
McCall, L. 2005. The complexity of intersectionality. *Signs*, 30(3): 1771–1800.
Muñoz, J.E. 1999. *Disidentifications: Queers of Color and the Performance of Politics*. Minneapolis, MN and London: University of Minnesota Press.
Muñoz, J.E. 2009. *Cruising Utopia: The Then and There of Queer Futurity*. New York and London: New York University Press.
Pérez, E. 2004. Queering the borderlands: the challenges of excavating the invisible and unheard. *Frontiers: A Journal of Women Studies*, 24(2): 122–131.
Pétursdóttir, Þ. 2013. Concrete matters: ruins of modernity and the things called heritage. *Journal of Social Archaeology*, 13(1): 31–53.
Rooke, A. 2009. Queer in the field: on emotions, temporality, and performativity in ethnography. *Journal of Lesbian Studies*, 13(2): 149–160.
Smith, L. 1999. *Decolonizing Methodologies: Research and Indigenous Peoples*. New York and London: Zed Books.
Smith, L. 2006. *Uses of Heritage*. London: Routledge.
Smith, L. and Akagawa, N. 2008. *Intangible Heritage*. London: Routledge.
Spivak, G. 1988. Can the subaltern speak? In C. Nelson and L. Grossberg (eds) *Marxism and the Interpretation of Culture*. London: Macmillan, pp. 271–313.
Stoetzler, M. and Yuval-Davis, N. 2002. Standpoint theory, situated knowledge and the situated imagination. *Feminist Theory*, 3(3): 315–333.
Tate, S.A. 2005. *Black Skins, Black Masks: Hybridity, Dialogism, Performativity*. Aldershot: Ashgate.
Tivers, J. 2002. Performing heritage: the use of live 'actors' in heritage presentations. *Leisure Studies*, 21(3–4): 187–200.
Yuval-Davis, N. 1999. What is 'transversal politics'? *Soundings*, 12(1): 94–98.
Yuval-Davis, N. 2006. Intersectionality and feminist politics. *European Journal of Women's Studies*, 13(3): 193–209.

Part IV
Politics

Chapter 11

Transversal dances across time and space

Feminist strategies for a critical heritage studies

Astrid von Rosen, Monica Sand and Marsha Meskimmon

Introduction

This chapter draws upon a three-year collaborative research project through which we have sought to explore and articulate a specifically *feminist* approach to dance and the city (as an emergent and corporeal archive) within the context of critical heritage studies. Looking particularly at the independent dance group Rubicon and the traces of the material, yet ephemeral, engagement they had with the city of Gothenburg during the 1980s, our research has enabled us to test the limits of interdisciplinary feminist theories of space, memory and intersectional agency within this particular case study. In so doing, we have developed a multi-modal, multi-disciplinary methodology that articulates a profoundly ethical approach to heritage studies through feminist engagements with embodiment (Grosz 1994), nomadism (Braidotti 1994) and materialisation (Barad 2007).

In what follows, we will introduce briefly the case study at the centre of our project, the Rubicon choreographers and dancers and their work in public spaces in Gothenburg during the 1980s, and then elaborate our critical, feminist approach to researching this particular historical instance of 'intangible heritage'. In our explorations of Rubicon, we have adopted and developed a dialogic, corporeal and multi-disciplinary method to facilitate an active engagement with heritage studies that is both *responsible* for its approach to the past and *responsive* to the ever-changing meanings that are configured in the present through the critical articulation of the concept of 'heritage'. The method that emerges at the dynamic intersection between heritage studies and feminism is, we argue, both contingent and strategic and, as such, suggests directions for future explorations of gender and heritage that reach far beyond our initial case study.

Rubicon in its political context

Inaugurated in 1978, Rubicon was founded by the four female choreographers and dancers: Eva Ingemarsson, Gunnel Johansson, Gun Lund and Gunilla Witt.[1] At this time and in this particular context, it was not commonplace to work as an independent choreographer and, arguably, founding Rubicon was a powerful feminist political strategy, centred on women joining forces in collaborative structures. While Rubicon spent its first years touring in the region performing for children, the choreographers also created their own works, and eventually formed their own companies. Rubicon ceased to exist in 1998, but to the dance community in Gothenburg, its venues and participants are still important.

Significantly, Rubicon was the first independent dance group outside the Swedish capital to receive government subsidy from the Swedish Arts Council. This not only indicates that Rubicon was esteemed for its high artistic quality, it also places the group firmly within the 1974 national cultural policies in Sweden, which consolidated the strong democratising tendencies of the 1960s. Looking back, the 1974 policies were – at least to some extent – successful in decentralising culture by means of building regional structures and support for independent artists (SOU 2009: 16).

Examining the types of independent dance that received public support in Sweden from 1974 until the 1990s, Lena Hammergren maps a one-sided focus on raising the status of dance as an art form through the promotion of contemporary postmodern dance believed to possess universal qualities, while excluding folklore, and other dance cultures. Thus, innovation and creativity overruled tradition and continuity in the field of independent dance (Hammergren 2011: 176–182). Rubicon was, in many ways, a typical exponent of postmodern dance, but the productive aspects of the group's work, as well as lasting impact, were distinctly local, democratic and in direct contrast to any universalising tendency. Indeed, as we will argue, the legacy of Rubicon can be considered as a particular form of *feminist critical heritage*, not to be safeguarded and preserved, but to be activated and learned from.

It was in the early 1980s, after experiencing a dance theatre performance by Pina Bausch, that the Rubicon choreographers became intrigued by the idea of exploring the foundations of dance and decided to start from what they regarded as its very basis: walking. The dancers began by walking together in a studio, and did so for almost a year, adding more and more everyday movements into a new, shared vocabulary. This story of the creative foundations of Rubicon functions as a 'master narrative', told already during the 1980s, and repeated today by the choreographers, as well as by scholars – and by us, here in this text. Yet walking, or more particularly, women composing new systems of walking and dancing in the city of Gothenburg, moving within and viscerally occupying public space with art, is arguably the most enduring legacy of Rubicon and where their practice is most clearly articulating a feminist critical heritage studies.

Looking at Rubicon's way of walking from a dance perspective, it is important to remember that three of the four founding choreographers had classical ballet as their basic training form and the walking sessions became a way creating another foundation for their work. As expressed by Lund (2013), walking like Rubicon was a most difficult and demanding task to undertake. Not only did such walking instigate change, it manifestly and persistently implemented it in the individual dancers' bodies and in the collective body politic. In this sense, it can be argued that Rubicon's walking through dance can itself be considered as a contribution to a dynamic, *critical* and responsive form of heritage.

The walking, in combination with the fact that Rubicon did not have any stage or venue of their own, led to the idea of performing outdoors, in the city, in the public sphere. In turn, this has several important resonances, one of them being with the 1968 political context and the idea that the streets were the 'natural place to be' (Persson 2013). Although Rubicon asked the authorities for permission when performing in the city, their appearance in urban space retained an anarchistic flavour that reached beyond the frame of 1970s cultural policy. According to Ingemarsson (2013), the opening of dance to an audience that could not be counted easily was completely alien to the bureaucratic structure of the funding bodies, who built their model on statistics that determined the number of paying audience members in venues with clear borders. By contrast, the choreographers of Rubicon met at cafés to discuss and make drawings of choreographic patterns and ideas. They also worked *in situ*, at the places selected for performances, making themselves visible in public space. Additional dancers would come in later in the process, as funding for rehearsal time was minimal.

Rubicon's 1986 performance on the stairs of the city art museum at Götaplatsen, a pivotal cultural space within Gothenburg to this day, provides a useful example of the way in which their city interventions made the socio-economic, cultural and sexual politics of the urban space evident through ephemeral as well as hyper-material dance actions. (Jackson 2010: 240–260). A documentary video made at the time demonstrates how the dancers in yellow moved – and did not move – on the stairs, as noises from the city and its inhabitants became entangled with the insistently hammering music for the performance. The event crystallises a number of identifiable principles within Rubicon's work and their legacy.

Zooming in on a particular sequence of the performance – the dancers crawling down the stairs – we see the principles in operation. The dancers form two groups (three in each) and these move as patterns of yellow colour in the larger space. Traversing the horizontal direction of the stairs, the bodies fill in the vertical and hierarchical dimension, while at the same time subverting it, as they glide down the stairs, head first, hands in white gloves. This movement is powerful in the way it activates and challenges the large neo-classical vaults in the museum façade, as well as the complex nexus of ideologies evoked by this architecture and its history.

During the performance on the Götaplatsen, the dancers were, for the first time clad in the yellow rainwear that would become their signature mark for several years, making them visible beyond gender notions. Notably, yellow rainwear was also used by the workers maintaining the city's public spaces. Thus, a metonymic relation is established between the dancers and the larger groups of workers. Of course, there is a pragmatic dimension to this, as dancing outdoors in a city where it often rains requires appropriate costuming – tights and tutus would not suffice – but the yellow dress also emphasised a political layer: dancers were important, professional '*kulturarbetare*' (cultural workers), potentially sharing their art with a large-scale audience. The term '*kulturarbetare*' was deployed in the early twentieth century, but during the 1960s and 1970s it specifically equated cultural workers with '*förvärvsarbetare*' (labourers) (SOU 2003: 21).

Though the audience members could move freely, the choreographers had ideal spaces for them in mind when creating the pieces. In particular, the dance movements engaged spectators in haptic (touching with the eyes) and kinaesthetic (body mirroring) ways, giving rise to manifold personal associations and critical judgements. In such a response to space, mind and body, thoughts and affects, are entangled and conjoined. Such an articulation of public space is in marked contrast to a mythic, masculine ideal of the public sphere as a place reserved for disembodied or 'objective' rationality. At play also were cultural imaginaries – mindsets, ideas, associations and fantasies many people agree upon – enlivened by the exchange between the dancers' actions, the spectators' experiences and the environment. For example, the idea of artistic dance as something to be performed indoors in a theatre building by artists in certain typical dance gear (such as tights, leotards, tutus or historical costume) may be challenged by an audience member experiencing a dancer in raingear crawling in public space. On the symbolic level (or ordering structure) Rubicon enacted the conflict between the ideology of the cultural policies and the dancers' activist agenda on the stairs of the prestigious art museum, in which they did not have a place. Without being deliberately hostile towards the art institution, Rubicon's engagement with the museum exterior can be interpreted as institutional critique – which bodies were inside the museum and which were kept at bay? How does urban architecture and the 'cultural capital' of fine art serve to constrain access to the public sphere? How do these nomads, walking, dancing and taking the space of the cultural plaza in their bright yellow rainwear call these imaginary limits into question and how might we reactivate their legacy in our present through an embodied and critical heritage studies practice?

Rubicon's formal endeavours were not only traversed and affected by the political discourse of their time, the group's dance figurations fed into them, with the specific aim of establishing a qualified as well as generously open community and a venue for non-institutional dance in the local context. As Rubicon repeatedly reappeared as nomads in yellow rainwear (and sometimes in other costumes) in various city spaces, they created an imaginary web of artistic presence – who knew when or where they would appear next time? Importantly, the notion of the nomad has not been forced upon Rubicon by us, but rather was used in their information materials, resonating at the time with interviews, introductions and in particular a translation into Swedish of a theoretical text by Gilles Deleuze. This text, in Swedish called '*Nomadtänkande*' ['Nomadic thinking'] originally written in 1973 was published in the Swedish journal *Res Publica* 5–6, in 1986. Moreover, *Capital aim is to explore and isme et Schizophrénie 2. Mille Plateaux* by Deleuze and Felix Guattari, published in French in 1980 would, of course, also be read within the Swedish cultural establishment, as would the first translation into English of *A Thousand Plateaus* from 1987.

Embarking upon the process of accessing Rubicon's legacy as more than an elegant coincidence within a nomadic narrative, we sought to work with, indeed to *walk with*, their performance legacy as an important form of critical heritage. Deploying the practice-led, artistic research method of *walking* as an exploratory strategy that might bring our enquiry closer to the physical and material intervention of Rubicon, we determined not to *recreate* the work of Rubicon, but to *reactivate* the dynamics of their gendered, ethico-political spatial practices so to create a vibrant dialogue with the past and reanimate the 'archive' with/in the city and the bodies of the dancers, spectators and researchers who worked together at the core of this project.

Subsequent explorations developed the experiential data of the 'walkshops' further by creating dialogues with the choreographers and dancers themselves (who have remained important and generous participants in this project) as well as scholars from a number of cognate fields ranging from the arts, social sciences and humanities. The dialogic approaches that have developed also extend to the sparse archival records that exist around Rubicon's interventions, which have been supplemented by still and moving-image documentary and memory-work from participants in the project. Through these varied and experimental processes, our emphasis has been on *resonance* and *reactivation*, ways to enable the feminist ethics and the legacy of the dancers of the city to continue to have an impact in the present rather than become a relic of the past. A more critical look at some of these strategies is instructive at this point.

Artistic re-activation of Rubicon's legacy

Rubicon's performances in the city were determined by a more or less pragmatic decision; without a permanent stage, the group performed in the city centre of Gothenburg as the *City Dancers*. Since they did not see themselves as homeless they called themselves 'nomads of the city'. The way they performed in the city underlined the concept of 'nomadism' in a new context developed through the mobile 'schizophrenic' forces of capitalism (Deleuze and Guattari 1980/2004). Thus Rubicon encountered the friction between the traditional nomadic body with its rhythmic walk in circles in a seasonal repetition and the modern body in a city organised for efficient walking forward in straight lines seemingly free from the rhythm of nature. Moreover, Rubicon identified, moved within, projected, and challenged these very lines (lines created and recreated by architecture, infrastructure and moving people) in and through their choreographic interventions.

Our 'walking', within the context of the collaborative research project, was also a more or less pragmatic decision; our task was not to reconstruct the choreography of Rubicon (that would be a different project, if equally valuable), but to create a space where scholars from several academic disciplines and practitioners from several artistic fields could engage bodily with the core concerns of Rubicon's project as it sought to articulate, through basic movement and gesture ('walking'), a resonant relationship with the spaces of the city. Many of the participants had not seen

Rubicon's choreography before and had little knowledge of the work of the group, but through the workshop participants were able to enter a sphere where the powers and potentialities of communal critical activation of city space became accessible at a profoundly experiential level. Monica Sand, artist and artistic researcher, introduced walking as a way of creating a corporeal and sensitive relation to the history of the *City Dancers*, returning participants to the places where Rubicon had performed. We walked, we worked together, we came to understand both the difficulties and the exhilaration of making a physical, gestural and collective intervention in the public sphere. We could not have gleaned the same insights through reading about Rubicon or by looking at the few small images or short snippets of film footage of their work in the archive. (Meskimmon *et al.* 2014). To be precise, through this practice our bodies became a form of corporeal repository – an archive of sorts – for a moving and living history. Reading about Rubicon would of course have had an affective dimension, but there would not have been any direct tracing, *in situ* (in place), of these activities into our bodies as living archives.

This was a different form of engagement and dialogue, arguably a feminist critical engagement, with the legacy of one specific instance of women's (the Rubicon choreographers) ephemeral hyper-material urban activism. However, the strategy itself was premised upon a more extensive theoretical lineage concerning the ethical implications of embodied research and situated knowledge; in particular what Kelly Oliver has so eloquently described as the relationship between 'response-ability' and 'responsibility':

> There is a direct connection between the response-ability of subjectivity and ethical and political responsibility . . . The responsibility inherent in subjectivity has the double sense of the condition of possibility of response, response-ability, on the one hand, and the ethical obligation to respond and to enable response-ability from others born out of that founding possibility, on the other.
>
> (Oliver 2001: 15)

Within the context of our project, these ethical and aesthetic interactions have centred on the concepts of resonance and materialisation as embodied and critical methodological tools bringing practice-led artistic research into close connection with feminist cultural geography, urban studies and the politics of the public sphere. Turning to that now helps to further unfold our argument for a multi-modal, multi-disciplinary feminist critical heritage studies.

Walking between matter and metaphors – the ethics and aesthetics of resonance

Our collaborative research project offered an inspiring invitation for artists and researchers to 'walk in the steps of Rubicon' with the focus on their project the *City Dancers* (1986–1989). The project posed a number of ethical questions throughout and we made particular decisions in relation to how we should conduct our critical explorations of the 'intangible' heritage left in the wake of the dancers of the city. Ethics and aesthetics meet where bodies are organised in space and time, in society and in research, and in this case, between the past and the present, art and politics, matter and language. Three questions emerged with pressing regularity:

1   What does it mean and in what sense do we walk in the steps of the dance performance group Rubicon?
2   By what means are we able to respond to the challenges of public space today beyond the 'neo-liberal' individual and commercialised paradigm?
3   If claiming the relation 'bodies–cities' as a living archive, how can we produce research that will continue to maintain the vitality and vibrancy of the original inscription of the city by its dancers so that it continues to make meaning in the present?

In short, these questions could be posed in terms of *response-ability* (the ability to respond to space and time in the proprioceptive, corporeal and vocal sense) and *responsibility*, here, towards history, in public space and through research (Meskimmon 2014). In the etymology of 'responsibility', relation is at the core (Sand 2014): without a relation to others you lose your ability to respond to the challenges of the space and of society. To express it in corporeal/vocal terms, if no body is able to respond, nobody becomes response-able/responsible.

The expression to 'walk in the steps of' can be understood as either a spatial-corporeal reality or a linguistic metaphor. In reality it is easy to walk in the steps of others on a snowy field, in sand or on a rainy street. The metaphor, meaning to follow the life path or imitate the example of either an historical or invented person, in life, profession or character, does not necessarily take the follower out on foot. In our project, the metaphor of walking is turned into reality in several ways; in the walking process itself, in mapping out and re-activating the places Rubicon once used as citizens in a society dedicated to the power of consumption. This strategy confronts us with the first ethical issues; does this walking process make sense to the history of the City Dancers? How and in what sense are we responsible for this history?

Without aiming to present a 'true story', or to repeat, re-perform or re-present the choreographic work by Rubicon, we, as a research group, collectively approached the places once used by the group. While the urban art performances of Rubicon were ephemeral, the places where they took place remain (sometimes re-built and re-organised). Walking enables the present to resonate with the past through daily routines and social rituals, such that the archive of the city activates both on a corporeal/spatial and an individual/social level. By activating our corporeal engagement with/in the same places as Rubicon, we began a process of walking through the archive of the city. Rather than historical layers, we created another spatial and corporeal *infrastructure* within the urban schema: an infrastructural cartography of places performed and inhabited by art, that are possible to *re*-inhabit and *re*-activate through our research method in the present.

In situ, a process of *resonance* takes place in the search to establish a communication with the specific place through movements, voices and rhythms. Through this process, the aim is to explore and re-activate artistic potential so that remembering becomes a rhythmic process between the past and the present urban organisation and social relations. By re-activating the living and lived archive of the city, with our bodies as research tools, and entering into a body-space remembering process, we create new body-space memories and take responsibility for our materialisation of the spaces and histories we engage. In our ways of walking in the steps of Rubicon, the archival relationship between 'bodies–cities' is set in motion in a rhythmic encounter between feet and surface, the past and present, re-activating the imaginative potential (and cultural imaginary) of places: their materiality, dimensions, associations, memories and fragments of stories.

In *A Philosophy of Walking*, Frederic Gros states that it is possible to escape identity, name and history by walking, yet refers only to male walkers through history (Gros 2014). In public space, throughout history, the ability to become no body, a neutralised body, has been a freedom reserved for bodies not defined by sex, race, class, or age, e.g. the white middle-class man. (Solnit 2001: 232ff.). If walking is defined by gender, Rubicon, as the City Dancers, re-invented walking to build a new collective public identity in relation to both an intentional and unintentional audience. As performers, they became visible as a new kind of 'urban labour' dressed in the bright yellow rainwear, similar to the common city labours at that time. As actors and subjects, prepared and dressed for hard physical work, the group occupied a new stage for performance art protected from both the unreliable weather and the common objectification of women in the public arena. Due to the extensive transformation of public space, public art performances that are not commercial have almost become impossible; seeing performers in yellow rainwear in the city today would be unlikely without the aid of commercial sponsorship. In the extreme commercialisation of cities worldwide, *public* space has decreased and much art has been incorporated into the entertainment industry: public art performances have become another way of promoting 'the creative city'.

Rubicon, engaging both female and male dancers performed a visible and audible response to public space, an alternative to the common location of art within the commercial power of urban places, and suggested among other things more varied roles for women in public. One of the questions this posed for our research into the critical heritage of these ephemeral yet hyper-material actions, was in what sense we as citizens, artists, researchers and visitors were able to respond to the city now, dominated as it is by commercialisation and private interests, in order to reactivate any sense of common ground? That brings us to a reconception of the idea of responsibility, moving away from a purely individualistic sensitivity toward an awareness of its transversal and collective effect. We are arguing that the capacity to respond is related not only to the individual, but to the entire organisation of space and the multidimensional communication between bodies in space and time.

Neutralisation of public space is part of an aggressive design ideology that separates places from users and the individual from the society as a common concern. The aim is to protect, not the visitor, but the private consumption domain, by keeping out the local climate, weather conditions or environmental sounds and get visitors to adapt to a commercial around the clock rhythm instead of a rhythm based in the seasons and the time of the day (Kärrholm 2012: 73). Seamlessly, without any friction, disconnected from spatial, temporal and corporeal rhythmic dimensions, inhabitants find themselves 'surfing' through an attraction, a historical scenography, serving an image rather than the organisation of daily life. It is a serious threat to the human being that the design tool of neutralisation forces inhabitants to adapt so that the real human body becomes an aesthetic problem – poor, aging, fragile, disturbing, ugly – an enemy of friction-less design.

In both research and life, visual metaphors create a language of spatial orientation, directed by vision, that seems to presume an immobile viewer with a *point of view; outlook, vision, overview, focus, general picture* and *reflection*. 'Go through the material', 'take one step at a time', as well as 'walking in circles' or 'moving forward' are metaphors performed every day. Our third research question raises the potential of our research as a powerful force to transform matter and direct knowledge – body, space and time – into more than mere abstractions, metaphors, words and afterthoughts. Metaphors can be more than abstractions; as linguistic and practical tools, we are able to live them and orient ourselves through them (Lakoff and Johnson 1980; Sand 2012). They structure our way of acting, mediating seamlessly from real life to abstraction and back again. Refusing to accede to the abstraction of 'space' and 'the body' within the research project has had a significant impact on both the methods and the results of our research.

In contrast to the neutralisation of space, resonance creates an active and critical response to the way we inhabit and act within public space that draws us out of the seemingly unmarked position of a disembodied, individual consumer. Both bodies and spaces are resonating systems, set in motion by vibrations within and in relation to each other (Gershon 2013). Those vibrations create an instant awareness and sensibility, almost on a cellular level, towards space and other bodies, a knowledge created in and through spatial embodiment and articulated in corporeal-materialist aesthetics. As an artistic research method, we deployed resonance in this project as an active response to, and a corporeal and sensorial dialogue with, public space. As the immaterial, continuous and elusive expressions of the rhythms of social content and meaning, based in movements, actions and voices, resonance is a response to and an art of resonating collectively with/in/through the city (Sand and Atienza 2012).

Drawing also on the insights of cultural geography and urban studies, *resonance* functions both as a descriptor for urban experience and as a practical tool for collective actions that remove neutrality. Engaging with the material reality in a collective engaged embodiment, the artists/researchers vibrate with the environment, between fiction and facts, feet and social rhythms, voice and spatial dimensions, matter and language. In this project we act and re-act together, using our bodies and voices as a collective, responding to the dynamic vibrations of the resonance of the past as it is materialised in the present. *Resonance* is to be understood as a frame and a figuration through which methods such as walking, re-actions, memory-work, archival research and critical writing for this project are developed.

It is significant here that resonance must be employed and explored in a real space, by real bodies and actions. In daily life the environment with its smell, sound and tactility activates the senses, we feel and react to the presence of other persons, spatial organisation, social and corporeal rhythms. As researchers in this project we entered the complex process of being both producers and observers within the same situation as other agents, others who are both actors and observers, similarly unable to fully control the outcome. Within this corporeal-materialist aesthetics, the immaterial and moving life is performed with hopes, expectations, associations, memories and projections of the becoming future (Meskimmon forthcoming). By taking up the invitation to walk in the steps of Rubicon and resonate with their legacy, our project stages a response to the past and the present gentrification and neutralisation of public space by developing research methods that are dependent on the creative human body and its spatial and rhythmic needs and desires. Resonance and materialisation, as method and concept, offer practical tools for space-body experiments. Thus by 'walking in the steps of Rubicon', metaphors and abstractions can be brought back into real places, in a rhythmic resonance between language and matter, ethics and aesthetics.

Crossing the Rubicon: towards a feminist critical heritage studies

Since its inception, our project has been multi-valent; it is a project absolutely centred on exploring the political and artistic legacy of Rubicon as a significant, yet under-researched, group of performers/choreographers who brought independent dance to Gothenburg in the 1980s, but it is also a research project that asks critical questions concerning the construction of the arena of 'heritage studies' in relation to academic disciplines, contemporary art theories and practices and feminist interventions in the cultural sphere. There are tensions between these various strands within the project, but more often than not, they are productive – they generate new perspectives and possibilities both for work on Rubicon and within the frame of a *critical* heritage studies.

Given the focus of the research upon the work of Rubicon, the cultural legacy of women artists, ephemeral performance practices and the sexual politics of urban space, it is not surprising to find that we would be in dialogue with feminist research in the arts and social sciences. In relation to the field of heritage studies, the insights of authors such as Laurajane Smith are important to our project in that they stress the idea of heritage as a *cultural process* rather than an *object*.

In many ways, the arguments Smith made following a period of work with Waanyi women in Australia, that heritage can be understood better as a form of experience forged through dialogue and activity (fishing, for example, in Smith's case study) is paralleled by our work with the legacy of the Rubicon city dancers described in this chapter (Smith 2006: 45–48). Smith's insights into heritage, derived through an astute analysis of empirical data and a clear social science methodology, bear remarkable similarities to work undertaken by feminist activist artists during the 1980s and 1990s as part of what came to be called 'new genre public art'. Suzanne Lacy remains a key voice in this field and her statement from 1995 on the interrelationship between marginal subjects, public spaces, the arts and heritage are instructive here:

> The construction of a history of new genre public art is not built on a typology of materials, spaces or artistic media, but rather on concepts of audience, relationships, communication, and political intention. It is my premise that the real heritage of the current moment in public art came from the discourses of largely marginalized artists.
>
> (Lacy 1995: 28)

The focus here on the role of the audience, relationships, communication and politics in shaping the public sphere through the arts and heritage reiterates a commitment to thinking through the processes by which cultural meanings are produced in the here and now, by active agency in the present. This is a direct move away from a focus on the objects of heritage (or public art), as if these have any innate, essential or intrinsic value or meaning.

These insights are crucial to the present project and to our attempts to begin to articulate a methodology that can adequately underpin a *critical feminist heritage studies*, which enables ephemeral, and sometimes marginalised, practices to come to the fore. We would argue that it is vital to the construction of our methodology both that we cross disciplinary boundaries (particularly between the arts, art practice and the social sciences), and that we find a means by which to think through processes rather than categories of objects. Taking the former point first, our project touches on established work in feminist art and performance history, theory and practice, feminist cultural geography and sociology (on sexuality and space), feminist philosophy (questions of embodiment and sexed subjectivity) and politics (especially women in the public sphere). Perhaps less expected routes within the project have come from the direction of feminist poetics, life-writing and art-writing, where the emphasis on finding textual modes that are dialogic, engaged and corporeal have been increasingly significant as the corollary to the affective and bodily engagements with space that we have enacted practically (through 'walkshops' and resonance). Likewise, in working more deeply with the issues of memory invoked by this project (the memories of the dancers themselves, participant-spectators in the 1980s and current users of the city's spaces), we quickly found that a feminist method ('memory-work', pioneered first in

Germany by social scientists exploring the acquisition of gendered identity and now more commonly undertaken by social scientists around the world) was crucial to the project, and that feminist methods of 'participatory action research' were inspiring as well as practically effective for us (Haug 1992; O'Neill 2013; Onyx and Small 2001).

In thinking through processes, the theoretical trajectories of our project have strong links with corporeal feminist perspectives that undo masculine-normative epistemologies premised on the binary logic of a sharp subject/object, mind/body split (cf. Braidotti 1994; Grosz 1994). They further incorporate a move away from *representation* where that term suggests that texts, images and objects (including, but not limited to, academic and theoretical writing, literature, performance and the visual and material arts) operate as a mute mirror of 'reality', rather than constitutive of any sense we might have of the 'reality' of ourselves, others and the world. In this way, our thinking and making take a lead from the feminist materialist critiques of 'objective' and/or 'reflective' knowledges (cf. Barad 2007; Braidotti 2002; Haraway 1991) that have turned toward 'materialisation' as a way to explore the mutable processes through which subjects, objects and meanings emerge in mutuality:

> *[M]aterialization is an iteratively intra-active process whereby material-discursive bodies are sedimented out of the intra-action of multiple material-discursive apparatuses through which these phenomena (bodies) become intelligible.*
> (Barad 2001: 108, emphasis in original)

The feminist theory that underpins our approach understands subjects to be embodied and situated within, rather than beyond, the world. In its anti-essentialism, it chimes with the more empirical claims of those strands of heritage studies that see heritage as a cultural process, but moves further in its acknowledgement of the contingency of meaning-in-making. Arguably, then, ours is not a *critical feminist* project because those are stable categories of meaning that we 'reflect' or 'represent' in our work, but because we are aware in using this epithet, that we cannot fix it fast, only materialise it in all its variant contingency. As Elizabeth Grosz argued so well in relation to the attempts to define feminist texts 'once and for all':

> [N]o text can be classified once and for all as wholly feminist or wholly patriarchal: these appellations depend on its context, its place within that context, how it is used, by whom and to what effect. These various contingencies dictate that at best a text is feminist or patriarchal only provisionally, only momentarily, only in some but not in all of its possible readings, and in some but not all of its possible effects.
> (Grosz 1995: 24)

Like the question of 'objectivity' that is unravelled by feminist philosophies of science, which acknowledge the intrinsic connections between the observer and the observed and the mutual emergence of the subject and object in and through the 'agential cut' (Barad 2007: 178) of the flow of life in every critical act, we embrace feminist contingency. Contingency does not negate meaning, but makes it animate in every instantiation; the body-archive of the city comes alive in its critical activation in the present, not its dusty entombment in the filing systems of the past. Our constitution of a feminist method-in-process does not pit the insights of the social sciences *against* those of the creative arts, humanities or pure sciences, but rather entangles these knowledges in a dynamic exchange.

We have actively sought a method for *walking/dancing in the steps of the past* that permits contingencies – the shift of weight and balance from foot to foot as we correspond and resonate with that which has come before. We have moved toward a *multi-modal, multi-disciplinary* method that can respond to, and be responsible for, the various forms in which our enquiry takes place, from the textual, archival, visual, material, spatial and gestural to the performed and remembered. This is not a fixed method, there are no absolute rules and steps that will once and for all define it, but there are key insights that our contingent strategy can provide for others working in what we would call a feminist critical heritage studies.

First, it is collaborative and dialogic, as well as sensorial and site-specific: it is a matter of speaking *with*, rather than *to* or *of* others. In this case 'speaking with' connects the contemporary disconnected bodies with the seemingly neutralised space of consumption and knowledge production. This collective process of resonance pertains even for the 'lone researcher'; heritage is not 'owned' by any one person/interest, but is always already collective and formed by the interlocutions of many different agents. Second, a feminist critical heritage studies is embodied and embedded; there is no 'outside' to knowing. By inhabiting and re-activating the urban art archive, we make space both for other kinds of knowledges and spatial structures to emerge. Third, our method is an ethics in that meanings are articulated through affective response-ability that engenders critical responsibility. This departs from a 'masculine, disembodied notion of the "public sphere" as a political space' premised upon 'objective' rationality and instead insists on the concept of an 'affective public sphere', 'a space of emotional exchange' (Perkovic 2015: 20–21). And finally, in our method there is a commitment to the interconnections between space, time and matter(ing); the past is made in the here and now, through ceaseless agential acts, both human and non-human.

It is our contention that a *critical* heritage studies ranges broadly across questions of cultural value, legacy, participant engagement and of course, the power politics of knowledge production and that none of these questions can be addressed from a neutral position. We argue that *feminist* theories and methods that make explicit the embodied and situated perspectives of knower and known, the significance of our corporeal engagements with the material traces of the past and the complexities of sexual and other forms of difference in negotiating the terrain of 'heritage', are a key element of any form of *critical* heritage studies. We thus propose the parameters of a *feminist critical heritage studies* (however contingent these may be), and suggest that these are important to future work in the arts, humanities and social sciences.

As a way of concluding we would note UNESCO's 2003 notion of 'intangible heritage', which includes a wide range of practices, traditions and artistic expressions such as dance (UNESCO 2003). For UNESCO, it is important to define 'intangible heritage' so it can be 'safeguarded' (UNESCO 2014). The approach to heritage that we are interested in exploring is not necessarily one that defines an object for safeguarding; rather, as we have sought to demonstrate, we are interested in activating forms of so-called intangible heritage because of their critical and constructive potential in the present. Thus, Rubicon's work for public space can be considered an important, historically specific example of 'dance as critical heritage', which transgresses artificial, and not particularly compelling, borders between intangible and tangible aspects of past events.

In developing approaches toward heritage that move beyond its preservation (in the past) and toward its activation (in the present), we are arguing that a collaborative, dialogic method of working is more powerful than methods premised upon disembodied, disengaged 'objectivity'. Our insights have their origins in decades of feminist work across the arts, social sciences and humanities and are pivotal to thinking about the significance of the past in the volatile circumstances of the present. What is happening in today's Europe, with cultural policies rapidly changing, and subsidies for independent culture being reduced or completely cut off, makes it even more relevant to explore and activate the dance heritage growing out of the Swedish 1974 cultural policies, in the present. And what we learn from that specific instance, we can develop toward further work in the future.

Acknowledgements

The authors are thankful to the Carina Ari Memorial Foundation and the Centre for Critical Heritage Studies at the University of Gothenburg and University College London for supporting the research.

Note

1 Johansson left in the mid 1980s when Rubicon stopped creating work for children only and started to perform outdoors in the city.

Bibliography

Barad, K. 2001. Getting Real: Technocscientific Practices and the Materialization of Reality. *Differences: A Journal of Feminist Cultural Studies* 10(2): 87–128.

Barad, K. 2007. *Meeting the Universe Halfway: Quantum Physics and the Entanglement of Matter and Meaning*. Durham, NC: Duke University Press.

Braidotti, R. 1994. *Nomadic Subjects: Embodiment and Sexual Difference in Contemporary Feminist Theory.* New York: Columbia University Press.
Braidotti, R. 2002. *Metamorphoses: Toward a Materialist Theory of Becoming.* Oxford: Polity.
Deleuze, G. 1973/1986. Nomadtänkande. *Res Publica* 5–6: 79–89.
Deleuze, G. and Guattari, F. 1980/2004. *A Thousand Plateaus: Capitalism and Schizophrenia,* trans. by B. Massumi. London Continuum.
Gershon, W. 2013. Vibrational Affect Sound Theory and Practice in Qualitative Research. *Cultural Studies Critical Methodologies* 13(4): 257–262.
Gros, F. 2014. *A Philosophy of Walking,* trans. by J. Howe. London: Verso.
Grosz, E. 1994. *Volatile Bodies: Toward a Corporeal Feminism.* Bloomington, IN and Indianapolis, IN: Indiana University Press.
Grosz, E. 1995. *Space, Time and Perversion: Essays on the Politics of Bodies.* London and New York: Routledge.
Hammergren, L. 2011. Dance and Democracy in Norden. In K. Vedel (ed.) *Dance and the Formation of Norden: Emergences and Struggles.* Trondheim: Tapir Academic Press, 176–182.
Haraway, D. 1991. *Simians, Cyborgs, and Women: The Reinvention of Nature.* London and NY: Routledge.
Haug, F. 1992. *Beyond Female Masochism: Memory-Work and Politics.* Trans. by R. Livingstone. London: Verso.
Ingemarsson, E. 2013. *Dance as Critical Heritage: Archives, Access, Action.* Seminar, 30 May. Gothenburg, Sweden: Critical Heritage Studies, University of Gothenburg.
Jackson, S. 2010. When 'Everything Counts': Experimental Performance and Performance Historiography. In C.M. Canning and T. Postlewait (eds) *Representing the Past: Essays in Performance Historiography.* Iowa City, IA: University of Iowa Press, 240–260.
Kärrholm, M. 2012. *Retailising Space: Architecture, Retail and the Territorialisation Of Public Space.* Burlington, VT: Ashgate.
Lacy, S. 1995. *Mapping the Terrain: New Genre Public Art.* San Francisco, CA: Bay Press.
Lakoff, G. and Johnson, M. 1980. *Metaphors We Live By.* Chicago, IL: University of Chicago Press.
Lund, G. 2013. *Dance as Critical Heritage: Archives, Access, Action.* Symposium, 28–29 October. Gothenburg, Sweden: Critical Heritage Studies, University of Gothenburg.
Meskimmon, M. 2014. Response and Responsibility: On the Cosmo-Politics of Generosity in Contemporary Asian Art. In C. Turner and M. Antoinette (eds) *Contemporary Asian Art and Exhibitions: Connectivities and World-Making.* Canberra: ANU Press, 143–159.
Meskimmon, M. Forthcoming. Art Matters: Feminist Corporeal-Materialist Aesthetics. In H. Robinson and M.E. Buszek (ed.) *The Companion to Feminist Art Practice and Theory.* Oxford: Blackwell.
Meskimmon, M., von Rosen, A. and Sand, M. (eds) 2014. *Dance as Critical Heritage: Archives, Action, Access, Symposium Report 1.* Gothenburg, Sweden: Critical Heritage Studies (CHS), Gothenburg University. Available at: http://criticalheritagestudies.gu.se/digitalAssets/1497/1497255_dach-report.pdf (accessed 4 November 2016).
Oliver, K. 2001. *Witnessing: Beyond Recognition.* Minneapolis, MN and London: Minnesota University Press.
O'Neill, M. 2013. Women, Art, Migration and Diaspora: The Turn to Art in the Social Sciences and the 'New' Sociology of Art? In M. Meskimmon and D. Rowe (eds)

Women, the Arts and Globalization: Eccentric Experience. Manchester: Manchester University Press, 44–66.
Onyx, J. and Small, J. 2001. Memory-Work: The Method. *Qualitative Enquiry* 7(6): 773–786.
Perkovic, J. 2015. An Ethics of Touch. *Dancehouse Diary* 8: 20–21.
Persson, L. 2013. *Dance as Critical Heritage: Archives, Access, Action.* Symposium, 28–29 October. Gothenburg, Sweden: Critical Heritage Studies, University of Gothenburg.
Sand, M. 2012. Spegelresa i Spegellandet – reflektionens begärliga och bedrägliga yta. *Arche* 40–44: 130–145.
Sand, M. 2014. Resonans – resonera med stadsrummet. In K. Olsson and D. Nilsson (eds) *Det förflutna i framtidens stad. Tankar om kulturarv, konsumtion och hållbar stadsutveckling.* Lund: Nordic Academic Press, 37–48.
Sand, M. and Atienza, R. 2012. Playing the Space: Resonance, Improvisations and Variations of Urban Ambience. In *Ambiances in Action/Ambiances en acte(s) – International Congress on Ambiances.* Montreal, Canada: International Ambiances Network, 153–158.
Smith, L. 2006. *The Uses of Heritage.* London and New York: Routledge.
Solnit, R. 2001. *Wanderlust: A History of Walking.* London: Verso.
SOU 2003: 21, *Konstnärerna och trygghetssystemen. Betänkande av Utredningen konstnärerna och trygghetssystemen,* Statens offentliga utredningar, Stockholm.
SOU 2009: 16, *Kulturutredningen del 2. Betänkande av Kulturutredningen: Förnyelseprogram.* Stockholm: Statens offentliga utredningar.
UNESCO 2003. Convention for the Safeguarding of Intangible Cultural Heritage. Available at: http://unesdoc.unesco.org/images/0013/001325/132540e.pdf (accessed 19 June 2015).
UNESCO 2014. Lists of Intangible Cultural Heritage and Register of Best Safeguarding Practices. Available at: www.unesco.org/culture/ich/index.php?pg=00011 (accessed 19 June 2015).

Chapter 12

Gendering 'the other Germany'
Resistant and residual narratives on Stauffenbergstraße, Berlin

Joanne Sayner and Rhiannon Mason

> On 20 July it will be exactly seventy years since the momentous attempt to overthrow Hitler took place in the Bendler Block. What better reason than to open this modernised permanent exhibition on resistance to National Socialism. For the dramatic and tragic events surrounding the 20 July 1944 still have a distressing effect today. Not only in relation to the brave men and women who dared to attempt the coup at Hitler's Headquarters or in the Bendler Block – and I particularly mention 'the women', in case some of you are wondering, because they gave their support in many cases – but also with regard to the family members who were at the mercy of the vengeful Nazis in the days following 20 July.
>
> (Wowereit 2014a)[1]

Introduction

Klaus Wowereit, then the Mayor of Berlin, spoke these words at the opening of the reconceptualised German Resistance Memorial Centre [Gedenkstätte deutscher Widerstand] in July 2014. Or, rather, he intended to speak these words. Instead, when he actually presented his speech Wowereit conflated reference to 'the women' with 'the families who were sympathetic [*Mitleidtragende*] to the work of the men' (Wowereit 2014b). The aside Wowereit originally intended is notable in a contemporary public German memory context where it is axiomatic that women were involved in the resistance to Nazism. Debates about women's lives and roles within the Nazi state and disputes about responsibility, perpetration and victimhood have persisted for several decades (Bock 1998; Koonz 1987). Recent scholarship and public forms of commemoration have increased the visibility of women who resisted (Sayner 2013; Schad 2010).[2] Until recently though, there has been little thematisation of gender, of masculinity and femininity, in exhibitions about Nazism (Paver 2009). Wowereit's slippage at the high-profile opening event raises questions about agency, about the extent to which women were involved in the resistance and about the ways in which women and gender are represented in the permanent exhibition 'Resistance against National Socialism' ['*Widerstand gegen Nationalsozialismus*']. It is this exhibition, and the adjacent commemorative site, which are the focus here. They are of particular significance in a context where resistance plays a minor role in contemporary exhibitions about Nazism, if it is present at all.[3]

In this chapter, we highlight how, amid competing narratives circulating within the Memorial Centre, the constitutive elements of this site of commemoration give rise to gendered tensions in the display. We maintain that narratives of heroicised, masculinised resistance are privileged by and dominant within the auratic site. Arguing for the continued relevance of a framework developed by Raymond Williams (1977: 122), we suggest that while 'residual' narratives within the display have the potential to productively unsettle these narratives, the opportunity for making the visitor aware of the gendered dimensions of life under Nazism is missed. As such, gender roles are taken for granted and normalised. We argue that this is significant in terms of contemporary museological practice, which should take gender into account, and also in terms of how resistance to Nazism itself is conceptualised. We suggest that thematising gendered resistance narratives onsite could provide the basis for an 'emergent' feminist practice within the commemorative space. We investigate how gender norms are represented at the Memorial Centre by focusing on four aspects where these issues are most prominent: the commemorative courtyard; the three introductory exhibition rooms; the representation of 20 July 1944 in rooms 8–11; and the use of photographs throughout the exhibition.

Locating the exhibition

In the heart of Berlin amid a dense memorial landscape but somewhat off the tourist trail, the Memorial Centre is located to the west of the Neue Staatsgalerie and Philharmonie and south of the Tiergarten. It is situated in the Bendler Block, a building surrounding a courtyard, which housed military officials during the Nazi regime. These included key players in the assassination attempt on 20 July 1944, among them Claus Schenk Graf von Stauffenberg who detonated a bomb at Hitler's headquarters, the Wolf's Lair in Rastenburg. Unaware that Hitler had survived the explosion, Stauffenberg returned to Berlin and attempted to initiate a coup. On its failure, he and three others (Friedrich Olbricht, Albrecht Ritter Mertz von Quirnheim and Werner von Haeften) were executed, while co-conspirator Ludwig Beck was shot after a failed suicide attempt.[4] The Memorial Centre comprises two elements, a commemorative courtyard where the men were executed and the exhibition sited on the second floor of the building, where Stauffenberg's office was located.

The Memorial Centre is therefore an auratic site, and one that stresses its links to the past. At the same time, as Aleida Assmann argues, places alone cannot signify. Cultural mnemonics keep memories bound to a place and allow them to signify beyond it (1999: 76). Indeed, the courtyard has hosted memorial ceremonies led by surviving relatives since 1952. A memorial statue by Richard Scheibe was inaugurated in 1953 by the then Mayor of West Berlin, Ernst Reuter.

The street outside was then renamed Stauffenbergstraße in 1955. A small exhibition about resistance opened in 1968. The commemorative courtyard was redesigned 12 years later, by Erich Reusch. In 1989, just before the unification of Germany and amid much controversy, the exhibition was considerably extended to include a broader range of resistance groups, sited in the rooms where the coup had been planned and attempted (Steinbach 1993). Extensions followed, which further increased the diversity of resistance represented. The exhibition closed on 20 July 2013 for a year of renovation and reworking and was recently reopened – work having been financed by the national Ministry for Culture and Media and the Berlin lottery. Since 1993, the Bendler Block has also housed elements of the Federal Ministry of Defence and is one of the sites where new army recruits are sworn in. A contemporary memorial to German soldiers was built in 2008 (Bundesministerium der Verteidigung Presse und Informationsstab 2010). Like many such memorial sites in Berlin, the spaces of the Memorial Centre and those surrounding it therefore 'bear [. . .] the traces of years of activity, [. . .] of erasure and marking' (Jordan 2005: 38–39).

In his reopening speech, Wowereit refers to the complex history of the site and to battles over memorialisation in the context of the Cold War, battles that were played out amid accusations that resisters had betrayed their country. Wowereit spoke alongside the Director of the Memorial Centre, Johannes Tuchel. Tuchel (2014) said that it was the aim of the exhibition to 'stimulate debate about the possibility of political action and individual responsibility in different political systems'. His speech was followed by that of the German Federal Chancellor, Angela Merkel. Addressing the women and men of the resistance and their surviving relatives in the audience, Merkel's speech described the resisters as 'role models who give us courage and who admonish us' [*Vorbild, Mutmacher und Mahner*] for contemporary society (Merkel 2014).

Taking a feminist approach, this chapter similarly insists that gendered representations of resistance in the Memorial Centre are significant for processes of recognition and identity formation in Germany today. Specifically, that within the many complex interactions present at the commemorative site, the Memorial Centre constructs spaces in which 'visitors search for features of their personal lives, both actual and imagined selves, [. . .] and their searches may lead to confirming, disconfirming or elaborating understandings of their own identities' (Paris and Mercer 2002: 402). The focus here is on representation, 'understood in terms of collections, sites and performances', and our investigation does not go beyond information that any visitor to the site would have (Reading 2015: 399). We are not, therefore, investigating consumption, production (defined as 'a concern with workplace structures, curatorial practices and heritage management') and heritage policies; aspects that might otherwise be considered as part of a gendered approach (Reading 2015: 399). Analysing discourses of representation in the museum and how they talk to each other and to the visitor (Muttenthaler and Wonisch 2006), we begin from the assumption that gender is performative (Butler 2006) and relational (Reading 2015: 403). We maintain that the Memorial Centre performs multiple gendered discourses and, in doing so, offers up subject positions with which the visitor can choose to identify. These positions are always circumscribed by prevalent gender norms and pre-existing structural power relations.[5]

Gender, museums and resistance in context

Gendered representations in museums matter. As Roswitha Muttenthaler and Regina Wonisch (2010: 4) point out:

> Differences based on gender – but also ethnicity, class etc. – determine social structures and debates about political, cultural and social capital. Therefore the category of gender is also central to the ways in which museums justify their existence and conceptualise their collections and exhibitions.

Museums, as prestige cultural forms, have the 'epistemic authority' of the 'Look!' and, as such, are embroiled in the politics of recognition (Bal 1999: 6; Smith 2008: 159–178; Sullivan 1994: 100). Building on a history of feminist interventions with the museum in Germany since the 1970s, Muttenthaler and Wonisch (2010: 8) reiterate the importance of asking how gendered role models are 'rendered invisible, strengthened, made obvious or made subject of discussion by the way in which they are displayed'.[6] They draw attention to strategies that encourage visitors to reflect on gendered representations and to 'question their own beliefs and habits of perception' (Muttenthaler and Wonisch 2010: 8). Taking these issues of visibility, perception and reflexivity as starting points, we investigate what (if any) gendered conversations may be prompted and supported in the Memorial Centre. Before we do so, however, it is necessary to address some specifics of the German memory context.

As David C. Large (1984: 499) wrote, 'every nation needs a useable past with which it can validate its present and inspire faith in its future'. In relation to Germany since 1945, this has always been a challenge. Sharon Macdonald (2009: 8) argues that it is the country 'that has struggled most and longest over its twentieth-century difficult heritage – with the eyes of the world relentlessly on it'. Divided into two states between 1949 and 1990, embroiled in the competing ideologies of the Cold War, and faced with the responsibility for the horrors of the Holocaust, politicians and other memory activists in Germany have often looked to resistance to Nazism as a way of asserting a better, 'other' Germany [*Das andere Deutschland*]. Different resistance groups have played different roles in these complex and highly politicised discourses at different times (Niven 2002; Steinbach and Tuchel 1994). In West Germany, for example, Chancellor Konrad Adenauer made recurrent reference to the military group of 20 July 1944 in speeches during the 1950s as he fought to bring prisoners of war home and make a case for rearmament to sceptical Western European neighbours. Shortly after the founding of East Germany, it was memories of the Communist resisters, including those who had spent time in exile in Moscow and who returned to a Germany in ruins, who promoted memories of 'antifascist fighters'. Unification in 1990 prompted contentious, high-profile, public reassessments of a wide range of institutionalised memory discourses, including those on resistance. In a contemporary 'Holocaust-centred' memory context where recognition of the responsibility for the genocidal atrocities is anchored in public commemoration (Langenbacher 2010), memories of resistance play a marginal but significant role. This is evidenced by the state as key funder of the Bendler Block exhibition and the symbolic presence of Angela Merkel at its re-opening.

Only a minority of German citizens were part of the anti-Nazi resistance, even allowing for broad definitions including civil disobedience (Broszat 1981). Women were part of this minority. Their involvement took diverse forms, as did that of the men (Elling 1981). The extent of their participation varied depending on the resistance group, with some groups comprising as many women as men (Coburger 1994). Their activities were inevitably shaped by dominant gender norms of the time, which regulated all spheres of women's and men's lives, including their ability to learn, work, travel, marry and reproduce. Referring to such regulation of gendered spheres of action, Claudia Koonz describes how 'Nazi power severed male from female worlds, but resistance networks depended upon women and men working closely together. [. . .] Opponents [to the regime] guarded their humanity in an integrated society of people from varied backgrounds and both sexes' (1987: 310). Yet, even in resistance groups where fascist ideology was wholeheartedly rejected and a worldview based on equality was professed, female resisters often found themselves constrained by prevailing conservative gender norms (Kuckhoff 1972).

Framing the visit through the courtyard: male, masculine, military and national

The commemorative courtyard is not only the first thing encountered by the visitor but it is central to the symbolic functioning of the space; it physically and metaphorically frames the visitor's experience. The leafy space contains several mnemonic features. Entering it, the visitor passes through an archway, whose stone bears the inscription: 'It was here in the former military headquarters that on 20 July 1944 Germans organised the attempt to overthrow the Nazi regime. In doing so they sacrificed their lives.' Following this, the visitor reads that the commemorative site was redesigned in 1980 with state and regional support. Through the generic reference to 'Germans', the text suggests the significance of their action for the nation, something recognised by federal support. The linking of nation and sacrifice pervaded early commemoration of this resistance group. In a ceremony marking the tenth anniversary of the attempted coup, for example, West German President Theodor Heuss claimed that '[t]he blood of the martyred resisters [. . .] has cleansed our German name of the shame which Hitler cast upon it'. Heuss made numerous references to the sacrificial act of 'the men', which he named 'a gift to the German future' (Heuss 1954; Large 1984: 500). These words are echoed at the site to the left of the courtyard where the men were shot, where a plaque declares that those named below 'died for Germany on 20 July 1944'. A list of their names and military honours then follows. Shame, resistance and sacrifice for 'freedom, justice and honour' are also encapsulated in a dedication 'to those who resisted' on a bronze plaque in front of the focal point of the courtyard – a bronze statue centred at the far end of the space, dating from 1953 (Figures 12.1 and 12.2).

The visitor is drawn towards this statue of a lone, naked man with his hands tied in front of him, situated on axis to the entrance. Its powerful masculine form draws the visitor's attention to the physicality of the space, its restraints signifying both the restraints of system and the physicality of the arrest. The aestheticised beauty of this statue is symbolic not indexical – the men were not executed on that spot and were not naked. The bodily inhabiting of this space of memory by the visitor is further emphasised by the additions to the memorial from 1980, intended as two 'symbolic thresholds' (German Resistance Memorial Centre Foundation 2014a: 8): bronze steps of varying heights that run horizontally in front of the statue, steps the visitor can climb up and over, walk around or sit on. They mark a physical and temporal distance between the visitor and the statue, albeit one that the visitor can choose to cross. They provide a space for contemplation in a courtyard that is usually absolutely quiet, with even the voices of tour guides and groups being absorbed by the buildings surrounding the commemorative space.

Figure 12.1 Commemorative Courtyard of the German Resistance Memorial Centre
Source: © 2015 Gedenkstätte Deutscher Widerstand

Gendering 'the other Germany' 191

Figure 12.2 Statue by Richard Scheibe

Source: photograph by Joanne Sayner, reprinted with permission of the German Resistance Memorial Centre.

The significance of this commemorative courtyard is explained by three panels on the left of the space, adjacent to the Memorial Centre entrance. In both German and English, they outline a condensed history of the site, the Memorial Centre and the 20 July 1944 plot, accompanied by uniformed photographs of the five men who were shot. These panels also help to signpost the unassuming entrance to the exhibition. For non-German speakers without a guide or pre-existing knowledge, these panels are the only curated point of orientation in the courtyard; the memorials themselves do not have captions or translations. In contrast to the information on the panels, the German-only text of the archway-thresholds-statue triptych emphasises sacrifice for the nation, thereby interpellating the German visitor.[7] The commemorative courtyard is, literally and metaphorically, inward-looking.

Notwithstanding the myriad ways in which the visitor might experience the space and the diverse forms of knowledge they bring, the memorials provoke dominant narratives of military men, hegemonic masculinity (as encapsulated by the strong, heroicised male body) and sacrifice in the name of Germany.

Entrance narratives: the exceptional and the everyday

In her chapter advocating a feminist strategy for museums, Hilde Hein (2010: 59) suggests that museums should stop foregrounding the exceptional, given that it tends to reinstate hierarchy and 'obscure continuity and the flow of phenomena'. In consequence, she argues, 'we are unable to imagine or understand the gradual processes leading up to the climax' (Hein 2010: 59). Yet, as Barbara Welter (2002: 105) maintains, representing moments of historical change can provide a perfect opportunity for thematising gender roles that are often brought into focus at such times. The Memorial Centre exhibition begins with both process and climax, focusing on the post-war reception of resistance, the rise of the Nazi Party during the Weimar Republic and the culmination of the 'Third Reich' in the horrors of the Holocaust. However, a tension between climax and process in historical narratives is played out in the visit as organised by the physicality of the space and the curation of the overall memorial complex. Having begun at the dramatic end of Stauffenberg's story, the visitor then climbs two flights of stairs to reach the permanent exhibition.

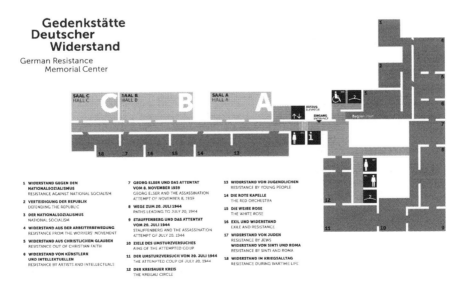

Figure 12.3 German Resistance Memorial Centre: plan of the permanent exhibition
Source: © 2014 Gedenkstätte Deutscher Widerstand

At this point the chronology and form of musealisation shifts (Figure 12.3). As the floor plan illustrates, on entering the exhibition the visitor is presented with three choices although the museum guide (available in English) recommends first visiting rooms numbered 1–3, which characterise in turn 'Resistance against National Socialism', 'Defending the Republic' and 'National Socialism'. In gender terms, these three opening rooms are particularly interesting.

Room 1 is painted in dark grey with a long white uplit panel on the corridor wall containing eight quotations in German and English thematising issues of resistance and betrayal. These are followed by three quotations set into the corridor leading to rooms two and three. The exhibition thus opens with the voices of the resisters themselves. Reading the panel from left to right, the first voice is that of journalist Ruth Andreas-Friedrich:

> The final victory: when the Allies march through the Brandenburg Gate. And once again I think, as so often: what an absurdity, for a German to pray for the enemies' victory! A strange patriotism that can wish for nothing better than the conquering of one's own country!

Andreas-Friedrich helped Jews in Berlin with food, false papers and accommodation. Her words pre-empt the post-war controversy about whether the resisters were traitors to Germany. Quotations follow from other resisters including: a member of the Kreisau Circle, Peter Graf Yorck von Wartenburg; journalist and Communist resister Julius Fučik; protestant pastor Dietrich Bonhoeffer; Claus Schenk Graf von Stauffenberg; and Ludwig Beck. There is also a quotation from a note written in exile by Constanze Hallgarten, a key figure in the women's and peace movements before 1933. It is the breadth of motivation for resistance and a shared need to justify acting against the state that stands out in these quotations. The voices chosen also already speak volumes about the gendered representation of resistance. All the men profiled were executed by the Nazis. Many had public and official roles before or during the Nazi regime. The two women survived. Their quotations are taken from non-published sources.

The Weimar Republic is the focus of room 2. It was a time of societal upheaval and alternating economic stability and crisis. A triptych of floor-to-ceiling images showing mass rallies in defence of the Republic conveys the extent of unrest. Documents from the time including newspapers and flyers detail the founding and collapse of the Republic and increasing violence from the National Socialist German Workers' Party (NSDAP). As Kathleen Canning (2009) has persuasively shown, gender roles were in significant flux during this time, something only hinted at in the display. Veterans of the First World War often faced unemployment and poverty. Many bought into the anti-semitic rhetoric that Germany was 'stabbed in the back' during the war and faced shame following the Treaty of Versailles. As Dick Schuman (2010: 247) has noted, attempts to reassert masculinity often manifested themselves in political violence as parties from the far left and far right fought for dominance in a fledgling democracy.

Women were given the vote in 1919 and the 'New Woman' was making claims to equality in education and political and cultural arenas (Canning 2009). Women's increasing demands in the public sphere are encapsulated in the gaze of a woman in the centre of the triptych's middle photograph. She looks directly into the camera. As if to emphasise the competing models of femininity at the time, directly opposite is an image from a theatre gala review with a line-up of scantily clad women. They are dancing beneath a large painting of a saxophone-playing bare-chested woman who sports the androgynous haircut of the 'New Woman'. Touch screens provide further information on socio-political events and key personalities at this time, including the campaign for equal rights for women. However, the emphasis of the display in this room is more on mass movement than gendered change.

The 10 large images in room 3, called 'National Socialism', are fascinating as gendered synecdoche. As noted above, Paver has argued that exhibitions on National Socialism rarely thematise gender; concurring with Bill Niven, Paver maintains that 'inclusiveness' in such exhibitions is usually understood to mean with regards to victim groups and not to women (2008: 43). However, these images do encapsulate key debates about gendered roles under Nazism and women's roles in particular. Pairs of images juxtapose different groups or crowds. Photographs on the top row show people supporting the regime and the process of bringing all aspects of society into line [*Gleichschaltung*]; from a group of very young boys in a school room doing the Hitler salute, to a field of SS men at a Nazi party conference, to a crowd of enthusiastic girls waving Nazi flags. This latter image can be read in several ways: as an often repeated trope of hysterical women who, once given the vote, catapulted Hitler into power; of vulnerable young women whose youthful enthusiasm was exploited by misogynist Nazi ideology; or of women who were able to enjoy freedoms (albeit restricted) within the Nazi youth groups (Heinsohn *et al.* 1997: 7–20; Paver 2008: 2, 8). What is not visible through the images' captions is that during the Nazi regime, anti-Semitic constructions of race first and foremost effaced gender as a determining marker of identity (Paver 2008). However, underneath these photographs thematising support for the regime are iconic images of the Holocaust, including: the young boy with his hands raised as part of a Jewish group at the Warsaw ghetto;[8] the process of 'selection' on the death ramp at Auschwitz-Birkenau; prisoners' roll call at Sachsenhausen; and soldiers carrying out executions in Serbia. These images are well known in Holocaust iconography (Wollaston 2010: 439) and the ethics involved in showing such (gendered) images have been discussed in detail (Brink 1998; Paver 2006; Wollaston 2010). For visitors who recognise these images, they serve to confirm knowledge, to reassure the 'good citizen' who 'knows' the story (Paris and Mercer 2002: 408). They do not necessarily prompt reflection on the gendered aspects of everyday life under Nazism. Indeed, as Paver (2008: 6) argues:

> [E]xamples from exhibition practice suggest that photographs showing a single-sex crowd tend to be displayed more prominently and to possess more potent symbolic meanings than images of mixed crowds. The fact that it

proves difficult to pick apart how much of this gender segregation and gender coding derives from the NS era and how much it is due to the choices of the curator calls attention to the fact that curators rarely aid visitors in making these distinctions.

The images represent gendered segregation of supporters and the victims of the regime alike but attention is not drawn to such segregation in either the captions or audio tour. For example, the image of young women waving flags is entitled 'Cheers for Hitler after German troops invaded Austria, Berlin, March 1938' and the image of the men and women and children being separated on arrival at Auschwitz-Birkenau refers only to 'Hungarian Jews'. While it was indeed the case that 'extreme forms of gender polarisation' characterised the Nazi regime and, as Paver further points out, were promoted in the Nazis' own propaganda materials (Paver 2008: 1), in this exhibition such images are also a product of selection by the curators; for example, a decision to display a photograph of an NSDAP party conference in Nuremberg that focuses only on SS men. On one level, this collection of images efficiently and effectively conveys the racist misogyny of the regime. On the other, it misses the opportunity to historicise and denaturalise these gendered relationships and to also point out, as many historians have done, that the policy of distinctly gendered spheres could not be maintained in practice (Noakes 1998).

Juxtaposed with these iconic images taken by the Nazis is a picture that has been less well known until recently. To get to room 3, the visitor walks down a corridor that terminates at arguably one of the key images of the exhibition: it looks at first glance like a large (all male) crowd with their hands raised in the Nazi salute. It is only as the visitor nears the picture that s/he sees a man in the centre with his arms folded. The photograph was taken at the launch of the Horst Wessel training ship in Hamburg in June 1936. It is unsurprising that the workers from this industry at that time are male, but it is interesting that this man is standing next to the only woman in the crowd. Popular and academic discussion has focused on the fact that little is known about the man; indeed his identity is contested (Wildt 2012). Why there is only one woman in the group is unclear. She, like the other men raising their arms in the Hitler salute, is rendered invisible. The image arguably functions as a symbol of agency amid conformism, and as a statement of simple, understated (male) resistance it marks a pivotal point in the display. Standing in front of this image the visitor either turns left, to the room entitled 'National Socialism', to the images of conformism and horror, or to the right and the rooms on resistance.

Representing 20 July 1944: gendered presences and absences

Turning right, the visitor enters an enfilade of 9 of 15 rooms about different resistance 'groups'. Returning to the entrance through a library of material that can be bought at the entrance desk, the visitor then turns down a corridor along whose left side are another five rooms with groups and types of resistance, opposite the museum's seminar rooms. These colour-coded rooms thematise resistance according to motivation for resisting and/or the name of the group (several groups had members with diverse motivations). Room 7 is different in that it focuses on one individual, Georg Elser, who worked alone in his attempt to assassinate Hitler. Four of these rooms (numbered 8–11) focus on 20 July 1944; the actual offices of Stauffenberg and the other plotters. The visitor is reminded of this in panels that detail, for example, the site of Friedrich Fromm's office where the coup was organised in 1944. These rooms occupy the largest part of the exhibition. The 20 July group is therefore at the centre of the exhibition physically and metaphorically.

Some 179 portrait photographs of the 'co-conspirators', all men in military uniform dominate this section of the exhibition, covering a large expanse of one wall (Figure 12.4). There are no pictures of women on this wall. Yet, women were involved in two key ways. First, direct professional involvement came in the form of secretarial work and three secretaries do receive a brief panel mention as 'reliable confidant(s) to the conspirators', including Margarethe von Oven,

Figure 12.4 Room 10: 'co-conspirators'

Source: photograph by Joanne Sayner, reprinted with permission of the German Resistance Memorial Centre.

Erika von Tresckow and Ehrengard Gräfin von der Schulenburg. Von Oven (later Hardenberg) copied the plans of the assassination plot on her typewriter. These plans were for dissemination following a successful coup and began with the sentence 'Our Führer, Hitler, is dead' (von Meding 1997: xvii). The pre-emptive copying of this text clearly amounted to treason under the prevailing law but it would have been vital in terms of dissemination had the coup been successful.

Second, these three women, among others, must be considered among those 'relatives, friends, colleagues and comrades' that the display reminds us were needed to enable the conspirators to act. At any point, the plotters could have been arrested had they been denounced to the authorities. As von Meding insists: 'The sacrifice of the women consisted of the fact that [. . .] they subordinated themselves to the imperative of secrecy' (1997: xx). The display includes several letters written by the military men to their wives, including to Freya von Moltke and Clarita von Trott zu Solz, the first of which records an account of the genocide in the extermination camps in Poland. The wives are present in family photographs displayed and are named in the captions but are not referred to in the explanation of the involvement of co-conspirators. A pattern that von Meding has highlighted predominates in the display: 'Time and again the direct life-risking participation of the men in the Attentat and coup has been seen as a sacrifice in comparison to which the activities of the women look rather unassuming, ordinary and self-evident' (1997: xx). It is taken for granted that the female resisters would support their husbands or colleagues. The implications of such support are, however, made very clear in a final panel, which refers to the process of '*Sippenhaft*', that is, the wholesale arrest of family members of those involved in the plot. Nina Gräfin Schenk von Stauffenberg, Stauffenberg's wife, endured five months in solitary confinement in Ravensbrück while pregnant, giving birth while still imprisoned. The children were taken to Nazi children's homes to be 're-educated' (von Meding 1997: 194).

The men of the plot are larger than life in the exhibition in two ways. If the visitor follows the route suggested by the room numbering, they see, on axis, a life-size poster of Stauffenberg and Albrecht Ritter Merz von Quirnheim standing in the doorway to Stauffenberg's office (Figure 12.5). Expressed as an object in a room, it is sited near another artefact from the time, a bust of Stauffenberg – notable items in an exhibition that purposefully does not contain three-dimensional objects (German Resistance Memorial Centre 2014b).[9] Given this insistence, the bust, sculpted by Frank Mehnert in 1929–1930, carries particular significance as a bodily synecdoche for the resistance as a whole. As Paver (2008: 8) notes, a bust comes from a tradition of 'celebrating "great men" [. . .], a tradition from which women were largely excluded in early twentieth-century Germany':

> Nevertheless, so long as the cultural impulse for the creation of the various busts is passed over in silence (a 1929 Stauffenberg bust, for instance, was presumably created to confirm Stauffenberg's social status as a male

member of the aristocracy, and it is only our understanding of the bust as an aggrandizing genre that allows it now to double up as a celebration of his role in a plot to assassinate Hitler) the museum arguably continues to validate a cultural tradition (bust = important person) that can only put historical women at a disadvantage.

(Paver 2008: 8)

The inclusion of this bust and no other is particularly interesting given that a bust was created of student resister Sophie Scholl for Germany's Hall of Fame 11 years before the reconceptualised museum opened.

The representation of the 20 July 1944 resistance group is emblematic of the broader gendered politics of the commemorative site. While we acknowledge that display always involves selection, selection in this part of the exhibition, however, reinforces the framing physicality and masculinity of the commemorative courtyard. Gendered relations during the Nazi regime were pivotal to the resistance of this group but these relationships are neutralised by the display, taken for granted in a way that renders the work of the women mostly invisible.

Figure 12.5 View from room 8 to room 9, picturing Claus Schenk Graf von Stauffenberg and Albrecht Ritter Mertz von Quirnheim

Source: photograph by Joanne Sayner, reprinted with permission of the German Resistance Memorial Centre.

Exhibiting diversity: photographic communities and the isolated individual

It is not only the spaces that convey these powerfully gendered messages but also the photographic images that dominate the exhibition. Rooms 4–6 and 12–18 follow a similar pattern to rooms 1–3: the walls contain numerous black and white photographic portraits of individual resisters, family and group photographs, and photographs of key sites (Figure 12.6). Bilingual text gives biographical and historical information. The images span a spectrum of 'socially sanctioned forms' (Olin 2012: 15); the forms and contexts in which they were taken during the Nazi regime and in which they are being used in the exhibition. These contexts include photographs taken by the Gestapo on the resisters' arrests although this is not always highlighted as such in the accompanying captions. For one group, 'The Red Orchestra' [*Die Rote Kapelle*], the images are recontextualised in a 'Book of the Dead', a book of photographs of those executed for their work in the resistance. As Margaret Olin insists, however, photographs are 'more than context: they touch one another and the viewer. They substitute for people. [. . .] Photographs act rather than represent' (Olin 2012: 16–17). The photographs in this museum are indexical witnesses to individual agency and to overlapping communities of resistance; that is, they insist on repeated moments of action against the Nazi regime. The repetition of portraits throughout the exhibition emphasises what the resisters have in common notwithstanding their different motivations.

In addition to the smaller portraits and the life-size image of Stauffenberg and Ritter Merz von Quirnheim, there are other full-size images in the exhibition.

Figure 12.6 Permanent exhibition, topic 04 'Resistance from the workers' movement'
Source: © 2015 Gedenkstätte Deutscher Widerstand.

Along the corridor wall adjacent to rooms 13 to 18 are black and white images of individuals and pairs of resisters who greet the visitors on their departure from their seminars. Given the pedagogical aims of the museum, the photographs seem part of a strategy of creating an antifascist community,[10] a community of visitors subscribing to the imperative of 'never again'. Indeed, it is the pedagogical imperative of showing diversity and breadth of resistance, insisting that people had choices in different spheres of action, which has structured the exhibition since the late 1980s (Steinbach 1993).

Following Olin (2012: 69), the indexical power of the photograph resides in the 'relation between the photograph and its beholder', something she calls the 'performative index', or 'index of identification'. Many of the photographs on display, and therefore points of identification, are of resisters who were executed. This also has a gendered dimension as more women resisters survived. At the same time, many of the photographs show the resisters within family contexts. Such family frames are known to be significant for visitor engagement. As Scott G. Paris and Melissa J. Mercer (2002: 404) explain:

> [O]bjects that evoke personal connections have both attraction and holding power, that is, visitors are drawn to them by recognition and are likely to view them carefully, read the labels, and talk about them with other people [. . .] Rosenzweig and Thelen (1998) found that family was the most often reported connection to the past and the most important source of identity.

Family is also a site of gendered relationships where individual identities and priorities are constantly being negotiated, even more so when the former Nazi state aimed to influence every aspect of family life. As such these family constellations would have provided an ideal opportunity for reflecting on multiple gendered positions; for example, how the Nazi role for women deemed acceptable to the regime supposedly focused on home and children (Noakes 1998), and at the same time how the domestic sphere could provide a space for resisters to meet and plan resistance activities (Kuckhoff 1972).

The exhibition's reliance on photographs is not limited to visuality. The introduction of touch screens and computer terminals means that viewers engage with texts and images in a tactile way, choosing whose biographies to engage (further) with. The touch screens and computer terminals replicate the physical displays and give further searchable information for each group. The effect here is to draw attention back to the individual and away from the group context of the display. It was, after all, the individual who decided to resist and who faced the consequences if, and usually when, they were discovered by the Gestapo.

Conclusion: resistant and residual narratives

Muttenthaler and Wonisch (2006: 39; 2010: 9), following Irit Rogoff, plead for a 'responsible gaze' when it comes to gendered exhibition spaces. They argue that museums lend themselves to engaging with issues of gendered representation because they allow the viewer to look again (and again) and therefore to reflect upon what they are seeing (Muttenthaler and Wonisch 2010: 189). As such, museums are important sites for increasing (gendered) visual literacy (Unger 2009: 38). Given its recent reconceptualisation, it is surprising that the Memorial Centre does not exploit the gendered dimensions of the resistance it represents physically, visually and symbolically. Gender is undoubtedly central to the construction of the representation of resistance in the Memorial Centre. Yet, while both women and men are included, the museum does not explicitly reflect on gendered conditions during Nazism or ask the viewer to reflect on representations of masculinity and femininity then or now. Given that the site does thematise definitions of resistance, stresses inclusivity in terms of the political motives of the resisters (in the face of significant criticism) and aims to 'engage [. . .] spectators in complicity with the social agenda of the institution' (Levin 2010: 5), this is a surprising missed opportunity.

There are multiple gendered narratives potentially operating in the spaces at the Memorial Centre. These interact with the primary emphasis of the exhibition, which is on the shared diversity of the resistance community. As such, it is possible to see these gendered narratives as evidence of what Raymond Williams calls 'the dominant' and 'the residual' (Williams 1977: 121). Writing of the 'dynamic interactions' in the cultural sphere and of social processes that are 'constitutive of and constituting' perception and identities, Williams argues that we can reflect on the complexity of cultural interaction through a focus on 'the dominant', that is, the hegemonic, and how it relates to 'the residual' and, potentially, to 'the emergent'. He defines the residual as that which has 'been effectively formed in the past, but is still active in the cultural process, not only and often not at all as an element of the past but as an effective element of the present' (Williams 1977: 121). The residual may be oppositional or alternative, archaic or incorporated into the dominant (Williams 1977: 122). Incorporation of certain elements of the residual into the dominant occurs during the work of 'selective tradition' (Williams 1977: 123).

In terms of gendered representations at the Memorial Centre, applying Williams's model, as we now show, allows us to read the display against the grain and to denaturalise the many gender roles taken for granted within the dominant discourse of diversity in resistance. His concept of the residual is useful because he suggests that, from within dominant discourses, it is possible to reach back

> to those meanings and values which were created in actual societies and actual situations in the past, and which still seem to have significance because they represent areas of human experience, aspiration, and achievement which the dominant culture neglects, undervalues, opposes, represses or even cannot recognise.
>
> (Williams 1977: 124)

The actively residual is valuable because it can provide the basis for the emergent, which comprises genuinely (and exceptionally) 'new meanings and values, new practices, new relationships and kinds of relationship' (Williams 1977: 123).

In terms of the dominant 'Stauffenberg narrative', the memorial site reproduces the masculinisation of Nazi politics and hegemonic postwar gender norms without explicitly thematising them. The impact of the courtyard entrance and the representation of the 20 July group in the exhibition itself, including the 'auratic intensification' (Muttenthaler and Wonisch 2010: 48) of the office spaces, conveys a gendered hierarchy that stresses masculinised sacrifice and heroism. On the face of it, therefore, to use a term Sullivan has applied to museums in general, the Memorial Centre remains a 'sexist institution' (1994: 100).[11] This has implications for the conceptualisation of resistance: it marginalises how some women were able to exploit gendered expectations of Nazi ideology, moving around more easily as couriers and, at least in the early years of the regime, not being subject to intensive interrogation (Kuckhoff 1972).[12] Without wanting to valourise a restricted sphere of action, women undoubtedly did 'more routine but equally lifesaving work than men' and so were sometimes able to escape detection or execution (Koonz 1987: 334–335). At the same time, men and women who resisted often refused the dominant gender norms of the Nazi time to work together. Neither these dominant gender norms nor the (resistant) work that women did in the domestic sphere to facilitate the resistance are reflected on. In particular, they are taken for granted in the display about the 20 July plot and as such rendered invisible.

Arguably, laudable political diversity is achieved in the Memorial Centre at the expense of gendered reflexivity.[13] Such reflexivity could draw the visitor's attention to the actively residual in the display. There will always be tensions about representing diversity within memorial practice, and it is not possible to fulfil all representational claims and to (re)present all identities at all times. This is, however, all the more reason for encouraging self-reflexivity on behalf of the visitor about what is being presented. As societies become more internally diverse, the implications for public commemoration based on competing political, ethnic and class identities become more acute. In Germany, fraught geo-political allegiances of the past now merge with demands for mainstream recognition and participation that stretch the political spectrum far wider than in many other European countries – from the far left to the far right. Within this context, notwithstanding the multiple and competing gendered identities that people inhabit today, gender identity is something everyone has in common. And yet it often remains the case that this is the one aspect of identity that is rendered invisible, taken for granted in exhibitions and memorial sites in Germany and beyond. Hilde Stern Hein reminds us that '[f]eminist theory [. . .] advocates diverting the focus on products and their consumption to the depiction of practices and processes that vitalise societies' (2007: 39). The resistant and residual narratives within the Memorial Centre are performances of gender, points of potential identification about the successes and failures of gendered relationships in times of immense social and political upheaval. As such, these narratives have potential to create new, and emergent, ways of understanding the past for the future. In the context of contemporary museum and heritage studies this is particularly significant given the continued underrepresentation of gendered perspectives, both theoretical and practical.

Notes

1 All translations from the German by Joanne Sayner.
2 Student resister Sophie Scholl was voted by the German public in 2003 into the 'Top Ten' Germans of all time.
3 In her survey of 200 exhibitions dealing with the National Socialist past, resistance exhibitions do not fall into the five main categories that Paver highlights (2009: 227).
4 For a history of the resistance plot see: Jochaim Fest (1997). The events were recently made famous by the film *Valkyrie* starring Tom Cruise (dir. Bryan Singer, 2008).
5 In contrast to Michael Haldrup and Jørgen Ole Bœrenholdt we suggest that, in terms of gender, heritage cannot 'always [be] performed as more-than-citational'. While a multiplicity of gendered identities exists, 'unpredictable, creative and non-stable [performances], arriving out of the dramas, improvisations and remakings of heritage' are policed within normative gender frameworks (Haldrup and Bœrenholdt 2015: 66).
6 For a history of feminist museology in Germany see Hauer *et al.* 1997. The periodisation outlined here in terms of an emphasis on gendered practices of collecting, attempts to anchor women in museums (either as part of existing exhibitions or as separate museums), a move away from essentialist notions of women and including different stories with their inherent contradictions, to a focus on gender more broadly, follows a similar pattern to that in an Anglo-Saxon context (Porter 2012).
7 The national significance of the site is further attested to by the publicity issued by the resident Ministry of Defence, which makes links between the contemporary memorial to Germany's military dead, situated on the other side of the Bendler Block, and the commemorative courtyard (Bundesministerium der Verteidigung Presse und Informationsstab 2010). Such narratives reinforce mythologies of a 'clean' Wehrmacht, narratives only partially destroyed by controversy about the so-called 'army exhibition' 20 years ago (Niven 2002).
8 Wollaston discusses the 'complex cultural afterlife' of this photograph (2010: 442).
9 Macdonald points to the difficulties that curators of sites of 'perpetration at a distance' have in Germany – that 'their preservation and public display might be interpreted as conferring legitimacy of sort [. . .] Moreover, there is also the risk that such sites might become pilgrimage destinations for perpetrator admirers' (2009: 3).
10 Olin relies on Benedict Anderson to suggest that photographs 'help create or maintain the wider community' (2012: 101). I am using the term antifascism here in full knowledge of the contentious nature of it. See Sayner 2013.
11 Sullivan maintains that this does not, in general, happen maliciously but thoughtlessly (1994: 100).
12 Any such leniency was short-lived. Hitler himself commuted the prison sentence of Mildred Harnack and imposed the death penalty. He also refused an appeal of clemency for Hilde Coppi, who gave birth in prison before being executed.
13 As Macdonald (2009: 198) writes for a different German context: 'performed openness can involve displacements of its own. Attention to certain areas may deflect attention from areas of remaining silence and avoidance'.

References

Assmann, A. 1999. Das Gedächtnis der Orte. In U. Borsdorf and H.T. Grütter (eds) *Orte der Erinnerung. Denkmal, Gedenkstätte, Museum*. Frankfurt am Main: Campus, pp. 59–75.

Bal, M. 1999. Introduction. In M. Bal (ed.) *The Practice of Cultural Analysis: Exposing Interdisciplinary Interpretation*. Stanford, CA: Stanford University Press, pp. 1–14.

Bock, G. 1998. Ordinary Women in Nazi Germany: Perpetrators, Victims, Followers, and Bystanders. In D. Ofer and L.J. Weitzman (eds) *Women in the Holocaust*. New Haven, CT and London: Yale University Press, pp. 85–100.

Brink, C. 1998. *Ikonen der Vernichtung. Öffentlicher Gebrauch von Fotografien aus nationalsozialistischen Konzentrationslagern nach 1945*. Berlin: Akademie.

Broszat, M. 1981. Resistenz und Widerstand. *Eine Zwischenbilanz des Forschungsprojekts*. In M. Broszat, E. Frohlich and A. Grossman (eds) *Bayern in der NS-Zeit IV. Herrschaft und Gesellschaft im Konflikt Teil C*. Munich: Oldenbourg, pp. 691–709.

Bundesministerium der Verteidigung Presse und Informationsstab. 2010. Der Bendlerblock. Available: www.bundeskanzlerin.de/Content/Infomaterial/BMVg/Der_Bendlerblock.pdf;jsessionid=B324FFDFB6B6EFE030D24B364BBF90C8.s3t2?__blob=publicationFile&v (accessed 17 December 2015).

Butler, J. 2006. *Gender Trouble*. Abingdon: Routledge.

Canning, K. 2009. Women and the Politics of Gender. In A. McElligott (ed.) *Weimar Germany*. Oxford: Oxford University Press, pp. 146–174.

Coburger, M. 1994. Die Frauen der Roten Kapelle. In H. Coppi, J. Danyel and J. Tuchel (eds) *Die Rote Kapelle im Widerstand gegen den Nationalsozialismus*. Berlin: Gedenkstätte Deutscher Widerstand, pp. 91–103.

Elling, H. 1981. *Frauen im deutschen Widerstand 1933–45*. Frankfurt am Main: Röderberg.

Fest, J. 1997. *Plotting Hitler's Death: The Story of German Resistance*. New York: Holt.

German Resistance Memorial Centre. 2014a. *Permanent Exhibition: 'Resistance Against National Socialism'*. Berlin: German Resistance Memorial Centre Foundation.

German Resistance Memorial Centre. 2014b. Main Exhibition Concept. Available: www.gdw-berlin.de/fileadmin/_migrated/content_uploads/Main_Exhibition_Concept.pdf (accessed 12 August 2015).

Haldrup, M. and Bœrenholdt, J.O. 2015. Heritage as Performance. In E. Waterton and S. Watson (eds) *The Palgrave Handbook of Contemporary Heritage Research*. Basingstoke: Palgrave, pp. 52–68.

Hauer, G., Muttenthaler, R., Schober, A. and Wonisch, R. 1997. *Das inszenierte Geschlecht: feministische Strategien im Museum*. Vienna: Böhlau.

Hein, H. 2010. Looking at Museums from a Feminist Perspective. In A.K. Levin (ed.) *Gender, Sexuality and Museums: A Routledge Reader*. Abingdon: Routledge, pp. 53–64.

Heinsohn, K., Vogel, B. and Weckel, U. (eds) 1997. *Zwischen Karriere und Verfolgung. Handlungsräume von Frauen im nationalsozialistischen Deutschland*. Frankfurt am Main: Campus.

Heuss, T. 1954. Der 20. Juli 1944. Available: www.20-juli-44.de/uploads/tx_redenj2044/pdf/1954_heuss.pdf (accessed 12 August 2015).

Jordan, J. 2005. A Matter of Time: Examining Collective Memory in Historical Perspective in Postwar Berlin. *Journal of Historical Sociology* 18(1/2): 37–71.

Koonz, C. 1987. *Mothers in the Fatherland: Women, the Family, and Nazi Politics*. New York: St. Martin's Press.

Kuckhoff, G. 1972. *Vom Rosenkranz zur Roten Kapelle: Ein Lebensbericht*, Berlin: Verlag Neues Leben.

Langenbacher, E. 2010. 'From an Unmasterable to a Mastered Past: The Impact of History and Memory in the Federal Republic of Germany. *German Politics* 19(1): 24–40.

Large, D.C. 1984. 'A Gift to the German Future?' The Anti-Resistance Movement and West German Rearmament. *German Studies Review* 7(3): 499–529.

Levin, A.K. 2010. Introduction. In A.K. Levin (ed.) *Gender, Sexuality and Museums: A Routledge Reader*. Abindgton: Routledge, pp. 1–5.

Macdonald, S. 2009. *Difficult Heritage: Negotiating the Nazi Past in Nuremburg and Beyond*. Abingdon and New York: Routledge.

Merkel, A. 2014. Sie sind uns Vorbild, Mutmacher und Mahner. Available: www.gdw-berlin.de/fileadmin/bilder/dauer/Eroeffnung/GDW_Rede_Dr._Angela_Merkel_1._Juli_2014.pdf (accessed 12 August 2015).

Muttenthaler, R. and Wonisch, R. 2006. *Gesten des Zeigens: Zur Repräsentation von Gender und Race in Ausstellungen*. Bielefeld: Transcript.

Muttenthaler, R. and Wonisch, R. 2010. *Rollenbilder im Museum. Was erzählen Museen über Frauen und Männer?* Schwalbach/Ts: Wochenschau.

Niven, B. 2002. *Facing the Nazi Past: United Germany and the Legacy of the Third Reich*. Abingdon: Routledge.

Noakes, J. (ed.) 1998. *Nazism 1919–1945, Volume 4: The German Home Front in World War II*. Exeter: University of Exeter Press.

Olin, M. 2012. *Touching Photographs*. London: University of Chicago Press.

Paver, C. 2006. 'Ein Stück langweiliger als die Wehrmachtsausstellung aber dafür repräsentativer': The Exhibition Fotofeldpost as Riposte to the 'Wehrmacht Exhibition'. In A. Fuchs, M. Cosgrove and G. Grote (eds) *German Memory Contests: The Quest for Identity in Literature, Film, and Discourse Since 1990*. Woodbridge: Camden House, pp. 107–126.

Paver, C. 2008. Gender Issues in German Historical Exhibitions About National Socialism. *The International Journal of the Inclusive Museum* 1(3): 43–55.

Paver, C. 2009. Exhibiting the National Socialist Past; an Overview of Recent German Exhibitions. *Journal of European Studies* 39(2): 225–249.

Paris, S.G. and Mercer, M.J. 2002. Finding Self in Objects: Identity Exploration in Museums. In G. Leinhardt, K. Crowley and K. Knutson (eds) *Learning Conversations in Museums*. Mahwah, NJ and London: Lawrence Erlbaum Associates, pp. 401–424.

Porter, G. 2012. Seeing Through Solidarity: A Feminist Perspective on Museums. In B.M. Carbonell (ed.) *Museum Studies: An Anthology of Contexts*. Second edition. Oxford: Blackwell, pp. 62–72.

Reading, A. 2015. Making Feminist Heritage Work: Gender and Heritage. In E. Waterton and S. Watson (eds) *The Palgrave Handbook of Contemporary Heritage Research*. Basingstoke: Palgrave, pp. 397–413.

Sayner, J. 2013. *Reframing Antifascism: Memory, Genre and the Life Writings of Greta Kuckhoff*. Basingstoke: Palgrave.

Schad, M. 2010. *Frauen gegen Hitler*. Munich: Herbig.

Schumann, D. 2010. Political Violence, Contested Public Space, and Reasserted Masculinity in Weimar Germany. In K. Canning, K. Barndt and K. McGuire (eds), *Weimar Publics/Weimar Subjects: Rethinking the Political Culture of Germany in the 1920s*. Oxford: Berghahn, pp. 236–253.

Smith, L. 2008. Heritage, Gender and Identity. In B.J. Graham and P. Howard (eds) *The Ashgate Research Companion to Heritage and Identity*. Aldershot: Ashgate, pp. 159–178.

Steinbach P. 1993. Die Rote Kapelle – 50 Jahre danach. *Zeitschrift für Geschichtswissenschaft* 41: 771–780.

Steinbach, P. and Tuchel, J. (eds) 1994. *Widerstand gegen die nationalsozialistische Diktatur 1933–1945*. Berlin: Akademie.

Stern Hein, H. 2007. Redressing the Museum in Feminist Theory. *Museum Management and Curatorship* 22(1): 29–42.

Sullivan, R. 1994. Evaluating the Ethics and Consciences of Museums. In J.R. Glaser and A.A. Zenetou (eds) *Gender Perspectives: Essays on Women in Museums*. Washington, DC and London: Smithsonian Institution Press, pp. 100–107.

Tuchel, J. 2014. Begrüßung. Available: www.gdw-berlin.de/fileadmin/bilder/dauer/Eroeffnung/GDW_Begruessung_Prof.Dr._Johannes_Tuchel_1._Juli_2014.pdf [accessed 12 August 2015).

Unger, P. 2009. *Gender im Blick: Geschlechtergerechte Vermittlung im öffentlichen Raum und in Museen*. Vienna: Bundesministerium für Unterricht, Kunst und Kultur.

von Meding, D. 1997. *Courageous Hearts: Women and the Anti-Hitler Plot of 1944*. Trans. M. Balfour and V.R. Berghahn. Oxford: Berghahn.

Welter, B. 2002. Weiblich? Männlich? Geschlechtergeschichtliche Ansätze in historischen Museen. *Zeitschrift für schweizerische Archäologie und Kunstgeschichte* 59: 103–108.

Wildt, M. 2012. Nationalsozialismus: Aufstieg und Herrschaft 'Volksgemeinschaft'?. Available: www.bpb.de/izpb/137185/volksgemeinschaft (accessed 14 July 2016).

Williams, R. 1977. *Marxism and Literature*. Oxford: Oxford University Press.

Wollaston, I. 2010. The Absent, the Partial and the Iconic in Archival Photographs of the Holocaust. *Jewish Culture and History* 12(3): 439–462.

Wowereit, K. 2014a. Gedenken als Ausdruck einer bürgerschaftlichen Verantwortung. Available: www.gdw-berlin.de/fileadmin/bilder/dauer/Eroeffnung/GDW_Rede_Klaus_Wowereit_1._Juli_2014.pdf (accessed 12 August 2015).

Wowereit, K. 2014b. Gedenken als Ausdruck einer bürgerschaftlichen Verantwortung'. Available: www.youtube.com/watch?v=MLgURT3gOLI&feature=youtube_gdata (accessed 12 August 2015).

Chapter 13

Gender and intangible heritage

Illustrating the inter-disciplinary character of international law

Janet Blake

Introduction

International law is increasingly stepping outside the confines of its own narrow discipline and has to engage directly with other universes of discourse (Prott 1998). The needs of modern societies have not only led to a much greater cross-fertilisation within international law, bringing with it theoretical challenges (Sands 1999), but have also required it to confront issues that cannot be addressed from a legal standpoint alone. International law has faced the need to engage directly with other universes of discourse in a number of areas, including environmental, trade and investment law, to name but a few. International law-making in all these areas has been heavily influenced by intellectual developments occurring outside the law (Sands 2003). This chapter takes as an illustrative case the question of the gender dynamics of intangible cultural heritage (ICH) in order to explore the ways in which developing new treaties in diverse fields has thrown up new challenges for international regulation that cannot be addressed through the legal discipline alone.

The current discussion is located within the context of UNESCO's 2003 Convention for the Safeguarding of Intangible Cultural Heritage ('2003 Convention'), which is an innovative heritage treaty in a number of ways, in particular in the central role it attributes to 'communities, groups and . . . individuals' in the safeguarding process (UNESCO 2003 at Articles 2(1), 11(b) and 15). Inevitably, then, implementing this treaty involves questions relating to human beings as cultural actors since it concerns a living form of heritage that is primarily located in human beings. Such a strong focus on the human context within which ICH is performed, practised, enacted and transmitted, and without which this heritage is no longer 'living', forces Governments (and other actors) to confront a variety of issues not usually addressed in implementing cultural heritage treaties. Many of the challenges posed by the first 10 years or so of implementing the 2003 Convention may broadly be characterised as being of an anthropological character. This immediately throws up a range of issues concerning social relationships and social power (such as age, disability, sexual orientation, ethnicity, etc.) and that include the gender dynamics at play not only in the creation, enactment, expression and transmission of this heritage but also in its safeguarding. Although I have named these issues as broadly 'anthropological' ones, they are also very closely intertwined with human rights; this is not surprising given that these rights attach to human beings simply by virtue of their being human. As a consequence, the discipline of anthropology has and continues to exert an extremely powerful influence on the development and application of this treaty.

The way in which this influence has played out and continues to do so in developing strategies for implementing the obligations it places on States Parties has, with the possible exception of environmental law, far-reaching impacts that go beyond those found in other fields of international law. Indeed, the current term of art introduced by the 2003 Convention into international law, namely 'intangible cultural heritage', had initially been employed by anthropologists before it entered the legal lexicon (Blake 2001, 2015). Once the General Conference of UNESCO decided to develop a new Convention for this heritage, the 'expert' draft for the treaty was prepared by a restricted drafting group made up of legal and non-legal experts (the latter mostly from anthropology and related disciplines) whose contribution to that text was significant (Blake 2006). In an unusual move within international law-making, with the possible exception of environmental law (Sands 2003), the negotiating teams fielded during the three inter-governmental sessions held in UNESCO headquarters between September 2002 and June 2003 included non-legal (cultural) as well as legal experts.

Anthropologists, ethnographers and other cultural heritage experts have continued to be deeply implicated in the process of implementation (often in their roles as government officials in national cultural bodies) and setting national policies for this. Moreover, unusually for an international treaty, their contribution to the academic literature on the Convention thus far has been much greater than that of lawyers; this, again, gives a clear signal both of the inter-disciplinary nature of this area of law and of the innovative approaches the Convention takes, which make many experts from a traditional international law background unwilling to engage in the discussion. This may have profound implications for the future development of the Convention and carries clear dangers since it is essential that the debate concerning its implementation is in the form of a dialogue between the law and anthropology (and related disciplines). In the absence of international lawyers engaging with the question, potentially damaging misconceptions about how the law operates are creeping into the literature, much of which is in the field of critical anthropology.

Of course, the law (and lawyers) need to be criticised from outside their discipline, but some of this criticism is poorly targeted and fails to comprehend the legal requirements of an international treaty. In particular, there is a general failure to appreciate the fundamental realities of international law including, for example, the principle of the sovereign equality of States (Crawford 2012: 16–17; Malanczuk 1997) and the difference between a binding treaty and non-binding instruments (Dixon 1990: 44–45). This may lead to the development of inappropriate policy approaches if it is not complemented by legal criticism, especially in view of the highly flexible structure of the 2003 Convention in which the Intergovernmental Committee of the Convention ('ICH Committee') develops Operational Directives for its implementation (UNESCO 2014), frequently based on reports produced by non-legal experts. Lixinski (2015) has addressed the role of experts from different fields (heritage studies and heritage law) in cultural heritage policy- and law-making and the need for a proper and mutually respectful dialogue between the two. Here, the main aim is to explore some of the challenges that the treaty's inter-disciplinary character poses to international law, taking as an illustrative case the myriad ways in which gender is expressed in, and even created by, ICH and the lack of fit of the human rights notions of equality and non-discrimination to this reality.

If we look at the experience of countries that are Parties to the 2003 Convention, it is clear that this heritage in all its various forms is a rich social, economic and even political resource that can provide a variety of possible routes towards sustainable models of development. However, regulating intangible heritage brings with it new challenges or, at least, ones that have only recently been appreciated as a result of a shift that has occurred in the cultural heritage protection paradigm within UNESCO's standard-setting. One of these relates to the question of how to address the gender dynamics of ICH and its safeguarding, which ties in with the broader issue of inter-disciplinary approaches in international law. Through the following examination of the gender dynamics of ICH and its relationship to gender equality as a human rights norm, I wish to illustrate (i) the inevitable interactions between the 2003 Convention and questions more commonly understood to fall within the domain of the social sciences and (ii) how these latter then interact with international (human rights) law through the Convention's operation.

Gender diversity and ICH: an anthropological approach

Before addressing the gender dynamics of ICH, however, it is helpful to clarify how the notion of gender is understood here. Gender is exceptionally complex and does not operate, as is often assumed in international law areas such as human rights, in simple terms of biological sex. It can be understood rather, as a notion that emphasises the social and cultural construction of femininity and masculinity to which sex is the biological counterpart. Hence, dualistic and biologically deterministic views of gender fail to appreciate its multi-layered character and, importantly for this discussion, the fact that gender identities are not fixed but can be subject to change. Indeed, ICH sometimes provides the locus in which shifts in gender identities occur. Of further significance to ICH, it has been argued that the use of gender as a *universal and timeless social category* must be read in relation to the global dominance of (Indo)European/American cultures and the ideology of biological determinism that underpins Western systems of knowledge (Oyeronke 1997).

The imposition of 'Western' gender roles and values can indeed be damaging to gender systems that operate in a different manner and that may be crucial to safeguarding certain cultural elements, as in the case of Papua New Guinea (Strathern 1988). As an illustration of the complexity of the relationship between gender and ICH, Hertz (2002) asks rather provocatively whether 'true' ICH is not really a *matrimoine* (a 'female inheritance') that has been placed within the essentially masculine framework of an inter-governmental organisation, namely UNESCO.

We can identify here potential tensions between what may broadly be called the anthropological and legal approaches: the former addressing the *gender dynamics* of ICH and the latter focusing on human rights questions concerned with *gender equality* in ICH and its safeguarding, which employs a notion of *sexual* equality. Here, I will attempt to explore the gender/ICH dynamic through an anthropological perspective although, as an international lawyer by training, I will no doubt do so through international law 'eyes'.

Gender has largely been ignored in the heritage discourse and, according to Laurajane Smith (2007a: 160) 'alongside concepts of ethnicity and class, is perhaps one of the most un-problematised and naturalised aspects of identity within heritage discourses'. In the rare cases when gender is directly addressed, it is frequently reduced to 'women's issues' as if men have no gender; the flip side of this, ironically, has been a tendency to ignore female-dominated ICH as just 'what women do'. The interactions between gender and ICH performance, enactment, practice and transmission are complex and are, to some degree, mutual (Torggler and Sediakina-Rivière 2013) since ICH not only provides a route for the performance and/or expression of gender identities, but can also be constitutive in their formation.

As a consequence, safeguarding approaches have the potential to impact on these in both positive and negative ways but the safeguarding actions proposed for this heritage tend to miss the larger, holistic aspect of culture of which gender dynamics form a part (Kurin 2004). Not only do we express our gender identities through ICH, but they are also shaped to some degree by it and this process can be affected by safeguarding practices and interventions. This underlines the necessity both of applying a gender-sensitive approach to ICH safeguarding and also, as this article seeks to demonstrate, of finding an appropriate balance between legal and non-legal (anthropological) expertise in this process in order to ensure a sufficiently nuanced but well-grounded approach towards gender.

Gender is expressed through and constituted by ICH in multiple ways and forms an important part of cultural diversity, given that the gender diversity in ICH has its roots in culture. Since cultural diversity now receives greater recognition following the adoption of UNESCO's International Declaration on Cultural Diversity (UNESCO 2001), it seems appropriate to regard the diversity of gender roles and relations in ICH as a human rights value (UNESCO 2001: Article 4). Moreover, the 2003 Convention springs directly from that instrument and so provides an excellent case for examining gender diversity in cultural heritage from a human rights perspective. The variety of gender roles manifested in (and also constituted through) ICH performance and practice include reversal of standard male/female gender roles, as in the *Châu van* shamanistic ritual from Viet Nam (Norton 2009) during which female mediums assume traditionally 'male' roles and male dress, while male mediums take on traditionally 'female' gender roles, dress and behaviours. Another example of crossing gender boundaries in ICH is found in the kabuki *onnagata*, a male actor who specialises in the art of performing 'female' gender roles (Mezur 1998). These performers have developed rigorous performance techniques and stylised performance codes, known as the *onnagata kata*, and have created roles marked by gender ambiguity and transformativity. Their performance is based on the inter-play between the 'female' gender acts performed and the male body beneath, through which we see that the body in performance is not a purely biological form but is, above all, a socio-cultural construct (Todorova Gabrovska 2009).

Perhaps an even more striking example of such inversion of gender roles in ICH is that of the pre-colonial culture of the indigenous Ibo people of Nnobi town (south-eastern Nigeria) whereby women could assume 'male' gender roles, daughters becoming sons (in order to inherit) and women practising woman-to-woman marriage (*igba-ohu*); in the latter case, a wealthy and successful woman (endowed with the title *Ekwe*, associated with the goddess Idemili) would marry a less powerful woman who rendered her services in return for enjoying the benefits of her higher status and wealth (Amadiune 1998). As Amadiune (1998: 15) notes: 'The flexibility of Ibo gender construction meant that gender was separate from biological sex. Daughters could become sons and consequently male. Daughters and women in general could be husbands to wives and consequently males in relation to their wives.' Here, then, women (and girls) are assuming the male gender roles of son and husband, but do not actually become men.

In other ICH elements through which gender is performed, men and women have clearly differentiated roles, as in the Song and Dance performances of the Acoli in Uganda where gender differentiation is used as a social resource by women to achieve their aspirations for a greater public role within the patriarchal social system (Okot 2012). A clear gender-based differentiation in the division of labour is found in *Taquile* textile weaving in Peru where men use different tools (the pedal loom and needles) from women (who use the plain loom) and make Spanish colonial-style trousers and hats in contrast to the more traditional garments, such as blankets, made by women (Peru 2012). This case demonstrates not only the differentiation in the gender roles, but also suggests that it was through men that colonial elements have entered into the indigenous cultural heritage while, at the same time, women kept pre-colonial traditions alive. Such examples clearly demonstrate that gender does not operate solely along biologically determined male or female lines, even though there may be social roles regarded as 'male' and 'female': In fact, the differences that are often attributed to a woman's or a man's biological nature may be the result of their relative positions within the social structure and the expectations placed on them by society (Lorber 1995).

Furthermore, gender is understood variously across different societies and, since there is no globally universal understanding of gender, we are in danger of making false culture-bound assumptions about ICH. For example, ICH documentation programmes in the Pacific region have at times misinterpreted the nature of traditional gender roles and, consequently, ignored the gender complementarities present (Bolton and Kelly 2001: 33). Strathern (1988) sought to avoid this trap by arguing that Papuan women are not being exploited, but rather that their definition of gender is different from the Western one. The approach taken up until recently of applying the 2003 Convention in a 'gender-blind' fashion might, therefore, result in culturally inappropriate responses and may even serve to reinforce discrimination and exclusion experienced by women and other gender-based groups (Moghadam and Bagheritari 2005). There is a danger inherent in viewing 'the cultural community' of the Convention as if it is a monolithic structure and ignoring the diversity of experiences and aspirations of its members; this may, for example, result in putting in place 'participatory' structures that favour certain community members' interests over others. It might also result in damaging gender balances within ICH (and the community) in favour of a more black and white conception of gender equality. Although such outcomes may be hard to avoid completely, a better awareness of gender and other diversities within communities can help in the design of participatory approaches that respond better to the wishes of all community members.

In order to address this gender diversity as manifested in ICH and to apply the gender equality and non-discrimination principles to such ICH in a way that does not damage either the heritage or gender balances within the cultural community, we need to be able to locate and contextualise gender within the activities of both men and women and understand the social power negotiations involved in these (UNESCO 2013). Heritage can be conceived as a point or *moment* of negotiation, which may occur during performances of ICH or in relation to sites and objects of symbolic value (Smith 2007b). Although human beings generally tend to assimilate/learn gender positioning by repeated acts right from childhood, gender identity is performative and it is possible to change the way we perform our gender (Butler 1990). Hence, heritage is one process through which identity (including gender identity) and social and cultural meaning are mediated, evaluated and worked out (Okot 2012).

In terms of safeguarding ICH we need, for example, to consider the effect on women and other gender-based groups of their marginalisation from the public sphere: the paradox we find here is that such marginalisation may actually lead them to become privileged reproducers of certain ICH elements in their communities. We can take as an example of this phenomenon the *hijras* in India, a non-mainstream and generally marginalised gender-based group that has gained a recognised position in society and earns a living through a ritual performance exclusive to them that is invested by Hindu mythology (Reddy 2005). Moreover, it may be necessary to re-examine the assumptions upon which certain ICH practices are described as predominantly 'female' (e.g. handicrafts and textile weaving) and others as 'male' (e.g. certain initiation rites). This may help us to identify more easily the differences and disparities that exist between individuals in society (rather than between men and women), allowing us to take better account of the processes of subordination and negotiation that are a part of social relations (Sigel 1996).

Gender equality and ICH: a human rights-based approach

There is a distinction to be drawn between the reality of the gender dynamics and diversity within ICH and the human rights-based notion of gender equality, which has important implications for approaches towards safeguarding of ICH. In this section, I propose that some of the predicates underlying these two ways of conceiving of gender are different and may prove potentially incompatible (Logan 2012). This presents a serious challenge if we wish to preserve the gender diversity of ICH while respecting the human rights of individuals in the associated cultural communities and social groups.

Human rights have generally been the area of international law in which anthropology as a discourse has been most directly engaged. With reference to cultural heritage, this debate has frequently been manifested in discussion of the relationship, and potential incompatibility, between cultural diversity and human rights (Logan 2008). Anthropology was implicated in the development of post-World War II human rights in the shape of the involvement of the American Association of Anthropologists' in the drafting of the 1948 Universal Declaration on Human Rights. Their Statement to the drafters championed a culturally relativistic approach and asserted that the rights of humans 'could not be circumscribed by the standards of any single culture, or be dictated by the aspirations of any single people' (AAA 1947). Until the mid-1980s, however, although anthropologists had expressed concern for human rights violations against the people they studied, the discipline itself generally remained aloof (Freeman 2008: 92). A significant milestone in the relationship between anthropology and human rights was the publication of *Human Rights and Anthropology* by Cultural Survival in 1988, an activist organisation working on behalf of indigenous and tribal peoples and a movement for the anthropological study of human rights developed around this time (Downing and Kushner 1988; Freeman 2008).

Messer (1993) pointed to an important distinction between the two disciplines, noting that the UN-sponsored human rights system is primarily legalistic, built around the primacy and sovereign equality of States. In contrast, anthropology approaches law simply as one type of cultural system, which results in very different conceptions of human rights. In addition, by clarifying how human rights relates to specific cultures, anthropologists are equipped to play a role in helping to resolve the universalism/relativism conflict inherent in human rights (Messer 1993). In many ways, the differences between the two fields essentially boils down to the high degree of certainty required by human rights law as a legal discipline, and the much messier and more uncertain reality of the human experience recorded by anthropologists. In this chapter, there is no attempt to claim a superior approach or position for either discipline, but rather to recognise how they interact. It seeks also to explore the ways in which an anthropological perspective (i) poses challenges for the human rights law within which the 2003 Convention is clearly framed (according to the first recitation in its Preamble where the main human rights treaties are cited) and (ii) can offer insights into weaknesses of the human rights vision, while respecting the requirements of the law as a discipline.

Human rights are 'literally, the rights that one has simply because one is a human being', as Donnelly (2003) reminds us, while emphasising the differences between (human) rights and other social practices and grounds for action. As a result, human rights are equal rights since 'one either is or is not a human being, and therefore has the same rights as everyone else (or none at all)' (Donnelly 2003: 10). If we refer to the Charter of the United Nations, we see that achieving equality between men and women is one of the fundamental objectives of that organisation and of the human rights treaties developed within it. Indeed, 'the inferior position of women in many cultures [with regard to labour and health rights, for example] has long occupied the concerns of the international community' (Smith 2007: 177). This goal of equality irrespective of a person's sex/gender is usually achieved in the first instance through the application of the principle of non-discrimination, but 'there have been almost insurmountable cultural barriers to cross in reversing sex discrimination' (Smith 2007: 177). We understand discrimination to mean any distinction, exclusion, restriction or preference or other differential treatment that is directly or indirectly based on the prohibited grounds of discrimination (including sex), which has the intention or effect of nullifying or impairing the recognition, equal enjoyment or exercise of human rights (Committee on Economic, Social and Cultural Rights 2009). The non-discrimination principle also provides an important legal basis in addition to the treaty-based cultural rights for defending the cultural practices and identities of minorities and other groups in society. Hence, the right to access and enjoyment of one's cultural heritage (based on the right to participate in cultural life) is one that all people and communities should enjoy equally with no discrimination on the basis, inter alia, of sex, age, race, etc.

Discrimination against women (on the grounds of their biological sex) is defined in the Convention on the Elimination of Discrimination Against Women (United Nations 1979) as

> [a]ny distinction, exclusion or restriction made *on the basis of sex* which has the effect or purpose of impairing or nullifying the recognition, enjoyment or exercise by women . . . on a basis of the equality of men and women of human rights.
>
> (United Nations 1979: Article 1, emphasis added)

Thus, in contrast with the anthropological view of gender presented above, the human rights principle of non-discrimination is primarily predicated upon the fact of biological sex, not on gender per se. As a consequence, it can be argued that the human right to sexual equality does not easily take account of the complexities of gender roles. Although the Human Rights Committee has, in the Toonen case heard in 1994, extended the prohibitive ground of 'sex' (in United Nations 1966a and 1996b: Article 2) to include sexual orientation, such a radical interpretation is unusual and the treaty law does not generally protect gender-based minorities against discrimination (Donnelly 2003: 224–239). Moreover, some feminist commentators have criticised the notion of equality as expressed in human rights discourse as failing to recognise differences in women's (from men's) experiences and wishing to replicate for women a masculine role and experience (Charlesworth and Chinkin 2000). As we have seen above, 'female' gender roles derive from the position of women in the wider social structure and the expectations placed on them by society and not, immediately, from their biological sex itself. There is some truth in the feminist position, but Freeman (2008: 129) advises caution, noting that 'the critique of equality for the sake of difference of women's experiences may be counter-productive because cultural groups often justify treating women unequally on the ground of cultural difference'. Gender equality, as Donnelly (2003: 120) notes 'is often a particularly sensitive matter in cross-cultural discussions. International standards do require that all human rights be available to men and women without discrimination. But that does not require the elimination of differentiated gender roles.' Hence, women should not be denied the right to run for public office, for example, but they are free to choose whether to do so or not. Of course, we need to recognise that 'free choice' may not, in reality, be open to women in many societies because of social pressures to conform.

One of the main areas in which questions concerning the human rights notion of sexual equality arise with regard to ICH concerns claims to preserve traditional cultural practices that include and may even promote non-egalitarian elements. When such claims are made, they should be balanced against the freedom to choose of women, children and others who may be marginalised and disempowered by traditional cultural practices. There are, therefore, human rights-based limitations placed on the right of everyone to take part in cultural life, in particular in the case of harmful practices attributed to customs and traditions that violate other human rights. Certain practices –such as forced marriage or foot-binding – are, of course, indefensible from a human rights perspective, but many others may lie in a grey area where it can be very challenging to determine the degree of harm to individuals. The UN Convention on the Elimination of Discrimination Against Women (CEDAW) (United Nations 1979) addressed the issue of gender roles with regard to cultural traditions in Article 5(a) by calling on Parties to take all appropriate measures to modify the social and cultural patterns of conduct of men and women, with a view to achieving the elimination of prejudices and customary and all other practices which are based on the idea of the inferiority or the superiority of either of the sexes or on stereotyped roles for men and women.

To the degree that it refers to 'stereotyped roles', it could be argued that it does take gender into account. It also implies that the *harm caused to individuals* by notions of inferiority or superiority of the sexes and from sexually stereotyped roles is the main target. What is, perhaps, of most relevance to the question of ICH and the treatment of women, girls and gender-defined minorities is the suggestion that social and cultural patterns of conduct that underlie harmful traditional practices can, and perhaps should, be modified. With regard to safeguarding ICH that contains prejudicial and potentially gender discriminatory aspects, this raises the question of whether Parties should seek to modify these to eliminate such elements and, if so, how this is to be done.

Bearing in mind the previous discussion of the gender dynamics of ICH, caution is required in applying a non-discrimination filter if we seek to avoid an overly strict or simplistic approach. It is essential that we appreciate the wider social context of the ICH element in question and the ways in which it may provide social benefits as well as losses to the various participants. Following this logic, ICH practices should not be discounted solely on the basis of the fact that they are, for example, sexually segregated: In societies around the world, many social and cultural practices are segregated (on the basis of age, sex and other criteria) and this fact alone should not be taken as a sign that discrimination is taking place. Only through applying a gender-based analysis can we recognise whether a particular social practice, ritual or oral tradition is truly discriminatory. From a human rights perspective, Donnelly (2003: 121) provides a nuanced reading of the operation of the non-discrimination principle in relation to women's traditional gender roles that is informative here. He states that the non-discrimination principle

> allows women to determine... the extent to which they will conform to, reject, or modify traditional gender roles. If they choose traditional gender roles, that choice is protected, no less (but no more) than the choice to challenge conventional definitions of what they ought to be and how they ought to act. Human rights simply seek to assure that no group of human beings is authorized to use the apparatus of the state to impose on any other group of human beings standards, rules, or roles that they do not impose on themselves.
> (Donnelly 2003: 121)

From this, we understand that a human rights-based approach requires that it is the members of groups who feel they are discriminated against on the basis of sex and/or gender in the practice, performance or transmission of ICH who should themselves make such a determination. This is not a matter that can be decided by others (even other members of the cultural community) except in the most egregious violations of rights, which, because of their extreme seriousness, may require action by all States to prevent them (such as slavery and genocide).

Conclusion

The interactions between gender and ICH performance (enactment, practice, etc.) are complex and have some degree of mutuality. As a consequence, safeguarding approaches have the potential to impact on these in both positive and negative ways. The examples given in this chapter illustrate the variety of gender dynamics at play in ICH and, hence, the complexity of safeguarding these appropriately. From this, we see clearly how applying an anthropological analysis of gender and gender roles is vital for the appropriate implementation of the 2003 Convention and that an inter-disciplinary approach is a pre-requisite for ensuring the proper and successful operation of this Convention over the long term. Therefore, in implementing the 2003 Convention, we need to consider a number of questions, which include: Does official recognition of women (and gender minority) practitioners and transmitters of ICH contribute to their empowerment in contemporary societies? To what extent does ICH depend on gender-specific transmission? Can the concept of gender equality always be compatible with preserving traditional cultures?

When we consider the illustrative examples of gender diversity in ICH set out in this chapter and the question of how to apply the theoretical and contextual considerations set out above to the implementation of the 2003 Intangible Heritage Convention, Kurin's observation that the Convention tends to reduce ICH to 'a list of largely expressive traditions, atomistically recognized and conceived' becomes relevant (Kurin 2004). As a result of this, he suggests, the safeguarding actions it proposes tend to miss the larger, holistic aspect of culture, the very thing that makes culture intangible, of which its gender dynamics form a part (Kurin 2004: 74–75). One of the conclusions we can draw from this is that not only do we express our gender identities through ICH, but they are also shaped by it to some degree and this process can be affected by safeguarding practices and interventions. This underlines the necessity both of applying a gender-sensitive approach to safeguarding and, as this chapter seeks to demonstrate, striking an appropriate balance between legal and non-legal (anthropological) expertise in this process in order to ensure a sufficiently nuanced but well-grounded approach towards gender.

Bibliography

Amadiume, I. 1998. *Male Daughters, Female Husbands: Gender and Sex in an African Society*. Sixth edition. London: Zed Books.
American Association of Anthropologists (AAA) 1947. American Anthropological Association's Statement on Human Rights. *American Anthropologist* 49: 542.

Arantes, A.A. 2007. Diversity, Heritage and Cultural Practices. *Theory Culture and Society* 4: 290–296.

Blake, J. 2001. *Developing a New Standard-Setting Instrument for Safeguarding Intangible Cultural Heritage: Elements for Consideration.* Paris: UNESCO.

Blake, J. 2006. *Commentary on the 2003 UNESCO Convention on the Safeguarding of the Intangible Cultural Heritage.* Leicester: Institute of Art and Law.

Blake, J. 2014. Seven Years of Implementing UNESCO's Intangible Heritage Convention – Honeymoon Period or the 'Seven-Year Itch?'. *International Journal of Cultural Property* 21: 1–14.

Blake, J. 2015. Safeguarding Intangible Cultural Heritage in the Urban Environment: Some Experiences Gained from Implementing the 2003 Convention. In S. Labadi and W. Logan (eds) *Urban Heritage, Development and Sustainability: International Frameworks, National and Local Governance.* Oxford: Routledge, pp. 114–133.

Bolton, L. and Kelly, S. 2001. *Women's Intangible Heritage and Development: A Feasibility Study – Pacific Regional.* Tehran: Iranian National Commission to UNESCO.

Butler, J. 1990. *Gender Trouble: Feminism and the Subversion of Identity.* New York and London: Routledge.

Crawford, J. 2012. *Brownlie's Principles of International Law.* Eighth edition. Oxford: Oxford University Press.

Charlesworth, H. and Chinkin, C. 2000. *The Boundaries of International Law: A Feminist Analysis.* Manchester: Manchester University Press.

Committee on Economic, Social and Cultural Rights (CESCR) 2009. *General Comment No. 20 on Non-Discrimination in Economic, Social and Cultural Rights* (art. 2, para. 2, of the International Covenant on Economic, Social and Cultural Rights). The Committee on Economic, Social and Cultural Rights at its 43rd Session 2–20 November 2009, Doc. E/C.12/GC/20.

Condé, H.V. 2004. *A Handbook of International Human Rights Terminology.* Second edition. Lincoln, NE and London: University of Nebraska.

Dixon, M. 1990. *Textbook on International Law.* London: Blackstone Press.

Donnelly, J. 2003. *Universal Human Rights in Theory and Practice.* Second edition. Cornell, NY: Cornell University Press.

Downing, T.E. and Kushner, G. 1988. *Human Rights and Anthropology.* Cambridge, MA: Cultural Survival.

Francesco F. 1996. International 'Soft Law': A Contemporary Assessment. In V. Lowe and F. Malgosia (eds) *Fifty Years of the International Court of Justice.* Cambridge: Cambridge University Press, pp. 167–178.

Freeman, M. 2008. *Human Rights: An Interdisciplinary Approach.* Cambridge: Polity Press.

Galia, T.G. 2009. Gender and Body Construction in Edo Period Kabuki. *Core Ethics* 5: 71–87.

Hertz, E. 2002. Le matrimoine. In M.O. Gonseth, J. Hainard and R. Kaehr (eds) *Le musée cannibale.* Neuchâtel: Musée d'ethnographie de Neuchâtel, pp. 153–168.

Kurin, R. 2004. Safeguarding Intangible Cultural Heritage in the 2003 Convention: A critical appraisal. *Museum International* 221(2): 66–67.

Lixinski, L. 2015. Between Orthodoxy and Heterodoxy: The Troubled Relationships Between Heritage Studies and Heritage Law. *International Journal of Heritage Studies* 21(3): 203–214.

Logan, W.S. 2008. Cultural Diversity, Heritage and Human Rights. In B. Graham and P. Howard (eds) *The Ashgate Research Companion to Heritage and Identity*. Farnham: Ashgate, pp. 439–454.

Logan, W.S. 2012. Cultural Diversity, Cultural Heritage and Human Rights: Towards Heritage Management as Human Rights-Based Cultural Practice. *International Journal of Heritage Studies*, Special Issue on World Heritage and Human Rights: Preserving our Common Dignity through Rights Based Approaches 18(3): 231–244.

Lorber, J. 1995. *Paradoxes of Gender*. New Haven, CT: Yale University Press.

Malanczuk, P. (ed) 1997. *Akehurst's Modern Introduction to International Law*. Seventh revised edition. London: Routledge.

Messer, E. 1993. Anthropology and Human Rights. *Annual Review of Anthropology*, 22: 221–249.

Mezur, K.M. 1998. *The Kabuki Onnagata: A Feminist Analysis of the Onnagata Fiction of Female-likeness*. Hawaii: University of Hawaii.

Moghadam, V.M. and Bagheritari, M. 2005. *Culture Conventions and the Human Rights of Women: Examining the Convention for Safeguarding Intangible Cultural Heritage and the Declaration on Cultural Diversity*. Paris: UNESCO (UNESCO Doc. SHS/HRS/GED).

Norton, B. 2009. *Songs for the Spirits: Music and Mediums in Modern Vietnam*. Champaign, IL: University of Illinois Press.

Okot, B. 2012. Striking the Snake with Its Own Fangs: Uganda Acoli Song, Performance and Gender Dynamics. In V.Y. Mudimbe (ed.) *Contemporary African Cultural Productions*. Dakar: CODESRIA, pp. 109–128.

Oyeronke, O. 1997. *The Invention of Women: Making an African Sense of Western Gender Discourses*. Minneapolis: University of Minnesota Press.

Peru 2012. *Periodic Report 00793*. Peru on the implementation of the Convention and on the status of elements inscribed on the representative list of the Intangible Cultural Heritage of Humanity, submitted by Peru to the seventh session of the Intergovernmental Committee for the Safeguarding of the Intangible Cultural Heritage. UNESCO Headquarters, December 2012.

Prott, L.V. 1998. Understanding One Another on Cultural Rights. In H. Niec (ed.) *Cultural Rights and Wrongs*. Paris: (UNESCO/UK) Institute of Art and Law.

Reddy, G. 2005. *With Respect to Sex: Negotiating Hijra Identity in South India*. Chicago, IL: University of Chicago Press.

Sands, P. 1999. Sustainable Development: Treaty, Custom and the Cross-Fertilization of International Law. In A. Boyle and D. Freestone (eds) *International Law and Sustainable Development: Past Achievements and Future Challenges*. Oxford: Oxford University Press, pp. 39–60.

Sands, P. 2003. *Principles of International Environmental Law*. Cambridge: Cambridge University Press.

Sigel, R.S. 1996. *Ambition and Accommodation: How Women View Gender Relations*. Chicago, IL: University of Chicago Press.

Smith, L. 2007a. Gender, Heritage and Identity. In B. Graham and P. Howard (eds) *The Ashgate Research Companion to Heritage and Identity*. Farnham: Ashgate, pp. 159–180.

Smith, L. 2007b. Empty Gestures? Heritage and the Politics of Recognition. In H. Silverman and D.F. Ruggles (eds) *Cultural Heritage and Human Rights*. New York: Springer, pp. 159–171.

Smith, R.K.M. 2007. *A Textbook on Human Rights*. Oxford: Oxford University Press.

Strathern, M. 1988. *The Gender of Gift*. Oakland, CA: University of California Press.

Todorova Gabrovska, G. 2009. Gender and Body Construction in Edo Period Kabuki. *Core Ethics* 5: 71–87.

Torggler, B. and Sediakina-Rivière, E. 2013. *Evaluation of UNESCO's Standard-Setting Work of the Culture Sector: Part I – 2003 Convention for the Safeguarding of the Intangible Cultural Heritage*. Paris: UNESCO.

UNESCO 2001. Universal Declaration on Cultural Diversity. Available at: unesdoc.unesco.org/images/0012/001271/127162e.pdf (accessed 4 October 2015).

UNESCO 2003. Convention for Safeguarding of the Intangible Cultural Heritage, 17 October 2003, in force 20 April 2006. Available at: unesdoc.unesco.org/images/0013/001325/132540e.pdf (accessed 4 October 2015).

UNESCO 2014. Operational Directives for the Implementation of the Convention for the Safeguarding of the Intangible Cultural Heritage, adopted by the General Assembly of the States Parties to the Convention at its second session (UNESCO Headquarters, Paris, 16 to 19 June 2008), amended at its third session (UNESCO Headquarters, Paris, 22 to 24 June 2010), its fourth session (UNESCO Headquarters, Paris, 4 to 8 June 2012) and its fifth session (UNESCO Headquarters, Paris, 2 to 4 June 2014).

United Nations 1966a. International Covenant on Economic, Social and Cultural Rights. Available at: www.ohchr.org/Documents/ProfessionalInterest/cescr.pdf (accessed 8 April 2016).

United Nations 1966b. International Covenant on Civil and Political Rights. Available at: www.ohchr.org/EN/ProfessionalInterest/Pages/CCPR.aspx (accessed 8 April 2016)

United Nations 1979. Convention on Discrimination Against Women. Available at: www.ohchr.org/Documents/ProfessionalInterest/cedaw.pdf (accessed 8 April 2016).

Chapter 14

Women of Steel at the Sparrows Point Steel Mill, Baltimore, USA

Michelle L. Stefano

Introduction

This chapter explores the experiences of women workers at the Sparrows Point Steel Mill, which was located – up until recently – at the mouth of the Patapsco River, adjacent to the city of Baltimore, Maryland. In particular, it frames these experiences as a certain living cultural heritage that remains an important part of their lives even though the steel mill is no longer in operation, nor are the majority of its buildings still standing. This cultural heritage is comprised of a deep sacrifice and pride – pride of the contributions they, as women, have made as steelworkers, providers for their families and in fighting for equality at the mill.

The following exploration stems from a larger project, Mill Stories, which aims to document, safeguard and promote the living cultural heritage of the Sparrows Point Steel Mill during its decline, grounded in the perspectives of its workers, both men and women.[1] Their stories and memories collectively form a narrative of pride and resilience, living cultural heritage that can often be neglected in both the mainstream media and heritage enterprise, or presented in far-too simplistic terms (Shackel *et al.* 2011; see also Smith *et al.* 2011).

With respect to dominant heritage practice, Shackel *et al.* (2011: 291) note that:

> The sites, places and intangible heritage of working-class people are often underrepresented in national and international heritage lists and registers. Moreover, when the sites of labour are present on such lists, they tend to be celebrated for technical or industrial innovations and often have little to say about the people whose labour underwrote those industries and their achievements.

In addition, through their review of critical scholarship on working-class and labour heritage, they underscore that official heritage discourse and practice can frequently paint working-class people as 'passive' and superficially 'nostalgic' when 'portraying their heritage' that relates to labour and industry, as well as its often devastating decline (Shackel *et al.* 2011: 292). However, local-level, community-based research, such as within the Sparrows Point community, can reveal far more complex processes at work, reflecting the intellectual and 'emotional acuity that communities and individuals can express in confronting dissonant and traumatic heritage and history' (Shackel et al. 2011: 292). These arguments are also true for the accomplishments and experiences of women workers in the steel industry, which have been commonly overlooked and, yet, have significantly shaped its history and continuing legacies.[2]

For a significant part of its 125 years, Sparrows Point was the largest steel-producing mill in the world, providing employment for hundreds of thousands of steelworkers and associated personnel. It was an integral force for the economic and social development of working-class people in greater Baltimore, and built the company towns of Sparrows Point (razed for plant expansion in the 1970s), the town of Dundalk, and the historically African-American neighbourhood of Turner Station. In late 2012, shortly after the mill's closure, folklorists (including the author) at Maryland Traditions, the folklife program of Maryland, honoured Sparrows Point through its state heritage award programme as a means of promoting its importance to the wider public, as well as to help keep alive the living heritage that persists in the hearts and minds of its former workers. Preliminary fieldwork in the mill's community, through the assistance of already active researchers and oral historians, such as Elmer Hall, Louis Diggs, William Barry and Deborah Rudacille, helped to shape the Mill Stories project, which began in early 2013. The project, developed from a partnership between the author and William Shewbridge in media and communication studies at the University of Maryland, Baltimore County (UMBC), is discussed in more detail later.

At its core, the ongoing project seeks to examine the sociocultural impacts of industrial decline through the documentation and promotion of the stories and memories of former workers shared through ethnographic interviews. Here, Mill Stories serves to connect the experiences of Sparrows Point workers to the broader narratives of industrial boom and bust, whether in Baltimore or beyond. Indeed, deindustrialization is an increasingly common phenomenon for regions across the world. The countless closures of manufacturing plants, mills and factories form a pattern that affects millions. For much of the past century, and through to today, industry not only provided jobs, but also shaped the lives of its workers through the development of housing, neighbourhoods and community life. Nonetheless, when presented in mainstream media, statistics are often employed to illustrate industrial decline and its impacts, with little interrogation of local-level, personal, as well as shared, experiences of it. The researcher and writer, Deborah Rudacille, highlights that:

> [E]very social movement of the 20th century played out at Sparrows Point – from agriculture to industry, from corporate paternalism to unionization, to the Civil Rights Movement and the struggle for equal opportunity by women, and then on through technology change and globalization, and now, post-industrialization.[3]

During interviews, steelworkers spoke of the legacies of the local union through which workers' rights were fought for over the course of the twentieth century, and the different ways in which they strove for better safety measures and regulations in recent decades. African-American workers recounted how the Civil Rights Movement impacted the mill, beginning with the integration of the bathrooms in the 1960s. Importantly, several women workers discussed the discrimination they faced and hardships encountered with respect to working at the mill while raising a family, among other issues.

As such, this chapter serves to not only add to the growing studies of working-class and labour heritage, but to also make room for explorations of women's contributions to it. In her valuable overview of the intersections between gender and heritage, Reading (2015: 398) outlines that a core category of a 'gendered approach' to heritage examines the ways in which gender is represented in the heritage sector, whether through museum exhibitions or heritage sites, as examples. Citing Smith (in Reading 2015: 401), she explains:

> Gendered approaches to heritage in the late twentieth and early twenty-first centuries have also tended to use a simplistic framework in which gender is telescoped into a focus on women, making gender and heritage into what is to be seen a women's problem (Smith 2008). A more productive way of understanding gender in relation to heritage is to frame it in terms of how changing constructions of masculinity and femininity interact with what is valued and included in heritage. The argument is that we need to consider whose identities are being 'represented and reinforced' and what the consequences are within contemporary culture for representing a primarily masculine perspective.

Here, it could be argued that steelmaking and its cultural heritage is most often associated with the masculine; that is, as a role played by men and as an industry that is generally perceived as having been shaped solely by men. Of course, from walking around steel manufacturing plants and attending meetings at local union halls, such as with respect to Sparrows Point, one will most likely see women working and conducting union business alongside men. Furthermore, historical research reveals that this was the case for much of the past century (see Reutter 1988; Rudacille 2010). Accordingly, the following sections focus on the history of women at Sparrows Point, the challenges they experienced within a male-dominated environment and the Women of Steel committee that was formed in response. First, a brief historical overview of the mill and the Mill Stories project is presented.

Sparrows Point and the Mill Stories project

Beginning with a brickyard, the first buildings of the Sparrows Point Steel Mill were constructed in 1887. Financed by the Pennsylvania Steel Company, in partnership with the Bethlehem Iron Company (later becoming Bethlehem Steel), the location for the mill was chosen due to its proximity to a deep-water port since the essential ingredient of iron ore was originally brought by steamships from Cuba. In the ensuing decades, railroads were laid, wharfs and piers were built and the first Sparrows Point Company Store opened. In the early 1890s, the first blast furnace was constructed, allowing for steel to be produced on site. In these early years, houses for workers were built and the company town of Sparrows Point blossomed. Up until the 1970s, the Sparrows Point town included its own police force, fire department, schools, churches, a bowling alley and cinema, among many other amenities (Reutter 1988). Based on the memories of those who have lived there, it is understood that the lifestyles of both workers and their families – through annual parades, company football and baseball games to segregation, gender discrimination, strikes and life-threatening conditions – were profoundly defined by the mill, a phenomenon that spread further over the course of the twentieth century into the surrounding areas.

The development of the Pennsylvania and Baltimore & Ohio (B&O) railroad lines at the turn of the twentieth century not only helped to transport resources and products in and out of 'the Point', but helped to bring in workers from numerous neighbourhoods in Baltimore city, the surrounding county, as well as from all over Maryland, Pennsylvania, West Virginia, Virginia and North and South Carolina, and as far away as Trinidad and Tobago (Reutter 1988). During the 1950s, Sparrows Point was the largest steel-producing plant in the world, having built ships used in the World Wars, and parts of the Empire State Building, the Golden Gate Bridge and the Chesapeake Bay Bridge, among other prominent US structures (Rudacille 2010). At its height, the mill employed roughly 33,000 steelworkers and associated personnel (Rudacille 2010). Common to many industries, a significant portion of the workforce was 'born into' life at the mill – that is, it was a place where one's grandparents, parents and children found employment up until 2012.

Sparrows Point Steel Mill became a complex constellation of factories, docks, cold and hot mills and numerous blast furnaces that covered several thousand acres. In this light, it can be viewed as a significant component of the occupational and industrial heritage of Baltimore, the mid-Atlantic region and far beyond, as well as a significant force in the labour, civil and women's rights movements within the US. In 2001, Bethlehem Steel went bankrupt and up until 2012, the mill underwent several changes of ownership with the workforce diminishing to roughly 1,500 personnel at its end. While parts of the mill have now been imploded, or sold and shipped to other industrial plants, and the surrounding region is economically suffering, the significance, values, memories and stories of Sparrows Point still live on. Over the course of its long history, hundreds of thousands of people have known Sparrows Point not only as a place of employment and economic stimulus for surrounding areas, but as a way of life, as a home and a place that has shaped memories and stories that still endure today.

Since early 2013, the Mill Stories project addresses how the socio-cultural effects of industrial decline can be better conceptualized, shared and connected. In other words, how can we learn to see the experiences of deindustrialization in a more complex light, and how can we make the sociocultural impacts of such decline more visible? The main aim of Mill Stories is to help amplify the voices of deindustrialization, grounded in the stories and memories of the mill workers. As such, the project is guided by the following objectives: (1) to examine the cultural heritage and significance of the mill from the perspectives of former workers and surrounding community members; (2) to audio-visually document the stories and memories of its community for the future; (3) to connect these distinctive voices (and experiences) to the broader narrative of industrial decline via a documentary film, the project's website and community discussion events; and (4) to engage undergraduate students in community-based and collaborative cultural research and documentation outside of the classroom (see Mill Stories 2016).

One of the most useful tools for publicly promoting the mill's living legacies, and for connecting to broader narratives of industrial boom and bust, has been the 35-minute documentary film, *Mill Stories: Remembering Sparrows Point Steel Mill*, which was developed over the past two years from interviews with mill workers.[4] The film – in both its rough and fine cut versions – has garnered significant attention; it has screened at several film festivals in the US and Europe, as well as at events in Baltimore and Bethlehem, Pennsylvania, the headquarters of the former Sparrows Point owner, Bethlehem Steel. Most importantly, the film has helped to build a sense of ownership over the project – and more so over the collaborative *process* of its creation, as well as the promotion and dialogue for which it strives – on behalf of those mill workers who have participated. The draft, or rough cut, versions of the film were first screened at community events during 2013 and 2014 as a means of seeking feedback and approval, as well as for enhancing its reach within the mill community and further sparking conversation on deindustrialization and its impacts. At such events, even though project participants and audience members reflect on their histories at the mill, discussions are also oriented towards the future, responding to the ever-present question of 'what is next?' Dialogues can become emotionally charged as participants express their anger over the mill's closure, the loss of jobs in Baltimore and beyond, and larger forces that they feel are to blame, such as global capitalism, among others.

The film is structured through 'chapters' that have emerged during interviews as key themes in the overall story of the mill. One such theme has focused on the experiences of women workers and their fight for gender equality on the job. Out of the 31 workers whose stories and memories have been documented so far, 8 are women. The following sections provide a history of women at Sparrows Point and an examination of their experiences with discrimination and the ways in which they pushed back against unfair treatment. Looking back on the progress she and other women steelworkers made, Paula Fleming – who was hired three decades ago – states that, eventually, 'we stopped being treated as second class citizens'.[5]

The Women of Steel

During World War II, a shortage of male workers led to a rise of 'Rosie the Riveters': women who filled their place in the many US industries of the time and who descended onto Sparrows Point in the hundreds. Reflective of the period, as well as the multi-cultural neighbourhoods of Baltimore, many of these women were émigrés, or children of immigrants, from Europe. As Reutter (1988: 360) notes, 700 women had been 'hired as crane operators and machine tenders' and worked in the Bethlehem-Fairfield shipyard on the wartime production of ships, as well as the associated airplane plants. However, during and after the war, the main job for which women were hired was to check for defects in the sheets of tin, rolled to paper-thin size in the tin mill. At a rate of 30 sheets per minute, Reutter (1988: 360) explains the process:

> At the tin mill tens of millions of dollars depended on the touch of a woman's hand [. . .] This was the task of women who worked at tables stacked high with freshly tinned steel and earned the nickname of 'tin floppers' from the sound of their work [. . .] The hand ran along the rim of a sheet, thumb and forefinger gauging whether the edge was straight, the surface unwavy. The eye patrolled for pinprick holes, black spots, scale pits, and other signs of machine defects. The wrist arched the sheet from front to back and into one of several classificatory bins, the trademark *flop* coming from sheet hitting sheet.

Men were considered 'ham-handed' when it came to flopping tin, so management believed that this was a perfect job for women, who could handle the speed and hand, eye and wrist coordination needed (Reutter 1988: 360–361). Based on the recollections of former tin floppers, who were in their 70s and 80s when interviewed, Reutter (1988) and Rudacille (2010) provide insight into how grueling a job this was. While their wages were higher than the clothing factories and oyster-canning plants that employed women in Baltimore, they were still paid significantly less than men at Sparrows Point (Reutter 1988: 364). In addition, the heat of the tin sorting room would frequently cause fainting, they had to wear gloves to avoid deep cuts, many thicker sheets were almost too heavy to carry and the atmosphere – under the constant supervision of foreladies – was extremely strict, down to the uniforms that they were required to purchase, which were 'never more than 12 inches from the floor' (Reutter 1988: 361). It was also commonplace for men to flirt with and 'silently appraise' the tin floppers, making for an uncomfortable environment that was exacerbated by the fact that men and women were forbidden to converse (Reutter 1988: 375).

In this rigid atmosphere, women had few moments to relax aside from their monitored 15-minute breaks, when coffee sipping and chit-chat would abound. One social event, held every two to three years, was the Kotex Ball, named after the feminine hygiene product popular at the time. Even though Bethlehem

Steel provided free Kotex pads, the head of the ladies' dressing room, Mrs Mary Gorman, would collect five cents each time one was needed. This 'tax' would fund what was officially called the 'Banquet and Dance by the Ladies of the B.H. Department', an evening of skits, music and dance at a hotel downtown. Based on a conversation with Gorman, Reutter (1988: 372–373) describes the stark contrast of the 'occasional pageant' and mill life:

> At the Kotex Ball the company rules were flouted by normally obedient workers, flouted to the applause of normally tyrannical bosses. Here was where young women could shed their blue uniforms for skirts far above the 12-inch rule. Where men and women could freely talk to one another. Where girls who sorted [the tin] in silence could sing before the glare of floodlights. Where children of immigrants could feel a part of America. Where on one night every two or three years those who would never cry in front of the boss lady could sniffle to the strains of a love song.

During the mid-1950s, a group of women began protesting against the working conditions of the sorting room, including the mandatory uniforms. Taking cues from the men workers, they sought representation by the union and their informal meetings in the dressing room led to several staged sit-ins in the lunchroom. With the retirement of their longstanding boss, who was both strict and yet protective of the women, the rules of the 1940s and early 1950s began to be lifted. The Kotex Ball was also terminated, and the pads were free for women workers to use. Nonetheless, as the post-war boom in steel and tin making dimmed over the course of the 1960s, so did the number of women working at the mill. Rudacille (2010: 165) describes how some tin floppers transferred to other jobs, such as working on the 'halogen line' of the tin mill and on 'labor gangs', after the closing of the sorting room. Yet, it was not until the early 1970s that another 'boom' – in terms of hiring women – took place.

The 1970s onwards: sacrifice and pride

In 1974, Loretta Houston Smith was part of a group of women newly hired at the mill. She recounts her first experiences, including the brief period when she was laid off, a common reality for many workers in the industry:

> I was hired as a laborer, and I was then hired in the pipe mill. And in the pipe mill, we had jobs like grinders, hookers, and it was funny, because when I had – when I first got laid off – my first experience with unemployment, I had to tell them the type of job that I worked, and I said: 'Well, I was a hooker,' you know . . . and the lady was like, 'you were what . . . at Bethlehem Steel?' And I said, 'Oh, let me explain the job to you: I was a crane follower, and I hooked up these long cables, and I would pick them up and hook it up to the cranes, and that was what a hooker did, you know.' And I made a lot of money doing that, so I didn't leave.[6]

The fight against racial discrimination at Sparrows Point, which included lawsuits and strikes throughout the 1960s and early 1970s, also affected the hiring of women. Specifically, in the spring of 1974, employment policies of the steel industry became more just with respect to the hiring and in-the-mill mobility of minority groups when the

> United Steelworkers of America and nine companies in the industry entered into a Consent Decree with the United States as represented by the Attorney General's Office, the Department of Justice, the Secretary of Labor, the Office of Federal Contract Compliance, and the Equal Employment Opportunity Commission.
>
> (Ichniowski 1981: 1)

Rudacille (2010: 165) highlights that while there were former tin floppers still working at the mill who benefitted from the consent decree, the hiring of new women was one of its greatest impacts. For instance, Mary Lorenzo was hired in 1971, but was laid off the following year. On Lorenzo's experience, Rudacille (2010: 165) writes:

> By then she was divorced and a single parent, so when they started hiring women in the coke ovens after the consent decree, she bid in. 'That must've been about '76 or '77,' she said. 'There were a lot of girls out in the coalfields then, but it was all still new, because some of the men acted like they've never seen women before, hanging out of the cranes whistling and hollering and carrying on.'

Houston Smith experienced similar responses from men at the mill. Eventually becoming a crane operator, she explains:

> Some of the cranes had what they called moving cabs – it's on a rail, like a train car. And it's just, a moving cab, you could move back and forth with it, OK? Well, my job was picking up coils, pipes and things like that. You know, loading railroad cars, and trucks [. . .] We had what they called C-hooks, we had hooks that rotated; I mean, it was really amazing. And a lot of times when I would come down, and for a lot of the female operators, the guys would look up when they see you come down and say, 'Were you up there?' You know, and it was like really amazing [for them] that it was a woman up there, you know.[7]

She also remembers men's reactions when she first started in the pipe mill in the mid-1970s:

> My first assignment was in the pipe mill. And when we entered the mill, the guy said to us, 'Ladies watch out for the moving cranes.' So, of course, none

of us had experienced working in the mill before at all. So, when the crane started moving, we all got up against the wall and we were petrified. And here comes this crane, moving, and we're like, 'Which way do we go?' But he forgot to tell us that it had a moving cab and to watch the cab [since it moved in many directions]. And we learned that later, but we were so petrified; we did not know what to do and the men thought it was so hilarious. They wouldn't tell us any different. They wanted to see how we would react.[8]

Rudacille (2010: 165–171) examines sexual discrimination and harassment issues, such as teasing, but also rampant displays of pornographic imagery throughout the mill. Mary Ellen Beechner, hired in 1975, remembers when she walked 'into one shop where I was going to do some lead sampling to make sure people weren't being overexposed, and they had pictures from *Hustler* magazine, I mean really hard-core stuff, wallpapering the walls [. . .] I felt so uncomfortable' (in Rudacille 2010: 167).

Despite strides made by women in the union, as discussed later, a male-dominated culture could still be felt in the 1990s, even with respect to basic amenities. For instance, in 1995, Natalie Johnson was hired as a housekeeper, which she notes was typical for many women, but she wanted a better job with a higher salary. She states:

Because I didn't like housekeeping, I went to Mobile Equipment, where I was told certain things like, 'You can't do this job' or 'You're not equipped for this job,' but overall I did every job that every guy could do – without hesitation. Sometimes, I did it better.[9]

As such, she became one of a few women in the Mobile Equipment Department, where one utilizes large vehicles for transport tasks throughout the mill complex. She explains:

I was originally a slab-haul operator, which I don't know if y'all know, but a slab-haul operator is a big carrier that picks up the slabs from the caster to put them on the ground, to pick them back up and to take them to the mill. And that's what we did: we just moved the steel around the mill in different buildings on this slab carrier and I was the only girl on that, but it was fun. It was one of the biggest pieces of equipment down there.[10]

However, she had to fight for a more respectful place to change into and out of her work clothes. She recalls:

I had no locker room personally to myself, you know. I wasn't actually in the locker room with the guys, but there was, like, a makeshift section off of it, but it was still in the same building [. . .] The guys were on one side of the locker and I was on the other side of the locker, which was totally

> uncomfortable, especially when you have to take your clothes off, alright? But after a while, I protested and got on my soapbox, and they got me a trailer. And that's when the other women started coming [getting hired] into the department. So, it was about a good five of us in a department of, like, sixty guys, and it was a mess because guys are nasty [laughs].[11]

Similarly, Paula Fleming, who started in 1996, recalls the lack of restrooms for women when she was working in the 'pickler' (the process of removing impurities from steel):

> You know, we didn't have the proper facilities. I remember in my unit, the pickler, we didn't have bathrooms. So, I would actually have to go outside to another building to go to the bathroom [. . .] Their solution was, after I was the main one making the ruckus, was to get us spot-a-pots [portable toilets]. And I'm like, 'How you gonna have me use a spot a pot that the guys use?' You know, women have different issues. I mean, it just wasn't cool. We managed to get them to fix up a bathroom. It was still in another building, but at least we had our own.[12]

Even though poor bathroom facilities for women may seem like a minor issue in the grand scheme of discriminatory practices, Loretta Houston Smith brings to light their importance as spaces where they could feel comfortable and bond, providing a deeper sense of relief. She notes: '[W]e fellowshipped a lot in the bathrooms, through tears. You know, to keep each other strong'.[13]

In addition to coping with life in a male-dominated environment, working conditions were extremely challenging and dangerous for all. Darlene Redemann, whose husband also worked at the mill, was hired in the mid-1970s and remembers:

> I was told that Sparrows Point was hiring, which was one of the better paying jobs with better benefits in the community [. . .] I started as basically a laborer and then I moved up into the cranes for twenty years.[14]

Redemann was one of the first women trained in crane operation. She subsequently moved up into the cold mill as the first female 'roller', which she describes as:

> Well, you stayed on your feet for 8 solid hours and you got a sheet of steel flying past you at 2,500 feet per minute. So, it was a very dangerous job; the environment was very greasy . . . in the summer time, you're looking at [temperatures] higher than a hundred degrees, and in the winter time, you're looking at freezing [temperatures]. There were no lunch breaks; you eat on the fly. So, here you got your sandwich with your hand full of grease. There were no breaks: if you had to go to the bathroom, well, you're just gonna have to wait. As far as the swing shift, that was just insane [. . .] It didn't matter if

it was Christmas, the Fourth of July, it didn't matter; you had to be at work. I mean, there was no 'I can't come to work today, my child is sick' – it didn't matter, it didn't matter what the situation was at home; you showed up for work or you didn't have a job. It was very simple.[15]

These demanding and dangerous conditions have been noted by almost all of the workers – female and male – interviewed. As 'Joe-Ed' Lawrence, an ironworker at the mill for decades, points out, 'You would not believe how many people have been killed at Sparrows Point. I'd say since the '60s, it's in the 200s.'[16] On one of the main thoroughfares in the mill's neighbourhood, in front of the local United Steelworkers (USW) union buildings, a monument was erected to workers who sacrificed their lives to the job, with too long a list of names etched onto its surface.[17] Having witnessed the death of a co-worker, who 'fell off of a transporter', Natalie Johnson comments that it is 'something you will never forget'.[18]

Although not exclusively, the women tend to frame the difficulties and dangers they faced as a necessary step towards ensuring that their children were raised with as many opportunities for success as possible, such as being able to attend college. While numerous workers commented on the relatively high wages and good benefits they received, which were good enough to outweigh the health and safety risks, the women also spoke about the extra challenges of raising a family. For instance, Houston Smith tells a bittersweet story about coping with a lack of childcare at the mill. She recounts:

> I had a babysitting problem and my foreman had me come in one night. I had to open the [pipe] mill; I had to turn the lights on to do my job. And during this time, I didn't have a babysitter; I didn't know what to do with my child. And like I said before, a lot of us had problems with our children. Where were we gonna leave them? You know, and this was on 11 [pm] to 7 [am] [shift]. And I looked at my daughter; she was two. I grabbed her little pillow, and she had on her little pajammies [pyjamas], and I drove to Bethlehem Steel, and I carried her up the ladder with me, into my crane. And there she stayed; she slept with her bottle until I completed the end of my shift.[19]

Redemann also discusses the sacrifices she made as a mother by adding: 'I mean, I worked 16 hours, I'd go home and, well, my son has a baseball game. You have to support your children in their sports, so it was like, when did you sleep? You didn't.'[20] Natalie Johnson shares a conversation she had with one of her children, reflecting the choices she made in order to raise them as best as she could:

> I tell [my kids] that Sparrows Point was a good place and that Sparrows Point was what fed you, so don't talk bad about it [. . .] My son, he goes, 'Well, Mom, you shouldn't have to work like that, you should have a sit down job.' I was like, 'Why is that?' He said, 'You need to just relax [. . .] You shouldn't have to work out in the cold.' I said, 'Well, I feel as though I shouldn't have

to go outside in the cold, but I went.' You gotta do some things you gotta do just because. But, he doesn't get it; he just thinks his mother is supposed to just sit down and, you know, put on a pretty dress and go to work, but that's not the mother he has.[21]

Here, it can be argued that pride is also being expressed – a pride derived from making difficult choices that supported their families, and also a pride of the roles they played at the mill. Gail Fleming, who started at the mill in 1979, also expresses this dual pride by commenting:

It was just being able to make the money that I needed to make in order to buy a house for my kids and myself and in order to, you know, progress. And I mean, there were hard times, night shifts, swing shifts; it wasn't an easy task in itself, but I became the first female dispatch operator where the dispatcher would dispatch me out to different jobs where they call for different pieces of equipment [. . .] I had the run of the whole plant.[22]

Many of the problems encountered by the women steelworkers, such as a lack of privacy, were resolved. As noted, they would speak up – as uncomfortable as that could be – and demand change. Furthermore, as examined in the following section, great strides were also made through their involvement in the local USW, especially with respect to forming a Women of Steel committee as a means of coming together and strengthening their efforts at the mill.

Women of Steel

While Natalie Johnson feels that she handled the problems she faced on her own, she does highlight how the union served as a 'back-up' support system:

Most things I handled myself. But you have others that, you know, won't speak up. They'll go to the union and have someone speak for them [. . .] But I know I have the backing of the union to help me if I needed it. [E]ven though we're not working there, if I'm having an issue or something is going on, I can call up here to the [union] hall and they'll do their best to address my issue, try to help me out with it and steer me in the right direction to go.[23]

This system was based on the idea of having strength in numbers, where union representatives were there to help resolve grievances and fight for better wages, safety measures, benefits and working conditions. For Darlene Redemann, the dangerous surroundings and the difficulties experienced as a mother led her to become involved in the union a year after getting hired. Describing her motivation, as well as her focus on women's rights, she notes:

> [S]ince I was a union rep, I went to different parts of the steel mill to find out how their environment was, how their wage tier was, trying to help with women's rights, because a lot of women really had to fight hard for the positions that they held.

For example, in 1982, she fought a sexist rule regarding the fact that women 'have to pick up 75 pounds to remain in the mill', but as she quips: '[Y]ou had men that couldn't pick up 75 pounds [. . .] I fought that really long and hard and finally won that case.'[24]

Redemann became a well-respected union representative for many workers – both women and men. Chris MacLarion, who started working at Sparrows Point in 1996 and eventually became Vice President of the union in the mill's final years, remembers Redemann as first encouraging him to become an active member, something of which he is very proud. He recalls:

> [Redemann] is a very outgoing woman, and she is not shy [. . .] So, we became friends and at one point she said, 'you're gonna be shop steward of this unit [the cold sheet mill]; things are changing and we need a young guy in here' . . . well, I couldn't tell you what a damn shop steward was.

However, he learned quickly and describes it as:

> [It] was the lowest elected officer in the union [. . .] the representative that will do first step grievances: if an employee has a complaint and management violated the contract, the labor agreement, you will facilitate his grievance, you will represent him [. . .] all those early stages of the complaint process.[25]

During the 1970s and 1980s, more women became active in the union, but it was not until the mid-1990s that their efforts in fighting for gender equality became considerably stronger, through the formation of their own Women of Steel committee. Loretta Houston Smith was also active in the union early on, citing discrimination against women, a lack of childcare, as well as racism, as issues she wanted to help change. As she explains, the committee was a tool for organizing women and to be able to meet regularly and discuss pressing issues. Gail Fleming remembers her first time engaging with the international Women of Steel 'activist arm'[26] of USW at a related convention in Las Vegas in 1995; soon after, she was involved with 'bringing Women of Steel back to Sparrows Point', as both she and Darlene have noted.[27]

The efforts of Sparrows Point women steelworkers reflected broader changes in USW at the time. As stated in an online pamphlet for Women of Steel, its origins date back to Canada in the 1980s:

Female activism within the USW has always been recognized. However, it wasn't until the establishment in Canada of the Women of Steel Leadership Development Course in the mid-1980s that the phrase Women of Steel first symbolized for women their identity within the union. At the 26th USW Constitutional Convention in 1992, the first Women of Steel resolution was introduced and stated: 'Our message must be clear to all our members; women are first-class citizens in the union and in the labor movement as well as in the workforce and society in general. Gender equality is a union issue – it is a source of our strength and solidarity.'[28]

As noted in a United Steel Workers of America (USWA) instructional booklet that provides guidance on how to form local Women of Steel committees, the mid-1990s was a time when 'one-third of union members are women and over 50% new members are women'. The booklet begins with '[USWA] Resolution Number 21: Women of Steel', which cites that, among others, the issues of sexual harassment and violence against women ought to be tackled through such committees. It states: 'The union can and has taken a strong stance on both of these issues. As we say – 'Let's Put It On The Table' – our table, the bargaining table, the community table, the government table, and the family dinner table.' Similarly, the 'women's issues' of 'childcare, parental leave, pay equity and freedom to develop as individuals are issues for all of us'. The booklet also reminds women workers that:

> [U]nionized women *working together* fare *much* better. Given the opportunity and security, women will share stories and experiences and work together to identify strategies for change that benefit all workers. Whether it is working toward workplace and union events free from harassment, scheduling union meetings and events that do not conflict with family responsibilities, or bargaining pay equity, we have all gained from the work of women and women's committees.[29]

Back in Baltimore, Houston Smith eventually became president of the local Women of Steel and states that she 'taught the women a lot of things, when we would have issues in the mill, we would have meetings once a month and any type of issue that needed to be resolved, I was the person'.[30]

It ought to be stressed that for a number of women, the struggles for gender equality and Civil Rights were tightly interwoven, especially since many women workers are African-American, such as Houston Smith, Gail Fleming, Paula Fleming and Natalie Johnson. Indeed, Paula and Gail have both mentioned that they were involved in the union's Civil Rights committee in addition to their becoming a part of Women of Steel. The positive impacts of all of their efforts, including Redemann's, were certainly felt by successive generations of women workers. For instance, Lettice Sims, who was hired in 2002 as a crane operator, fondly calls Houston Smith the 'Rosa Parks' of Sparrows Point as a result of her support for and protection of women at the mill. Even Loretta calls herself a 'trouble maker', someone who 'wanted something done, you know, and I would talk about the issues that involved myself and a lot of other women'.[31] Sims continues:

> Loretta was a legend in her own right [. . .] It's just like Rosa Parks; you got to stand for something. She was that stronger person that stood for us to make it easier for us coming in the door, because everything was already paved there – I had it easy, believe me [. . .] When Loretta left, it was two Afro-American females [. . .] It was around sixty crane operators and there was two Afro-American crane operators and I was one of them. During my generation, [nobody] was prejudiced; I was never discriminated against, or nothing like that. I thank Loretta and Darlene, because they made the path for women like me to come along . . . because that was a hard road that they had to go through and I couldn't endure nothing like that.[32]

In the mid-2000s, Sims joined the Women of Steel 'just to see' what it was like. She remembers that: 'Kathy Garrison was our leader and just to see strong women like her – Loretta, Darlene, Gail Fleming – pave the way for us [. . .] I wanted to take initiative and make a step.'[33]

Unfortunately, by the late 2000s, the mill was in sharp decline in terms of financial stability and with a future that was increasingly uncertain. Sims, having only worked for a decade as a crane operator, was looking – at the time of her interview in 2013 – for new employment in the food service industry. The accomplishments of women steelworkers and Women of Steel over the years were overshadowed by the prospect of a closing mill, as well as the loss of pensions and healthcare benefits that are today still being fought for today. Redemann, who has sadly passed away in spring 2016 at too young an age, was particularly angered by the broken promises given by the series of mill owners during the last ten years. She states:

> But all the women down there really suffered as far as a family life so they could have security when they left, and that was lost. You know, [my] union job towards the end really got rough, because that's when we going through all the job eliminations and I was trying to make the best grievance possible to secure some type of income for the people that were losing that position, but it was a no win situation. [I]f you helped out the junior guy, now you screwed with the senior guy; if you helped out the senior guy, now you screwed with the junior guy. So, that was just a catastrophe trying to deal with that making everybody happy, but . . . I made it![34]

What remains?

The contributions women made in shaping the culture and living heritage of the mill extend far beyond what has been learned and documented through the Mill

Stories project. Nonetheless, the chapter has provided valuable insight into their experiences as steelworkers in a male-dominated mill, as well as their progress in striving for equality, including just working conditions and compensation. These are narratives that need to be shared and more widely promoted as a means of complicating and deepening discussions on the history of industrial boom and bust, and the cultural heritage of labour. Women steelworkers often coped with strict rules and supervision, teasing and sexual harassment, as well as a lack of basic amenities that were already guaranteed to men, and that could only be won with a hard fight. Moreover, it has become clear that manufacturing jobs are dangerous and full of life-threatening risks, which is of no surprise; yet, as the women here have expressed, there is a strong sense of pride for both the sacrifices they have made for raising their families and bettering themselves, as well as for their own, individual advancements up through the ranks of the various mills, units and departments.

Redemann and Houston Smith were one of the first women crane operators, and Gail Fleming was the first female dispatch operator, proud of her wide reach across the mill's complex. Natalie Johnson was one of the first women working in mobile equipment, securing for herself and subsequent women a proper place to change clothes. In recent decades, the women came together to help protect each other – including men – against larger, more powerful forces that would soon lead to the mill's demise. In big and small ways, all were instrumental in ensuring a path with fewer racist and sexist barriers for younger generations of women steelworkers. At the end of the day, and despite an industrial landscape that is forever gone, what remains is resilience. Through frustration, anger, tears and laughter, a powerful dignity is what lives on.

Acknowledgements

Thanks to William Shewbridge, who also runs the Mill Stories project, and the steelworkers with whom we have been fortunate to work. This chapter is dedicated to Darlene Redemann.

Notes

1. See http://millstories.umbc.edu/our-story/.
2. Olsen (2005) and Walkerdine (2010) both examine the experiences of women living in the deindustrializing steel communities of Sparrows Point and Steel Town, South Wales, respectively.
3. As stated in the film, *Mill Stories: Remembering Sparrows Point Steel Mill*.
4. To view the film's trailer, see http://millstories.umbc.edu/documentary/.
5. Interview with author, United Steel Workers Union local 2609, 28 March 2013, Baltimore, Maryland. It is important to note that interviews with the women excerpted throughout this chapter derive from two, full-day interview 'sessions' held at the local union hall. In order to maximise the opportunity to interview as many steelworkers as possible, both women and men, setting up all-day 'share your story' events was beneficial.

6 Interview with author, 26 March 2013, United Steel Workers Union local 2609, Baltimore.
7 Interview with author, 26 March 2013, United Steel Workers Union local 2609, Baltimore.
8 Interview with author, 26 March 2013, United Steel Workers Union local 2609, Baltimore.
9 Interview with author, 28 March 2013, United Steel Workers Union local 2609, Baltimore.
10 Interview with author, 29 March 2013, United Steel Workers Union local 2609, Baltimore.
11 Interview with author, 28 March 2013, United Steel Workers Union local 2609, Baltimore.
12 Interview with author, 28 March 2013, United Steel Workers Union local 2609, Baltimore.
13 Interview with author, 26 March 2013, United Steel Workers Union local 2609, Baltimore.
14 Interview with author, 26 March 2013, United Steel Workers Union local 2609, Baltimore.
15 Interview with author, 26 March 2013, United Steel Workers Union local 2609, Baltimore.
16 Interview with author, 28 March 2013, United Steel Workers Union local 2609, Baltimore.
17 The monument has since been relocated to a nearby public park.
18 Interview with author, 28 March 2013, United Steel Workers Union local 2609, Baltimore.
19 Interview with author, 26 March 2013, United Steel Workers Union local 2609, Baltimore.
20 Interview with author, 26 March 2013, United Steel Workers Union local 2609, Baltimore.
21 Interview with author, 28 March 2013, United Steel Workers Union local 2609, Baltimore.
22 Interview with author, 28 March 2013, United Steel Workers Union local 2609, Baltimore.
23 Interview with author, 28 March 2013, United Steel Workers Union local 2609, Baltimore.
24 Interview with author, 26 March 2013, United Steel Workers Union local 2609, Baltimore.
25 Interview with author, 17 July 2013, Belcamp, Maryland.
26 See www.usw.org/act/activism/women-of-steel.
27 Interview with author, 26 March 2013, United Steel Workers Union local 2609, Baltimore.
28 See www.uswlocal1999.org/files/wos_what_its_all_about.pdf.
29 Emphasis in original; from an instructional booklet (n.d.) entitled, 'Women of Steel: Building Solidarity: What's It All About?', which was given out at one of the United Steel Workers of America (USWA) conventions that Houston Smith lent to the author. It was probably produced in the mid-1990s as it cites a 1996 USWA District 3 meeting.
30 Interview with author, 26 March 2013, United Steel Workers Union local 2609, Baltimore.
31 Interview with author, 26 March 2013, United Steel Workers Union local 2609, Baltimore.
32 Interview with author, 26 March 2013, United Steel Workers Union local 2609, Baltimore.

33 Interview with author, 26 March 2013, United Steel Workers Union local 2609, Baltimore.
34 Interview with author, 26 March 2013, United Steel Workers Union local 2609, Baltimore.

Bibliography

Ichniowski, C. 1981. Have Angels Done More? The Steel Industry Consent Decree. National Bureau of Economic Research, Inc. and the Sloan School of Management at the Massachusetts Institute of Technology. Available at: https://dspace.mit.edu/bitstream/handle/1721.1/48047/haveangelsdonebe00ichn.pdf?sequence=1 (accessed 25 January 2017).

Mill Stories 2016. Homepage. Available at: www.millstories.org (accessed 23 May 2017).

Olsen, K. 2005. *Wives of Steel: Voices of Women from the Sparrows Point Steelmaking Communities*. University Park, PA: Penn State University Press.

Reading, A. 2015. Making Feminist Heritage Work: Gender and Heritage. In E. Waterton and S. Watson (eds) *The Palgrave Handbook of Contemporary Heritage Research*. London: Palgrave Macmillan, pp. 397–413.

Reutter, M. 1988. *Sparrows Point Making Steel: The Rise and Ruin of American Industrial Might*. New York: Summit.

Rudacille, D. 2010. *Roots of Steel: Boom and Bust in an American Mill Town*. New York: Pantheon.

Shackel, P., Smith, L. and Campbell, G. 2011. Editorial: Labour's Heritage. *International Journal of Heritage Studies*, 17(4): 291–300.

Smith, L., Shackel, P. and Campbell, G. (eds) 2011. *Heritage, Labour and the Working Classes*. London and New York: Routledge.

Walkerdine, V. 2010. Communal Beingness and Affect: An Exploration of Trauma in an Ex-Industrial Community. *Body and Society*, 16(1): 91–116.

Chapter 15

'Does it matter?'
Relocating fragments of queer heritage in post-earthquake Christchurch

Andrew Gorman-Murray and Scott McKinnon

Introduction

'Does it matter?' This was a response from an interviewee, a 60-something gay man (Interview 9: 02/06/2015), to our question about the loss of contemporary and historical LGBT[1] social spaces in Christchurch, Aotearoa New Zealand, after the earthquake that devastated the city on 22 February 2011. As we outline later in this chapter, this was among the most destructive disasters to strike the country, causing massive damage to buildings and infrastructure, as well as 185 deaths and many more non-fatal injuries (Swaffield 2013). Yet for other respondents, the loss of space mattered a great deal. A 30-something lesbian told us that 'the impact on LGBT social spaces was and is huge' (Survey 91: 15/04/2015), while a 50-something gay man claimed that 'life in the LGBT community died after the earthquake' (Survey 20: 23/04/2015). These divergent responses to material losses to the LGBT community compel us to explore the meaning of queer heritage – by which we mean LGBT spaces and the communities of practice that they enable – in post-earthquake Christchurch. Following Denis Byrne (2005: 1), we understand queer heritage in the Asia-Pacific as a 'queer geography' that materialises 'a tradition of what it has meant to be queer in this part of the world'. This heritage is tangible and intangible, encompassing places, landscapes and the practices, memories and meanings associated with those sites.

The aim of this chapter is to relocate fragments of queer heritage in post-earthquake Christchurch and to explore LGBT and mainstream responses to the loss of queer heritage. Christchurch is a compelling site for this work: a city steeped in particular notions of heritage, where people and authorities must make decisions about rebuilding and recovering heritage in a post-disaster context (Bowring and Swaffield 2013). Where does queer heritage figure in the deliberations? Our data are from a project on LGBT experiences of disasters in Australia and Aotearoa New Zealand – in which Christchurch is a key case study – and include surveys, interviews with LGBT residents, and analysis of media and policy discourse. In this chapter, we analyse the data through five thematic frames. *Displacement*, by which respondents indicated their awareness of lost or changing social spaces, practices and everyday geographies, and four responses to displacement: *ambivalence* (does queer heritage matter?), *invisibility* (of queer heritage in Christchurch's heritage recovery programme); *reminding* (of queer presence and history by transient appropriation of urban ruins); and *remembering* (through which some seek to recover the memories, if not the sites, of queer heritage). We begin with some framing on queer heritage and the Christchurch context.

Queer heritage from below

Since our interest in this chapter is *queer heritage* in post-earthquake Christchurch, we first need to discuss what we mean by our deployment of these terms. We use the term *queer* to encompass a diversity of sexual and gender minorities, or LGBT subjects, spaces, cultures and practices. On the one hand, queer is being used as an alternative umbrella term for LGBT. On the other hand, we also have in mind the more radical conceptual use of queer in scholarship. In queer theory, queer also signals a counter-normative disposition that contests and opposes the naturalisation of conventional identities, relationships and communities (Oswin 2008). Queer, in this sense, seeks to open up new ways to understand the lives and practices of LGBT and other non-conventional subjects, and advocates for the recognition and validity of counter-normative identities, relationships and communities (Ahmed 2006). Used in this way, queer seeks to challenge and subvert the centring of (hetero)normative subjectivities and traditions (Browne and Nash 2010). This sense of queer is taken forward in the idea of queer *heritage*.

Heritage refers to a range of 'things' that are inherited from the past, and also to the effect of that inheritance on contemporary activities, meanings and behaviours (Robertson 2012). Heritage includes both tangible and intangible things: landscapes, structures, buildings, objects, traditions, events, literature, language and social and cultural practices (Harrison 2013). But the things that are preserved and remembered, and with what effect, are informed by cultural and social values, conventions and power (Smith 2006). What kinds of heritage are included, and what is left out or overlooked, in these decisions? Perhaps more critically, *whose* heritage is overlooked (Hall 1999)? As Laurajane Smith (2006: 38) contends, heritage is 'inherently political and discordant', divided and used by different interest groups to create hegemony or counter-claims. Yet if heritage is used – as it often is – to buttress hegemonic national, mainstream or valued identities (Waterton 2014), what happens to the memories and practices of marginal social groups? How do we find 'alternative' heritage and consider its relationship to larger narratives of inheritance?

Iain Robertson (2012) offers the idea of 'heritage from below' as a localised, vernacular and democratic form of heritage. The spatial metaphor – heritage from below – is suggestive of the flow of power in heritage practice. Robertson (2012: 1) argues that 'mainstream manifestations of heritage' are 'nationalist, top-down, commercial and tourism-focussed perspectives' that are concerned with 'visitors, audience and consumption'. He instead seeks other avenues of heritage that are 'anti-hegemonic . . . resources for expression of identity and ways of life that run counter to the dominant' (Robertson 2012: 2). Heritage from below is 'a sense of inheritance that does not seek to attract an audience' but foregrounds 'interconnections between identity, collective memory and sense of place' (Robertson 2012: 2). Such heritage is often local rather than national, marginal rather than mainstream. Heritage from below is intimate, and it is also vital and active, suffusing the performativity of identity: 'Heritage, wrapped up in and constitutive of identity as it is, can be understood as an active and dynamic central part of the performance of our sense of self (individually and collectively)' (Robertson 2012: 14; see also Waterton 2014). As such, heritage from below can become an important part of social movements in the present, buttressing senses of place, identity and collectivity.

Queer heritage – the heritage of LGBT communities – neatly exemplifies heritage from below. For a start, in almost any country around the world, queer heritage comprises a set of inheritances that would be devalued and marginalised in the discourses and practices of nationalist heritage industries (Andersson 2012; Forsyth 2001). How, then, might we recover queer heritage? In his discussion of 'queer heritage in the Asia-Pacific', Denis Byrne (2005) offers some ideas to use in our attempt to relocate queer heritage in post-earthquake Christchurch. While his scope for queer inheritance includes all queer traditions, including language and literature, he focuses in particular on 'physical places and landscapes', including the practices, memories and meanings associated with those sites (Byrne 2005: 1). Byrne (2005: 1–2) contends that:

> Queer heritage is a whole queer geography or topography. That is to say, a constellation of sites of homosexuality scattered across the landscape along with the conceptual and physical linkages ('pathways') between them. . . . Inevitably, many 'places' eventually cease to be represented on the ground . . . Even so, the places may continue to live in people's memories and have a presence in the books, magazines, and photos that 'capture' and evoke them.

Byrne thereby suggests we might recover and remember queer heritage by *locating* it.

Queer heritage in a post-disaster city

Following Robertson's (2012) emphasis on local, vernacular heritage from below, this chapter takes a specific case study: we locate, excavate and remember queer heritage in Christchurch, Aotearoa New Zealand, in the wake of the devastating earthquake of February 2011, which brought permanent material changes to the city. We believe this is an important and telling context for exploring the constitution of queer heritage. Christchurch was, and is, a city famed for its construction and celebration of heritage – 'the most English of all cities', was a common phrase – and its place-identity and city-marketing programmes have traded heavily on its heritage tourism industry (Schöllman *et al.* 2000). In the wake of the earthquake and destruction of significant parts of the iconic urban landscape, issues of rebuilding and reconstituting heritage have loomed large in public, media and planning discussions (Swaffield 2013). The sudden shattering of the urban fabric has also been a sudden and ongoing recalibration of the city's cultural and material heritage. What is to be recovered of Christchurch's pre-earthquake heritage, and what is to be transformed or left behind? These wider debates open cracks in and through which we might locate and excavate queer heritage from below in Christchurch.

Queer heritage did not figure in Christchurch's pre-earthquake heritage industry (Brown 2000). Yet, LGBT people have long made their homes and communities in the city (Brickell 2008; Brown 2000), and have constituted heritage from below – their own places, landscapes, practices and traditions. These, too, were turned upside-down in the wake of the material and social dislocation wrought on 22 February 2011. Our fieldwork suggests that LGBT community places and networks that were shattered in the event have not been re-knitted the same as before. For the respondents, transformations in the landscapes, traditions and practices of the queer community impelled awareness of, and reflection on, queer heritage – on the queer topography of pre-earthquake Christchurch that has been 'lost'. The legacy of this 'fateful moment' has been productive in one sense, leading to the constitution of memories about queer places and networks in Christchurch. In this chapter, we draw on our data to explore the complexity of queer heritage in Christchurch through five thematic frames: *displacement* (lost or shifting spaces and practices), *ambivalence* (does the loss of queer heritage matter?), *invisibility* (silence around queer heritage in Christchurch's recovery programme), *reminding* (transient queer appropriation of urban ruins), and *remembering* (recovering the memories of queer heritage).

First, we give a brief outline of the research context and data. Our Christchurch case study is part of a larger project on LGBT experiences of disasters in Australia and Aotearoa New Zealand.[2] On 22 February 2011, a 6.2 magnitude earthquake struck Christchurch; it was part of a sequence that began with a 7.1 magnitude earthquake on 4 September 2010. However, it was the February event that devastated Christchurch due to its shallow depth and proximity to the city centre. It is the deadliest and costliest disaster in Aotearoa New Zealand since WWII: 185 deaths, 6,500 people injured and thousands of buildings damaged or destroyed, including historic structures and much of the Central Business District (CBD), many requiring subsequent demolition. Rebuilding costs are *c.* NZ$30 billion (Swaffield 2013). There have been thousands of aftershocks, and rebuilding continues. We used multiple methods to collect data on LGBT experiences during and after this event. These include a survey on LGBT disaster experiences (127 respondents), semi-structured interviews with LGBT residents (19 participants), and analysis of LGBT and mainstream media and local policy discourse.[3] Loss, meaning and recovery of queer spaces figured prominently in the data.

Displacement

After the 2011 earthquakes, Christchurch residents were forced to renegotiate and reinterpret their understanding of place in the city. In the course of a remarkably short space of time, the city was no longer as it had been. As Lachlan[4] (gay man, 30s) remembered, 'So where you'd normally walk through to get somewhere didn't exist anymore. The whole landscape had changed' (Interview 8: 02/06/2015). Indeed, the sense of security, belonging and identity that may be drawn from traversing familiar, everyday spaces was massively disrupted. As with other city residents, many of the LGBT individuals we interviewed experienced feelings of displacement resulting from the loss of the familiar. Adding to this troubling personal loss was concern that their community had also been displaced. After the earthquakes, many of the spaces of the city in which LGBT identity, community and safety had been located no longer existed.

For several interviewees, negotiating the post-earthquake city was made all the more difficult because the everyday landmarks – the unremarkable sites, buildings and locations that nonetheless marked a pathway through the city – were no longer present. Simon (gay man, 40s), stated:

> It is really hard to get your orientation in Christchurch because I drive in the city every day and ... I don't even know which street I'm on because you've got nothing – there are no landmarks – so you go about and you get the hang of the new landmarks.
>
> (Interview 19: 07/06/2015)

As the city rebuilds, this process of negotiating everyday displacement, or of undertaking a process of re-placement, is made all the more challenging because so little is fixed in place. A road that was open one day may be closed for repairs the next. A building that had been awaiting demolition for several years may be gone overnight. Simon said, 'It's the constant change, and constant change is really tiring, really exhausting.'

The need to secure some form of heritage in the post-earthquake city may be seen as a response to the everyday experience of displacement and as an attempt to fix at least some aspects of the pre-disaster city in place. Queer heritage might equally be seen here as a response to displacement. It is an attempt to maintain an attachment to lost places or practices and thus to renew feelings of security and safety (or of fun and sociability) for often marginalised identities.

A widely recognised dimension of the emergence of LGBT identities since WWII has been the establishment, in many larger cities of the Global North, of neighbourhoods marked by their inhabitation by mainly gay men (Knopp 1998), but also lesbians (Podmore and Chamberland 2015). Although Christchurch could not be said to have contained a 'gaybourhood' in the manner of New York's Chelsea or Sydney's Oxford Street, in the years prior to 2011 the major spaces of

LGBT sociality in the city were located in a particular area of the CBD. Several of our interviewees, particularly gay and bisexual men, remembered that their social lives had centred on a small number of bars, clubs and sex-on-premises venues in the CBD area. Tim (gay man, 50s) created a memory map of these spaces during our interview, stating:

> There was, like Litchfield Street, I guess at one stage it was, we called it the 'gay ghetto' because you had Litchfield and Colombo Street and at one stage there was a bar on Colombo Street. Across from that was the Colombo Sauna, on the corner there was Bar Particular which was a bar run by a couple of lesbians, then there was, turn the corner on Litchfield Street, there was Platinum Bar, then there was UBQ which became Cruz, and the Ministry nightclub ... and then across from that was my friend's sauna and then further down the road was the Box which was another sex-on-site venue, and there was also Camellia. So it was like this little area that you felt reasonably safe in on the weekends.
> (Interview 5: 30/05/2015)

Tim's narrative offers a trip through queer space over the course of some years in which he and his friend's had enjoyed an active social life within this precinct – a constellation of queer sites, constituting a topography of queer heritage (Byrne 2005). By the time of the earthquake, many of the venues he lists were closed and only Cruz bar and several sex-on-premises venues remained. The earthquake forced the closure of even these remaining businesses. The CBD was so badly damaged during the earthquake that much of the area was labelled a 'red zone', entry was forbidden by local authorities, with entry points guarded by army personnel (Canterbury Earthquake Recovery Authority 2016). Those business owners able to do so would gradually reopen their businesses in a range of other areas of the city. But an easily locatable and fixed site of LGBT community has not since been re-established. In the course of one day in February 2011, the small 'gay ghetto' of Christchurch had become a memory.

Below, we explore how the displacement of the LGBT community from this city space (and others) in Christchurch was incorporated into or excluded from narratives of the city's heritage. Among the LGBT community, a certain ambivalence exists about the loss of this space, in which the sense of loss experienced by some is resisted by those who see post-disaster reinvention as a positive process. Among wider and official heritage processes, any notion that pre-disaster queer spaces or practices should be acknowledged as an element of the city's heritage is largely absent, only visible in occasional acts of queer heritage from below.

Ambivalence

When asked how the loss of pre-disaster queer spaces had impacted on their community, LGBT residents of Christchurch offered a wide variety of viewpoints. Several respondents emphasised the fact that the queer spaces of the city had, even before the disaster, begun an inevitable process of decline or, at least, of significant change. The earthquake merely hastened that which had already begun. Some interviewees and survey respondents also commented positively on new forms of LGBT sociality appearing in the post-earthquake city. And yet, even among this ambivalence, there lay acknowledgement of loss and expressions of concern that queer visibility – including a connection to past queer cultural practices – needed to be maintained in the post-disaster city.

In many cities of the Global North, changes in identity formation and shifts in the uses of urban space have seen significant changes in the construction and meanings of LGBT neighbourhoods, revealing these spaces as mobile rather than immutable (Gorman-Murray and Nash 2014). One interviewee, Richard (gay man, 50s), described some of the changes taking place in Christchurch even before the earthquake:

> When I first moved to Christchurch 14 years ago, I wouldn't set foot in a straight bar. It's just not what you did. But, over time, before the earthquakes, I much preferred going to straight bars. They were much more fun and everyone was there to have a good time . . . I think young people still go out. They just don't feel the need to go somewhere that's solely gay.
> (Interview 18: 07/06/2015)

Greater acceptance of LGBT identities had gradually opened up more spaces of the city as safe and accessible to queer people. As a result, the importance of exclusively or predominantly queer spaces had been somewhat reduced, leading to ambivalence about their loss in the disaster.

Nonetheless, post-disaster LGBT social practices indicate that opportunities for participation and collaboration in identifiably queer spaces were of continued importance to some LGBT community members. Queer heritage was not reflected in the preservation or commemoration of material sites so much as it was adapted into new cultural processes designed to maintain community connections (Robertson 2012). A group called the UpRising Trust was established in the six months post-earthquake with the aim of promoting 'social cohesion of rainbow peoples and rainbow communities' (D'Aeth 2014: 2). UpRising responded to the sudden absence of queer spaces by organising one-night LGBT social events at otherwise 'straight' bars and clubs around Christchurch. In the four years after the earthquake, groups such as LYC and Pride would also organise dance parties and other LGBT community events in a range of venues across the city.

For some LGBT locals, these events meant that their access to and participation in the LGBT community actually increased after the earthquake. Nathan (gay man, 20s) stated:

> I think for me personally there's been more going on since the quake, since the loss . . . LYC kept the community together, I think . . . it was quite good after the earthquake. So I think I was going out to more events than I was going out before the earthquakes.
> (Interview 1: 28/05/2015)

A gay male survey respondent (26–35 years old) wrote, 'The presence of LYC has been one of the most encouraging [things] in post-quake Christchurch ... I have become more involved in the LGBT community since the quakes' (Survey 12: 10/05/2015). Rather than ensuring the preservation of material sites, queer heritage operated within moments of queer collaboration designed to maintain the community that had existed prior to the earthquakes. Even if the earlier spaces of that community were no longer available, and if the desire to use those spaces had significantly changed, there nonetheless remained a need, at least from time to time, to connect to queer cultures and to surround oneself with other LGBT people.

While some LGBT people saw increased opportunities post-disaster, others, however, experienced only loss. A trans survey respondent (FtM, 26–35 years old) wrote, 'Most of my LGBT friends have moved away. I miss feeling like part of an established community' (Survey 22: 20/04/2015). Emily (lesbian, 20s) described a sense of sadness that seemingly fixed places of queer life no longer existed, stating:

> Sometimes you'd like to just be able to go to some place gay where you could like blend in among your own rather than among everyone else ... if there isn't a consistent physical space there's at least a consistent time when you know that your people will descend upon a particular venue.
> (Interview 16: 03/06/2015)

None of our respondents or interviewees expressed a desire for the preservation or re-establishment of specific material sites. Those who expressed a sense of loss did not mourn a specific location, but rather the opportunities of community collaboration that had been possible within lost spaces. When queer heritage was enacted in the post-disaster city, it was expressed in the preservation of a community through cultural and social practices.

Invisibility

Unsurprisingly, given the centrality of heritage to the city's pre-disaster identity, the fate of historically or architecturally significant buildings and places was of considerable public concern in post-earthquake Christchurch (Swaffield 2013). In response, the Ministry for Culture and Heritage issued the 'Heritage Buildings and Recovery Programme for Greater Christchurch' (2014). The stated objective of the programme was to balance 'the need for wider earthquake recovery to proceed quickly and within available funding' with 'retaining heritage buildings and places as an important part of greater Christchurch's identity' (Ministry for Culture and Heritage 2014: 6). Containing costs and returning the city to some sense of normality were often in conflict with the possibility of expensive and time-consuming restoration and preservation projects. Moreover, the Heritage Recovery Programme was primarily concerned with 'land-based heritage' (Ministry for Culture and Heritage 2014: 7) and focused on buildings that had been registered as heritage sites prior to the earthquake. The city's losses in terms of such sites were substantial. By 2014, close to half of the registered heritage buildings in the city centre had been lost, either collapsing in the earthquake or subsequently demolished due to earthquake-related damage (Ministry for Culture and Heritage 2014: 7).

Although stating that 'Heritage recovery recognises and celebrates all cultural influences that contributed to heritage of greater Christchurch' (Ministry for Culture and Heritage 2014: 7) there is no mention of queer heritage as of interest to the programme. Indeed, places of queer heritage appear to have been entirely ignored within official heritage policy. In the version of the past reconstructed through official policy, queerness was entirely invisible. Official policy constructed a heteronormative historical vision from which the city's material LGBT heritage was excluded. Spaces of importance to the LGBT community of the pre-disaster city were not understood as significant spaces worthy of preservation or official commemoration. The programme did, however, acknowledge the need to keep 'memory and awareness alive' and to create 'spaces to remember' (Ministry for Culture and Heritage 2014: 4, 8). It was within these spaces of remembrance that small acts of queer heritage from below were carried out. Although 'official' heritage was comprised largely of the preservation of architectural styles and celebrations of Christchurch's 'most English of all cities' past, reminders of queerness could nonetheless be found among the ruins.

Reminding

The earthquakes' devastating impacts on Christchurch's landscape left large areas of the city in ruins. As collapsed buildings were cleared away, entire city blocks were left as empty, gravelled spaces. The enormous amount of work to be done meant that damaged buildings might sit empty for years, often held in place by temporary supports. Among these ruins, grassroots and community-based art projects flourished. In response to the destruction of the disaster, deliberate attempts were made by artists and community members to create beauty, humour and commemoration. As Jason Prior (2015: 168) argues: '[U]rban ruins enable and affirm nonnormative identities and sexual practices through their unique materiality and relationship to memory, as well as their ability to develop an independent existence from the everyday lived spaces of the city.' It was often within the ruins of post-earthquake Christchurch that moments of material queer heritage could be found.

If not always explicitly connected to LGBT identities or communities, there was at times an implicit queerness to the artworks produced among the ruins. Artists were, in effect, queering the ruins by transforming spatial meanings from destruction and loss to creativity and renewal, as well as by creating nonnormative uses for these spaces. One of our interviewees had felt empowered as a queer person by the appearance of what she interpreted as queerness in the post-disaster city. Rachel (lesbian, 50s) described an art project in which heavily decorated statues of giraffes were placed in various locations around the city:

> We had I think 50, maybe more, giraffes around the city and people would go and see and they'd all be decorated differently. So there was a glitter ball giraffe. I mean it was deeply camp. I don't think there was a gay element to it but it was deeply camp. So we don't do traditional queer stuff here, like there is a Pride Week, but I don't go to it. There is enough camp quirkiness in the city that it's all good.
> (Interview 11: 03/06/2015)

Rachel found that this camp art project allowed her to feel in place within post-earthquake Christchurch. The 'disco-ball giraffe' acted as a humorous reminder of long-term – and enduring – queer cultural practices.

Others in Christchurch made more explicit connections to LGBT identities through the creation of artwork among the ruins. An interactive installation titled 'Words of Hope' was established in one vacant block (Gap Filler 2011). Furniture and other abandoned objects were arranged on the site as a symbolic re-creation of the city. Members of the public were encouraged to spray-paint words, messages or drawings on to the installation. One participant took the opportunity to remind others of the presence of LGBT people in the city by spray-painting the messages 'Gay Pride!' and 'One Love' and adding a drawing of a rainbow, a well-known Gay Pride symbol (QuakeStudies 2011). This small act of heritage from below created a connection to past queer cultural practices and deliberately situated an enduring LGBT community as an element of the post-disaster city. Although official heritage responses to the disaster concentrated on material heritage and the preservation of a heteronormative vision of the past, these grassroots cultural responses reveal both implicit and explicit queerness appearing among the ruins. Either through acts of queer humour or deliberate expressions of gay pride, the past and ongoing place of an LGBT community in Christchurch was made visible.

Remembering

In Christchurch, the earthquakes of February 2011 are, quite literally, unforgettable. Their impacts are inscribed on the material spaces of the city. One interviewee, James (gay man, 40s) told us:

> There's never a day goes by without me being confronted by it . . . but, you know, sometimes you can be on the bus and you can pass a building site and it's just a building site, it's nothing more. And some days you can walk through town and you turn a corner and you . . . it sounds a bit dramatic, you get a flashback to what was there before and it will be like, 'Oh my god', you know? This is . . . it's all changed, it's all gone.
> (Interview 2: 28/05/2015)

James makes clear that to travel through the post-earthquake city was to be reminded, not only of the disaster itself, but also of the buildings and sites that had been lost. Another interviewee, Matt (bisexual man, 30s), described the challenges of constructing memories in a city without landmarks. He described as 'a sort of game' his attempts to remember the buildings that had stood in particular spots before the earthquake and to connect lost sites with memories of events in his life. Matt stated:

> [I'll be] driving, trying to remember what was there and 'Oh yeah, we did that thing there' and 'I remember that night that we did that thing outside this [building] – Actually, no it's over there' and 'Oh no, there's that building, so that must . . .' – It was trying to reconfigure understanding.
>
> (Interview 4: 29/05/2015)

A disaster not only has the capacity to destroy physical spaces, but may also place at risk memories once evoked by those spaces. This may impact both personal memory and the memories of wider communities, including the LGBT community (McKinnon, *et al.* 2016). Marginalised communities may argue for their right to inclusion within the present-day city by drawing on a long heritage as remembered through material sites in the urban landscape. Without these sites, do the memories of the community also disappear?

An article on LGBT news website GayNZ.com expressed concern that the loss of LGBT material heritage was a significant loss for the community. Journalist Jay Bennie set out to record the lost spaces of queer Christchurch, stating 'it's now clear that the Christchurch earthquakes wiped out all physical evidence of most of the places gay men, and occasionally lesbians, used to congregate' (Bennie 2013). The article listed bars, nightclubs, community meeting rooms, beats, bookshops and other important queer spaces dating back to the 1980s. Bennie concluded, 'Almost all are now gone, but their place in Christchurch's GLBTI memory is undeniable.'

Although that place may be undeniable, the possibility that these spaces will evoke community memories through their presence in the city has been entirely removed by the disaster. As we have seen, queer spaces were not included in official heritage efforts and the desire of the LGBT community to seek their preservation or commemoration was uncertain. When asked whether the loss of such spaces was important, Clark (gay man, 60s) replied, 'There's a sadness that these places have gone, but they were already . . . they'd already finished before the earthquakes anyway, so it's just the buildings that were there' (Interview 9: 02/06/2015). Yet journalist Bennie's attempt to forge a place for these sites in the collective memory of LGBT Christchurch suggests that others in the community did feel a significant sense of loss. Although the LGBT community of Christchurch has ensured its ongoing place in the city through the maintenance of queer cultural practices and small acts of heritage from below, the material heritage of the community was almost completely destroyed.

The ongoing consequences of this loss remain to be seen. It is perhaps only in the longer term that we will discover if the loss of material forms of memory matter to the ongoing success of a community.

Conclusion

Acts of queer heritage in post-earthquake Christchurch confirm the fact that 'official' heritage practices remain only one element of how heritage is created, enacted or performed in urban spaces (Robertson 2012). Although invisible in the forms of heritage enacted by government agencies, LGBT people in Christchurch found ways to maintain a connection to past cultural practices (Byrne 2005). Indeed, many in the LGBT community of Christchurch appeared uncertain as to whether the place of their community in the 'land-based' forms of heritage prioritised by governments was even necessary. It was largely the loss of opportunities for collaboration or participation that was mourned by many LGBT people.

The February 2011 earthquake in Christchurch produced significant tension between plans for the future and memories of the past. The desire to see the city quickly rebuilt and normal life resumed at times conflicted with concerns that the city's once cherished material heritage was being insufficiently considered. Spaces tied to queer identities played, at best, a negligible role in these discussions. Amid the ruins, however, queerness was made visible and through opportunities for queer collaboration and sociality, the community acknowledged its past while creating space for itself in the recovering city.

Notes

1 LGBT refers to lesbian, gay, bisexual and trans, and is a familiar acronym for sexual and gender minorities in Anglophone countries, now used in the mainstream media and government policies.
2 The three main case study sites are Brisbane (following the catastrophic floods of January 2011), Christchurch (following the devastating earthquake of February 2011) and the NSW Blue Mountains (following the bushfires of October 2013).
3 These response figures are for Christchurch only, not the entire multi-country study.
4 All respondent names have been changed to preserve anonymity.

Bibliography

Ahmed, S. 2006. *Queer Phenomenology: Orientations, Objects, Others*. Durham, NC: Duke University Press.

Andersson, J. 2012. Heritage discourse and the desexualisation of public space: the 'historical restoration' of Bloomsbury's Squares. *Antipode* 44: 1081–1098.

Bennie, J. 2013. The gaping holes in gay Christchurch history. GayNZ.com. Available at: www.gaynz.com/articles/publish/45/printer_13279.php (accessed 31 March 2016).

Bowring, J. and Swaffield, S. 2013. Shifting landscapes in-between times. *Harvard Design Magazine* 36: 96–104.

Brickell, C. 2008. *Mates and Lovers: A History of Gay New Zealand*. Auckland: Random House.

Brown, M. 2000. *Closet Space: Geographies of Metaphor from the Body to the Globe*. London: Routledge.

Browne, K. and Nash, C.J. 2010. Queer methods and methodologies: an introduction. In K. Browne and C.J. Nash (eds), *Queer Methods and Methodologies: Intersecting Queer Theories and Social Science Research*. Farnham: Ashgate, pp. 1–23.

Byrne, D. 2005. Excavating desire: queer heritage in the Asia-Pacific Region. In *Sexualities, Genders and Rights in Asia: 1st International Conference of Asian Queer Studies*. Bangkok, Thailand. Published by AsiaPacifiQueer Network, Australian National University, ANU Digital Collections. Available at: https://digitalcollections.anu.edu.au/handle/1885/8660 (accessed 31 March 2016).

Canterbury Earthquake Recovery Authority, 2016. *CBD Rebuild Zone: The History of the CBD Red Zone*. Available at: http://cera.govt.nz/cbd-rebuild-zone (accessed 18 March 2016).

D'Aeth, L. (2014) *Canterbury Rainbow Communities Vision Workshop: Report Prepared for the Uprising Trust*. Available at: www.healthychristchurch.org.nz/media/141229/canterburyrainbowcommunitiesvisionworkshopssurveyresults.pdf (accessed 18 March 2016).

Forsyth, A. 2001. Sexuality and space: nonconformist populations and planning practice. *Journal of Planning Literature* 15: 339–358.

Gap Filler, 2011. *May 23, 2011–June 2, 2011: CPIT Design/Build – 19 Ferry Rd & 270 St Asaph St (#5 & 6)*. Available at: www.gapfiller.org.nz/gap-5-6-19-ferry-rd-270-st-asaph-st/ (accessed 30 March 2016).

Gorman-Murray, A. and Nash, C.J. 2014. Mobile places, relational spaces: conceptualizing change in Sydney's LGBTQ neighbourhoods. *Environment and Planning D: Society and Space* 32: 622–641.

Hall, S. 1999. Un-settling 'the heritage', re-imagining the post-nation: whose heritage? *Third Text* 13: 3–13.

Harrison, R. 2013. *Heritage: Critical Approaches*. London: Routledge.

Knopp, L. 1998. Sexuality and urban space: gay male identity politics in the United States, the United Kingdom, and Australia. In R. Fincher and J.M. Jacobs (eds), *Cities of Difference*. New York: Guilford Press, pp. 149–176.

McKinnon, S., Gorman-Murray, A. and Dominey-Howes, D. 2016. 'The greatest loss was a loss of our history': natural disasters, marginalised identities and sites of memory. *Social and Cultural Geography* 17(8): 1120–1139.

Ministry for Culture and Heritage, 2014. *Heritage Buildings and Recovery Programme for Greater Christchurch Wellington, NZ*. Available at: www.mch.govt.nz/files/Heritage%20Recovery%20Programme%20%28D-0588813%29.PDF (accessed 31 March 2016).

Oswin, N. 2008. Critical geographies and the uses of sexuality. *Progress in Human Geography* 32: 89–103.

Podmore, J. and Chamberland, L. 2015. Entering the urban frame: early lesbian activism and public space in Montreal. *Journal of Lesbian Studies* 19: 192–211.

Prior, J. 2015. Amongst the ruins. *Journal of Homosexuality* 62: 167–185.

QuakeStudies, 2011. *Photograph of Gap Filler project 5 (19)*. Christchurch, NZ: University of Canterbury. Available at: https://quakestudies.canterbury.ac.nz/store/part/95506 (accessed 30 March 2016).

Robertson, I. 2012. Introduction: heritage from below. In Iain Robertson (ed.) *Heritage from Below*. Farnham: Ashgate, pp. 1–27.

Schöllman, A., Perkins, H. and Moore, K. 2000. Intersecting global and local influences in urban place promotion: the case of Christchurch, New Zealand. *Environment and Planning A* 32: 55–76.

Smith, L. 2006. *The Uses of Heritage*. London: Routledge.

Swaffield, S. 2013. Place, culture and landscape after the Christchurch earthquake. In Helen Sykes (ed.) *Space, Place and Culture*. Sydney: Future Leaders, pp. 144–169.

Waterton, E. 2014. A more-than-representational understanding of heritage? The 'past' and the politics of affect. *Geography Compass* 8(11): 823–833.

Part V

Conclusion

Chapter 16

The politics of heritage
How to achieve change

Wera Grahn

As many of the previous chapters in this volume have shown, together with a large amount of at least 30 years of previous research within the field, gender issues have very seldom been integrated and problematised in museum and heritage management work.[1] The politics of heritage seem to a high degree still to be the same as at the birth of the museum in the late 1800s, i.e. a celebration to men and masculinities in a well-to-do, heteronormative, white, Western context. This chapter will discuss what can be done in order to achieve change at both a structural and a concrete, individual level.[2]

In this chapter, the concept 'gender' will be used as an umbrella term to embrace all theoretical perspectives within the field today, from women's history, gender equality work, sexual difference, queer studies, masculinity studies to feminist technoscience/posthuman studies and intersectionality, just to mention a few. Intersectionality is a gender perspective that emphasises how gender acts and works together with other social categories, such as class, ethnicity, sexual preferences, dis/ability, age, etc.[3] I especially want to pay attention to this in this chapter, as it is important for heritage institutions to be aware of this complexity when narrating the past. How can gender, as well as other categories such as class, ethnicity, sexuality, dis/ability, age, etc. be integrated into museum and heritage management work?

I also want to draw attention to the fact that there is no single general solution that can be applied in all circumstances, but various solutions will have to be adjusted and adapted to fit the specific institution and the specific context in each and every single case. My suggestions below come from a Swedish context, where an extensive consensus of the importance of gender issues prevails. Gender issues are accepted within a broad public consensus, politicians of almost all parties agree on the importance of these issues and gender studies is an established discipline within Swedish universities. In another context, other measures may have to be taken first in order to reach such a societal agreement; for instance, an active lobbying of politicians, arranging of debates, demonstrations and special actions, etc. This chapter, apart from being inspired by the earlier work that has been done within this field, is based on my previous experience of working at several museums of cultural history from 1993–1999 as well as on my own research and knowledge of heritage issues within a Nordic context from 1999–2016.[4] But before I go into this, I would like to emphasise some major reasons why it is important to problematise what heritage institutions do in terms of gender constructions.

The importance of gender

Apart from the importance of nuancing the given picture of a reduced and truncated exaggeration of the past (cf. Said 1978: 142) that exists in many Western museums today (see e.g. Grahn 2006; Haraway 1989; Losnedahl 1993; Porter 1987; Vanegas 2002), one major reason for discussing representations of gender constructed by heritage institutions is because of its strong link to the modern project. This connection gives these institutions a very high credibility in society at large (e.g. Amundsen and Brenna 2003; Bennett 1995/1999; Hooper-Greenhill 1992; Smith 2006). The heritage institutions are often understood as privileged places for construction of a true past. People most often believe these institutions to be presenting the truth about past events and interpret the selected parts according to a modern pattern (cf. Grahn 2006; Hooper-Greenhill 2000: 151). However, what happens when an artefact is being selected and preserved at a museum is that certain parts of the past are being materialised into the present. They are thus acquiring a meaning that is not only localised to a historic time and setting, but also to a contemporary situation for the visitors of today and it even has the potential of shaping our understanding of the future (Bennett 1995/1999: 162; Nietzsche 1974: 14).

With this approach, it becomes crucial to understand how images and stories of the past are constructed in the heritage sector and how artefacts are selected to become a part of our cultural heritage. They shape our 'cultural imaginary' (Dawson 1994: 48) of those who inhabited the past, and, following Nietzsche, at the same time also have the potential to affect our understanding of who belongs to the present and future. In other words, cultural heritage has a strong symbolic potential for constructing identities (e.g. Smith 2006: 87). It is most often shaping images and narratives around those people that are regarded as officially honourable, memorable and desirable in a society. This makes it even more important to reflect upon and problematise the identities a society wants to preserve and remember.

In addition to strengthening identities, cultural heritage can also have the function of building barriers and boundaries toward those whose cultural heritage is not regarded, which for instance is what has happened when heritage has been destroyed in recent conflicts in Iraq, Syria, Egypt, the Balkans and in Afghanistan. Similar processes – achieved by building barriers without necessarily destroying but ignoring the heritage of 'the others' – can also be noticed in more peaceful parts of the world, such as Scandinavia, where the heritage of, for instance, the Sámi people seems to be more absent than present in several national heritage institutions (see e.g. Grahn 2009, 2011a, 2011b; Spangen 2015). Cultural heritage can, in other words, function as a vehicle for both opening the door for a more inclusive and diverse society or closing it. This underlines even more the potential importance of the cultural heritage.

But this is also important in relation to the democratic function of cultural heritage. This means the right of all people to be able to identify, relate to and benefit from the cultural heritage. The foundation of the democratic function of heritage is formulated in several international conventions, such as: The UN Universal Declaration of Human Rights (United Nations 1948); The Council of Europe the European Landscape Convention (Council of Europe 2004); The UNESCO Convention on the Protection and Promotion of the Diversity of Cultural Expressions (UNESCO 2005); The Council of Europe FARO-Convention (Council of Europe 2005). These are conventions that a majority of countries have signed and ratified that emphasise the importance of cultural diversity for democratic reasons. This is underlined in an official report like The UNESCO report *Gender Equality: Heritage and Creativity* (UNESCO 2014). The same intention is also expressed explicitly in several Swedish official policy documents and reports for the heritage field (DS 2003:61; Prop. 2009/10:3; Prop. 1996/1997: 3; SOU 1999:18). This means that the democratic reason for implementing gender in heritage work is actually already authorised by a majority of countries, however, this does not always show in their heritage institutions. Therefore, there are many reasons why it is important to integrate and problematise gender issues in heritage work. But what can be done in order to integrate gender in the museum work? I will first consider what can be done at a structural level and then at an individual level when working with exhibitions.

Support of the highest management team

One of the most important structural factors for a successful integration of gender issues, or some of the other above-mentioned categories, is that the people in charge of a museum or heritage management institution must have some kind of basic knowledge of these perspectives, understand their importance and have an affirmative attitude towards these issues (Grahn 2007). Even the most knowledgeable, competent and skilled employee or small group of employees will very likely meet difficulties to integrate these perspectives in the workplace without a clear support from the highest management team. An example of an institution that has had a long-term commitment towards diversity perspectives is the Swedish Exhibition Agency, which together with some other actors in the field have recognised the broad needs among all heritage institutions for specific training in gender studies for leaders. Since 2012, a course to promote training in gender equality and diversity for leaders within this sector has been launched.[5]

The highest management team needs, in addition, to be engaged and a driving force for change to come true. It will not be enough to silently give the blessing to integrate these perspectives in the daily work, but an explicitly active and outspoken support is needed. Apart from speaking in support of implementing specific ideas including a gender perspective, the leading team should in addition have a long-term strategy for developing the competence and skills in the subject area of all the employees at the institution (Grahn 2007). This is especially important as statistics show that the average age of employees at Swedish museums is very high. This implies that majority of the staff went to university and finalised their studies before gender studies and other disciplines focusing on diversity had been launched as university subjects, hence most of the staff lack this competence in their educational background. One museum in Sweden that has been making such special efforts to develop the competence and skills of the staff for a long time is Uppland's museum in Uppsala. Without the support and engagement from the management team, this would very likely not have occurred. This has among other actions been done in form of a series of lectures and seminars on the theme, with mandatory participation for the whole staff. It has been shown that it is very important that everybody from the management team is present during such events, showing curiosity and being actively engaged in the discussions (Grahn 2007). To sum up, to have people in charge of an institution with grounded knowledge of gender and diversity is one of the key factors that have the potential to bring about a successful integration of these perspectives in the daily work.

The position of research

Another important factor in order to achieve change seems to be the position research has within the institution. The stronger position research has, the more easily an integration of gender and other diversity perspectives seems to become (Grahn 2007). Those institutions that already have a strong commitment to research appear to better integrate these perspectives in their activities. This can be understood as a result of a readiness and a familiarity to assimilate and implement theories into practice at large in these institutions. They have a profound epistemological ground to stand on, which makes it obvious to assimilate and implement new perspectives into their daily work. To have this ability is particularly important in this case, as gender issues most often are based on research and are only available in the form of research publications.

Usually, these institutions have a research and action plan focusing several years ahead. These institutions have also actively sought to employ a high number of employees with a doctoral degree. This is, for instance, the case at the previously mentioned Upplands museum, and also at the Museum of Work in Norrköping and the Swedish Museum of History in Stockholm. This makes the museum work at large to be permeated by a scientific approach, which becomes an integral part of the daily work there (Grahn 2007). This facilitates an integration of gender and other diversity perspectives as it creates a familiarity with scientific thinking in everyday practices.

Gender as a qualification for new positions

It is also crucial to employ persons who have documented experience and education in gender studies and/or other diversity perspectives. If a museum should be able to integrate gender in its daily work it needs to have people on the staff that have in-depth knowledge of gender and diversity issues (Grahn 2007). Today the field of gender studies is an extremely wide area, which embraces almost all the disciplines and in which a lot of advanced epistemological and ontological discussions are being addressed (see, for instance, Barad 2007; Haraway 1997; Lykke 2010). To apply a gender perspective is not something you can do just because you, for instance, are a woman. Even if women are structurally treated as subaltern in a large part of the world today and, therefore, might have more experience in issues related to key questions in gender studies, it does not mean that women automatically have access to gender theories. In the same way as you are not born as a woman, but become one (Beauvoir 1993), women are not born with a gender equality gene, but women can, as well as men, acquire knowledge within the field by thorough studying. Gender studies is today, as mentioned, an extensive field of knowledge that is constantly expanding and changing and you must most likely have been studying the subject in order to grasp the area and to be able to see the possibilities of different perspectives and to make appropriate choices. To apply a gender or diversity perspective requires skills, competence and acquired knowledge, which surprisingly enough is not especially evident in current job advertisements for new positions in heritage institutions. Only very seldom are such requirements demanded. In addition, there must be a critical mass of highly qualified people working at the museum or heritage institution for change to occur. A small number of stakeholders will very easily become isolated and will very likely not have any cardinal impact on the focus of activities. A group of people working together with a joint aim would have a much better chance of succeeding. These are some structural factors influencing if gender issues might be integrated in the work of a museum or heritage institution. But how can gender be integrated on an individual daily basis when working for instance practically with exhibitions?

How to think about gender integration in exhibitions

Even if museums conduct a wide range of activities, it is above all the artefacts and exhibitions that characterise a museum. It is this that distinguishes museums from other cultural institutions and makes them unique. Although museums of today have almost stopped adding artefacts to their collections and have already completed a large part of their permanent displays, a gender perspective or various gender aspects could, however, always be applied in order to ask new questions for change. This can be done no matter which collection of items the institution has and no matter how the exhibitions on display are constructed.

Gender research is today an extensive field that includes many different theories and perspectives as indicated previously. The research has during the years evolved and developed within and between various disciplines, but also within the subject of gender studies as such. As indicated at the beginning of this chapter, there exists today a wide scope of various gender perspectives, ranging from women's history, gender equality studies, sexual difference, masculinity studies, queer studies, trans* studies, feminist technoscience/posthuman studies, to intersectionality. Moreover, each and every one of the various strands comprise a multitude of different trajectories, depending on which discipline they have developed within and what kind of material that has been studied. The field of masculinity studies includes, for example, at least the different strands of men's studies, masculinity studies and critical studies of men and masculinity. This applies also to most parts of the other fields mentioned.

Although gender perspectives can be applied to almost all exhibitions, some perspectives might work better in one context than another. If a museum, for instance, has been collecting artefacts, images and archives from an exclusively masculine sphere, various forms of masculinity studies could be fruitful. Such a collection could, for instance, be taken as a point of departure to narrate how hegemonic masculinity has been constructed, maintained, reproduced and maybe modified in one or another direction within a specific area.

Degrees of gender integration

A vast number of different gender perspectives can be applied when an exhibition is being made: when planning the exhibition, during the process when building it up and afterwards to see where it landed. In addition, various *degrees* of gender aspects can be integrated when making an exhibition. Below, a suggestion for a model of how to think about this is presented. This is a modification and an adjustment of the Swedish Research Council's recommendation on how to evaluate applications for funding when various degrees of gender awareness are being included (Ganetz 2006: 12ff.). This constitutes the basis of the suggestion below of a model for to determine if and how gender could be integrated into museums, focusing especially on exhibitions.

To be able to determine to which degree of gender awareness an application for funding has, the Swedish Research Council has identified three categories that are crucial to determine the degree of gender awareness. The categories are: *gender research, gender perspectives* and *gender aspects*. In order to make this model compatible with museums' exhibitions I have in addition added some further categories: *gender visibility, gender registering, history of addition* and *gender-blind history*. I find it important to add these categories to the model, as according to my research within the field, these four last types are the most common when it comes to museums (Grahn 1999, 2004, 2006, 2007). It is important to see them, but also to see the difference between them. In the following, I will go through all the phases one by one.

The first category proposed by the Swedish Research Council, i.e. a project that could be described as Gender research, should be emphasised (Ganetz 2006: 13). In such a project, gender is allowed to permeate the whole area of inquiry. Usually the gender focus will show already from the title and the work should relate clearly to theories and methods within the area. Translated into the world of museums, this could be called an exhibition with *gender focus* and implies that the display in question is dominated by making a conscious gender integration that clearly shows that the project group is very well acquainted with the theories within gender studies at both a general level and in a more concrete way related to the theme of the exhibition. The title and the various parts of the exhibition are clearly manifesting a gender focus.

To continue the Swedish Research Council's presentation a project with gender perspective is defined as one that explicitly applies some kind of gender perspective. In this case, gender is not the only theoretical approach being used, but one of several equally important techniques to interpret the empirical data. Even this requires a well-developed overarching knowledge of gender studies and in addition in-depth knowledge of one or several specific gender theories and methods that have been chosen. This could within the museum's sector be called an exhibition with *gender perspective(s)* and an overview as well as a presentation of the special theories and methods chosen should be explicitly articulated.

Other projects where the researchers as a minor part of their work seek to answer gender-specific aspects is, according to the Swedish Research Council, called a project with *gender aspects*. Also, this builds on a broad knowledge of gender theories. Even if a fully developed understanding of gender theories is not explicitly being shown, at least a description of previous research within the particular field that will be applied and a clarification of which specific kind of gender theories and methods that will be used, should be included. Transferred to the museum sector, this could be called an exhibition with *gender aspects*. This implies that a fully developed overview does not have to be presented, however, good knowledge about the specific gender theoretical direction chosen has to be explicitly stated.

It is important to notice that according to the Swedish Research Council it is not enough to use women and men as variables in order for the research to be regarded as belonging to any of the three mentioned approaches (Ganetz 2006: 14). In order to be able to be included as gender-sensitive research it is necessary to show that the visible knowledge has been analysed from some kind of gender theoretical perspective. A plain accounting and sorting by gender can, in other words, not be regarded as applying a gender approach to a project. This does not, however, mean that this kind of research is worthless. On the contrary, this can be the first step to raise awareness of differences and inequalities that can form the ground of new research questions and projects. Put another way, in order to be included in one of the three categories something more must be done with the empirical observations than just an elementary accounting, but it can nevertheless be useful as a method.

Translated to the museum field this type would be exhibitions considering equally both men's and women's relation to what is shown. This implies, in other words, that attention is paid towards both women's and men's relation to the subject of the display. However, this cannot be understood as gender integration as it only implies a sorting of artefacts on gender. A simple counting is not necessarily equivalent to a gender analytic thinking and thus would not fall under such a classification. But just as in the case of research, these kinds of displays should not be regarded as drained of meaning. To pay attention to the numerical representation, to count how many gendered representations – men, women, queer, ethnical groups, dis/abled, etc – exist and to try to get an equal representation, is a fundamental issue as the first step towards a more gender-sensitive approach in museums. As the numerical representation – in terms of gender, class, ethnicity, sexual preferences, dis/ability, etc. – is often being overlooked in much museum work, this practice deserves especial mentioning and a special category if it is done. This variation of display could be named *gender registering*.

According to previous research, one of the other types of exhibition that can be identified is *gender visibility* (Grahn 1999, 2004, 2006, 2007). Compared to *gender registering*, an exhibition with *gender visibility* has taken one more step towards gender awareness, as the display would make visible a subordinate group's relation to a theme shown and let it dominate the narration of the whole display, but without explicitly linking this to some of the theories within the field of gender studies and without showing any knowledge of the overall view of the field. This type of exhibition would be localised between *gender registering* and *gender aspects* on a scale. On the other side of *gender registering*, displays can be found that altogether lack any awareness of gender. Even if all exhibitions might not need to have a gender approach, all displays need to have an adequate answer to why not, if that is the case. Such a choice should be well thought through and include strong arguments.

An example of an exhibition that lacks gender awareness altogether is a display that has added the underrepresented group as a minor part of an exhibition, but as a part that has been separated from the grand narrative of the past. This can be named *history of addition* (cf. Hirdman 1993: 33). No critical gender perspective exists here. Even if the underrepresented group is not totally eroded, the small part dealing with the subordinate history is usually being placed in a marginal position of a display in a not so easily visible way. Moreover, there are also examples of exhibitions made without problematising or questioning the domination of one gender at all. No gender awareness exists in this type of display. The gender being on display in this kind of setting is usually of one single kind, i.e. coded by masculinity. The dominating position is, moreover, constructed as a naturalised and self-evident position that is allowed to dominate the scene without being questioned. This type of exhibition could be called *gender blind*. The following model is a suggestion for how this could be visualised (see Figure 16.1).

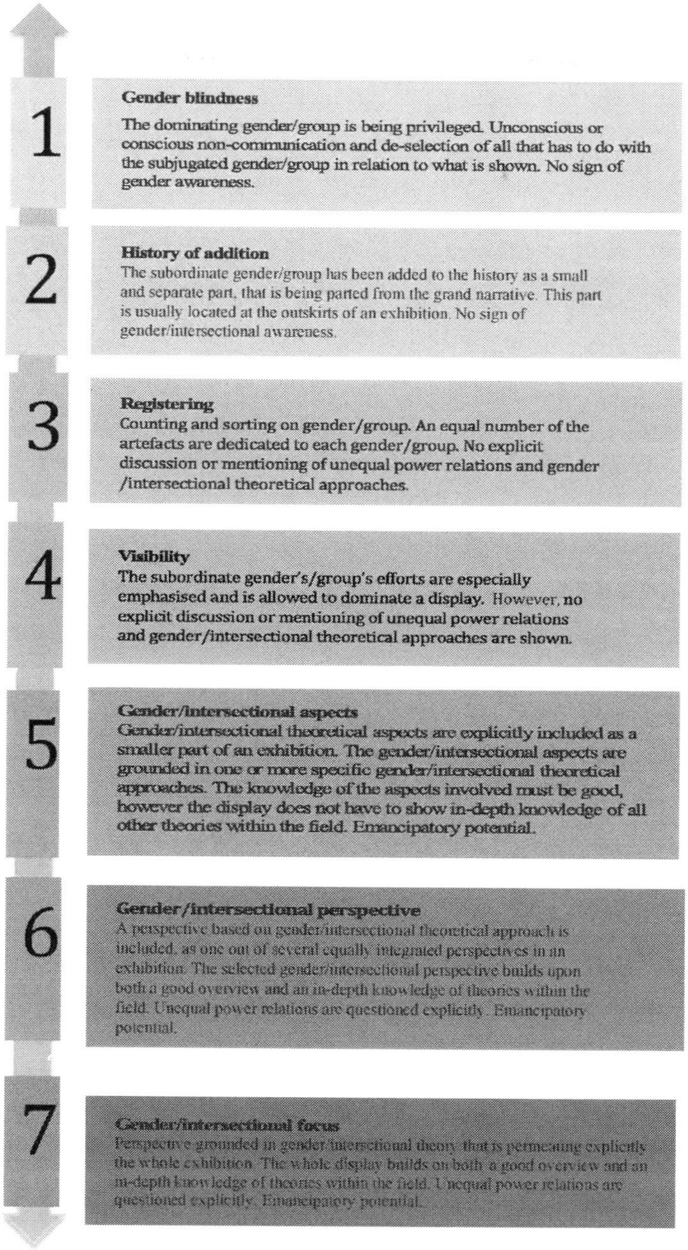

1 Gender blindness
The dominating gender/group is being privileged. Unconscious or conscious non-communication and de-selection of all that has to do with the subjugated gender/group in relation to what is shown. No sign of gender awareness.

2 History of addition
The subordinate gender/group has been added to the history as a small and separate part, that is being parted from the grand narrative. This part is usually located at the outskirts of an exhibition. No sign of gender/intersectional awareness.

3 Registering
Counting and sorting on gender/group. An equal number of the artefacts are dedicated to each gender/group. No explicit discussion or mentioning of unequal power relations and gender/intersectional theoretical approaches.

4 Visibility
The subordinate gender's/group's efforts are especially emphasised and is allowed to dominate a display. However, no explicit discussion or mentioning of unequal power relations and gender/intersectional theoretical approaches are shown.

5 Gender/intersectional aspects
Gender/intersectional theoretical aspects are explicitly included as a smaller part of an exhibition. The gender/intersectional aspects are grounded in one or more specific gender/intersectional theoretical approaches. The knowledge of the aspects involved must be good, however the display does not have to show in-depth knowledge of all other theories within the field. Emancipatory potential.

6 Gender/intersectional perspective
A perspective based on gender/intersectional theoretical approach is included, as one out of several equally integrated perspectives in an exhibition. The selected gender/intersectional perspective builds upon both a good overview and an in-depth knowledge of theories within the field. Unequal power relations are questioned explicitly. Emancipatory potential.

7 Gender/intersectional focus
Perspective grounded in gender/intersectional theory that is permeating explicitly the whole exhibition. The whole display builds on both a good overview and an in-depth knowledge of theories within the field. Unequal power relations are questioned explicitly. Emancipatory potential.

Figure 16.1 Gender blind model

This categorisation is rough and many mixed and in-between versions may exist. Moreover, in this model both ends continue with an arrow, which indicate that exhibitions with a more extreme approach could also be imagined to exist. One could, for instance, imagine exhibitions being, on the one hand, misogynist or, on the other hand, being pro-feminist to a degree that might approach historical revisionism. Apart from gender discrimination, this model can also be used to identify other forms of oppression existing within various forms of representations, for instance, class, ethnicity, sexual preferences, etc. and also the interrelation of these categories as in intersectionality. It is, however, always important to keep in mind that this is not a fixed and static model, but a suggestion of how empirical material can be understood visually at a general level. The model is *one* of many ways of understanding how an exhibition can be related to a gender-sensitive way of thinking in a specific context.

This implies that each and every museum must relate these aspects and modify them to their specific remit and the specific exhibition currently being discussed. In other words, each institution has to adapt and apply these aspects in a way that is individually tailored for every production. Museum institutions, exhibitions, the surrounding displays and the society at large – only to mention a few factors affecting an exhibition – are part of an on-going process of negotiations of meaning (cf. Hodge and Kress 1988). Put differently, the answers will not be identical from museum to museum and not even from one exhibition to another within the same institution. The world, as well as the museum's work at large, is much more diversified for one universal and all-encompassing model to be launched. Hopefully, this model can act as a point of departure for others to think and discuss further in the future.

As indicated above this model could be used in many different ways and be applied at many different times in the production of an exhibition. The suggested model could, for example, be used:

- When a display is being planned, in order to raise the awareness of which degree of gender integration the institution regards as the most desirable for an exhibition to apply, and to map out an approximate course for how to get there.
- During a production as a tool to check that the exhibition process keeps to the planned track.
- At the end of a production, as a tool to evaluate if the exhibition has reached the planned aims.
- To assess and make changes in already finalised exhibitions, by making manifest if and how earlier productions relate to gender issues and to identify which measures need to be taken in order to avoid possible inadequacies.

Conclusion

Heritage institutions have shown to be constantly constructing past identities in their narratives that do not only have a meaning in the past, but also create meaning in the present and future. As previous research has shown, prejudice in society has been strengthened by museum exhibitions putting on display reduced and stereotyped images of past masculinity, femininity, class and ethnic belonging, sexual preferences, dis/ability, etc. (Grahn 2006; Sandell 2007). Due to heritage institutions' strong link to the modern project, the museums have also benefited from a high credibility compared to other cultural institutions, and thus influences people's minds in general about a 'true' past. However, the high credibility of museums and other heritage institutions could, for instance, instead be used to combat prejudice rather than reinforcing gender stereotypes.

How heritage institutions construct the past is also important with regard to the democratic function of heritage, which implies that everybody should be able to identify and benefit from the selected collections of cultural heritage belonging to a certain society. The democratic function of cultural heritage is part of many international treaties and conventions signed by most countries and thus should be on the agenda of these states. Even if this does not seem to always be the case, it nevertheless underlines the importance for heritage institutions to raise their awareness of the importance of integrating gender perspectives into their daily work.

This chapter has given examples of what can be done in order to integrate gender issues and strengthen the awareness of the importance of heritage institutions to include gender perspectives when narrating about the past at both a structural and practically concrete level. At a structural level, it is most important that the leading management team of an institution have knowledge, awareness and an interest of integrating gender in the daily work. If not, it is not very likely that individual staff members or smaller groups will be successful in their efforts. It is also important for the institutions to demand documented knowledge and skills when new positions are being created. This knowledge today is, as shown, large and complex and something that has to be learned in academic contexts. In addition, it seems important if research in general has a high position in the institution or not. The more frequent research is in general and thus the more familiar the institution is in regards to using and transforming abstract ideas into practice, the more likely it seems that gender issues will be attended to.

On a more practical daily level, I have suggested a model for how to think about gender issues while working with exhibitions. Seven steps have been identified regarding how an exhibition can relate to gender issues. Of course, there are mixed and in-between forms that also exist, but these have crystallised clearly in my previous research. These are exhibitions that can be characterised as: *gender blindness, history of addition, gender registering, gender visibility, gender aspects, gender perspectives* and *gender focused.* This model can be used when planning an exhibition, during the process of making one, to check up when it is done or to evaluate and change already finalised displays.

Notes

1 See for instance (Glaser and Zenetou 1994; Grahn 2006; Haraway 1989; Losnedahl 1993; Porter 1987, 1988/1995, 1990, 1991a, 1991b, 1996).
2 This chapter will above all deal with making gender perspectives more present and visible in museum and heritage work. However, like Bergsdóttir and Hafsteinsson have shown in Chapter 7 of this volume, absence could be another factor to work with. This chapter will not deal with this aspect, as it needs to be further researched and developed.
3 Intersectionality is a perspective that is problematising that gender most often is intertwined and interacts with other social categories such as class, nationality, ethnicity, sexual preferences, dis/ability, etc. and that certain combinations get privileged in a society while others get subordinated. Intersectionality grew out of the writings of Black feminists and this approach was applied already during the 1970s (Crenshaw 1994). It is a perspective that has grown stronger during above all the 1990s (Collins 1998). In its present form intersectionality appears in the interstices between post-structuralism, feminist theory, post-colonial theory, black feminism and queer theory. Among its predecessors are Crenshaw (1994), Collins (1998), and Young (1997). This perspective has received an increasing interest in the Scandinavian academic context during recent years (see e.g. de los Reyes and Mulinari 2005; de los Reyes et al. 2002; Lykke 2003, 2005, 2010).
4 This chapter is partly based on an earlier publication in Swedish (Grahn 2007).
5 The course is organised jointly by DIK, JÄMUS/Statens Historiska museer and the Swedish Exhibition Agency in collaboration with Ledarna and Riksförbundet Sveriges museer. For more information see (Swedish Exhibition Agency 2016): www.riksutstallningar.se/node/1024?language=en (accessed 1 April 2016)

Bibliography

Amundsen, A.B. and Brenna, B. 2003. Museer og museumskunnskap. Et innledende essay. In A.B. Amundsen, B. Rogan and M. Stang (eds) *Museer i fortid og nåtid: essays i museumskunnskap*. Oslo: Novus forlag, pp. 9–24.

Barad, K. 2007. *Meeting the universe halfway: quantum physics and the entanglement of matter and meaning*. Durham, NC: Duke University Press.

Bennett, T. 1995/1999. *The birth of the museum: history, theory, politics*. London and New York: Routledge.

Collins, P.H. 1998. It's all in the family: intersections of gender, race and nation. *Hypatia*, 13(3): 62–82.

Council of Europe 2004. *The Council of Europe and the European Landscape convention 2004*. Strasbourg: European Treaty Series No. 176.

Council of Europe 2005. *The Council of Europe FARO convention 2005*.

Crenshaw, K.W. 1994. Mapping the margins: intersectionality, identity politics, and violence against women of color. In M.A. Fineman and R. Mykitiuk (eds) *The public nature of private violence*. New York: Routledge, pp. 93–118.

Dawson, G. 1994. *Soldier heroes: British adventure, empire and the imagining of masculinities*. London: Routledge.

de Beauvoir, S. 1993. *The second sex*. London: Campbell.

de los Reyes, P. and Mulinari, D. (eds) 2005. *Intersektionalitet. Kritiska reflektioner över (o)jämlikhetens landskap*. Liber: Stockholm.

de los Reyes, P., Molina, I. and Mulinari D. (eds) 2002. *Maktens (o)lika förklädnader: kön, klass & etnicitet i det postkoloniala Sverige: en festskrift till Wuokko Knocke*. Atlas: Stockholm.

DS 2003:61. *Genus och museer*. Departementsskrift, Sveriges regering, Kulturdepartementet. Stockholm.

Ganetz, H. 2006. *Gender research applications in the human and social sciences: a follow-up of Swedish Research Council's 2004 review process and its outcome*. Stockholm: Swedish Research Council.

Glaser, J. and Zenetou, A. (eds) 1994. *Gender perspectives: essays of women in museums*. Washington, DC: Smithsonian Institution Press.

Grahn, W. 1999. Tekniska museet – den manliga teknikens tempel? In *Dædalus 2000*. Stockholm: Tekniska museet, pp 190–209.

Grahn, W. 2003a. Könsmedvetna museiberättelse. *Samtid & museer*, 3–4 November. Stockholm: Samdok, pp. 11–12.

Grahn, W. 2003b. Museer och genus: En analys av Månadens föremål. In L. Palmqvist (ed.) *Minnets miljöer. Rapport från Museivetenskapliga dagarna 21–22 November 2002*. Stockholm: Aktantus Förlag, pp. 18–29.

Grahn, W. 2004. Representationer av kön på Tekniska museet. In C. Trenter (ed.) *Tankar och texter om industrisamhällets kulturarv*. Härnösand: ISKA, pp. 82–89.

Grahn, W. 2005a. Från vardagsartefakter till museala fakta. In I.L. Aronson and B. Meurling (eds) *Det bekönade museet*. Uppsala: Etnolore, pp. 95–124.

Grahn, W. 2005b. Inbyggda genusskript. Föreställningar om kön på museifasader. In T. Friberg, C. Listerborn, B. Andersson and C. Scholten (eds) *Speglingar av rum*. Stockholm: Symposion, pp. 51–67.

Grahn, W. 2005c. *The artifact of the month*. Internetpublicerat konferenspaper från Museum and the Web 2005. Available at: www.archimuse.com/mw2005/papers/bowen/bowen.html (accessed December 12 2007).

Grahn, W. 2006. *'Känn dig själf'. Genus, historiekonstruktion och kulturhistoriska museirepresentationer*. Diss. Linköping: Tema Genus, Linköpings universitet.

Grahn, W. 2007. *Genuskonstruktioner och museer. Handbok för genusintegrering*. Uppsala, Stockholm: Upplandsmuseet, Statens kulturråd.

Grahn, W. 2009. *Intersektionella konstruktioner och kulturminnesförvaltning*. NIKU-rapport 27. Oslo: NIKU.

Grahn, W. 2011a. Intersektionella konstruktioner av norskhet i nutida kulturminnesförvaltning. *Sosiologi dag* 41(3–4): 35–66.

Grahn, W. 2011b. Intersectionality and the construction of cultural heritage management. *Archaeologies: Journal of the World Archaeological Congress* 7(1): 222–250.

Haraway, D. 1989b. *Primate visions: gender, race, and nature in the world of modern science*. London: Routledge.

Haraway, D. 1997. *Modest_Witness@Second_Millennium.FemaleMan©_Meets_Onco Mouse: Feminism and Technoscience*. New York: Routledge.

Hirdman, Y. 1993. Kvinnohistoriens historia. In E. Persson (ed.) *Det dolda budskapet: kön och makt – kvinnor och män i museiutställningar*. Norrköping: Arbetets museum, Riksutställningar, pp. 28–38.

Hodge, R. and Kress, G. 1988. *Social semiotics*. New York: Cornell University Press.

Hooper-Greenhill, E. 1992. *Museum and the shaping of knowledge*. London: Routledge.

Hooper-Greenhill, E. 2000. *Museums and the interpretation of visual culture*. London: Routledge.

Losnedahl, K.G. 1993. *Kvinne + museum = kvinnemuseum?* Bergen: Senter for humanistisk kvinneforskning.

Lykke, N. 2003. Intersektionalitet – ett användbart begrepp för genusforskningen. *Kvinnovetenskaplig tidskrift* 1(3): 47–56.

Lykke, N. 2005. Nya perspektiv på intersektionalitet. Problem och möjligheter. *Kvinnovetenskaplig tidskrift* 2–3: 7–17.

Lykke, N. 2010. *Feminist studies: a guide to intersectional theory, methodology and writing.* New York: Routledge.

Nietzsche, F. 1974. *The use and abuse of history.* New York: Gordon Press.

Porter, G. 1987. Gender bias: representations of work in history museums. *Bias in Museums.* Museum Professional Group Transactions 22: 11–15.

Porter, G. 1988/1995. Putting your house in order: representations of women and domestic life. In R. Lumley (ed.) *The museum time-machine.* London: Routledge, pp. 102–127.

Porter, G. 1990. Are you sitting comfortably? *Museums Journal*, 90 (November): 102–127.

Porter, G. 1991a. Partial truths. In G. Kavanagh (ed.) *Museum languages: objects and texts.* Leicester: Leicester University Press, pp. 103–117.

Porter, G. 1991b. How are women represented in British history museums? In *Museum 171: Focus on Women* 63(3): 159–162.

Porter, G. 1993. Reading between the lines: gender and history in museums. In E. Persson (ed.) *Det dolda budskapet: kön och makt – kvinnor och män i museiutställningar.* Norrköping: Riksutställningar, Arbetets museum, pp. 50–59.

Porter, G. 1996. Seeing through solidity: a feminist perspective on museums. In S. Macdonald and G. Fyfe (eds) *Theorizing museums.* Oxford: Blackwell, pp. 83–104.

Prop. 1996/1997: 3. Swedish Government's Proposition on Politics of Culture.

Prop. 2009/10: 3. Swedish Government's Proposition on Politics of Culture.

Said, E. 1978. *Orientalism.* Stockholm: Ordfront.

Sandell, R. 2007. *Museums, prejudice and the reframing of difference.* London: Routledge.

Smith, L. 2006. *Uses of heritage.* London: Routledge.

SOU 1999:18. *Statens offentliga utredningar. Frågor till det industriella samhället. Slutbetänkande av Utredningen om en statlig satsning på det industrihistoriska kulturarvet.* Stockholm: Fritzes.

Spangen, M. 2015. Without a trace? The Sámi in the Swedish History Museum. *Nordisk Museologi* 2: 17–32.

Swedish Exhibition Agency 2016. *Gender and leadership course.* Available at: www.riksutstallningar.se/node/1024?language=en (accessed 1 April 2016).

UNESCO 2005. *The UNESCO convention on the protection and promotion of the diversity of cultural expressions.* Paris: UNESCO.

UNESCO 2014. *Gender equality: heritage and creativity.* Paris: UNESCO.

United Nations 1948. *The UN universal declaration of human rights 1948.* New York: United Nations.

Vanegas, A. 2002. Representing lesbians and gay men in British social history museums. In R. Sandell (ed.) *Museums, society, inequality.* London and New York: Routledge, pp. 98–109.

Young, I.M. 1997. *Intersecting voices: dilemmas of gender, political philosophy, and policy.* Princeton, NJ: Princeton University Press.

Index

access 33, 35–37, 83, 149–151, 158–159, 161, 173, 214, 245, 259
accessible 75, 140, 151, 174, 245
accountability 99, 102–105, 110
advocacy 86–87
aesthetics 46, 175, 177–178
agency 4, 7, 18, 92, 100–102, 109–110, 132, 135, 137, 169, 179, 185, 195, 199
agential realism 102
alternative 7, 26, 64, 68, 74, 91, 96, 130, 140, 156, 159, 161, 164, 176, 201, 240
ambiguity 23, 73, 91, 154, 156, 163–164, 211
androgynous 194
animal 35, 61, 63, 65–73, 100, 120, 125
archaeology 5, 113, 115, 120, 124
archaeological 113, 115
architecture 18, 53, 118, 171–173
archives 45, 49, 57, 152, 154, 157–159, 174, 260
artefacts 256, 259–260, 262
artifacts 107
audience 22, 47, 53, 84, 90, 93, 130, 134, 136, 141–144, 171–172, 176, 179, 187, 225, 240–241
authority 3, 7, 8, 10–11, 47, 56, 62, 95, 103, 159, 188, 244
authorized heritage discourse 9, 46–47, 52, 151

Barad, K. 4, 99–100, 102–106, 108–109, 169, 180–181, 259
belonging 48, 101, 138, 160, 243, 261, 265
biological 4, 34, 47, 61–65, 67, 94, 118, 122, 133, 209, 211, 214–215
biological determinism 209
bisexual 20, 25, 244, 249
black feminist 19, 130, 144, 160, 26n3

body 4, 9, 19, 23–24, 31, 33–36, 46, 53–54, 56, 66, 70, 83, 90, 118, 155, 170, 172–173, 175–178, 180–181, 192, 211
bourgeois 24, 47, 53, 57, 62, 64, 67–68
bourgeoisie 23, 48, 64,
Butler, J. 4, 24, 46–47, 56, 68, 149, 187, 212

capitalism 4, 11, 172–173, 225
case study 31–33, 35, 37–38, 100, 169, 179, 239, 241–242
change 20, 30–33, 35, 37, 45–46, 51, 64, 70–71, 74, 85, 86, 90, 92, 105, 108, 109, 116, 118, 120, 122, 125, 138–139, 145, 155–156, 158, 163, 170, 192, 194, 209, 212, 222, 224, 229, 232–234, 236, 241, 243, 245–246, 248, 256–259, 264–265
class 5, 9, 11, 17–18, 20–24, 26–27, 45, 51–54, 56–57, 61–62, 66, 92, 131, 133, 135, 156, 159–160, 176, 188, 202, 210, 221–223, 225, 255, 262, 264–265
collaboration 21, 25, 74, 131–132, 135–136, 152, 157, 161, 245, 246, 250
collection(s) 3, 5, 9–11, 44–45, 49, 51, 75, 100, 132, 134–136, 139, 141–142, 150 153, 158, 187–188, 195, 226, 259–260, 265
colonialism 50, 131, 143, 157, 160
communication 27, 40, 95, 138, 176–177, 179, 222
community 14, 25–26, 30–40, 71, 92, 115–116, 119, 133, 135, 140, 151, 154, 156, 160–162, 164, 170, 172, 200–201, 212, 214, 217, 221–222, 225, 230, 234, 239, 242–250
conflict 18, 20–21, 27, 29, 61, 125, 155, 172, 213, 234, 246, 250, 256
corporeal 4, 9, 101, 169, 174–175, 177–178, 181

craft(s) 30, 33, 38, 45–54, 56–57
credibility 256, 265
Crenshaw, K. 5, 149–151, 160–162, 266n3
critical theory 133, 148, 151
cultural heritage 5, 10, 18, 44, 56–57, 67, 76, 99, 101, 103–104, 107, 109–111, 141, 149–150, 157, 207–211, 213–214, 221, 223, 225, 236, 256–257, 265
cultural imaginaries 172
cultural imaginary 176, 256
custom(s) 7, 35, 65, 71–72, 85, 91, 124, 215–216

deconstruction 74, 99, 163
design 45, 48, 49, 51, 53–54, 56, 67, 136, 142, 177, 212
deviant 7
dialogue(s) 74–75, 95, 99, 131, 133, 134, 136–139, 145, 148, 157, 162–164, 173–174, 177–179, 208–209, 225
dichotomies 100
dichotomy 57, 150
difference 14, 18, 20, 27, 33–35, 37, 44, 46, 51, 54, 56–57, 71, 102, 107, 118, 131–132, 139–140, 145, 148, 150–152, 154, 156–158, 160–164, 181, 188, 208, 211, 213–215, 255, 260–261
difference(s) 18, 20, 27, 33–34, 36–37, 44, 46, 51, 54, 56–57, 71, 107, 118, 131–132, 139–140, 145, 148, 150–152, 154, 156–158, 160–164, 181, 188, 208, 211, 213–215, 255, 260–261
differentially 100, 109–110, 149, 151, 214
discourse 3–5, 9–10, 44–45, 47–48, 52, 61, 76, 82, 84–86, 90–91, 93, 130–131, 136, 140, 150–151, 153, 172, 179, 187–189, 201, 207, 210, 213, 215, 221, 239, 241–242
discursive 46, 63, 103, 108–110, 148–149, 151, 180
disembodied 172, 177, 181–182
displacement 239, 242–244
diversity 6, 9, 18, 31–32, 61, 75, 93, 132, 149–151, 156, 160, 162, 187, 200–202, 210, 212–213, 217, 240, 257–259
doing gender 31
dominance 93, 114, 118, 134, 193, 209
dualism 71

economics 4, 8–10, 82, 93
embodied 30, 32–34, 86, 130, 133, 146, 150, 172, 174, 180–181

embody 22, 31
emotional(ly) 20, 67, 69–70, 73, 130, 133, 181, 222, 225
enslavement 130, 133–134, 142–144
epistemological 74, 100, 103, 106, 110, 148, 156, 158, 164, 258–259
epistemology 99, 103, 131, 140
equality 5–6, 8, 9, 11, 21–22, 31, 33, 115, 189, 194, 208–210, 212–215, 217, 221, 225, 233–234, 236, 255, 257, 259–260
essentialism 132–133, 149, 155–156, 180
ethics 10, 99–100, 102–107, 110–111, 173, 175, 178, 181, 194,
ethnicity 6, 9, 11, 45–46, 70, 74, 135, 166, 207, 210, 255, 262, 264
ethnography 113, 119
excavation 153
exclusion(s) 90, 99, 103, 114, 118, 124–125, 212, 214
exhibition(s) 20, 68, 73, 75–76, 82, 87, 89, 94, 99–103, 105, 109–111, 125, 185–189, 191–202, 223, 255, 257, 259–262, 264–265
experience(s) 5–6, 8–9, 11, 17, 23, 25–27, 31, 38, 56, 60, 84, 89–90, 93–94, 96, 102–103, 105, 110, 119, 129, 134–138, 140, 142, 148–152, 154, 156, 158–161, 164, 172, 177, 179, 189, 192, 201, 209, 212, 214–215, 221–223, 225, 227–229, 232, 234, 236, 239, 242–244, 246, 255, 259
exploitation 73, 140

female(s) 13, 17–18, 20, 22–23, 26–27, 31–32, 34, 36, 38–39, 46–47, 52–53, 56, 61, 63, 67, 70–71, 73, 90–94, 101, 113–115, 119, 122, 124–125, 143, 148, 150, 159, 162, 169, 176, 189, 197, 210–212, 215, 228, 230–232, 234–236
femininity 4, 18–19, 22, 27, 47, 53, 57, 67, 69–70, 74, 76, 185, 194, 201, 209, 223, 265
feminist 4–5, 10, 18–19, 22–23, 27, 31, 45, 47, 57, 76, 92, 100–102, 104–105, 109–110, 113, 124, 129–130, 133–139, 141, 144–145, 148–150, 152, 156, 160, 164, 169–170, 173–174, 176, 179–182, 186–188, 192, 215, 255, 260, 264
fieldwork 18, 32, 35, 37–38, 40, 43, 148, 152, 155, 222, 242
Foucault, M. 4, 7, 82

Index   271

gay 20, 26, 239, 243–246, 248–249
gender 3–11, 17, 20, 23–26, 30–38, 40, 44–47, 49, 51, 53–54, 56–57, 61–64, 67–68, 71–76, 81–83, 90–92, 94, 99–101, 113–115, 118, 120–125, 130, 133, 135, 149–150, 158–160, 162, 169, 171, 173, 176, 185–189, 192–195, 201–202, 207, 209–217, 223–225, 233–234, 240, 255–265
gendered 4–5, 8–10, 26, 31–35, 37, 40, 44, 47, 62, 72, 75, 81–83, 85, 91–95, 99, 101, 110, 113–114, 116, 120, 124–125, 150, 164, 173, 180, 186–189, 193–196, 198–203, 262
genealogical 86, 92
genealogy 4
globalization 64, 222
government(al) 7, 10, 85, 113–114, 116, 118, 122–123, 149, 159–160, 162, 170, 207–208, 210, 234, 250

Haraway, D. 4, 62–63, 101, 103–104, 107–108, 131, 136, 139, 148, 161, 180, 256, 259
hegemonic 7, 10–11, 93, 101–102, 115, 149–151, 155–156, 161, 163–164, 192, 201–202, 240, 260
heritage 3–11, 17–19, 26–27, 30–35, 37, 40, 44–47, 49–50, 52–53, 57, 64, 67, 70, 74–76, 81–82, 84, 87, 90–92, 94–95, 99, 101–104, 107–111, 113–115, 118, 121–122, 124–125, 129–130, 132, 136, 138, 141, 148–153, 155–164, 169–176, 178–182, 187–188, 203, 207–215, 217, 221–225, 235–236, 239–250, 255–257, 259, 264–265
heritage-making 18–19, 44, 48–47, 56–57
hermaphrodite(s) 70, 73
hermeneutics 130–131, 136, 139, 144
heteronormative 61–64, 67–68, 70–71, 73–74, 76, 156, 247–248, 256
historical(ly) 7, 18, 20–22, 26, 45, 47–48, 52, 61–62, 64, 69, 71, 86, 89, 92, 94–95, 101–103, 110, 129–130, 132–133, 135–136, 142–143, 149, 151, 155, 159, 161, 169, 172, 175, 177, 182, 192, 198–199, 222–223, 239, 246–247, 264
history 18–19, 27, 30, 32, 44–49, 51–53, 56–57, 59, 62, 64, 78, 81–82, 84, 87, 89–95, 115–118, 124–125, 129–130, 135, 138, 140–142, 144, 151, 153–155, 157, 161, 171, 174–176, 179, 187–188, 191, 222–225, 236, 240, 255, 258, 260, 262
homophobia 17
homophobic 17, 19
homosexual 7, 63, 241
human–animal 71–72
humanities 3, 129–130, 173, 181–182
hybridity 133

identity 3, 5–11, 21, 61, 64–66, 83, 86, 94, 105, 117–118, 129–130, 135, 139, 143–144, 149–151, 154–155, 158–164, 176, 180, 187, 194–195, 200, 202, 210, 212, 234, 240–241, 243, 245–246
ideology 4, 90, 172, 177, 189, 194, 202, 209
image(s) 18, 38, 53–54, 65, 87, 89, 94–95, 101, 120, 124, 173–174, 177, 180, 193–195, 199–200, 256, 260, 265
imaginary 155, 172, 176, 256
in-between 24, 72, 106, 139, 264–265
inclusion 11, 122, 125, 156, 162, 198, 249
indigenous 83, 89–90, 153–154, 211, 213
inequalities 25, 27, 31–32, 133, 139, 160, 261
inferior 90, 120, 214
institution 24, 46, 67, 132, 134, 172, 201–202, 255, 257–259, 264
intangible 30, 34, 44, 132, 136, 150, 169, 175, 182, 207–209, 217, 221, 239–240
integrate 66, 82, 94–95, 257–259, 265
interdisciplinary 6, 129, 136, 169
intersectional 19, 161, 169
intersectionality 5, 8, 11, 27, 101, 149–150, 156–257, 161, 163, 255, 260, 264, 266n3
intersexual 25
intervention 173–174
interview 22, 38, 152, 159, 163, 235, 239, 243–246, 248–249
intra-action 104, 106, 108, 180

knowledge 37, 47, 49, 54, 61–64, 72–75, 86, 89, 100, 103–105, 122, 129–131, 133, 137, 139–141, 144, 148–151, 155–157, 161, 163–164, 174, 177, 181, 191–192, 209, 256–259, 261–262, 265
knowledges 39, 62, 103, 129, 140, 148, 180–181

landscape(s) 9–10, 17–23, 25–26, 74, 89, 114–115, 124–125, 157–158, 186, 236, 239–243, 249, 257

language 31, 33, 37, 61, 71, 82, 115, 117, 133, 136–138, 144, 175, 177–178, 240–241
law 10–11, 89, 114, 142, 197, 207–210, 213–215
lesbian 17, 19–21, 23–27, 135, 239, 243–244, 246, 248–249,
linguistic 135, 175, 177
local 17–19, 21,25–26, 32, 37–38, 40, 45–48, 51, 53, 61–62, 64, 71–72, 74–75, 87–89, 92, 100, 123, 130, 150, 152, 154–157, 159–162, 164, 170, 172, 177, 221–223, 231–232, 234, 241–242, 244,

mainstream 3, 6–7, 9, 11, 150, 161, 202, 221–222, 239–242
male(s) 17, 27, 45, 47, 56, 34, 38, 40, 57, 61–63, 67, 69–71, 73, 81, 84, 86, 91, 93–94, 100–101, 113–116, 118–122, 124–125, 130, 134, 143, 159, 176, 189, 192, 195, 197, 211, 213, 223, 226, 229–231, 236, 246
man 72, 74, 99–100
management 5, 44, 153, 187, 226, 233, 255, 257–258, 265
map(s) 67, 70–71, 73, 141, 170, 244, 264
masculinities 266, 81, 91, 93–95,
masculinity 4, 61, 67, 69–70, 72–73, 83, 93, 113, 115, 118, 125, 144, 159, 185, 192–193, 198, 201, 209, 223, 255, 260, 262, 265
master narrative 170
material-discursive 103, 108–109, 180
material-semiotic 104
materiality 34, 100, 102, 150, 176, 247
matter 4, 19, 49, 82, 99–111, 175, 177–178, 181, 188, 215–216, 230–231, 239, 242, 250, 259
meaning(s) 40, 62, 68, 86, 95, 103, 108–109, 122, 125, 131, 136–138, 142, 150, 163, 169, 175, 177, 179–181, 194, 201, 212, 239–242, 245, 247, 256, 262, 264–265
memory 87, 113, 116, 118, 169, 173, 178–179, 185, 188–190, 241, 244, 247, 249, 250
men 5, 20–23, 27, 31–38, 45, 47, 56–57, 69–74, 83–84, 89–95, 99, 101, 113–115, 118–121, 123, 125, 141–142, 159, 185–187, 189–197, 201–202, 210–216, 221, 223, 226–229, 233, 236, 243–244, 249, 255, 259–260, 261–262

methodology 148–149, 152, 156, 160–161, 169, 179
method(s) 3, 8, 131, 140–141, 152, 169, 173, 176–182, 242, 261
mind(s) 106, 110, 134, 145, 172, 180, 216, 222, 240, 264–265
modern 9, 18, 40, 45, 47–48, 51–52, 56–57, 81, 84, 90–93, 119, 173, 207, 256, 265
monument 10, 113–124, 231
moral(e) 20, 53, 120, 131
mother(s) 23, 34, 65, 67, 73, 86, 88, 90–91, 93–94, 125, 135, 231–232
multi-disciplinary 169, 174, 181
multi-modal 169, 174, 181
multiple 5, 48, 72–73, 86, 106, 130, 138–139, 149, 151, 153, 155–156, 162–163, 180, 188, 200–202, 210, 242
museum(s) 2, 8–11, 17–18, 20, 23, 25–26, 44–45, 47, 49, 57, 61–76, 99–111, 115, 117–118, 121–122, 124, 129–145, 171–172, 187–188, 192–193, 196, 198–203, 223, 255, 262, 264–265
museology 5, 101–102

narrative 8, 11, 17, 27, 49, 73–74, 76, 81–84, 87, 89–95, 99, 101–105, 107, 110, 113, 151–157, 159–161, 163–164, 170, 173, 186, 192, 201–202, 221–222, 225, 236, 240, 244, 256, 262, 264
nation 84, 92–93, 95, 117, 119, 121, 135, 188–189, 191–192
national 23, 33, 45, 49, 51, 56, 66, 87, 113, 115–119, 121–125, 152, 154, 170, 187, 208, 221, 240–241, 257
nationalism 81
nationalist 116–117, 140–141
natural 21, 23, 32, 53, 62–65, 74, 171
nature 35, 61–65, 68–70, 73–74, 83, 86, 91–92, 100, 102, 115, 130, 132–134, 173, 208, 211–212
Nazi(sm) 185–186, 188–189, 192–195, 197–202,
network(s) 10, 26, 48–49, 110, 129, 149, 151, 153, 189, 242
nomadic 173
non-heteronormative 73–74
non-human 4, 100–102, 104–105, 110, 181
non-normative 147, 156
normal(ly) 3, 11, 22

norm(s) 7–8, 19, 23–24, 31, 34–35, 39, 47, 53, 56–57, 61, 63, 70–71, 95, 114, 186, 188–189, 202, 209
normative 5, 7, 10, 19, 26, 162, 180, 240, 247

object(s) 22, 30, 35, 37, 44, 49, 54, 57, 61–62, 65, 67, 99–105, 108–110, 132–145, 164, 172, 176–182, 197, 212, 240, 248
objectivity 103, 139, 181–182
ontological 100, 103, 106, 109–110, 148, 259
ontology 105, 108–109, 152, 158
oppression 20, 134–135, 138, 142, 159, 164,
oppressive 22
origin 54, 65, 81, 83, 91, 118, 138, 154, 162–163, 182, 233,
otherness 46, 107

pansexual 25
partial 85, 140
patriarchal 33–34, 35, 38, 40, 45, 81, 84, 91, 113, 115–116, 118, 161, 180, 211
patriarchy 91, 93, 95, 114–116, 122
performative 19, 26, 46, 21, 54, 101, 149–150, 154–155, 157, 159, 162–164, 187, 200, 212,
performativity 4, 44, 46, 149–150, 163, 241
phalluses 101, 107–108
phenomena 99, 103, 105, 108, 192
philosophy 4, 117, 130, 176, 179
political 6, 8–10, 17, 18, 25, 27, 40, 62–64, 81, 84–85, 91, 94, 99, 102–103, 109, 116, 119, 121, 129, 135, 139, 143, 153, 156–158, 160, 163, 170–174, 178–179, 181, 187–188, 193–194, 201–202, 209, 240
politics 4, 7–10, 22–23, 25, 27, 63, 81, 85, 90, 93, 99–100, 102, 114, 130, 132, 134, 140, 149, 156–161, 163, 171, 174–175, 178–179, 181, 188, 198, 202, 255
positivism 161
positivistic 62, 74
postcolonial 118, 163–164
posthuman 110, 255, 260
postmodern 40, 138, 170
poststructuralist 106
power 3–4, 6–11, 19, 27, 45, 47, 49, 67, 81, 89, 91–93, 99, 104, 113, 116, 118, 125, 129–133, 136, 138–140, 142, 144,
149, 151, 157, 159–161, 163, 170–171, 174–177, 181, 188–189, 194, 200, 207, 212, 240
privilege(d) 6, 23, 25, 38, 65, 130, 137, 157, 159, 160, 186, 212, 256

queer(s) 7–8, 10, 19, 24, 56, 75, 108, 148–151, 156–157, 162–164, 239–250, 255, 260, 262

race 5, 107, 130, 133, 135, 150, 160, 176, 194, 214
racism 132–135, 139, 140–141, 233
reality 62, 75, 84, 103, 109, 148, 154, 175, 177, 180, 209, 213–215, 227
reason(s) 17, 38, 57, 70, 91, 123, 153, 185, 197, 202, 256–257
reflexivity 158, 161, 163, 188, 202
relativism 138, 213
representation(s) 3, 5–6, 9–10, 31, 44–45, 47, 53–54, 56, 61–69, 72–75, 81–84, 88–91, 93–95, 115, 124, 130, 136, 149–151, 155–161, 164, 180, 186–188, 193, 198, 201–202, 227, 256, 262, 264
reproduction(s) 23, 61–71, 73, 138, 151, 160–162
resistance(s) 4, 7–8, 10–11, 32, 90, 130, 135, 153–154, 158–159, 185–193, 195–202
responsibility 53, 102–104, 135, 137, 174–176, 181, 185, 187–189

science 3–5, 63, 103–104, 110, 173, 178–179, 181–182, 209
scientific 45, 62–63, 75, 100, 103, 109–110, 130, 139, 258
sex(es) 20, 25, 31, 47, 56, 61–63, 66, 70–71, 122, 125, 162, 176, 189, 194, 209, 211, 214–215
sexist 17, 202, 233, 236
sexual 5, 19–20, 25, 207, 210, 215, 229, 234, 236, 240, 237, 255, 260, 262, 265,
sexual difference 255, 260
sexuality 4, 7, 17, 45, 63, 133, 158, 179, 255
site(s) 4–10, 18, 35, 37, 44, 57, 82–83, 94, 114–115, 120, 123, 129–130, 132, 149–153, 156–158, 163, 186–187, 189–191, 196, 198–202, 212, 221, 223–224, 239–241, 243–249
situated knowledges 62, 103, 130, 148, 174
social construction(s) 64, 73

society 3–11, 21, 33, 37, 40, 45, 47–49, 53, 63, 75, 86, 90, 92, 94, 114–115, 118, 134, 142–144, 150, 154, 156, 161, 175, 177, 187, 189, 211–215, 234, 256–257, 264–265
sociology 4, 129, 179,
solidarity 21–22, 135, 234
stereotype(s) 31, 73, 91, 95, 99, 122, 133, 216,
stereotypical 63–64, 68, 70, 101–102, 132, 136
structuralism 120
subject(s) 3–4, 6, 9, 20, 35, 47, 56, 88, 90, 93, 102, 104, 109, 114, 135, 137–138, 176, 179–181, 188, 202, 209, 240, 258–260, 262
subjectivity 174, 179
subordinate 4, 90, 94, 102, 157, 197, 262
subversive 11, 155, 163
symbolic 7, 18, 34, 62–63, 65, 83, 125, 172, 189–190, 194, 201, 212, 248, 256

technology 67, 73, 104, 110, 122
technoscience 100, 104, 255, 260
theology 83
theory 3–4, 7, 10, 19, 47, 56, 93, 108, 115, 131, 133, 136, 139–140, 144, 148–151, 156, 160, 162, 164, 179–180, 202, 240
theoretical 4, 18, 44, 46, 62, 100, 102, 130, 134, 148, 150, 153, 172, 174, 180, 203, 207, 217, 255, 261
transgender 8, 20, 25
transsexual 63
trans* studies 260
transversal 149, 157, 163, 176

unconscious 81
universal 35, 140, 170, 209, 212–213, 257, 264
universalism 133, 213
university 17–18, 20, 22, 114–115, 129–134, 136–137, 144, 222, 258

validity 240
violence 92, 140, 151, 193, 234
vision 109, 177, 214, 247–248
visual 9, 38, 44, 47, 53–54, 56, 67, 177, 180–181, 201

white 17, 19, 24–26, 48, 51, 54, 61–62, 92, 120, 130, 132, 134–135, 141, 156, 159–160, 171, 176, 193, 199–200, 212, 255
whiteness 159
woman 18, 21, 23–26, 31, 33–36, 38–39, 41, 56, 69, 71–72, 92, 94, 101–102, 115–116, 119–121, 123, 125, 135, 138, 140, 142, 144, 154, 160–161, 194, 211, 226, 228, 233, 252
women 4–5, 17–27, 30–31, 33–38, 40, 45, 47–48, 51–53, 56–57, 62–63, 69–74, 76, 84, 88, 90–95, 99, 101–103, 110, 113–115, 118–119, 122, 124–125, 129–132, 135, 139–142, 158–160, 162–163, 170, 176, 178–179, 185, 187, 189, 193–198, 200, 202, 210–212, 214–217, 221–223, 225–236, 259–262
working class 17–18, 21–24, 27, 131, 135, 221–223
writing 45, 57, 69, 85, 131–132, 135, 143, 178–180, 201